We Want To Hear From You!

As the reader of this book, *you* are our most important critic and commentator. We value your opinion and want to know what we're doing right, what we could do better, what areas you'd like to see us publish in, and any other words of wisdom you're willing to pass our way.

As an associate publisher for Que, I welcome your comments. You can email or write me directly to let me know what you did or didn't like about this book—as well as what we can do to make our books better.

Please note that I cannot help you with technical problems related to the topic of this book. We do have a User Services group, however, where I will forward specific technical questions related to the book.

When you write, please be sure to include this book's title and author as well as your name, email address, and phone number. I will carefully review your comments and share them with the author and editors who worked on the book.

Email: feedback@quepublishing.com

Mail: Greg Wiegand
         Que Publishing
         800 East 96th Street
         Indianapolis, IN 46240 USA

For more information about this book or another Que title, visit our Web site at *www.quepublishing.com*. Type the ISBN (excluding hyphens) or the title of a book in the Search field to find the page you're looking for.

Contents

Adobe® Photoshop® CS2 On Demand

Andy Anderson

Steve Johnson

Perspection, Inc.

Que Publishing
800 East 96th Street
Indianapolis, IN 46240 USA

Adobe Photoshop CS2 On Demand

International Standard Book Number: 0-7897-3390-0

Library of Congress Catalog Card Number: 2005922647

Printed in the United States of America

First Printing: May 2005

06 05 04 03   4 3 2 1

Que Publishing offers excellent discounts on this book when ordered in quantity for bulk purchases or special sales. For information, please contact:

U.S. Corporate and Government Sales

1-800-382-3419

corpsales@pearsontechgroup.com

For sales outside the U.S., please contact:

International Sales

1-317-428-3341

International@pearsontechgroup.com

Trademarks

Warning and Disclaimer

Publisher
Paul Boger

Associate Publisher
Greg Wiegand

Managing Editor
Steve Johnson

Author
Andy Anderson

Contributor
Steve Johnson

Project Editor
Holly Johnson

Technical Editor
Matt West

Production Editor
Beth Teyler

Page Layout
Beth Teyler
Matt West

Interior Designers
Steve Johnson
Marian Hartsough

Indexer
Katherine Stimson

Proofreader
Beth Teyler

Team Coordinator
Sharry Lee Gregory

Acknowledgements

Perspection, Inc.

Adobe Photoshop CS2 On Demand has been created by the professional trainers and writers at Perspection, Inc. to the standards you've come to expect from Que publishing. Together, we are pleased to present this training book.

Perspection, Inc. is a software training company committed to providing information and training to help people use software more effectively in order to communicate, make decisions, and solve problems. Perspection writes and produces software training books, and develops multimedia and web-based training. Since 1991, we have written more than 70 computer books, with several bestsellers to our credit, and sold over 4.7 million books.

This book incorporates Perspection's training expertise to ensure that you'll receive the maximum return on your time. You'll focus on the tasks and skills that increase productivity while working at your own pace and convenience.

We invite you to visit the Perspection web site at:

www.perspection.com

Acknowledgements

The task of creating any book requires the talents of many hard-working people pulling together to meet impossible deadlines and untold stresses. We'd like to thank the outstanding team responsible for making this book possible: the author Andy Anderson; contributor, Steve Johnson; the project editor, Holly Johnson; the technical editor, Matt West; the production team, Beth Teyler, and Matt West; the proofreader, Beth Teyler; and the indexer, Katherine Stimson. A special thanks to Beth Teyler for your tireless efforts to make this book possible.

At Que publishing, we'd like to thank Greg Wiegand and Stephanie McComb for the opportunity to undertake this project, Sharry Gregory for administrative support, and Laurie Casey for your production expertise and support.

Perspection

About The Author

Andy Anderson is a graphics designer and illustrator who has worked with Photoshop since it was released. A university professor, Andy is a sought-after lecturer in the U.S., Canada, and Europe. The remainder of his time is split between writing graphics and fiction books, and developing graphics, animations, and resource materials for various corporations and seminar companies. His clients include designers and trainers from the U.S. Government, Boeing, Disneyland, and other Fortune 500 companies.

Contributor

Steve Johnson has written more than thirty-five books on a variety of computer software, including Microsoft Office 2003 and XP, Microsoft Windows XP, Apple Mac OS X Panther, Macromedia Flash MX 2004, Macromedia Director MX 2004, Macromedia Fireworks, and Web publishing. In 1991, after working for Apple Computer and Microsoft, Steve founded Perspection, Inc., which writes and produces software training. When he is not staying up late writing, he enjoys playing golf, gardening, and spending time with his wife, Holly, and three children, JP, Brett, and Hannah. When time permits, he likes to travel to such places as New Hampshire in October, and Hawaii. Steve and his family live in Pleasanton, California, but can also be found visiting family all over the western United States.

5 Working with Layers 97

6 Working with the History Palette 119

9 Using the Paint, Shape Drawing, and Eraser Tools 205

17   Working with Automate Commands   397

18   Managing Color from Monitor to Print   419

Introduction

Welcome to *Adobe Photoshop CS2 On Demand*, a visual quick reference/training book that shows you how to work efficiently with Adobe Photoshop CS2. This book provides complete coverage of basic and intermediate Photoshop CS2 skills.

How This Book Works

You don't have to read this book in any particular order. We've designed the book so that you can jump in, get the information you need, and jump out. However, the book does follow a logical progression from simple tasks to more complex ones. Each task is presented on no more than two facing pages, which lets you focus on a single task without having to turn the page. To find the information that you need, just look up the task in the table of contents, index, or troubleshooting guide, and turn to the page listed. Read the task introduction, follow the step-by-step instructions in the left column along with screen illustrations in the right column, and you're done.

What's New

If you're searching for what's new in Photoshop CS2, just look for the icon: New!. The new icon appears in the table of contents and throughout this book so you can quickly and easily identify a new or improved feature in Photoshop CS2. A complete description of each new feature appears in the New Features guide in the back of this book.

Keyboard Shortcuts

Most menu commands have a keyboard equivalent, such as Ctrl+P (Win) or ⌘+P (Mac), as a quicker alternative to using the mouse. A complete list of keyboard shortcuts is available on the web at *www.perspection.com* in the software downloads area.

Step-by-Step Instructions

This book provides concise step-by-step instructions that show you "how" to accomplish a task. Each set of instructions include illustrations that directly correspond to the easy-to-read steps. Also included in the text are time-savers, tables, and sidebars to help you work more efficiently or to teach you more in-depth information. A "Did You Know?" provides tips and techniques to help you work smarter, while a "See Also" leads you to other parts of the book containing related information about the task.

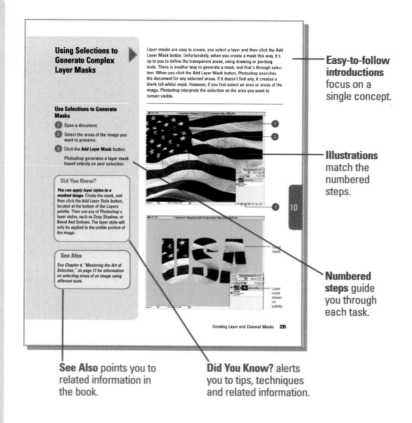

Easy-to-follow introductions focus on a single concept.

Illustrations match the numbered steps.

Numbered steps guide you through each task.

See Also points you to related information in the book.

Did You Know? alerts you to tips, techniques and related information.

Real World Examples

This book uses real world examples files to help you perform a task. The examples give you a context in which to use the task. By using the example files, you won't waste time looking for or creating sample files. The Photoshop example files that you need for project tasks are available on the web at *www.perspection.com*.

Real world examples help you apply what you've learned to other tasks.

Andy's Workshop

This book shows you how to put together the individual step-by-step tasks into indepth projects with Andy's Workshop. You start each project with a sample file, work through the steps, and then compare your results with Andy's project file at the end. The project files are available on the web at *www.perspection.com.*

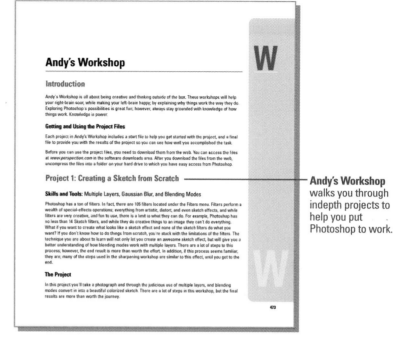

Andy's Workshop walks you through indepth projects to help you put Photoshop to work.

Photoshop for Windows and Macintosh

This book is written for the Windows and Macintosh version of Adobe Photoshop CS2. Both versions of the software are virtually the same, but there are a few platform differences between the two versions. When there are differences between the two versions, steps written specifically for the Windows version end with the notation (Win) and steps for the Macintosh version end with the notation (Mac). In some instances, tasks are split between the two operating systems.

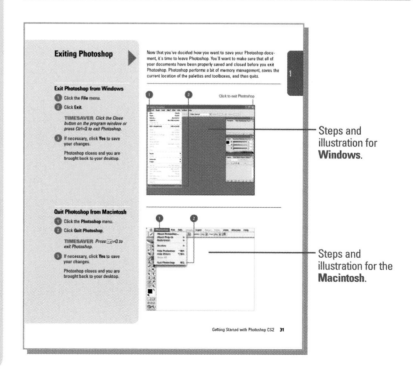

Steps and illustration for **Windows**.

Steps and illustration for the **Macintosh**.

Adobe Certified Expert

This book prepares you fully for the Adobe Certified Expert (ACE) exam for Adobe Photoshop CS2. Each Adobe Certified Expert certification level has a set of objectives, which are organized into broader skill sets. To prepare for the certification exam, you should review and perform each task identified with a Adobe Certified Expert objective to confirm that you can meet the requirements for the exam. Throughout this book, content that pertains to an objective is identified with the Adobe Certified Expert logo and objective number next to it.

Adobe Certified Expert

About the Adobe Certified Expert (ACE) Program

The Adobe Certified Expert (ACE) program is for graphic designers, Web designers, systems integrators, value-added resellers, developers, and business professionals seeking official recognition of their expertise on Adobe products.

What Is an ACE?

An Adobe Certified Expert is an individual who has passed an Adobe Product Proficiency Exam for a specific Adobe software product. Adobe Certified Experts are eligible to promote themselves to clients or employers as highly skilled, expert-level users of Adobe software. ACE certification is a recognized worldwide standard for excellence in Adobe software knowledge. There are three levels of ACE certification: Single product certification, Specialist certification, and Master certification. To become an ACE, you must pass one or more product-specific proficiency exam and sign the ACE program agreement. When you become an ACE, you enjoy these special benefits:

- Professional recognition
- An ACE program certificate
- Use of the Adobe Certified Expert program logo

What Does This Logo Mean?

It means this book will prepare you fully for the Adobe Certified Expert exam for Adobe Photoshop CS2. The certification exam has a set of objectives, which are organized into broader skill sets. Throughout this book, content that pertains to an ACE objective is identified with the following Adobe Certified Expert logo and objective number below the title of the topic:

 PS 3.1, 3.3

Logo indicates a task fulfills one or more Adobe Certified Expert objectives.

495

Getting Started with Photoshop CS2

Introduction

Adobe Photoshop CS2 is a graphics design and image enhancement program that runs seamlessly on the Windows and Macintosh platforms. Adobe Photoshop is a standalone program, but it's also part of Adobe's Creative Suite of professional programs, which includes Illustrator, InDesign, and Version Cue for the standard edition, and adds GoLive and Acrobat Professional for the professional edition. All Creative Suite 2 programs also include Adobe Bridge and Adobe Stock Photos. Bridge (New!) lets you organize, browse, and locate the different types of images you need to create content for print, the Web, and even mobile devices. Stock Photos (New!) is an integrated service available within Bridge that lets you search, view, try, and buy over 230,000 royalty-free stock photographic images.

Creative artists from Hollywood, brochure designers, as well as casual users turn to Photoshop for its proven ability to create special effects and image composites; however, Photoshop's ability to manipulate digital images, restore old photographs, as well as create digital artwork from scratch, has made Photoshop the undisputed leader in the digital industry. When it comes to digital photography, Photoshop is literally the best the computer industry has to offer.

Photoshop accepts images created with any digital camera, or traditional photographic film images, converted to the digital format through the use of a scanner. Once an image is opened in Photoshop, the designer can manipulate the image thousands of ways, everything from color correction, reducing dust and scratches in an old image, to removing a tree, or adding a missing friend. After creating and editing images using Photoshop, you can use ImageReady—a companion standalone program that comes with Photoshop—to prepare them for the Internet.

What You'll Do

Install and Launch Photoshop CS2

View the Photoshop Window

Work with Palettes

Work with Photoshop Tools

Use the Status Bar

Open Images

Work with Images Using Adobe Bridge

Create a New Document

Select Color Modes and Resolution

Create a New Document for Video with Auto Guides

Work with Non-Squared Pixels

Import Raw Data and Insert Images

Work with Smart Objects

Change Image Size and Resolution

Check for Updates and Patches

Get Help While You Work

Create Personalized Tips

Save and Close a Document

Exit Photoshop

Work with Adobe Creative Suite 2

Installing Photoshop CS2 ▶

To perform a standard program install, insert the Photoshop CS2 CD into the CD or DVD player on your computer, and follow the onscreen instructions. Make sure to have your serial number handy because you'll be asked to enter it during the installation process. If you're updating from a previous version of Photoshop, you'll be required to verify the older version by instructing Photoshop where on your hard drive the old version exists, or by inserting the previous version's install disk. Adobe, in an attempt to thwart software piracy, now requires online or phone activation of the program. The process can be postponed for 30 days. However, at the end of 30 days, the Photoshop program will shut down if it has not been properly activated. You can't blame Adobe for attempting to protect their products, since some surveys suggest there are more pirated versions of Photoshop than those purchased.

Install Photoshop CS2 in Windows

① Insert the Photoshop CS2 CD into your CD ROM drive.

② If the auto install does not begin, click **Start** on the taskbar, click **My Computer**, and then double-click the **Photoshop CS2 CD** icon.

③ Follow the on-screen instructions.

> **IMPORTANT** *During the installation process, Photoshop requires you to activate the program. Activation (using the Internet or by phone), must be accomplished within 30 days of installation, or Photoshop will cease to function.*

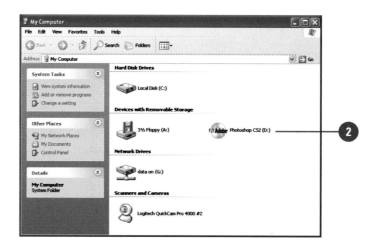

Did You Know?

The CD comes with bonus content. The Resources and Extras CD included with Adobe CS2 products includes bonus content and files in the Goodies folder. Check it out! For more free on-line resources, go to *www.adobe.com* and visit Adobe Studio Exchange.

Install Photoshop CS2 in Macintosh

① Insert the Photoshop CS2 CD into your CD ROM drive.

② Double-click the **CD** icon on the desktop to open the CD.

③ Double-click the **Install Photoshop CS2** program.

④ Follow the on-screen instructions.

Did You Know?

You can create a shortcut on the Macintosh. Drag and drop the Photoshop program to the bottom of the monitor screen, and then add it to the shortcuts panel.

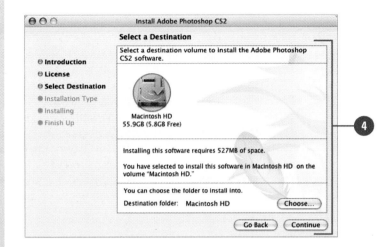

Photoshop CS2 System Requirements

Hardware/Software	Minimum (Recommended)
WINDOWS	
Computer Processor	Intel Pentium III or 4 (Intel 4)
Computer Speed	300 MHz (500+ MHz)
Operating System	Microsoft Windows 2000 (XP)
Hard Drive	280 MB (6+ GB)
Available RAM	192 MB (256+ MB)
Video Card	16-bit (16-bit)
Monitor Resolution	1024 x 768 (1024 x 768 or dual monitors)
MACINTOSH	
Computer Processor	PowerPC G3, G4, or G5 (PowerPC G5)
Computer Speed	250+ MHz (400 MHz)
Operating System	Macintosh OS X 10.2.8 - 10.3.4 (OS X 10.3.4)
Hard Drive	320 MB (6+ GB)
Available RAM	192 MB (256+ MB)
Video Card	16-bit (16-bit)
Monitor Resolution	1024 x 768 (1024 x 768 or dual monitors)
Additional Compatibilities	
Computer Processor	AMD Opteron, Opteron Dual, Athlon 64/64 FX

Launching Photoshop CS2

You can launch Photoshop like any other program. When you launch Photoshop, a Welcome Screen dialog box appears, displaying easy access links to new features, tutorials, tips and tricks from the experts, color management, informative movies, and more. When you access a link, your browser or Adobe Acrobat Reader opens to display the information or media you want to see. If you don't want to display the Welcome Screen dialog box every time you launch Photoshop, you can clear a check box on the dialog box. After you dismiss the Welcome Screen dialog box on first use, the Adobe Updater Preferences dialog box (**New!**) appears, asking you to select options to update Photoshop and it's related software. If you want to access the Welcome Screen or Adobe Updater Preferences dialog box later, you can use the Help menu.

Launch Photoshop CS2 in Windows

1 Click **Start** on the taskbar.

2 Point to **All Programs**.

3 Click **Adobe Photoshop CS2**.

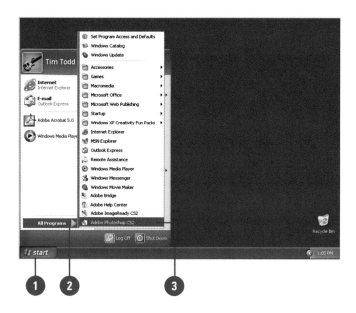

Did You Know?

You can create and use a shortcut icon on your desktop to start Photoshop (Win). Click Start on the taskbar, point to All Programs, right-click Adobe Photoshop CS2, point to Send To, and then click Desktop (Create Shortcut). Double-click the shortcut icon on your desktop to start Photoshop.

You can create and use a keyboard shortcut to start Photoshop (Win). Click Start on the taskbar, point to All Programs, right-click Adobe Photoshop CS2, and then click Properties. In the Shortcut Key box, type or press any letter, number, or function key, such as P, to which Windows adds CTRL+ALT. Click OK to create the keyboard shortcut. From anywhere in Windows, press the keyboard shortcut you defined (Ctrl+Alt+P) to start Photoshop.

For Your Information

Using Adobe Updater Preferences

The Adobe Updater Preferences dialog box (**New!**) allows you to set update options for installed Adobe products, such as Photoshop, Adobe Bridge, Adobe Help Center, and Adobe Stock Photos. When you select the Automatically Check For Updates Monthly check box, you can select options to automatically download or ask before performing the download. See "Checking for Updates and Patches" on page 24 for information on using the Adobe Updater Preferences dialog box.

Launch Photoshop CS2 in Macintosh

1. Open the **Programs** folder (located on the main hard drive).

2. Open the **Adobe Photoshop CS2** folder.

3. Double-click the **Adobe Photoshop CS2** program icon.

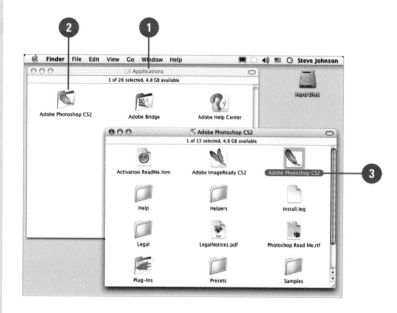

Shortcut for Photoshop CS2

Use the Welcome Screen

1. Launch Photoshop, if necessary, or click the **Help** menu, and then click **Welcome Screen**.

2. Click the item you want to learn more about, and then close it when you're done.

3. If you don't want to display the Welcome screen at startup, clear the **Show This Dialog At Startup** check box.

4. Click **Close**.

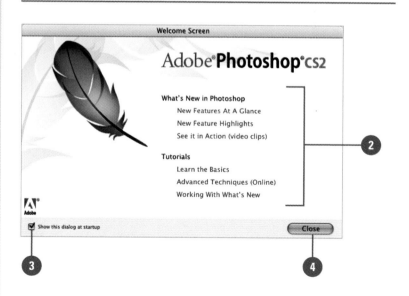

Viewing the Photoshop Window

Options Bar
Displays options for the active tool.

Docking Well
Let's you drag palettes into the well for quick access.

Toolbox
Gives you access to all of the drawing, painting, and selection tools.

Floating Palettes
Gives you access to all of Photoshop's palettes.

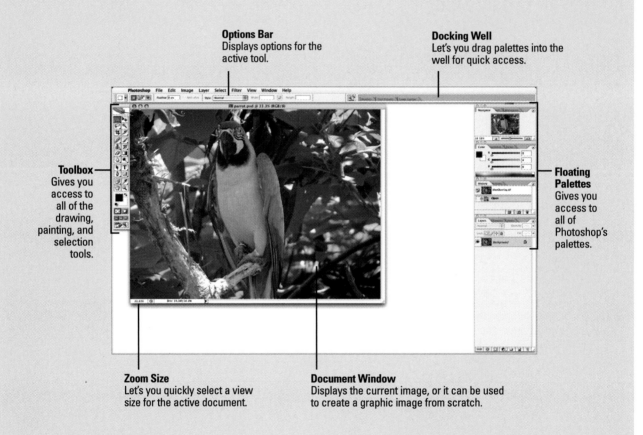

Zoom Size
Let's you quickly select a view size for the active document.

Document Window
Displays the current image, or it can be used to create a graphic image from scratch.

Working with Palettes

Photoshop's palettes give you access to everything from color control to vector path information. By default, the main palettes in Photoshop display along the right side of your monitor window. When you work in Photoshop, you may find it necessary to add or subtract specific palettes from your workspace; or you may just want to place several high-use palettes into one group. Controlling your workspace in this manner gives you a greater sense of control over the creative process. According to one study, the more control and organization you exert over a program, the more your creative side (right brain) is free to think creatively.

Add a Palette

1 Select a palette by clicking on the named palette.

2 Drag the palette into another group.

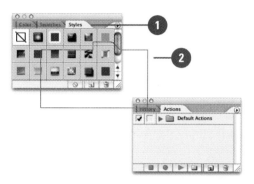

Subtract a Palette

1 Select a palette by clicking on the named palette.

2 Drag the palette out of the group.

3 Drop it onto the desktop (Mac) or click **Close** (Win).

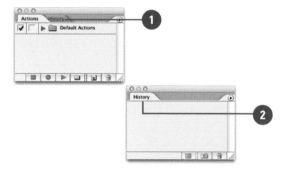

For Your Information

Hiding Palettes

If Photoshop's palettes get in the way, just press the Tab key to temporarily hide all the palettes. Or hold down the Shift key, and then press the Tab key to hide the palettes, but not the Toolbox and Options bar. Press the Tab key again to restore all the palettes, including the Navigator palette, to their last used positions.

Working with Photoshop Tools

Photoshop has an abundance of tools; located in the toolbox, they give a Photoshop designer tremendous control over any creative designing problems that may crop up. For example, the Photoshop toolbox contains eight selection tools (you can never have enough selection tools), 10 painting or shape tools, 4 type tools, and 12 tools dedicated to restoring and manipulating old images. Add to that mix, slicing, sampling, and view tools and you have a total of 59 dedicated tools. When you work on a document, it's important to know what tools are available, and how they help in achieving your design goals. Photoshop likes to save space, so it consolidates similar tools under one button. To access multiple tools, click and hold on any toolbox button that contains a small black triangle, located in the lower-right corner of the tool button. Take a moment to explore the Photoshop toolbox and get to know the tools.

The Photoshop toolbox contains the tools needed to work through any Photoshop job, but it's not necessary to click on a tool to access a tool. Simply using a letter of the alphabet can access all of Photoshop's tools. For example, pressing the V key, switches to the Move tool, and pressing the W key, switches to the Magic Wand tool. In addition, if a tool has more than one option, such as the Gradient and Paint Bucket tool, pressing the Shift key, along with the tool's shortcut lets you cycle through the tool's other options. You can refer to Adobe Photoshop CS2 Keyboard Shortcuts (available for download on the Web

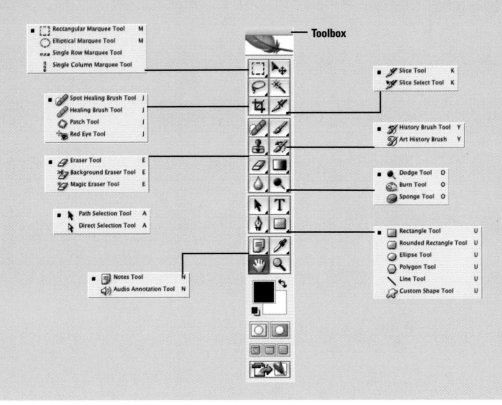

at *www.perspection.com*) for more information on all the letter assignments for the various tools. To really get efficient in Photoshop, you need to learn to use both hands. Use one hand for your mouse or drawing tablet, and the other on the keyboard to make quick changes of tools and options. Think of playing Photoshop, like a piano—use both hands.

Using the Options Bar

The Options bar displays the options for the currently selected tool. If you are working with the Shape Marquee tools, options such as

Feather, Styles, Width, and Height appear. When working with Brushes, tool options such as Brush size, Mode, Opacity, Style, Area and Tolerance appear. Airbrush and Paintbrush tools shows some of the Brushes options, but also includes Flow. The Pencil tool shows Auto Erase, along with the standard Brushes options. The Standard Shape tool Options bar includes Fill Pixels, Geometry, Blending Modes, Opacity, and Anti-alias. The important thing to remember is that the Options bar is customized based on the tool you have selected. For more information on these options, refer to Chapters 4, 6, and 9.

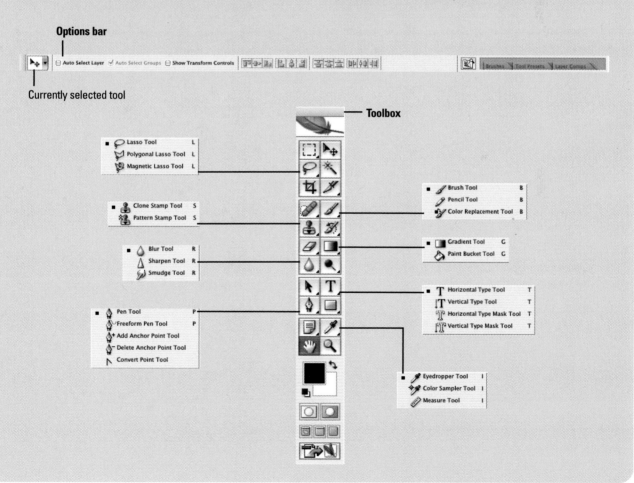

Using the Status Bar

To work efficiently in Photoshop you need information about the active document. Details about the document's size, resolution, color mode, and current size all help in the design and preparation of the final image. Photoshop displays current information about the active document through the Status bar, located at the bottom of the program window (Win), or document window (Mac).

Use the Status Bar

1 Click the **black triangle** near the Status bar info box, and then select from the following options:

- ◆ **Version Cue.** Indicates whether Version Cue file management has been enabled (New!).

- ◆ **Document Sizes.** The left number indicates the flattened size of the image file, and the right number indicates the size of the open file, based on layers and options.

- ◆ **Document Profile.** Displays information on the color profile assigned to the document.

- ◆ **Document Dimensions.** Represents the width and height of the image.

- ◆ **Scratch Sizes.** The left number indicates the scratch disk space required by Photoshop, and the right number indicates the available scratch disk space.

- ◆ **Efficiency.** Displays a percentage that represents Photoshop efficiency based on available RAM and scratch disk space.

- ◆ **Timing.** Records the amount of time required to perform the last command or adjustment.

- ◆ **Current Tool.** Displays the current tool.

- ◆ **32-bit Exposure.** Lets you control the overall image exposure (New!).

Opening Images

Photoshop lets you open image files created in different formats, such as TIFF, JPG, GIF, and PNG, as well as open Photoshop documents in the PSD or PSB formats. If you want to simply open an image or Photoshop document, the Open dialog box is the most efficient way. However, if you need to mange, organize, or process files, Adobe Bridge is the way to go. You open an existing Photoshop document or image file the same way you open documents in other programs. However, you have two Open dialog box display options: Adobe or OS (**New!**).

Open an Image

1. Click the **File** menu, and then click **Open** to display all file types in the file list of the Open dialog box.

   TIMESAVER *Point to the Open Recent command on the File menu to quickly open a recent file.*

2. To use a different Open dialog box display, click **Use Adobe Dialog** or click **Use OS Dialog**.

3. Click the **Format** (Win) or **Enable** (Mac) list arrow, and then select a format.

4. Click the the **Look In** (Win) or **Where** (Mac) list arrow, and then choose the location where the image you want to open is stored.

5. Click the image file you want to open.

   TIMESAVER *Press and hold the Shift key to select multiple files to open in the Open dialog box.*

6. Click **Open**.

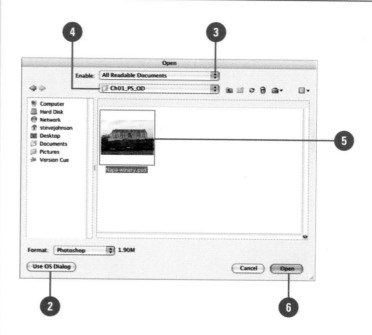

See Also

See "Understanding File Formats" on page 381 for information on the different file formats.

For Your Information

Opening a File as Another Format

The Open As command on the File menu allows you to open a file in Photoshop as another format, which can save you time by opening and saving a file in separate steps. Click the File menu, click Open As, select the file you want to open, display all files, select the desired format from the Open As (Mac) or Format (Win) list arrow, and then click Open. If the file does not open, then the chosen format may not match the file's true format, or the file may be damaged.

Working with Images Using Adobe Bridge

PS 1.2, 6.2, 10.1, 10.2

The Adobe Bridge (**New!**) is a stand-alone program (just like Photoshop), which lets you view and open images from any Adobe Creative Suite 2 program—Photoshop, Illustrator, InDesign, and GoLive. The Bridge is literally the glue that binds all of the Adobe Creative Suite 2 programs together into one cohesive unit. Bridge lets you organize, browse, and locate the different types of images you need to create content for print, the Web, and even mobile devices. You can drag assets into your layouts as needed, preview them, and add metadata to them. Bridge allows you to search, sort, manage, and process image files one at a time or in batches. You can also use Bridge to create new folders; rename, move, and delete files; edit metadata; rotate images; and run batch commands. You can also view information about files and data imported from your digital camera. In addition, Bridge integrates well with Adobe Version Cue, a file tracking project management program, and Adobe Stock Photos (**New!**), a service that lets you search, view, try, and buy royalty-free stock photography.

Work with Images Using Bridge

1. Launch Photoshop, and then click the **Go To Bridge** button on the Options bar (on the right side).

2. Click the **Folder** list arrow, and then select a folder. You can also select Adobe Stock Photos or Version Cue.

3. Click the **Folders** tab and choose a folder from the scrolling list.

4. Click the **Favorites** tab to choose from a listing of user-defined folders, such as My Pictures.

5. Click an image within the preview window to select an image.

6. Click the **Metadata** tab to view image information; including date and time the image was shot, and aperture, shutter speed, and f-stop.

7. Click the **IPTC Core** arrow to add user-defined metadata, such as creator and copyright information, or captions to an image.

8. Click the **Preview** tab to view a larger thumbnail of the selected image.

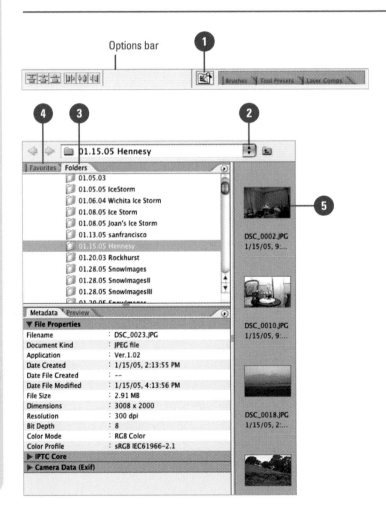

9 Drag the **Zoom** slider to increase or decrease the thumbnail views.

10 Click the preview buttons to select a different view.

◆ **Thumbnail.** Default view, displays the images as small thumbnails with the file name underneath. Use this view to see a large number of images at the same time.

◆ **Filmstrip.** Creates thumbnails across the bottom of the preview area. Clicking on a thumbnail creates a larger view, directly above the filmstrip view. Use this view to roll though a linear display.

◆ **Details.** Displays a thumbnail of each image with details as to date created and file size. Use this view to get basic information on an image.

◆ **Versions and Alternate.** Works in conjunction with Version Cue to display information on the number of versions of the original. Use this view to check out the current status of your Version Cue documents.

11 Use the file management buttons to sort thumbnails by star rating or color labels, rotate or delete images, or create a new folder.

12 Double-click on an thumbnail to open it in Photoshop, or drag the thumbnail from the Bridge into an open Photoshop document.

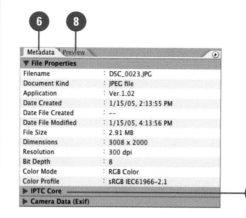

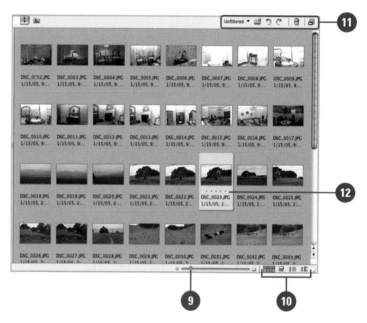

See Also

See "Working with Adobe Creative Suite 2" on page 32 for information on using Adobe CS2 with Photoshop.

For Your Information

What is Metadata?

Metadata is information about an image file, such as its author, copyright, creation date, size, version, color space, resolution, and searchable keywords, which is stored in the file or in a separate file, known as a **sidecar file**, using a standard method called **Extensible Metadata Platform (XMP)**. Bridge and Version Cue use XMP (**New!**) to help you organize and search for files. Metadata is stored in other formats, such as EXIF (digital camera data), IPTC (Core data), GPS (global positioning system data), and TIFF, which are all synchronized with XMP.

Creating a New Document

Creating a new Photoshop document requires more thought than creating a new word processing document. For example, there are resolution and color mode considerations to make. You can create as many new documents as you need for your current project. However, since opening more than one document takes more processing power, it's probably best to work on one new document at a time. Once a new document is created, you have access to all of Photoshop's design and manipulation tools to create anything your imagination can see.

Create a New Document

1. Click the **File** menu, and then click **New**.

2. Type a name for the document.

   IMPORTANT *Typing a name does not save the document. You still need to save your document after you create it.*

3. Click the **Preset** list arrow, and then select a preset document, or choose your own options to create a custom document.

   - **Width and Height.** Select from various measurements, such as points, centimeters, and inches.

   - **Resolution.** Select a resolution, such as 72 pixels/inch (ppi) for online use and 300 ppi for print.

   - **Color Mode.** Select a color mode, such as RGB for color and Grayscale for noncolor.

   - **Background Contents.** Select a background color or a transparent background.

4. Click **OK**.

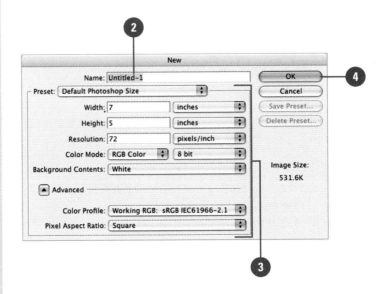

Selecting Color Modes and Resolution

Selecting a Color Mode

A **color mode**, also known as **color space**, determines how Photoshop displays and prints an image. You choose a different color mode (based on models using in publishing) for different tasks. You can choose a color mode while you create a new document or change a color mode for an existing document. The common color modes include:

Grayscale. Best for printing black-and-white and duotone images. This mode uses one channel and has a maximum of 256 shades of gray.

RGB (Red, Green, and Blue). Best for online and multimedia color images. RGB are also the primary colors on a monitor.

CMYK (Cyan, Magenta, Yellow, and Black). Best for commercial printing color images.

LAB (Luminosity A and B channels). Best for performing image correction. This mode puts all grayscale information on the L channel and splits the colors on the A and B channels.

For more information on color, see Chapter 8, "Understanding Colors and Channels."

Selecting Image Resolution

Photoshop works primarily with raster documents. **Raster** documents are images composed of pixels. A **pixel** is a unit of information that holds the color and detail information of the image. Thinking of a Photoshop image as a brick wall, with the individual bricks in the wall representing the individual pixels in the image, is an excellent way to envision a Photoshop document. Documents opened in Photoshop have a specific resolution. The **resolution** of the image, along with its width and height, represents how many pixels the image contains.

Since pixels (the bricks in a wall) represent information, the more pixels a document contains, the more information Photoshop has to manipulate or enhance the image.

A typical 17-inch monitor displays pixels at a resolution of 1024x768. You can figure out how many pixels are present on a monitor at 1024x768 by multiplying 1024 x 768, which equals to 786,432 pixels on the screen. The resolution is equal to how many pixels fit into each monitor inch, which is known as **ppi** (pixels per inch). A typical monitor displays pixels at 72ppi.

To determine the size of an image in inches, we divide the pixels by the ppi. For example, for an image 1024 pixels wide, 1024 / 72 = 14.2 inches. To determine the pixels present in an image, you multiple the size by the ppi. For example, for a 3 inch image, 3 x 72 = 216. As the image resolution drops, so does the output quality of the image. **Pixelization** occurs when the resolution is so low that the edges of the pixel begin to appear. The higher the resolution (more pixels), the sharper the image. However, the higher the resolution, the larger the file size. To optimize the use of a file, you need to use the correct resolution for a specific task. Use 72ppi for Web pages, CD-ROMs, and Multimedia; use 150ppi for an Inkjet printer; use 200ppi for Photo printers; and use 300ppi for commercial printing.

When working with images, it's always a good idea to start with a larger image size. You can always reduce the size of the image (subtract pixels) without losing any quality. If you need to enlarge an image, you run the risk of losing image quality. When you enlarge an image, the number of pixels doesn't increase as the image does, so the pixels become larger which mean a rougher image.

Creating a New Document for Video with Auto Guides

 PS 5.1, 5.2

When you work in video production, you know the importance of creating documents that will perfectly match the requirements of output to a video screen. The preset file sizes available in the new Preset menu let you create images at a size and pixel aspect ratio that compensate for scaling when you incorporate them into video. The presets also define, using non-printing guides, (the action and title areas of the document). When you work with the new Preset menu, the guesswork of creating compatible, NTSC, PAL, or even HDTV documents in Photoshop is a thing of the past.

Create a New Document Using Video Presets

1. Click the **File** menu, and then click **New**.

2. Click the **Preset** list arrow, and then select from the available video presets:

   ◆ NTSC DV 720x480 (with guides)

   ◆ NTSC DV Widescreen, 720x480 (with guides)

   ◆ NTSC D1 720x486 (with guides)

   ◆ NTSC D1 Square Pix, 720x540 (with guides)

   ◆ PAL D1/DV, 720x576 (with guides)

   ◆ PAL D1/DV Square Pix, 768x576 (with guides)

   ◆ PAL D1/DV Widescreen, 720x576 (with guides)

   ◆ HDTV, 1280x720 (with guides)

   ◆ HDTV, 1440x1080 anamorphic (with guides) (**New!**)

   ◆ HDTV, 1920x1080 (with guides)

3. Click **OK**.

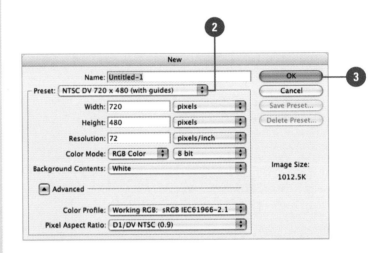

For Your Information

Using a Video Preview Option

Photoshop now includes a Video Preview option (**New!**) that lets you preview your documents on a display device, such as a standard or DVD screen. The device must be attached to your computer through the use of the FireWire port. Once the device is attached, open a document, click the File menu, point to Export, and then click Send Video Preview To Device. To set output options before viewing your document on the device, click the File menu, point to Export, and then click Video Preview. The Video Preview option supports RGB, grayscale, and indexed images, either 8 or 16-bits per channel. You can adjust the aspect ratio for proper display of images. First, select the aspect ratio of the display device, either Standard (4:3) or Widescreen (16:9), and then select a placement option, such as Center or Crop to 4:3, for the image. To maintain an image's (non-square) pixel aspect ratio, select the Apply Pixel Aspect Ratio To Preview check box.

Working with Non-Squared Pixels

PS 5.1, 5.2

Images displayed on a computer monitor are made up of square pixels. Conversely, an image displayed on a video monitor is analog and does not involve pixel shape. Non-square pixels are the most commonly used by encoding devices for video production. When importing an image created by a square-pixel graphics program into a video editing program such as Adobe Premiere, the square pixels are automatically scaled to the non-square pixels for video encoding. This scaling results in a distorted image. By default, non-square pixel documents open with Pixel Aspect Ratio Correction enabled. This enables you to preview how the image will appear on the output device such as a video monitor, and see how it will appear when exported to an analog video device. In keeping with an ever-changing industry, Adobe added three new Pixel Aspect Ratio options: D4/D16 Standard (0.95), HDV Anamorphic (1.333), and D4/D16 Anamorphic (1.0) (**New!**).

Work with Non-Squared Pixels

1 Click the **File** menu, and then click **New**.

2 On the bottom of the New dialog box, click the **Pixel Aspect Ratio** list arrow, select any of the non-square pixel settings, and then click **OK**.

3 Click the **Window** menu, point to **Arrange**, and then click **New Window** to create a new window for the active document.

4 Click the **Window** menu, point to **Arrange**, and then click **Tile** to view both images side-by-side.

5 Select the new window.

6 Click the **View** menu, and then click **Pixel Aspect Ratio** to toggle between corrected view and uncorrected view. (The default is corrected.)

The original window shows the corrected aspect ratio, and the new window displays the same document without pixel aspect ratio correction.

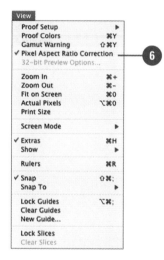

Image with a non-square pixel ratio

Importing Raw Data from a Digital Camera

PS 6.4, 10.3, 11.1, 11.2, 11.3, 11.4

Camera raw image file formats are created by most mid to high-end digital cameras and contain all the information about how the image was taken. The raw format turns off all camera adjustments, and simply saves the image information to the digital film. Using the raw format is as close to using traditional film as a digital camera can get. When you open a raw image file, Photoshop opens the Camera Raw Plug-in, which allows you to adjust the image details. For example, you decide where white point, shadows and highlights appear, not the camera. The adjustments available with the Camera Raw Plug-in provide flexibility to produce the best image possible from a camera raw image file. Raw images are larger; however, the increase in file size is actually more information that can be used by the Camera Raw Plug-in to adjust the image. In addition raw images can be converted into 16-bit. When a 16-bit image is opened, you have more control over adjustments, such as tonal and color correction. Once processed, raw images can be saved in the DNG, TIF, PSD, PSB, or JPG formats. You can create an action, or use the Batch, Image Processor or Create Droplet commands, to automate the processing of camera raw files. When a raw file is placed as a Smart Object, Photoshop embeds the raw data within the document, making it possible to change the raw settings and automatically update the converted layer.

Import a Camera Raw File

1. Click the **File** menu, and then click **Open**.

   To place a raw file as a Smart Object, click the File menu, and then click Place.

2. Click the **Format** (Mac) or **Files Of Type** (Win) list arrow, and then click **Camera Raw**.

3. Select a single camera raw image file, or Ctrl (Win) or ⌘ (Mac)+ click to select more than one file.

4. Click **Open**.

   Photoshop opens the image into the Camera Raw dialog box.

5. Click the **Settings** list arrow, and then select from the following options to load a previously used setup, or to create and save the current setup.

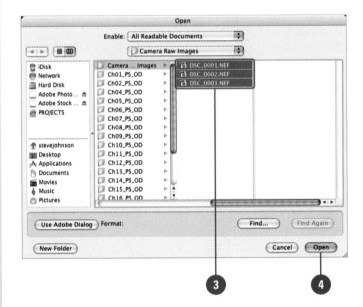

6 Use the Zoom, Hand, Rotate, Crop, and Straighten tools to change the size, orientation, and position of the image in the view window, or use the White Balance tools to set the image white balance or the Color Sample tool to sample a color from the image.

7 Select from the available image view options:

◆ **Image Preview.** Displays the active image.

◆ **Zoom Level.** Changes the view of the active image.

◆ **Histogram.** Displays information on the colors and brightness levels in the active image.

8 Click the **Adjust**, **Detail**, **Lens**, **Curve** , or **Calibrate** tabs, and then drag desired adjustment sliders to modify the color and tonal values of the active image.

9 Select the list arrows to change the (color) Space, (bit) Depth, Size, and Resolution of the image.

10 Click **Save** to specify a folder destination, file name, and format for the processed images.

11 Select the images you want to synchronize (apply settings) in the Filmstrip (if desired, click Select All), and then click **Synchronize**.

12 Click the **Camera Raw Menu** button to Load, Save, or Delete a specific set of Raw settings, or to modify the Camera Raw dialog box settings.

13 When you're finished, click **Done** to process the file, but not open it, or click **Open** to process and open it in Photoshop for further editing.

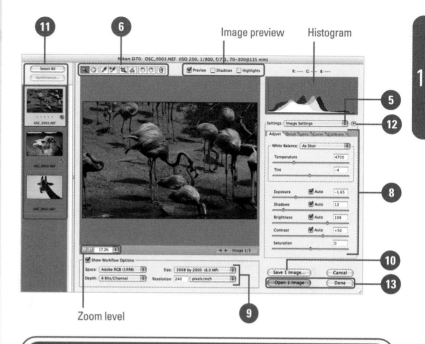

Image preview   Histogram

Zoom level

For Your Information

What is the DNG File Format?

The DNG (**New!**), or Digital Negative, format is an openly published raw file format that stores "raw" pixel data captured by digital cameras before it has been converted to another format, such as TIFF, or JPEG. In addition, it captures standard EXIF metadata, date, time, camera used, and camera settings. Saving RAW files in the DNG format provides several advantages. DNG files are smaller than uncompressed TIFFs, and they do not have the artifacts of compressed JPEGs. Many key camera parameters, such as white balance, can be modified even after the image is captured, You have access to 16-bit data for greater detail and fidelity, and the flexibility of converting a single file using multiple conversion settings. When you convert RAW images into the DNG format, you are using a format that is openly published by Adobe and other software and hardware vendors, which makes it a safe format for the long-term storage and archiving of digital images. The RAW format used by digital cameras is proprietary to the specific camera, so the format might not be supported once that camera goes obsolete, which means you might not be able to open any of your archived RAW images. The DNG format solves that problem. To get a free copy of the DNG converter, go to *www.adobe.com*, proceed to the download area, and then select DNG converter.

Inserting Images in a Document

You can use Photoshop's Place command to insert artwork into an open document. To increase your control of the new image information, Photoshop places the new image into a separate layer. Photoshop lets you place files in PDF, Adobe Illustrator, and EPS formats. When you first place a vector-based image into Photoshop, you have the ability to modify the width, height, and rotation as a pure vector image. However, since Photoshop is primarily a raster program, when you finalize your changes, Photoshop rasterizes the file information (converts the vector into pixels), and saves it as a Smart Object (**New!**). Which means you cannot edit the placed documents as you would a vector shape or path.

Insert an Image in a Document Using the Place Command

1 Open a Photoshop document.

2 Click the **File** menu, and then click **Place**.

3 Select the document you want to place into the active document.

4 Click **Place**.

Photoshop places the image in a new layer, directly above the active layer, and then encloses it within a free-transform bounding box.

5 Control the shape by manipulating the corner and side nodes of the freeform bounding box.

6 Press Enter (Win) or Return (Mac) to rasterize the image at the resolution of the active document.

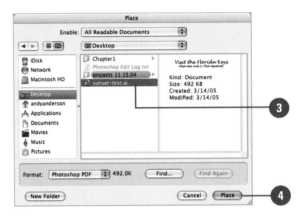

Freeform bounding box

New layer placed

Did You Know?

You can scan images into Photoshop. With the scanner hardware and software connected and installed (including the Twain plug-in), click the File menu, point to Import, click Twain, set scan settings, and then click Scan.

Working with Smart Objects

PS 3.8

A **Smart Object** (**New!**) is a container that you can embed raster/pixel (e.g. PSD, Camera Raw) or vector (e.g. AI, PDF, EPS) image data, for instance, from another Photoshop or Adobe Illustrator file that retains all its original characteristics and remains fully editable. A Smart Object can be scaled, rotated, and warped nondestructively without losing original image data in Photoshop. Smart Objects store source data with the original object, so you can work on a representation (composite data) of the image without changing the original—one file embedded within another. For example, when an Illustrator Smart Object is double-clicked in the Layers palette, Photoshop launches Illustrator and opens a working copy of the artwork. When Illustrator makes changes and saves the file, Photoshop automatically re-rasterize the file. If you duplicate a Smart Object, Photoshop stores only one copy of the source data while creating a second instance of the composite data. When you edit one Smart Object, Photoshop updates all copies. You can create Smart Objects from one or more selected layers in Photoshop, by pasting Illustrator data from the clipboard, or by using the Place command to insert a file.

Work with Smart Object

1. Open a Photoshop document.

2. Click the **File** menu, and then click **Place**.

3. Select the file you want, and then click **Place** to insert it in a new layer above the active layer.

4. Use the bounding box to modify the image to the shape you want.

5. Press Enter (Win) or Return (Mac) to convert the image to a Smart Object (in the Layers palette).

6. To make a copy, drag the Smart Object layer to the New Layer button.

7. Double-click the thumbnail of the original or copy to open the editor for the Smart Object.

8. Use the transform tools to make the desired changes to the image, save, and then close the editor window.

9. To convert a Smart Object into a normal layer, click the **Layer** menu, point to **Smart Objects**, and then click **Convert To Layer**.

Copy of Smart Object

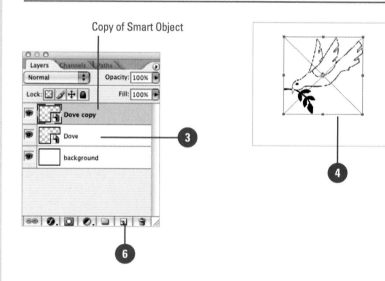

Changes made to one Smart Object impacts all Smart Objects.

1

Changing Image Size and Resolution

You can modify the size and resolution of a document after opening. However, be aware that changing the size and/or the resolution of an image forces Photoshop to add or subtract pixels from the image in a process called **interpolation**. For example, when you change the resolution of an image from 72 ppi (pixels per inch) to 144 ppi, Photoshop must add more pixels. Conversely, if you reduce the resolution, Photoshop must remove pixels. The image interpolation method determines how Photoshop completes this process. You can use the Nearest Neighbor method for the fastest way, but it produces the poorest visual image. Or, you can use the Bicubic Sharper method which takes the longest to perform, but produces the best visual results.

Change Image Size

1 Open an image.

2 Click the **Image** menu, and then click **Image Size**.

3 Select the **Resample Image** check box.

4 Click the **Resample Image** list arrow, and then select an option:

   ◆ **Nearest Neighbor.** Best for quick results with low quality.

   ◆ **Bilinear.** Best for line art.

   ◆ **Bicubic.** Default, best for most purposes with high quality.

   ◆ **Bicubic Smoother.** Best for enlarging an image.

   ◆ **Bicubic Sharper.** Best for reducing an image.

5 To maintain image proportions, select the **Constrain Proportions** check box.

6 Enter the desired sizes in the image size boxes.

   If you choose to constrain proportions in step 5, when you change a size, the other boxes will adjust automatically.

7 Click **OK**.

Icon indicates constrained proportions

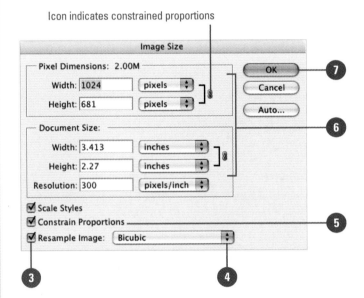

For Your Information

Using a Large Canvas Size

Photoshop supports documents up to 300,000 pixels in either dimension, and with up to 56 channels per file. Photoshop offers three file formats for saving documents with file sizes greater than 2 GB: PSD, RAW, and TIFF. It's important to note that most programs, including an older version of Photoshop (before the CS version), support a maximum file size of 2 GB.

Change Image Resolution

1. Open an image.

2. Click the **Image** menu, and then click **Image Size**.

3. Clear the **Resample Image** check box.

4. Enter a resolution, which automatically adjusts the Height and Width fields.

5. Click **OK**.

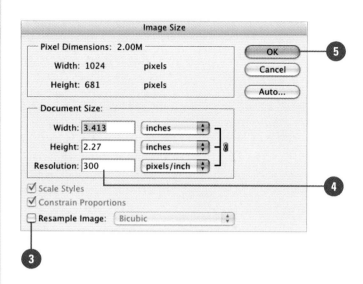

Change Image Size Using the Resize Image Wizard

1. Open an image.

2. Click the **Help** menu, and then click **Resize Image**.

   The Resize Image Wizard dialog box appears.

3. Click the **Print** or **Online** option, and then click **Next**.

4. Specify the image size you want, and then click **Next**.

5. If you selected the Print option, select a halftone screen, click **Next**, use the slider to select the image quality you want, and then click **Next**.

6. Click **Finish**.

   Photoshop makes a copy of the image and leaves the original alone.

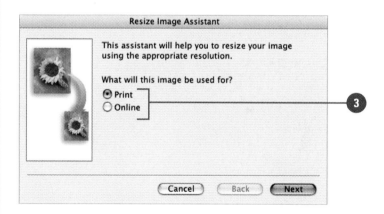

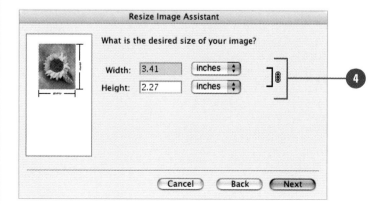

Checking for Updates and Patches

As time passes, Photoshop—like any other program—will change. There are two types of changes to an program: updates and patches. Updates are enhancements to a program such as a new feature, option, or command. Patches are problems discovered after the public release of the program. The good news is that both updates and patches are free, and once downloaded are self-installing. Adobe gives you two ways to check for changes. You can check on your own from the Adobe Web site, or directly through the Adobe Updater. The Adobe Updater Preferences dialog box (**New!**) allows you to set update options for Photoshop and other installed Adobe products, such as Bridge. You can set the update preferences to check for updates monthly and automatically download them or ask before performing the download.

Check for Updates Directly from the Internet

1 Open your Internet browser.

2 Go to the following Web address: *www.adobe.com/support/downloads/main.html*

3 Scroll down to Photoshop, and then click the Macintosh or Windows link.

Any updates or patches appear in a list.

4 Based on your operating system, follow the on-screen instructions to download and install the software.

IMPORTANT *Checking on your own requires a computer with a connection to the Internet. Since some of the updates can be rather large, it's recommended you have high-speed access; 56k is good, DSL or cable modem is better.*

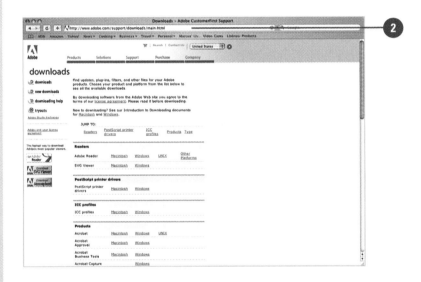

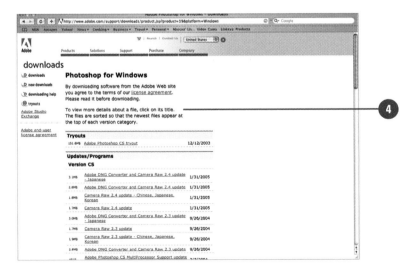

Check for Updates from the Photoshop Help Menu

① Launch Adobe Photoshop, if necessary.

② Click the **Help** menu, and then click **Updates**.

Photoshop automatically connects you to the Internet, and checks for updates. If there are any updates available, Adobe downloads and installs them.

IMPORTANT *Remember, these files can be quite large. So, if you're running with a slow Internet connection speed, you might want to perform downloading files at a low traffic time. Also, by making sure you don't have other programs running, you can maximize your system's resources for the downloading of files.*

When the check or download is complete, the Adobe Updater dialog box opens.

③ To change Adobe Updater preferences, click **Preferences**, select the **Check The Automatically Check For Updates Every Month** check box, select the update and program options you want, and then click **OK**.

④ Click **OK**.

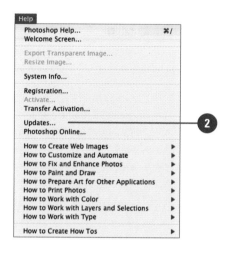

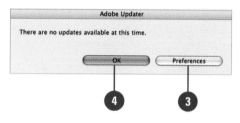

Select to update an application.

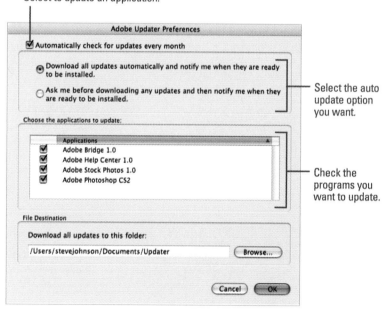

Select the auto update option you want.

Check the programs you want to update.

Getting Help While You Work

Working in Photoshop can be a rewarding experience, but it can also be frustrating when you're looking for that specific piece of information to complete a project. Adobe understands how important it is to have access to information quickly, so they created the Adobe Help Center (**New!**) with different types of help options, including product Help, Adobe Expert Support, and access to learning resources on *adobe.com*. Clicking the Help menu gives you access to an entire range of Help options, including dozens of tips and tricks. Adobe Help Center is a free, downloadable program that is updated periodically and can be downloaded through Adobe Help Center preferences.

Get Help While You Work

① Click the **Help** menu, and then select from the available options:

- ◆ Photoshop Help
- ◆ How to Create Web Images
- ◆ How to Customize and Automate
- ◆ How to Fix and Enhance Photos
- ◆ How to Paint and Draw
- ◆ How to Prepare Art for Other Applications
- ◆ How to Print Photos
- ◆ How to Work with Color
- ◆ How to Work with Layers and Selections
- ◆ How to Work with Type

② When you're done reading about your help topic, click the **Close** button.

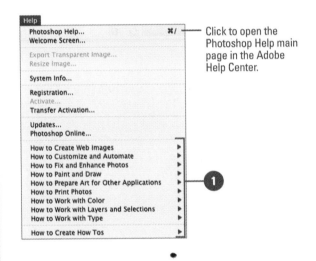

Click to open the Photoshop Help main page in the Adobe Help Center.

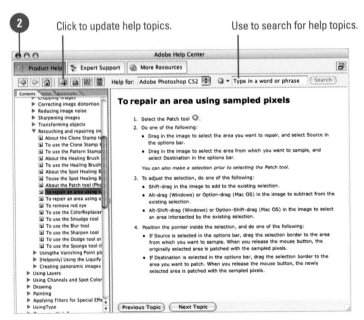

Click to update help topics.

Use to search for help topics.

Did You Know?

You can get help with Photoshop through the Internet. Click the Help menu, and then click Photoshop Online (requires an Internet connection) to display the Adobe Web site, where there is more helpful information.

Creating Personalized Tips

Not only does Photoshop give you access to helpful information, but it also lets you create you own personalized tips. **Personalized tips** allow you to create your very own Help system. For example, you discover this great way to color-correct an image that involves 6 or 7 steps; you've written the steps down, but you keep losing the paper. Creating a customized tip requires a bit of Web programming knowledge, but the time spent learning how to create a basic Web page is worth the effort. As a matter of fact, you could use an program such as: GoLive to generate the pages, and then save them in a format acceptable to the Photoshop Help menu.

Create Personalized Tips

1. Click the **Help** menu, point to **How To Create How Tos**, and then click **Create Your Own How To Tips**.

   Photoshop opens BB Edit (Mac) or your browser with instructions to open a text editor (Win).

2. Open the HTML template Add_001.html, located in the *Adobe Photoshop CS2/Help/Additional How To Content* folder, or create you own html document from scratch.

3. Save the new help document using a descriptive name, such as How to Template, in the Adobe *Photoshop CS2/Help/Additional How To Content* folder, and then close the editor.

4. Restart Photoshop, and then click the **Help** menu to access your new help document.

> **Did You Know?**
>
> *You can use any Web editing program to create help tips.* Open a Web program, such as Adobe GoLive, and then create the help tip. Make sure you save the file in the *Adobe Photoshop CS2/Help/Additional How To Content* folder.

Saving a Document

When you finish working on your Photoshop document, you need to save it before you close the document or exit Photoshop. While this may seem like a simple task, there are questions that must be asked before saving a file, like *What is the final output of the image?* For example, if the document is destined for the Internet, you'll probably save the document using the JPEG, GIF, or PNG formats. Each output device, whether monitor or paper, requires a specific format, and it's best to know this information at the beginning of the creation process. Knowing the final output of an image helps you create the design with the output in mind.

Save a Document

1 Click the **File** menu, and then click **Save**.

2 Enter a name for the file in the File Name (Win) or Save As (Mac) box.

3 Click the **Format** list arrow, and then select a format.

4 Click the **Save In** (Win) or **Where** list arrow, and then choose where to store the image.

5 Select from the available Save options:

- ◆ **As A Copy.** Saves a copy of the file while keeping the current file on your desktop.

- ◆ **Alpha Channels.** Saves or removes alpha channel information for the image.

- ◆ **Layers.** Maintains all layers in the image. If this option is cleared or unavailable, all visible layers are flattened or merged (depending on the selected format).

- ◆ **Annotations.** Saves annotations with the image.

- ◆ **Spot Colors.** Saves or removes spot channel information for the image.

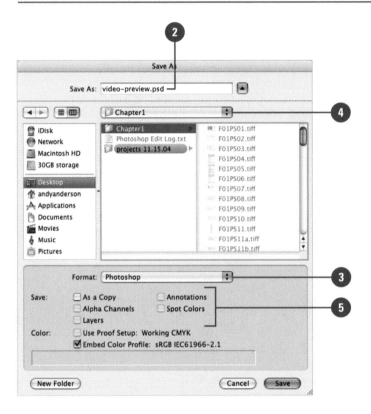

6 Select from the available Color options:

◆ **Use Proof Setup.** Creates a color-managed document.

◆ **Embed Color Profile** (Mac) or **ICC Profile** (Win). Embeds proof profile information in an untagged document. If the document is tagged, the profile is embedded by default.

7 Select from other available options (Win):

◆ **Thumbnail.** Saves thumbnail data for the file.

To use this option, you need to select Ask When Saving for the Image Previews option in the File Handling area of the Preferences dialog box.

◆ **Use Lower Case Extension.** Makes the file extension lowercase.

8 Click **Save**.

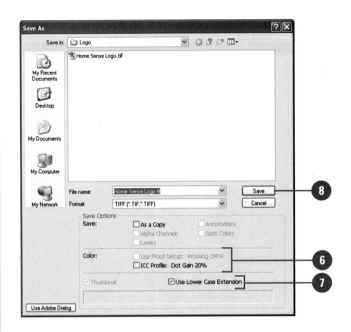

See Also

See "Saving a Document with a Different File Format" on page 382 for information on the save options.

See "Understanding File Formats" on page 381 for information on the different file formats.

For Your Information

Understanding the Save Commands

When you use the Save command on the File menu to save an existing document, Photoshop performs the save without opening a dialog box. That means the original document file has been replaced with the current state of the image. To preserve the original document, use the Save As command on the File menu, and then give the document file a new name. For example, a file originally named landscape.psd could be saved as landscape_1.psd. Every hour, stop, select Save As, and create another version of the file (landscape_2.psd, landscape_3.psd). That way you have an historical record of the progress made on the document, and if you ever need to go back in time, you have the image files necessary to make the trip easy.

Closing a Document

To conserve your computer's resources, close any Photoshop documents you are not working on. You can close open documents one at a time, or you can use one command to close all open documents without closing the program. Either way, if you try to close a document without saving your final changes, a dialog box appears, prompting you to do so.

Close a Document

1 Click the **Close** button in the document window.

> **TIMESAVER** *Press Ctrl+W (Win) or ⌃⌘+W (Mac) to close the active document.*

2 If necessary, click **Yes** to save your changes.

Did You Know?

You can close all documents in one step. Click the File menu, and then click Close All. If necessary, click Yes to save your changes for each document. You can also press Alt+Ctrl+W (Win) or Option+⌃⌘+W (Mac) to close all documents.

You can close documents and open the Bridge in one step. If you wish to close the open document or documents and then open the Bridge, click the File menu, and then click Close And Go To Bridge (**New!**).

1 For the Macintosh

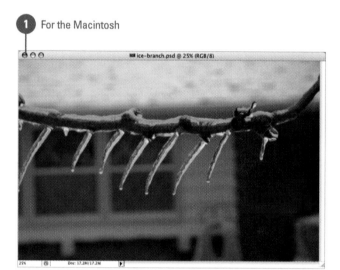

For Windows **1**

Exiting Photoshop

Now that you've decided how you want to save your Photoshop document, it's time to leave Photoshop. You'll want to make sure that all of your documents have been properly saved and closed before you exit Photoshop. Photoshop performs a bit of memory management, saves the current location of the palettes and toolboxes, and then quits.

Exit Photoshop from Windows

1 Click the **File** menu.

2 Click **Exit**.

> **TIMESAVER** *Click the Close button on the program window or press Ctrl+Q to exit Photoshop.*

3 If necessary, click **Yes** to save your changes.

Photoshop closes and you are brought back to your desktop.

Click to exit Photoshop

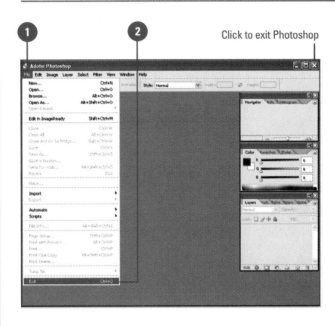

Quit Photoshop from Macintosh

1 Click the **Photoshop** menu.

2 Click **Quit Photoshop**.

> **TIMESAVER** *Press ⌘+Q to exit Photoshop.*

3 If necessary, click **Yes** to save your changes.

Photoshop closes and you are brought back to your desktop.

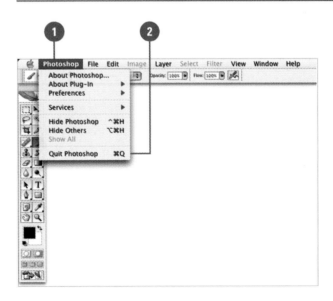

Working with Adobe Creative Suite 2

Adobe Creative Suite 2 is an integrated collection of programs that work together to help you create designs in print, on the Web, or on mobile devices. Adobe's Creative Suite 2 of professional programs, which includes Illustrator, InDesign, Version Cue, Bridge, and Stock Photos for the standard edition, and adds GoLive and Acrobat Professional for the professional edition.

Adobe Bridge

Bridge (**New!**) is a stand-alone file management/batch program that frees up Photoshop to process images across programs while you work. To use Bridge, open Photoshop, and then click the Go To Bridge button on the Options bar or click Browse on the File menu, or from the desktop use the Start menu (Win) or Applications folder (Mac). For more information on how to use Bridge, see "Working with Images Using Adobe Bridge" on page 12.

Adobe Stock Photos

Adobe Stock Photos (**New!**) is an integrated service available within Adobe Bridge that lets you search, view, try, and buy over 230, 000 royalty-free stock photographic images. With Stock Photos, you can download low-resolution, complementary (comp) versions of images you like at no charge and edit them in Photoshop. Each stock photo includes embedded metadata about the image, such as its author, copyright, creation date, size, color space, and resolution, to make it easier to find and track. You can work with the comps until you decision to use them, at which time you can purchase and download a high-resolution image. Downloaded images are automatically saved in folders in Adobe Bridge. To display stock photos, open Bridge, click the Folder list arrow, and then click Adobe Stock Photos, or use the Favorites pane, where you can also access downloaded comps.

Adobe Version Cue

Adobe Version Cue is a file tracking file management program you can use to keep track of changes to a file as you work on it. You can use Version Cue as an individual user or within a workgroup to manage project files in a single program, such as Photoshop, or from any of the Creative Suite programs. You can also keep track of non-Adobe files (**New!**), such as text documents or presentations. You use Adobe Bridge as a central location from which to use Adobe Version Cue. To use Version Cue, open Bridge, click the Folder list arrow, and then click Version Cue. The Version Cue Administration utility makes it easy to set up an online PDF review (**New!**) of the entire project.

Understanding Navigation and Measurement Systems

Introduction

When you go on a road-trip vacation, you need two things to make the trip a success-good navigational aids (maps), and an understanding of how to measure distances between two points on a road map (1 inch equals 100 miles). When you are working with Adobe Photoshop, one of the keys to making the journey a success is to understand the navigational and measurement aids available. Photoshop lets you choose a measurement system to fit a specific project. For example, if you're working on images destined for the Web or a monitor, you'll be using pixels as a measurement system.

Conversely, if you're outputting to paper, or possibly a 4-color press, you'll likely choose inches or picas. Selecting between different measurement systems does not impact the quality of the final image; only how you measure distance. Trust me on this one; understanding how to measure distance helps to make the journey an enjoyable experience (I know from experience).

Having problems squinting at the small details of a photographic image? Using the Zoom tool is a great way to gain control over a document. Zooming into a section of a document makes touching-up the fine details just that much easier. In addition, the Info palette gives you up-to-date information on the exact position of the cursor inside the document, as well as detailed color information that can be indispensable in color-correcting an image.

The ability to create text, and even audio annotations, gives you the capacity to record document information that might be vital to the processing of the image, and pass it on to anyone who opens the document. Photoshop's navigation and measurement systems are more that just information; they represent control of the document and control of the creative process.

What You'll Do

Change the View Size and Area with the Navigator Palette

Change the Color of the Navigator Palette View Box

Change the Screen Display Mode

Change the View with the Zoom Tool

Increase or Decrease Magnification

Move Images in the Document Window

Move Layers Between Two Open Documents

Work with the Info Palette

Change How the Info Palette Measures Color

Work with One Image in Multiple Windows

Work with Rulers

Create Notes

Create an Audio Annotation

Changing the View Size with the Navigator Palette

Photoshop's Navigator palette gives you an overall view of the image and the ability to navigate through the document or change the zoom size. Viewing images at different sizes gives you the ability to focus on small elements of the design, without impacting the overall quality of the image. Once small areas of an image are enlarged, it's easier for you to make minute changes. Zoom size determines the visible size of an image, as seen in the document window. Zooming in (enlarging the image) gives you a handy magnifying glass that lets you work on and manipulate fine details, and then you can zoom out (reducing the image) to view how the changes impact the entire image. The Navigator palette contains a thumbnail view of the image, and under the thumbnail are easy-to-use controls that let you adjust the zoom of the image. In addition, changes made in the Navigator palette, are immediately viewable in the active document window (what you see is what you get).

Change the View Size with the Navigator Palette

1. Select the **Navigator** palette.

2. Use one of the following methods to change the view size:

   ◆ Drag the triangular slider to the right to increase the zoom or to the left to decrease the zoom.

   ◆ Click the small and large mountain icons, located to the left and right of the triangular slider, to decrease or increase the zoom.

   ◆ Enter a value from .33 to 1600 percent into the Zoom box.

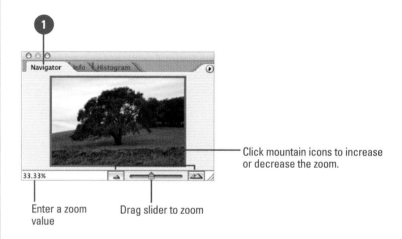

Click mountain icons to increase or decrease the zoom.

Enter a zoom value

Drag slider to zoom

Did You Know?

There are additional ways to zoom in using the Navigator palette. In the View box, hold down the Ctrl key, and then drag to resize the active document.

You can constrain the view box to drag horizontally or vertically. Hold down the Shift key, and then drag the view box horizontally or vertically.

For Your Information

Navigator Palette Shortcut

You can control the view of the document through a great shortcut. Simply click once in the Zoom input box on the Navigator palette, and then use the Up/Down arrow keys to increase or decrease the zoom value of the document 1 percentage point at a time. Not fast enough for you? Then hold down the Shift key, and use the Up or Down arrow keys to change the zoom size 10 percentage points at a time. Press the Enter key to see your changes reflected in the active document window.

Changing the View Area with the Navigator Palette

Zoomed images are typically larger than the size of the document window. When this happens, Photoshop adds navigational scroll bars to the bottom and the right of the document window. However, using awkward scroll bars is not the only way to change the viewable area of the image; the Navigator palette gives you a visible approach to changing the view area of the image. The view box in the Navigator palette represents the visible boundaries of the active document window, which is the viewable area of the image.

Change the View Area with the Navigator Palette

1. Select the **Navigator** palette.

2. Drag the view box in the thumbnail of the active image.

3. Click within the thumbnail.

   The position of the view box changes, which also changes the viewable area of the image in the document window.

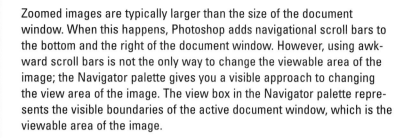
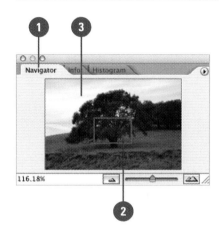

Did You Know?

You can show the Navigator palette. If the Navigator palette is not visible, click the Window menu, and then click Navigator.

You can change Zoom size of an image using the Navigator thumbnail. Hold down the Ctrl key (Win) or the ⌘ key (Mac), and then drag in the thumbnail. When you release your mouse, the selected area expands. It's just like using the Zoom tool, except you're dragging in the Navigator's thumbnail. Conversely, if you drag a second time (this time using a larger rectangle), the image zooms out.

Changing the Color of the Navigator Palette View Box

The view box defines the viewable area of the image—the default color of the view box is blue. It's important for the color of the view box to stand out against the image. However, some documents contain images that are the same color as the view box, making the view box difficult to identify. By changing the color of your view box to work with your image, you can make sure your view box stands out against the image. This may seem like a small thing to do, but it significantly cuts down on my frustration level, when I'm attempting to identify the view box.

Change the View Box Color

1. Select the **Navigator** palette.

2. Click the **Navigator Options** button, and the click **Palette Options**.

3. Click the **Color** list arrow, and then click a pre-defined color, or click **Custom** to select a color from the Color Picker dialog box.

4. Click **OK**.

Did You Know?

You can increase the size of the Navigator palette's thumbnail. Drag the lower-right corner of the Navigator palette to expand the size of the palette. As the Navigator palette increases in size, so does the thumbnail.

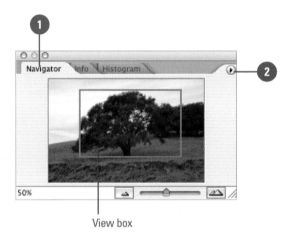

View box

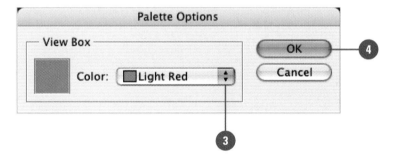

Changing the Screen Display Mode

In Photoshop, the Screen Display mode determines the background displayed behind the active image. For example, you can change the Screen Mode to black, and hide all the palettes. Since monitors, combined with Photoshop's palettes create a very colorful screen, changing the Screen Mode gives you a chance to see your image against a solid color background. Viewing your images against a black or gray background helps your eyes identify the true colors within an image.

Change the Screen Mode

1. Click one of the Screen Mode buttons at the bottom of the toolbox:

   ◆ **Standard Screen Mode.** Displays the image against a gray background (Win), or with the visible desktop (Mac). All menus and palettes are visible.

   ◆ **Full Screen Mode with Menu Bar.** Centers the image, and displays it against a gray background.

   ◆ **Full Screen Mode.** Centers the image, and displays it against a black background.

Did You Know?

You can temporally hide all of Photoshop's palettes and toolbox. Press the Tab key to hide the toolbox and palettes. If you press the Tab key while using Full Screen Mode with Menu Bar, or Full Screen Mode, the image is displayed against a gray or black background, respectively, without the distraction of the menus. Press the Tab key a second time to display the hidden toolbox and palette.

You can selectively hide just Photoshop's palettes. Hold down the Shift key, and then press the Tab key to hide the palettes, but not the Toolbox or Options bar.

Standard Screen Mode

Full Screen Mode with Menu bar

Full Screen Mode

2

Changing the View with the Zoom Tool

Working with the Zoom tool gives you one more way to control exactly what you see in Photoshop. Just like the Navigator palette, the Zoom tool does not change the active image, it only lets you view the image at different magnifications. The Zoom tool is located towards the bottom of Photoshop's toolbox, and resembles a magnifying glass. The maximum magnification of a Photoshop document is 1600 percent, and the minimum magnification is less than 1 percent of the original image size. Increasing the magnification of an image gives you control over what you see and gives you control over how you work. Large documents are difficult to work with and difficult to view. Many documents, when viewed at 100 percent, are larger than the maximized size of the document window. When this happens, viewing the entire image requires reducing the zoom.

Zoom In the View of an Image

1. Select the **Zoom** tool on the toolbox.

2. Use one of the following methods:

   ◆ **Click on the document.**

   The image increases in magnification centered on where you clicked.

   ◆ **Drag to define an area with the Zoom tool.**

   The image increases in magnification based on the boundaries of the area you dragged.

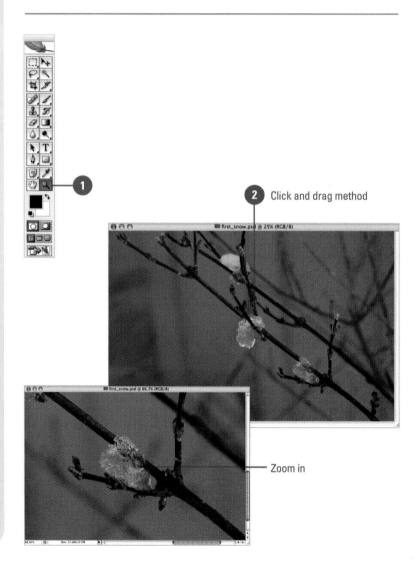

Click and drag method

Zoom in

Zoom Out the View of an Image

1 Select the **Zoom** tool on the toolbox.

2 Hold down the Alt (Win) or Option (Mac) key, and then click on the screen to reduce the zoom of the active document.

The zoom reduction centers on where you click on the active document.

IMPORTANT *Since images viewed in Photoshop are composed of pixels (like bricks in a wall), the only way to really see what the printed results of your artwork will look like is to view the image (even if it is to big for the screen) at 100 percent.*

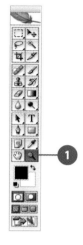

Did You Know?

You can zoom in or out using shortcut keys regardless of what tool you're currently using. To zoom in, press Ctrl+Spacebar (Win) or ⌘+Spacebar (Mac) and click or drag to define an area. To zoom out, press Ctrl+Spacebar+Alt (Win) or ⌘+Spacebar+Option (Mac) and click or drag to define an area.

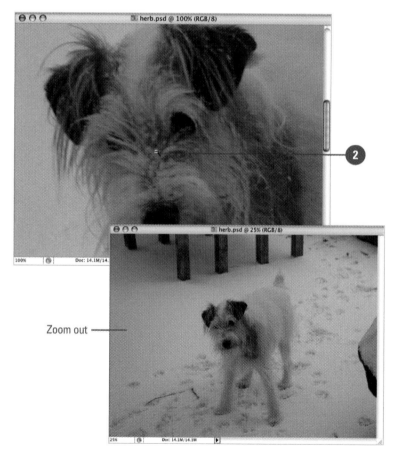

Zoom out

Increasing or Decreasing Magnification

Since changing the zoom size of an image is fundamental to the creative process, Photoshop gives you several ways to accomplish zooming. An additional way to zoom is using the options on the Options bar. To access the Zoom tool options, you must have the Zoom tool selected. Photoshop gives you two handy zoom preset values. To automatically zoom the document to 100 percent, double-click the Zoom tool. To automatically fit the image to the monitor, double-click the Hand tool.

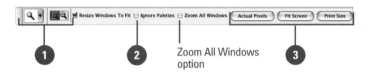

1

2   Zoom All Windows option

3

Increase the Magnification of an Image

1 Click the **Zoom In** or **Zoom Out** buttons on the Options bar, and then click in the document window to increase or decrease the zoom.

2 Click **Ignore Palettes** to zoom the active document beyond the boundaries of the floating palettes.

This causes the zoomed document to expand to the size of the monitor window.

3 Click **Actual Pixels**, **Fit Screen**, or **Print Size** to quickly zoom the screen to a preset size.

TIMESAVER *It's possible to change the zoom of a document without ever leaving the keyboard. Hold the Ctrl (Win) or* ⌘ *(Mac) key, and then press the plus "+", or minus "-" keys. The plus key increases the zoom size, and the minus key decreases the zoom size.*

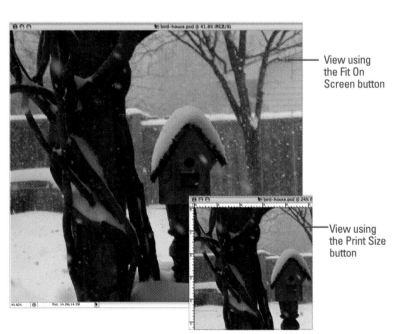

View using the Actual Pixels button

View using the Fit On Screen button

View using the Print Size button

Did You Know?

You can zoom in on more than one document. If you have more than one open document, click Zoom All Windows on the Options bar.

Moving Images in the Document Window

One of those little used, but handy tools to have is Photoshop's Hand tool. The Hand tool (called so because it resembles an open hand) lets you quickly move the active image within the document window without ever using the scroll bars. For example, you've zoomed the image beyond the size that fits within the document window and you need to change the visible portion of the document. It's a simple operation, but a handy one to know.

Move an Image in the Document Window

1 Select the **Hand** tool on the toolbox.

2 Drag in the active document to move the image.

Did You Know?

You can quickly access the Hand tool whenever you need it. Hold down the Spacebar to temporarily change to the Hand tool. Drag in the active document to the desired position, and then release the Spacebar. You're instantly returned to the last-used tool. It's important to note that you cannot use the spacebar to access the Hand tool if you are currently using the Type tool.

Moving Layers Between Two Open Documents

Photoshop has a lot of tricks up its electronic sleeves, and one of the handiest is the ability to move layers between open documents. For example, you have an image of a landscape and sky, but you don't like the sky, so you erase it. You then open another document with a sky that suits the design of your document. It's a simple matter to move the layer containing the sky into any other open document.

Move Layers Between Documents

1 Open two or more documents.

2 Click on the document containing the layer you want to move to make it the active document.

3 Select the **Move** tool on the toolbox.

4 Drag the layer you want to move from the open document window into the second document.

> **IMPORTANT** *If the document you're moving a layer into contains more than one layer, Photoshop places the layer you're moving directly above the active layer in the second document. If the layer is in the wrong stacking order, drag it up and down in the Layers palette until it's correctly positioned.*

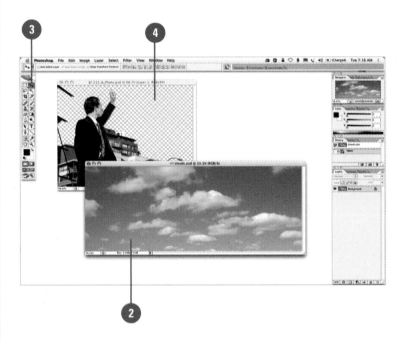

> **Did You Know?**
>
> ***You can also drag a layer thumbnail onto a document.*** Drag the layer thumbnail from the Layers palette into the document window of the second document.

From the Experts Corner

Removing the Excess

If you're dragging a layer from a document that contains more pixels than the receiving document, the areas of the image outside the viewable area of the document are still there, taking up file space. To delete them, first position the image exactly where you want, click the Select menu, and then click Select All. Select the Image menu, and then click Crop. That's it. All the image information outside the viewable window is removed.

Working with the Info Palette

Photoshop's Info palette gives you a wealth of data on the current document's color space, as well as information on the x/y position of your mouse cursor within the active document window. In addition, when you're using one of Photoshop's drawing or measuring tools, the Info palette gives you up-to-date information on the size of the object you're creating. Photoshop works with black, white, shades of gray, and every color in between. By creating color markers you help identify the location of specific color points within an image, which is indispensable for performing color correction, and the Info palette displays color information about the marked color and on how the color has shifted.

Create a Specific Size Object

1. Select the **Info** palette.

2. Select a drawing tool on the toolbox.

3. Drag in the document window to create a shape.

4. Release the mouse when the Info palette displays the correct dimensions.

> **IMPORTANT** *The bottom of the Info palette now displays tips on how to use the current tool, and the current size of the working document (**New!**).*

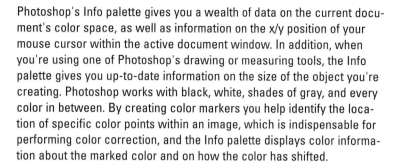
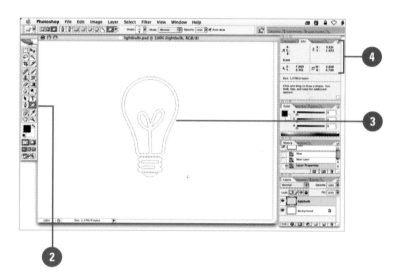

Create a Color Marker

1. Select the **Info** palette.

2. Select the **Eyedropper** tool on the toolbox.

3. In the document, hold down the Shift key, and then click once to create a color marker. You can have a maximum of four Color Markers in a single document.

Repositioning a marker is easy, simply press the Ctrl (Win) or ⌘ (Mac) key, and then click and drag the marker to a new position, or drag it off the document window to delete it.

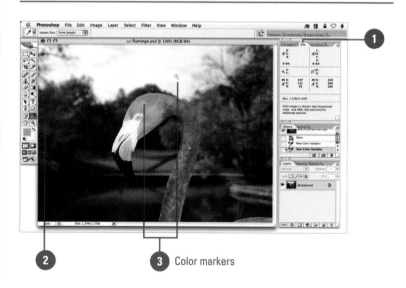

Color markers

Changing How the Info Palette Measures Color

Knowledge of the colors used in a document is important, but so is a thorough understanding of the color mode of the document. Different documents require different color modes. For example, images displayed on a monitor use the RGB (red, green, blue) color mode, and images sent to a 4-color press, use CMYK (cyan, magenta, yellow, black). Not only does the Info palette measure color, it also measures color in specific color modes.

Change How the Info Palette Measures Color

1. Select the **Info** palette.

2. Click the **Info Options** button, and then click **Palette Options**.

3. Click the **Mode** list arrows for First Color and Second Color Readout, and then select from the available options.

4. Click **OK**.

The Info palette now measures color based on your selections.

Did You Know?

The Info palette now allows you display information such as: Document Size, Efficiency, Scratch Sizes, and more. Simply click the Info Options button, and then select from the available options. The Info palette now displays whether the image is using 8, 16, or 32 bit color channels (**New!**).

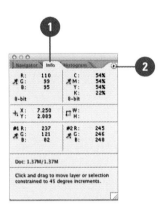

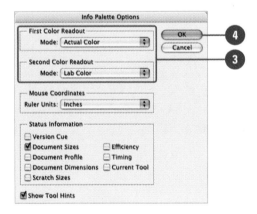

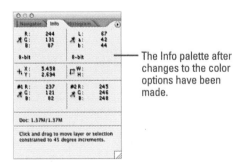

The Info palette after changes to the color options have been made.

Working with One Image in Multiple Windows

There are times when you're working on an image in Photoshop, and you need to see two separate views of the image. For example, you're working on retouching a photo and you need a zoomed in view to do fine detail work. At the same time, you want to see a normal view to get an idea of how the retouching is affecting the normal-sized image. Being able to view one image at two different views is a valuable tool.

Create Two Views of One Image

1. Open a document.

2. Click the **Window** menu, point to **Arrange**, and then click **New Window**.

   A copy of the active document is created in a new document window.

3. Select the **Zoom** tool on the toolbox, and then increase the zoom of the new document to the desired level.

4. Select an editing or painting tool, and then begin work on the new image in the zoomed window.

   The effects of your work instantly display in the normal image window.

5. When you're done with the new window, click the **Close** button.

New window with zoomed document

Did You Know?

You can prevent the zoomed window from expanding. With the Zoom tool selected, move into the Options bar and deselect Resize Windows To Fit.

Working with Rulers

Carpenters know that precise measurements are essential to making things fit, so they have a rule: Measure Twice, Cut Once. In keeping with the idea that precise measurements are essential, Photoshop gives you several measuring systems-among them are the ruler bars. Ruler bars are located on the top and left sides of the active document window, and serve several purposes. They let you measure the width and height of the active image, they let you place guides on the screen to control placement of other image elements, and they create markers that follow your cursor as you move. As you can see, Rulers serve a very important role. Ruler guides help you correctly align image design elements. As a matter of fact, if you're not working on a flat glass or LCD monitor, the curvature of the monitor can give you a false impression of the vertical and horizontal. By using guides you have access to precise alignment systems. To use the Ruler guides, the ruler bars must first be visible.

Change Ruler Options

1. Click the **Edit** (Win) or **Photoshop** (Mac) menu, point to **Preferences**, and then click **Units & Rulers**.

2. Select Ruler measurements and Type from the available options.

3. Click **OK**.

   IMPORTANT *If the Rulers are not visible in the active document, click the View menu, and then click Rulers.*

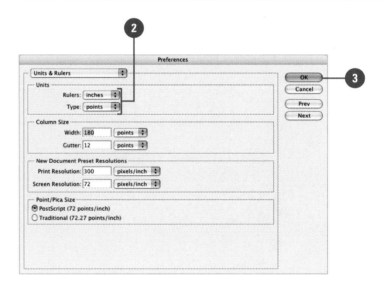

Did You Know?

You can choose what type of Point/Pica size to use. Click Postscript (72 points/inch) or click Traditional (72.27 points/inch). Postscript is more widely used, and Photoshop defaults to this option.

See Also

See "Working with Units & Rulers" on page 62 for more information on setting Units and Rulers preferences.

Use Ruler Guides

1. Click the **View** menu, and then click **Rulers** to display the ruler bars within the document window.

2. Move to the vertical or horizontal Ruler bar, and then click and drag into the document.

3. Return to the Ruler bar and continue to drag until you have all your guides properly set.

4. Click the **View** menu, and then click **Lock Guides** to lock the existing guides in place, or click **Clear Guides** to remove all guides.

5. Click the **Move** tool on the toolbox to drag existing guides to a new position (make sure Lock Guides is not selected).

Did You Know?

You can remove one guide at a time. Make sure Lock Guides is clear, and then click the Move tool. Drag the existing guide you want removed back to the corresponding Ruler bar.

You can switch guides on the fly. If you're dragging a vertical or horizontal guide onto the document window, when in fact you wanted the opposite guide, press the Alt (Win) or Option (Mac) key, while still dragging the guide. Vertical guides become horizontal, and horizontal guides become vertical.

See Also

See "Working with Guides, Grids & Slices" on page 64 for more informa-tion on setting guide preferences.

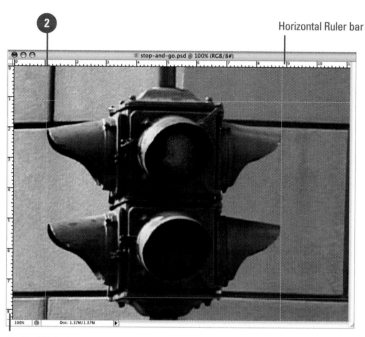

Horizontal Ruler bar

stop-and-go.psd @ 100% (RGB/8#)

Vertical Ruler bar

Creating Notes

Notes can be found everywhere—you see them stuck to the side of refrigerators, bulletin boards, and even covering your computer monitor. Notes serve a purpose to remind you of important duties and events. When you work in Photoshop, the ability to save notes can help you remember an important part of the design, or they can instruct another designer to the how's and why's of your document. For example, specific instructions to your service bureau on the printing of a document might be helpful in obtaining the best output.

Create a Note

1. Select the **Note** tool on the toolbox.

2. Click on the active document to create a blank note.

3. Enter the text for your note.

   TIMESAVER *Double-click the note icon to open and close a note. You can also right-click a note icon to access a shortcut menu with note commands.*

4. Click the **Close** button.

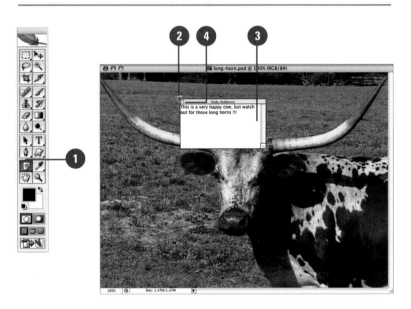

Did You Know?

You can change the Author, Font, and even the default color of a Note. Select a note, and then use the font, size, and color options on the Options bar to create a personalize note style; however, if the font you choose is not available on another computer, a default font will be substituted.

See Also

See "Saving a Document with a Different File Format" on page 382 for more information on saving note annotations with a document.

Working with Notes

Action	Keystrokes
Collapse a note	Click the Close button in the upper left-hand corner of the note
Reopen a note	Double-click on the Note icon
Delete a note	Select the note icon, and then press Delete

Creating an Audio Annotation

In addition to text notes, Photoshop lets you create audio notes. To create an audio note, your computer needs to have the ability to record sound. The good news is that most computers sold today, especially laptops, have the ability to record sound. Besides being an excellent way to communicate information, audio annotations give a sense of emotion or urgency, which sometimes can't be communicated using the written word. Audio notes require that the receiving computer has an audio output, and while this might seem quite common with today's technology, you might want to include a text note along with the audio note.

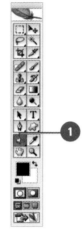

Create an Audio Annotation

1 Click and hold the **Note** tool on the toolbox, and then click the **Audio Annotation** tool.

2 Click on the active document to access the Audio Annotation dialog box.

3 Click **Start** to begin recording.

4 Click **Stop** to end the recording.

5 Double-click the **Audio Annotation** button to play the new message.

IMPORTANT *Notes and Audio Annotations are not contained on a specific layer; they are part of the Photoshop document and therefore visible in the document window at all times.*

Did You Know?

You can delete an audio annotation. Click on the speaker symbol, and then press the Backspace (Win) or Delete (Mac) key.

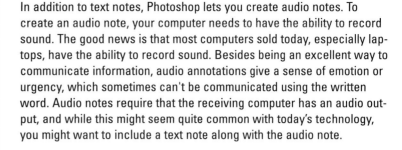

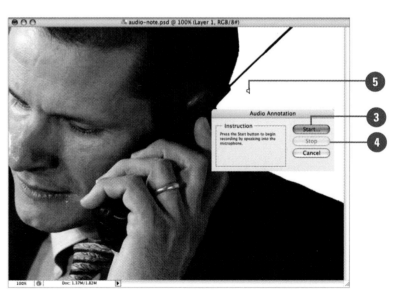

Customizing the Way You Work

Introduction

No description of Adobe Photoshop would be complete without that well known, but little utilized area called Preferences. Photoshop preferences serve several purposes. They help customize the program to your particular designing style, and they help you utilize available computer resources to increase the overall performance of the program.

By modifying File Handling preferences, such as appending a file extension on the file, or being asked when saving a layered TIFF file, you can streamline file saving process. In addition, you can change the way your cursors look. For example, do you want your paintbrush to look like a paintbrush when you paint, do you prefer a precession crosshair or the actual brush size shape, or the shape with a crosshair?

As you use Photoshop, you'll come to realize the importance of working with units and rulers. Precision is the name of the game when you are working with images. What about the color of your guides, grids, and slices? No big deal, you say. Well, if you've every tried viewing a blue guide against a blue-sky image, you know exactly why color is important. By working through preferences such as Image Cache, Scratch Disks, and RAM Memory, speed increases of up to 20 percent can be achieved.

In addition, customizing the program, helps make you more comfortable, and studies show that the more comfortable you are as a designer the better your designs. Plus, being comfortable allows you to work faster, and that means you'll accomplish more in the same amount of time. What does setting up preferences do for you? They make Photoshop run faster (up to 20 percent), you work more efficiently, and your designs are better. That's a pretty good combination. Photoshop doesn't give you preferences to confuse you, but to give you choices, and those choices give you control.

Optimizing Photoshop

Photoshop is a powerful program, and as such, requires a tremendous amount of computing power. When working on large documents, a poorly optimized Photoshop will translate into long wait times. That's the bad news if you have a deadline to meet. The good news is that Photoshop can be configured to run more efficiently. To optimize Photoshop, click the Edit (Win) or Photoshop (Mac) menu, and then point to Preferences. Of the available preferences, General, Plug-ins & Scratch Disks, and Memory & Image Cache contain options that will help increase the performance of Photoshop.

General Preferences

History States control the number of undos available. In fact, you can have up to 1000 undos (ever wonder who would make so many mistakes that they would need 1000 undos?). Unfortunately, increasing the number of History States will ultimately increase the amount of RAM Photoshop uses to manage the History palette. Assigning more RAM memory to manage History means less memory for Photoshop to perform normal operations, and will reduce the performance of the program. If you are experiencing slow performance problems, lowering the number of History States frees up more RAM, and permits Photoshop to operate more efficiently.

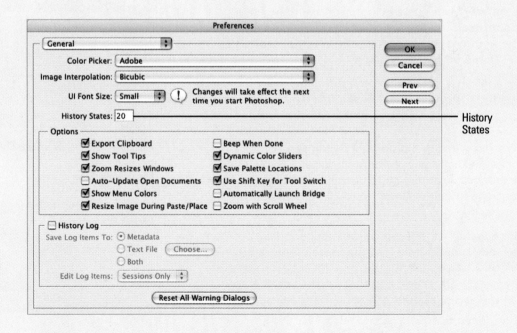

Plug-Ins & Scratch Disks Preferences

Scratch Disks are additional hard drives assigned to Photoshop. Photoshop requires 5 times the working size of the file in contiguous hard drive space. For example, if the working size of your file is 100MB, you will need 500MB of contiguous hard drive space, or you will receive an error message: Out of Scratch Disk Space (I hate it when that happens). Assigning additional hard drives gives Photoshop the ability to divide the processing load, and will increase performance. Scratch disks must be physically attached to your computer (avoid networks and removable media, such as zip drives, or rewriteable CD's). For maximum speed, avoid USB, and use 4 or 6-pin Firewire drives. Benchmark tests show Firewire drives provide up to a 20 percent speed improvement when used as Scratch Disks. Think of saving one hour out of every five, or one full day out of every five. That's not too bad.

Memory & Image Cache Preferences

Photoshop functions in RAM memory (actually all applications work within RAM). To run efficiently, Photoshop requires five times the working size of the open document in available memory (some tests indicate 6 to 8 times). Strictly speaking, the more RAM memory you can assign to Photoshop, the more efficient the program operates, especially when opening large document.

RAM memory usage is determined by the working size of the document, not its open size. As you work on a document, you will eventually add additional layers to separate and control elements of the image. As you add these new layers, the working size of the file increases.

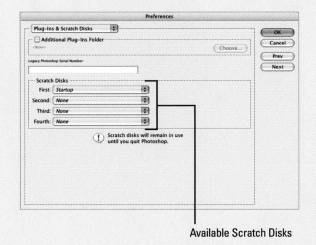

Available Scratch Disks

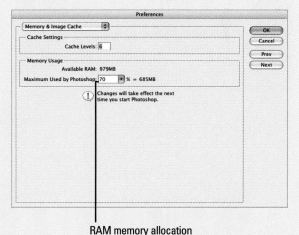

RAM memory allocation

Setting General Preferences

Photoshop's General preferences help you configure some of the more common features of the program. Image quality settings, as well as the new History log are setup in General preferences. Other options, such as showing tool tips, beeping when an operation is finished, and using Smart Quotes, can all be turned on or off in the options area. The History Log lets you save all the History States performed on a particular document. For example, when you open an image, all the adjustments and actions performed are saved in a text file. This gives you access to valuable information, and lets you reproduce the steps performed on one image, to correct the contents of another. You can also change the size of the small font text on the Options bar, palettes, and tool tips (**New!**).

Work with General Options

1. Click the **Edit** (Win) or **Photoshop** (Mac) menu, and then point to **Preferences**.

2. Click **General**.

3. Click the **Color Picker** list arrow, and then select Adobe or another operating system (Windows or Macintosh).

4. Click the **Image Interpolation** list arrow, and then select Nearest Neighbor (Faster), Bilinear, or one of the Bicubic options.

5. Click the **UI Font Size** list arrow, and then select a size for the user interface fonts (**New!**).

   The change takes effect the next time you start Photoshop.

6. Enter the amount of History States steps you want to keep as undos; you can enter up to 1,000.

   IMPORTANT *History States impact Photoshop's performance by holding the History States using a combination of RAM and Scratch Disk space. The more History States used, the more RAM memory is required. Using an extensive number of History States can impact Photoshop's performance.*

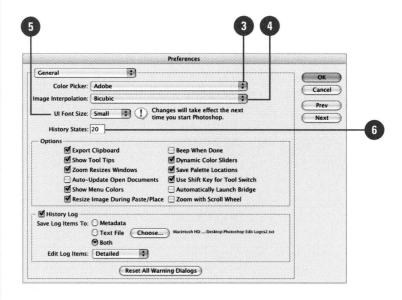

⑦ Select the various options you want to use:

◆ **Export Clipboard.** Transfers a copied image to the operating systems clipboard.

◆ **Show Tool Tips.** Shows labels when your cursor is placed over an option.

◆ **Zoom Resizes Windows.** Forces the image window to resize when zoom is selected.

◆ **Auto-Update Open Documents.** Creates a link between the open image and the image file on disk.

◆ **Show Menu Colors.** Displays selected menu items in user-defined colors (**New!**).

◆ **Resize Image During Paste/ Place.** Allows you to resize an image during a Paste or Place.

◆ **Beep When Done.** Sounds when an operation is complete.

◆ **Dynamic Color Sliders.** Previews color effects within the slider bars.

◆ **Save Palette Locations.** Defaults the palette locations.

◆ **Use Shift Key For Tool Switch.** Allows you to use the keyboard shortcut when two tools share the same slot in the toolbox.

◆ **Automatically Launch Bridge.** Automatically launches the Bridge in the background every time Photoshop is launched (**New!**).

◆ **Zoom with Scroll Wheel.** Determines whether zooming or scrolling is the default operation of the scroll wheel (**New!**).

⑧ Select the History Log options you want to use.

⑨ Click **OK**.

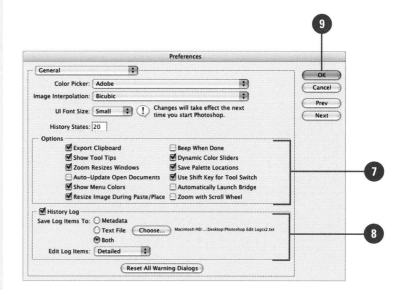

Modifying File Handling Preferences

Sooner or later, you'll have to save the file (document) you've created in Photoshop. The final output of any document is contained within a specific file format such as tif, eps, jpg, or even bmp. In fact, Photoshop lets you save files using over 18 different formats. The File Handling preferences provide several options that modify what information is saved with a file. Image previews are typically very small; add very little to the file size of the saved document. Once saved you will want to open, print, and possibly even modify the document using other image-editing applications. The File compatibility options help you save a file that will be transportable to other applications.

Work with File Handling Options

1. Click the **Edit** (Win) or **Photoshop** (Mac) menu, and then point to **Preferences**.

2. Click **File Handling**.

3. Select the File Saving Options you want to use:

   ◆ **Image Previews.** Select Always Save, Never Save, or Ask When Saving.

   ◆ **Icon.** Saves previews of the images (Mac).

   ◆ **Full Size.** Saves full-size previews for use as FPO (For Placement Only) objects in Desktop layout programs (Mac).

   ◆ **Mac Thumbnail.** Saves previews viewable when using the Mac File Open command (Mac).

   ◆ **Win Thumbnail.** Saves previews viewable when using the Win File Open command (Mac).

   ◆ **Append File Extension.** Lets you choose whether to append the file extension (Mac).

   ◆ **Use Lower Case.** Choose to have upper or lower case extensions.

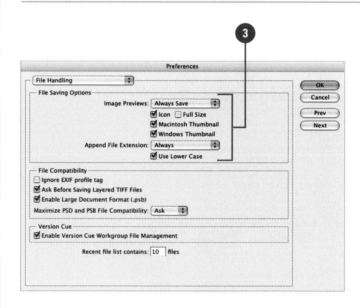

4. Select the File Compatibility options you want to use:

- ◆ **Ignore EXIF Profile Tag.** Ignores color space metadata attached to digital camera images.

- ◆ **Ask Before Saving Layered TIFF Files.** Lets you create multi-layered documents, and then save them using the TIFF format.

  This is a distinct advantage when you need to use multi-layered files and you don't want to save them using Photoshop's proprietary format .psd.

- ◆ **Enable Large Document Format.** Lets you create and save large files (up to 6 GB) (**New!**).

- ◆ **Maximize PSD File Compatibility.** Lets you save .psd files that can be opened in earlier versions of the program.

5. Select the **Enable Version Cue Workgroup File Management** check box to save files compatible with Adobe's Version Cue Workgroup File Management System.

6. Enter the number of files (up to 30) to keep in the Recent Files List box.

   IMPORTANT *The recent file list is not a function of RAM; therefore increasing the number of recent files will not impact Photoshop's performance.*

7. Click **OK**.

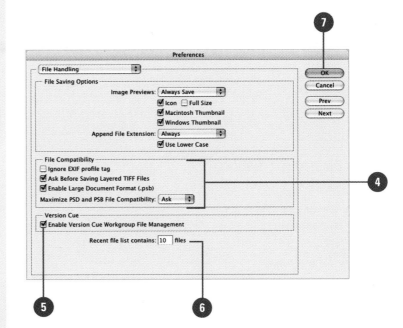

See Also

See "Understanding File Formats" on page 381 for information on some of the various file formats available in Photoshop.

3

Working with Display & Cursors Preferences

We communicate with Photoshop using various devices, such as a drawing table, mouse, touch screen, track pad, and a keyboard. Photoshop communicates with us using visual cues, the most prominent one is the shape of the cursor. For example, when a cursor looks like an I-beam, this typically means it's time to enter text, or when the cursor looks like a magnifying glass, clicking on the image expands the view size. Working with the Display & Cursors preferences, gives you control over how Photoshop communicates with you.

Work with Display and Cursors Options

① Click the **Edit** (Win) or **Photoshop** (Mac) menu, and then point to **Preferences**.

② Click **Display & Cursors**.

③ Select the Display options you want to use:

◆ **Color Channels In Color.** Allows you to view channels in the Channels palette in color.

For example, the red channel displays using shades of red, the green channel using shades of green, and the blue channel using shades of blue. When this option is not selected, color channels display, using shades of gray (does not affect printing).

◆ **Use Pixel Doubling.** Creates a low-resolution copy of the selected pixels during the drag, and then restores the dragged area to its original, high-resolution when you release the mouse (does not affect printing). Select this option to speed up the selecting and dragging of large areas of an image.

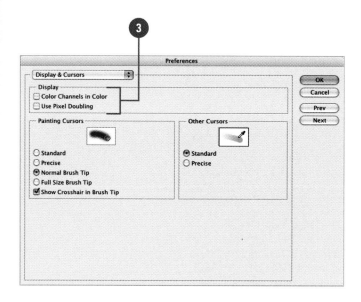

4 Select the Painting Cursors options you want to use:

◆ **Standard.** Painting cursors appear as their toolbox buttons.

◆ **Precise.** Painting cursors appear as cross-hairs.

◆ **Normal Brush Tip.** Painting cursors appear with the shape of the active brush tip.

◆ **Full Size Brush Tip.** Shows the full size of the brush tip, including feathered edges (**New!**).

◆ **Show Crosshair In Brush Tip.** Displays a crosshair in the center of the brush tip (**New!**).

5 Select the Other Cursors options you want to use:

◆ **Standard.** Painting cursors appear as their toolbox buttons.

◆ **Precise.** Painting cursors appear as cross-hairs.

6 Click **OK**.

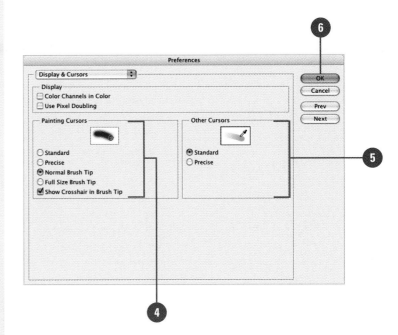

Did You Know?

You can toggle between precise and standard tools. Pressing the Cap Lock key while using a painting cursor, toggles the tool between the precise and brush size options, and pressing the Cap Lock key when using any other cursor, toggles between standard and precise.

Controlling Transparency & Gamut Preferences

The Transparency & Gamut preferences control how Photoshop displays transparent areas of a document (commonly called the tablecloth), as well as the color and opacity of areas of an image that fall outside of the CMYK (Cyan, Magenta, Yellow, Black), color mode. It's important to understand that transparency in Photoshop does not always translate into transparency, after you save the file. For example, the JPEG format is used primarily for images saved for the Internet, and does not support transparency. When you save the file, Photoshop will fill the transparent areas of the image with a matte color (default white). In addition, the Gamut Warning mask is used because a monitor displaying color information using RGB, and has more saturation values than a 4-color press (CMYK). Using new inks and spot colors can sometimes overcome an out-of-gamut color. For transparency it's important to remember that unless you're printing the document directly in Photoshop, it's the format that determines if the transparent areas will be saved, and the Gamut Warning is there to warn you of any areas that may not be saved.

Control Transparency & Gamut Options

1. Click the **Edit** (Win) or **Photoshop** (Mac) menu, and then point to **Preferences**.

2. Click **Transparency & Gamut**.

3. Select the Transparency Settings options you want to use:

   ◆ **Grid Size.** Allows you to select a transparency grid size.

   ◆ **Grid Colors.** Allows you to choose the color scheme for the transparency grid.

   ◆ **Use Video Alpha.** Allows you preview certain transparency settings. However, it requires hardware support.

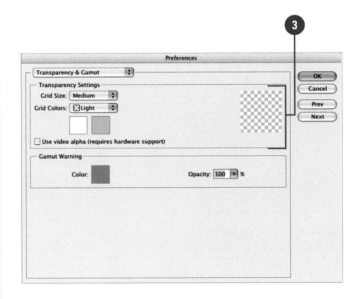

④ Select the Gamut Warning options you want to use:

◆ **Color.** Choose a color to mask areas of an image that move out of the CMYK color space.

◆ **Opacity.** Enter a value from 0 to 100 percent.

Opacity determines how much of the Color Overlay masks the original image pixels.

For example, if you choose the color gray, and an opacity of 100 percent, areas of an image that fall outside of the CMYK color space will be masked with gray.

⑤ Click **OK**.

IMPORTANT *To activate the gamut warning option, open a document in Photoshop, click the View menu, and then click Gamut Warning. Out of Gamut areas of the image will display with the color and opacity chosen in the Transparency & Gamut preferences.*

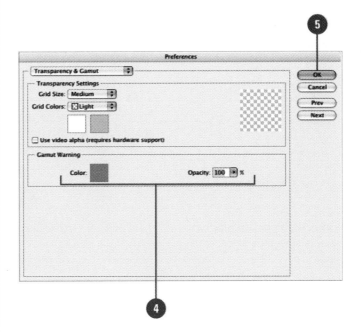

3

Working with Units & Rulers

While changing the measurable units and rulers do not affect output quality, they do help to measure information in a document consistent with the specific output device. Ruler units give you precise information on the width and height of the active document. The column size measurements provide information that Photoshop needs to create documents in the column and width of newspapers, magazines, brochures, etc. The Preset Resolutions lets you select specific resolution values for creating new documents. Insert the values you'll use most often in the creation of a new Photoshop document.

Work with Units & Rulers Options

1. Click the **Edit** (Win) or **Photoshop** (Mac) menu, and then point to **Preferences**.

2. Click **Units & Rulers**.

3. Select the Units options you want to use:

   ◆ **Rulers.** Sets a default measuring system for the Ruler bar.

   For example, pixels would be most common for images displayed on a monitor, and pica or inches most common for output to press or printer.

   ◆ **Type.** Sets to measure type with a default value of points or millimeters.

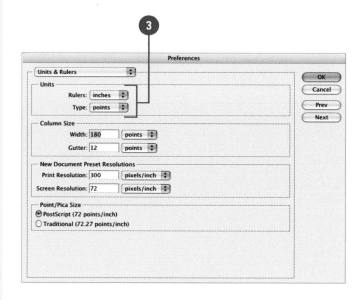

Did You Know?

You can switch between ruler measurements without going to preferences. To change the default measurement system of the Ruler bar, simply move into the Ruler bar, and then right-click your mouse. A list of available measurement options will be instantly available.

④ Select the Column Size settings you want to use:

◆ **Width.** Choose a measurement system and numerical value for column width.

◆ **Gutter.** Choose a measurement system and numerical value for gutter (the space between the columns).

When you choose a measurement system (points, inches, or cm), Photoshop changes the value to correspond to the type of measurement system.

⑤ Select the New Document Preset Resolutions settings you want to use:

◆ **Print Resolution.** Select a print resolution and measurement value for default printing.

◆ **Screen Resolution.** Select a print resolution and measurement value for default screen display.

⑥ Click the **Postscript** or **Traditional** option measuring systems for Photoshop's type tool (Postscript is the most widely used).

⑦ Click **OK**.

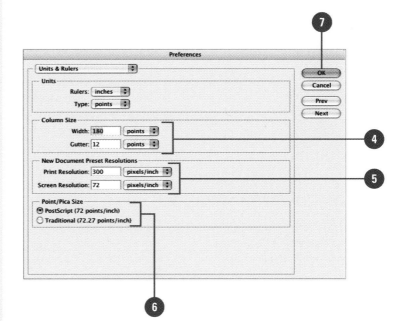

3

Working with Guides, Grid & Slices

The Guides, Grid & Slices preferences help keep a multi-layered document in proper order. For example, lining up buttons on a Web interface, or making sure specific design elements are exactly in place within the document window. The Guides option lets you select the color and style of the guides placed within a Photoshop document. Guides are placed within the image by dragging them from the horizontal or vertical Ruler bars in the active document. The Grid options let you decide on a color, style, and layout for Photoshop's grid system. The Slices option defines the visible color of a slice, and whether Photoshop displays a number value for each slice.

Work with Guides, Grid & Slices Options

1. Click the **Edit** (Win) or **Photoshop** (Mac) menu, and then point to **Preferences**.

2. Click **Guides, Grid & Slices**.

3. Select the Guides options you want to use:

   ◆ **Color.** Select a default color for displaying guides.

   ◆ **Style.** Select a default (Lines or Dashed) for displaying guidelines.

4. Select the Smart Guide options you want to use:

   ◆ **Color.** Chose a color for use with Smart Guides (**New!**).

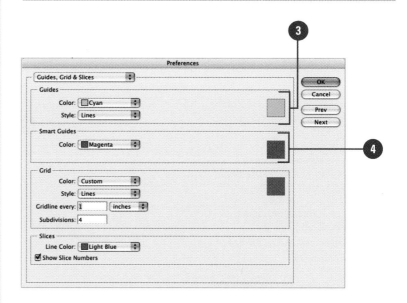

> **Did You Know?**
>
> **You can change a horizontal guide into a vertical guide, and vise versa.** Move into the Ruler bar and drag guide into the document window. Before releasing the mouse, hold down the Alt (Win) or Option (Mac) key. The guide automatically switches directions.

⑤ Select the Grid options you want to use:

◆ **Color.** Select a default color for displaying grids.

◆ **Style.** Select a default style (Lines, Dashed Lines, or Dots) for displaying the grid.

◆ **Gridline Every.** Enter a value for how often the grid lines appear within the active document.

◆ **Subdivisions.** Enter a value for how many subdivisions (lines) appear between each main gridline.

⑥ Select the Slices options you want to use:

◆ **Line Color.** Select a default line color for displaying document slices.

◆ **Show Slice Numbers.** Select the check box to display a number for each slice in the upper-left corner of the slice.

IMPORTANT *When you select a line color, choose a color that is different than the guide and grid line colors. That way you can easily identify grids and guides for user-created lines.*

⑦ Click **OK**.

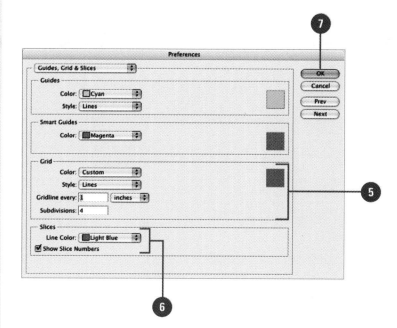

Did You Know?

You can change colors choices for Guide, Grid & Slices. Not satisfied with the color choices offered by the color and style menus. Click on the Color boxes located on the right side of the Guides, Grid & Slices dialog box, and select any color from the Color Picker.

Selecting Plug-Ins & Scratch Disks

The Plug-Ins & Scratch Disks preferences are designed to help you get the best performance out of your computer, by letting you choose more than one hard drive for scratch operations. Photoshop runs faster when you divide the Scratch Disk workload. Scratch operations are performed on your hard drive, and take place when Photoshop is using one of its many filters and adjustments. By assigning additional hard drives to the task, you speed up Photoshop's overall performance. Photoshop gives you the ability to organize your plug-ins by saving them in one or more folders. These additional folders are typically used to hold additional third-party plug-ins. When selected, plug-ins contained within the folder will be available from Photoshop's Filters menu.

Work with Plug-Ins and Scratch Disks Options

① Click the **Edit** (Win) or **Photoshop** (Mac) menu, and then point to **Preferences**.

② Click **Plug-Ins & Scratch Disks**.

③ Select the **Additional Plug-Ins Folder** check box to store additional plug-in.

> **IMPORTANT** *The first time you select this option, Photoshop asks you where to store the plug-ins. The next time you want to store plug-ins or add additional plug-ins, click Choose.*

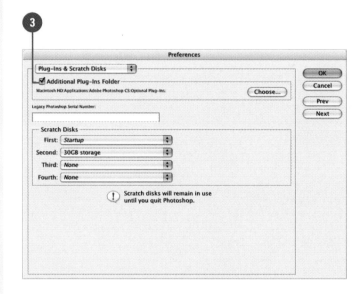

Did You Know?

You can keep a vast stock of plug-ins organized with multiple folders.
Organize your plug-ins into folders by subject, like restoration plug-ins, color correction plug-ins, etc. Then, when you have a specific project, enter the appropriate folder into the Additional Plug-Ins Folder option. Organizing your plug-ins into folders helps keep your project focused and reduces the clutter of plug-ins when you select the Filter menu.

④ If necessary, click **Choose** to identify the folder where you want to store plug-ins, and then click **OK**.

⑤ Enter in your Legacy Photoshop Serial Number.

Some third-party plug-ins require access to Photoshop's old style Serial Number. If you've been upgrading Photoshop, and you have the old style serial number (starts with PS) enter that number in the Legacy input box.

⑥ Select the Scratch Disks options you want to use:

◆ **First.** Select to see the available hard drives attached to your computer, and then switch first to an alternate drive.

◆ **Second.** If available, select an alternate drive.

◆ **Third.** If available, select an alternate drive.

◆ **Fourth.** If available, select an alternate drive.

IMPORTANT *Photoshop holds scratch disk space as long as the application is open. To delete scratch disk space you must close Photoshop.*

⑦ Click **OK**.

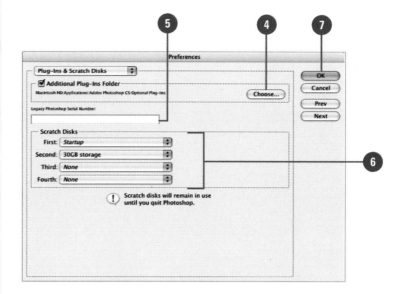

Allocating Memory & Image Cache

The Memory & Image Cache preferences give you control over how much RAM memory is assigned to Photoshop, and how much memory is allocated to screen draws (Image Cache). Photoshop, being a high-performance application, requires a fairly large amount of RAM memory. Adjusting these options can help increase Photoshop's overall speed performance. Photoshop has many names for RAM memory: History States, Undo, Clipboard, and Cache. When you modify the cache settings, you are increasing or decreasing the amount of RAM Photoshop uses for various tasks. Experimentation is the key here. Try different settings and record Photoshop's performance. By fine-tuning Photoshop's engine, you increase it's overall speed, and you'll get more design miles to the gallon.

Allocate Memory & Image Cache Options

1. Click the **Edit** (Win) or **Photoshop** (Mac) menu, and then point to **Preferences**.

2. Click **Memory & Image Cache**.

3. Select the Cache Settings options you want to use:

   ◆ **Cache Levels.** Select a number from 1 to 8.

See Also

See "Installing Photoshop CS2," on page 3 for information on RAM and other system needs.

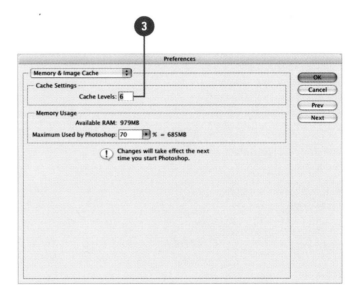

For Your Information

Setting the Cache Levels

Cache Levels are screen redraws. It's how many versions of the current active document Photoshop saves. When you're working on large documents, Cache Levels helps speed up the redraw function, and makes image manipulation proceed faster. However, they are held primarily in RAM memory, so the more Cache Levels you select, the less RAM memory is available for other Photoshop functions.

④ Enter the percentage of RAM used in the Maximum Used By Photoshop box.

Photoshop needs RAM memory to work efficiently (5 times the size of the open document).

IMPORTANT *Any setting changes made for allocating memory and image caching will take place the next time you start Photoshop. Please see the message at the bottom of the screen.*

⑤ Click **OK**.

IMPORTANT *Never select 100 percent Memory Usage. Selecting 100 percent gives Photoshop your entire available RAM, leaving nothing for the operating system or any other open programs. If you are experiencing more than your usual share of Photoshop crashes, experiment with reducing memory usage.*

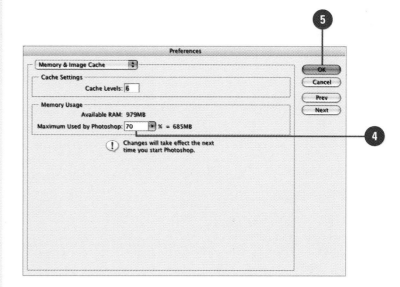

3

Working with Type

Although Photoshop is not by definition a type setting application, such as Adobe InDesign, it does have some very powerful type features. For example, Adobe Photoshop allows you to output PostScript text to a printer with a PostScript option. This way you will not need to place Photoshop images into type intensive applications, such as InDesign or Illustrator, just to create a few lines of text. In addition, Photoshop's new type menu lets you see fonts as they will print or display. For designers that use a lot of fonts, this WYSIWYG (What You See Is What You Get) font menu is a timesaver. You can use Type preferences (New!) to help you select the type and font options you want to use in Photoshop.

Work with Type Options

1 Click the **Edit** (Win) or **Photoshop** (Mac) menu, and then point to **Preferences**.

2 Click **Type**.

3 Select the Type options you want to use:

- **Use Smart Quotes.** Select to use left and right quotations.

- **Show Asian Text Options.** Select to display Japanese, Chinese, and Korean type options in the Character and Paragraph palettes (**New!**).

- **Show Font Names in English.** Select to display non-Roman fonts using their Roman names.

- **Font Preview Size.** Select to display fonts on the menu in small, medium, or large size.

4 Click **OK**.

IMPORTANT *Photoshop uses PostScript measuring systems to size fonts. Therefore a 72 point font will print 1 inch tall. Using this number as a yardstick lets you know how big the fonts will appear when output to print.*

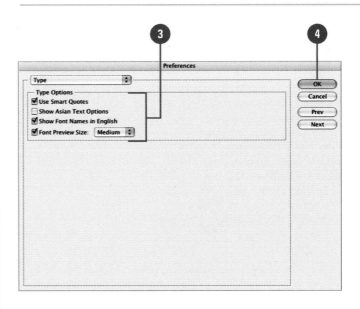

Managing Libraries with the Preset Manager

 PS 1.3

The Preset Manager gives you one place to manage brushes, swatches, gradients, styles, patterns, contours, custom shapes, and preset tools. The Preset Manager can be used to change the current set of preset items and create new libraries of customized sets. Once a library is loaded in the Preset Manager, you can access the library's items in all locations the preset is available. Changes made in the Preset Manager are global, and are applied every time you open Photoshop. When you save a new preset, the name appears in the dialog box for the specific option you selected.

Create a New Preset

1. Click the **Edit** menu, and then click **Preset Manager**.

2. Click the **Preset Type** list arrow, and then select the options.

3. Click the **Options** list arrow, and then select from the available presets to add them to the current item list.

4. To remove any items in a new preset, click a **thumbnail**, and then click **Delete**.

5. To reorganize their order, click and drag the thumbnails to new positions within the view window.

6. To change a preset name, click a **thumbnail**, click **Rename**, change the name, and then click **OK**.

7. Click a thumbnail, and then click **Save Set**.

8. Enter a new set name, and then select a location to store the set.

9. Click **Save**, and then click **Done**.

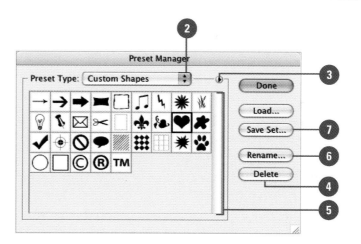

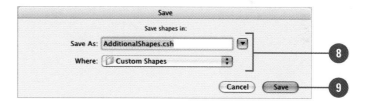

> **Did You Know?**
>
> **You can save specific items in the view window as a preset.** Press Ctrl+click (Win) or ⌘+click (Mac) on only those items you want in the new set, and then click Save Set.

Customizing the Workspace

 PS 1.1

Photoshop consists of a document surrounded by an Options bar, tool-box, and up to 19 floating palettes. Depending on how you work, your workspace may reflect any combination of the above. For example, when you work with text, you would need the Character and Paragraph palettes, but you might not need the Styles or Histogram palette. To work efficiently, each job requires a certain organization of the workspace. Rather than making you redesign your workspace every time you begin a new project, Photoshop gives you ways to create and save your own customized workspaces.

Create a Customized Workspace

1 Arrange the palettes into a specific working order.

2 Click the **Window** menu, point to **Workspace**, and then click **Save Workspace**.

3 Type a name for the workspace.

4 Select check boxes to save Palette Locations, Keyboard Shortcuts, or Menus.

5 Click **Save**.

Delete a Customized Workspace

1 Click the **Window** menu, point to **Workspace**, and then click **Delete Workspace**.

2 Click the **Workspace** list arrow, and then click the workspace you want to delete, or click **All**.

3 Click **Delete**, and then click **Yes** to confirm the deletion.

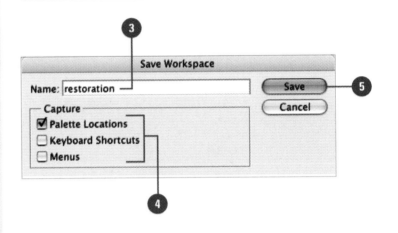

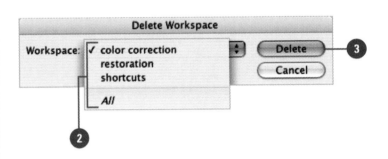

> ### Did You Know?
>
> **You can reset all Photoshop palettes back to their original configuration.** Click the Window menu, point to Workspace, and then click Reset Palette Location. Photoshop resets all palettes, regardless of current settings.

Defining Shortcut Keys

 PS 1.4

A wise man once wrote "time is money," and Photoshop is a program that can consume a lot of time. That's why the Photoshop application uses shortcut keys. **Shortcut keys**, as their name implies, let you perform tasks in a shorter period of time. For example, if you want to open a new document in Photoshop, you click the File menu, and then click New, or you can abandon the mouse and press Ctrl+N (Win) or ⌘+N (Mac) to use shortcut keys. Using shortcut keys reduces the use of the mouse and speeds up operations. In fact, a recent study in the American Medical Journal, suggested that the use of shortcut keys significantly cuts down on repetitive stress, and reduces instances of carpal tunnel syndrome. Photoshop raises the bar by not only giving you hundreds of possible shortcut keys, but also actually allowing you to define you own shortcuts.

Create a Keyboard Shortcut

1. Click the **Edit** menu, and then click **Keyboard Shortcuts**.

2. Click an arrow (left column) to expand the menu that contains the command you want to create a shortcut.

3. Select an item from the commands list.

4. Use the keyboard to create the new shortcut. For example, press Ctrl+N (Win) or ⌘+N (Mac).

5. Click **Accept**.

6. Click **OK**.

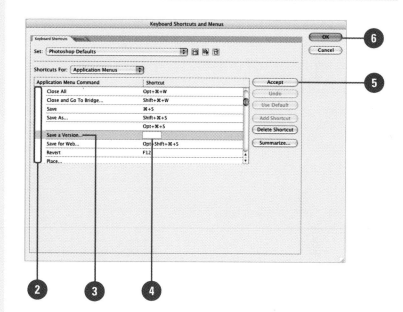

Did You Know?

You can save time using shortcut keys. According to several time and motion studies, using shortcut keys can actually save a computer user 1 hour out of every 8 in a work day.

See Also

See "Keyboard Shortcuts" on page xvii for information on getting a listing of common shortcut key assignments.

For Your Information

Working with Shortcuts

In addition to adding shortcuts, you can delete, add additional shortcuts, and even print out a summary of shortcuts defined in Photoshop. Shortcuts can be used for the Application and Palette menus, as well as for your tools in the toolbox. Click the Edit menu, click Keyboard Shortcuts, and then use the appropriate buttons, such as Delete Shortcut, Add Shortcut, or Summarize, to perform the tasks you want.

Creating a Customized User Interface

 **PS 1.4**

Photoshop's pull-down menus actually contain hundreds of options (yes, I did said hundreds). If you find navigating through menus a hassle, then Adobe has the answer to your problem with a customizable user interface. In Photoshop CS2, you have the ability to choose what menu items appear on the pull-down menus and even colorize certain menu items for easier visibility (**New!**). For example, if your curious about all the new features in Photoshop CS2, you can create a drop-down menu system with all the new features highlighted. Or, perhaps, you wish to create a menu system that highlights all the specific tools you're planning to use in a photo-restoration project. In fact, Photoshop includes several predefined user interface sets just to get you started in the right direction.

Use a Predefined User Interface

1. Click the **Window** menu, and then point to **Workspace**.

2. Click one of the predefined sets, such as: Automation, Web Design, or What's New in CS2.

   A dialog box displays asking whether you want to apply the new changes

3. Click **Yes** to apply the changes.

   The Photoshop menus will now display with highlighted options based on your selection.

Did You Know?

You can restore menus to original settings. To restore all of the Photoshop menu settings to the original values, click the Window menu, and then click Reset Menus.

You can turn a text box into a slider. You can use any text box which displays a numerical value, such as font size, like a slider. Point to the text box, press and hold down the Ctrl key (which changes the cursor to a hand with arrows), and then move the mouse left to decrease or right to increase the displayed number.

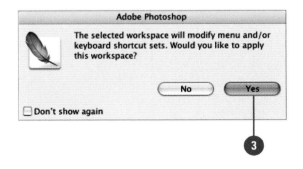

Create a Customized User Interface

1. Click the **Window** menu, point to **Workspace**, and then click **Keyboard Shortcuts & Menus**.

2. Click the **Menus** tab.

3. To create a new set, based on the current active set, click the **Create New Set** button, enter a name, and then click **Save**.

4. Click the **Set** list arrow, and then select a listing of modified User Interfaces.

5. Click the **Menu For** list arrow and then click **Application Menus** or **Palette Menus** with the items you want to modify.

6. Click an arrow (left column) to expand the menu that contains the command you want to modify.

7. Click the **Visibility** icon associated with a command to show or hide the command.

8. Click the **Color** list arrow, and select a color for the selected command.

9. Click the **Save All Changes** button to save the new customized User Interface.

10. Click **OK**.

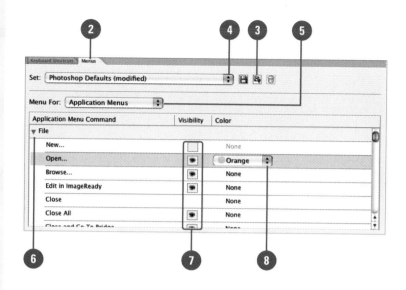

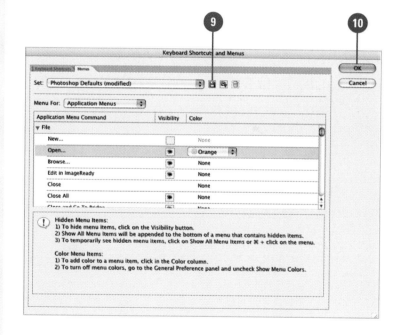

Did You Know?

You can delete a user interface set. Click the Windows menu, point to Workspace, click Keyboard Shortcuts & Menus, click the Menus tab, click the Set list arrow, click the set you want, and then click the Delete button.

Using Drawing Tablets

When you design on a computer, you're leaving the natural world of oil, watercolor, and canvas, for the electronic world of computer monitors and pixels (don't worry, it's a relatively painless transition). Without a doubt there are many differences between traditional and digital design; however, it's not necessary to abandon all aspects of the natural media world. For example, the computer mouse has always been a problem with designers who miss the feel and control of a brush in their hands. Fortunately, technology came to the rescue several years ago, with the invention of the drawing tablet. Drawing tablets incorporate a drawing surface, and a brush-like drawing tool. A designer picks up the brush and moves it across the drawing tablet surface. In turn, the drawing tablet interprets those movements as brush strokes. Not only does

Photoshop fully support drawing tablet technology, it also interprets the particular drawing style of the designer. For example, pushing harder with the brush against the drawing tablet, instructs Photoshop to create a wider stroke, or even to apply more color. Drawing tablets have helped to translate the control of working with real art brushes against canvas, into the world of the digital designer. Of all the manufacturers, Wacom stands out as the leader in drawing tablet technology. Wacom returns the feel of designing with a brush to the digital designer's world, and the software required to power the tablet works seamlessly with Photoshop and the Windows or Macintosh operating systems. To check out what tablet might be right for your needs, point your browser to *www.wacom.com* and check out the available options.

Wacom tablet

Drawing pen

Mastering the Art of Selection

4

Introduction

Mastering Adobe Photoshop requires skill in many diverse areas. While modifying an image's color, enhancing an old photograph, removing dust and scratches, may require different skills, they have one common thread-selection. Without selection, Photoshop gives you total access to the active document. If you choose to paint a black stroke, select the Paint Brush tool, the color black, and begin painting. Photoshop will let you apply black paint to any portion of the image. Selection is your way to instruct Photoshop what portions of the active document you want to change.

The Marquee tools are considered Photoshop's "good old" selection tools. In fact they've been a part of Photoshop since the early days. Where the marquee tools let you select areas of an image in a structured way (squares, circles, lines), the lasso tools add a bit of freeform selection to the mix. Lasso tools require a certain amount of hand/eye coordination. For example, you can use the lasso tool to create a customized selection area around just about any object in a document, be it an animal, vegetable, or mineral. It just requires a good eye, a steady hand, and a really big mouse pad (I hate it when I run out of mouse pad).

Selection lets you influence a specific area of the image, for example, changing the color of a car from red to blue. This is where selection really shows its strength. When you select an area of a Photoshop document, the selection becomes the work area-filters, adjustments, and brushes will only work within the selection boundary. Since selection is such an important aspect of controlling what happens in a document, Photoshop gives you many ways to create your desired selection. Mastering the art of selection gives you control over not just what you do, but where you do it.

What You'll Do

Use the Rectangular Marquee Tool

Use the Elliptical Marquee Tool

Use the Single Row and Single Column Marquee Tools

Use the Magic Wand Tool

Use the Lasso Marquee Tool

Use the Polygonal Lasso Tool

Use the Magnetic Lasso Tool

Select by Color Range

Modify an Existing Selection

Use Free Transform and Transform

Add, Subtract and Crop a Selection

Use Channels to Create and Store Selections

Use Smart Guides

Organize with Multi-Level Groups

Use the Quick Mask Option

Using the Rectangular Marquee Tool

The Rectangular Marquee tool lets you create rectangular and square selection marquees. the Rectangular Marquee tool is excellent for a quick crop, or selecting and moving blocks of image information. Select the Rectangular Marquee tool on the toolbox from the available Marquee options, and then drag the tool using the mouse (or drawing tablet) to control your movements. To further control a selection, hold down the Shift key to produce a perfect square, and hold down the Alt (Win) or Option (Mac) key to create a selection marquee from center out. Releasing the mouse instructs the Rectangular Marquee tool to create the selection.

Use the Rectangular Marquee Tool

1 Select the **Rectangular Marquee** tool on the toolbox.

2 Click the **Tool Preset** list arrow, and then select from the available tool presets.

3 Use the selection options on the Options bar to create a new selection, or add, subtract, or intersect an existing selection.

4 Enter a numerical value (0 to 250) in the Feather box to create a feathered selection edge.

5 Click the **Style** list arrow, and then select from the available styles:

- **Normal.** Lets you create freeform rectangular, or square marquee selections.

- **Fixed Aspect Ratio.** Lets you create selections using a specific ratio, such as a 2 to 1 ratio. Enter the Fixed Aspect Ratio values in the Width and Height boxes.

- **Fixed Size.** Lets you create selections based on an absolute size such as 30 pixels by 90 pixels. Enter the Fixed Size values in the Width and Height boxes.

6 Drag the selection area you want.

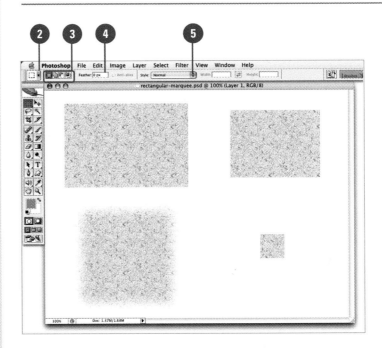

For Your Information

Selecting Areas for a Standard Monitor

If you are selecting areas of an image and plan to display them on a standard monitor (not DVD), then click the Fixed Aspect Ratio option on the Options bar, and then enter a width value of 4, and a height value of 3. Since a normal computer monitor (regardless of resolution) has a 4 by 3 ratio, then selection you make will fit a computer monitor perfectly.

Using the Elliptical Marquee Tool

 PS 4.1

The Elliptical Marquee tool lets you create oval or circular selection marquees. When used with the Layer Mask option, and a couple of creative filters, you can create some awesome vignettes. Select the Elliptical Marquee tool on the toolbox from the available Marquee options, move into the document, and drag the tool using the mouse to control your movements. To further control a selection, hold down the Shift key to produce a perfect circle, and hold down the Alt (Win) or Option (Mac) key to create a selection marquee from center out. Releasing the mouse instructs the Elliptical Marquee tool to create the selection.

Use the Elliptical Marquee Tool

1 Select the **Elliptical Marquee** tool on the toolbox.

2 Click the **Tool Preset** list arrow, and then select from the available tool presets.

3 Use the selection options on the Options bar to create a new selection, or add, subtract, or intersect an existing selection.

4 Enter a numerical value (0 to 250) in the Feather option to create a feathered selection edge.

5 Select the **Anti-alias** check box to create a softer selection.

6 Click the **Style** list arrow, and then select from the available styles:

◆ **Normal.** Lets you create freeform elliptical, or circular marquee selections.

◆ **Fixed Aspect Ratio.** Lets you create selections using a specific ratio, such as a 1 to 1 ratio (perfect circle). Enter the Fixed Aspect Ratio values in the Width and Height boxes.

◆ **Fixed Size.** Lets you create selections based on an absolute size, such as 100 pixels by 200 pixels (oval). Enter the Fixed Size values in the Width and Height boxes.

7 Drag the selection area you want.

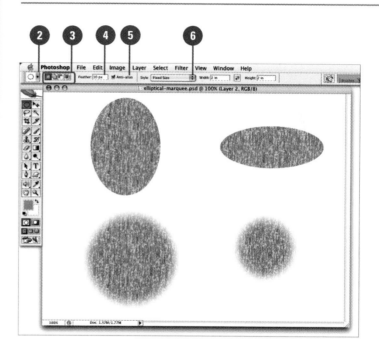

4

Using the Single Row and Single Column Marquee Tools

 PS 4.1

Use the Single Row and Column Marquee Tool

1 Select the **Single Row Marquee** or **Single Column Marquee** tool on the toolbox.

2 Click the **Tool Preset** list arrow, and then select from the available tool presets.

3 Use the selection options on the Options bar to create a new selection, or add, subtract or intersect an existing selection.

4 Drag the selection area you want.

Did You Know?

The Column Marquee tools doesn't have an Anti-Alias option. The reason is that a monitor displays digital information using pixels. Since the pixels fit together just like bricks in a wall, and the Column Marquee tools can only draw horizontal, or vertical lines, there is no need to make them look smoother because they're following the horizontal and vertical lines of the pixels.

The Single Row/Column Marquee tools lets you create a 1-pixel wide horizontal or vertical selection. Select the Single Row or Single Column Marquee tool on the toolbox from the available Marquee options, and then click the tool within the active document to create a single-pixel vertical or horizontal selection. To move the selection, place your cursor on the selection; when you see the cursor change to an arrow, then click and drag. Release the mouse when you have the selection correctly positioned. For precise positioning, press the arrow keys to move the selection 1-pixel at a time.

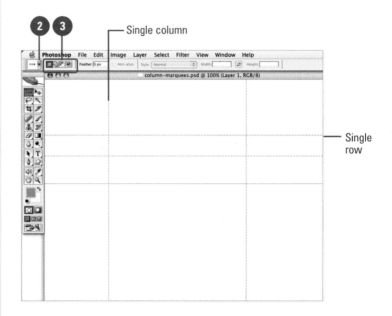

For Your Information

Creating Customized Guides

Have you ever needed a 45 degree angled guideline? Create a new layer, select the single row (or column) marquee tool, and then click to create a selection in the active document. Now, select black (or any other color) and press Alt+Backspace (Win) or Option+Delete (Mac) to fill the 1-pixel selection with the default color. Click the Edit menu, point to Transform, and then click Rotate. Enter a value of 45 in the Angle option on the Options bar, and then you'll have an instant 45-degree guide. Since the guide is in a separate layer, you can use the Move tool to reposition it anywhere it's needed.

Using the Magic Wand Tool

 PS 4.1

The Magic Wand tool (so named since it appears like a magic wand) is unique in the fact that you do not drag and select with this tool, you simply click. The Magic Wand tool creates a selection based on the shift in brightness range within an image. If there is a definable shift in the brightness of the pixels, it can be a very powerful tool for the selection of odd shaped areas. For example, a bright colored sunflower contrasted with a bright blue sky would be a snap for the Magic Wand tool. To use the Magic Wand, click on the Magic Wand Tool button on the toolbox—this tool does not have any other sub tools. Sometimes it's easier to select what you don't want. In this example, the blue sky was selected and removed. However, you might have wanted to select the sunflower, and move it into another image. If that's the case, it was still easier to select the sky using the Magic Wand, clicking the Select menu, and then clicking Inverse to reverse the selection.

Use the Magic Wand Tool

1 Select the **Magic Wand** tool on the toolbox.

2 Use the **Preset Tool** list arrow, and then select from the available tool presets.

3 Use the selection options on the Options bar to create a new selection, or add, subtract or intersect an existing selection.

4 Enter a Tolerance value (0 to 255). The higher the value the more information the Magic Wand tool selects.

5 Select the **Anti-alias** check box to create a softer selection (useful with intensely rounded or curved selections).

6 Select the **Contiguous** check box to select adjacent pixels within the active document.

7 Select the **Sample All Layers** check box to sample image information from all layers.

8 Click an area to make a selection.

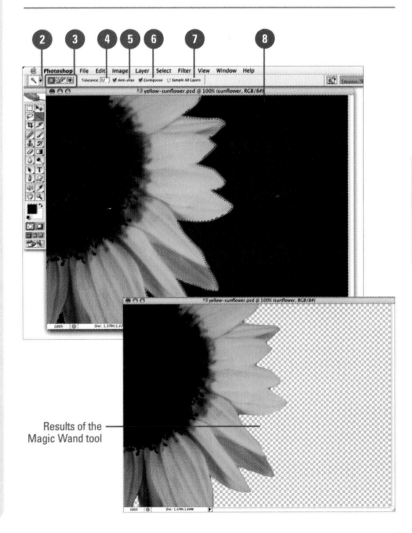

Results of the Magic Wand tool

Using the Lasso Marquee Tool

PS 4.1

The Lasso Marquee is a freeform tool that requires a bit of hand-to-eye coordination. Select the Lasso tool on the toolbox from the available Lasso options, move into the active document, and then drag the tool, using the mouse (or drawing tablet) to control your movements. Hold down the Alt (Win) or Option (Mac) key, and then drag to draw straight-line segments. Releasing the mouse instructs the Lasso tool to close the selection shape. That's all there is to it. I did mention that it requires good hand-to-eye coordination, didn't I? When you use this tool, don't drink too much coffee, and have a really big mouse pad.

Use the Lasso Marquee Tool

1. Select the **Lasso** tool on the toolbox.

2. Click the **Tool Preset** list arrow, and then select from the available tool presets.

3. Use the selection options on the Options bar to create a new selection, or add, subtract or intersect an existing selection.

4. Enter a numerical value (0 to 250) in the Feather box to create a feathered selection edge.

5. Select the **Anti-alias** check box to create a softer selection (useful with intensely rounded or curved selections.

6. Drag the selection area you want.

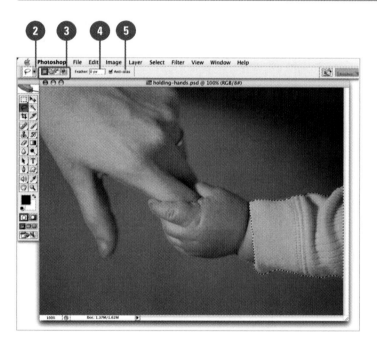

Did You Know?

You can temporarily convert the Lasso tool into a straight-line drawing tool (called the Polygonal Lasso tool). Hold down the Alt (Win) or Option (Mac) key, then release the mouse, move to a different area of the document window and click to draw a straight line between the two points.

Using the Polygonal Lasso Tool

 PS 4.1

The Polygonal Lasso creates straight-line selections. Perfect for creating a selection around a windowpane, or the roofline of a house. Select the Polygonal Lasso tool on the toolbox from the available Lasso options, and click to create a point; then move and click to create straight lines between the two points. Keep clicking and moving your mouse until the desired selection shape appears. Double-clicking the mouse instructs the Polygonal Lasso tool to close the selection shape.

Use the Polygonal Lasso Tool

1. Select the **Polygonal Lasso** tool on the toolbox.

2. Click the **Tool Preset** list arrow, and then select from the available tool presets.

3. Use the selection options on the Options bar to create a new selection, or add, subtract or intersect an existing selection.

4. Enter a numerical value (0 to 250) in the Feather box to create a feathered selection edge.

5. Select the **Anti-alias** check box to create a softer selection (useful with intensely rounded or curved selections.

6. Click to create anchor points, and then double-click or click the starting point to complete the selection.

> ### Did You Know?
>
> *You can temporally use the Polygonal Lasso tool as a freeform Lasso tool.* Hold down the Alt (Win) or Option (Mac) key, and then drag to draw. Release the mouse to return to the Polygonal Lasso tool.

4

Using the Magnetic Lasso Tool

 PS 4.1

The Magnetic Lasso creates a selection by following along the edge of a visible object. For example, it will follow around the edge of a building that contrasts against a bright blue sky. In reality there are no edges in a photographic document, so the tool follows along the shifts of brightness created when one image interacts with another. Select the Magnetic Lasso tool on the toolbox from the available Lasso options. Click on the visible edge of an image (like the edge between building and the sky), and then move (don't' drag) abound the object. The Magnetic Lasso will follow the visible edge of the object; occasionally adding anchor points to the line as you move. Double-clicking the mouse instructs the Magnetic Lasso tool to close the selection shape.

Use the Magnetic Lasso Tool

1. Select the **Magnetic Lasso** tool on the toolbox.

2. Click the **Preset Tool** list arrow, and then select from the available tool presets.

3. Use the selection options on the Options bar to create a new selection, or add, subtract or intersect an existing selection.

4. Enter a numerical value (0 to 250) in the Feather box to create a feathered selection edge.

5. Select the **Anti-alias** check box to create a softer selection (useful with intensely rounded or curved selections.

6. Enter a Width value (0 to 256) to instruct the Magnetic Lasso tool how many pixels to consider for the edge.

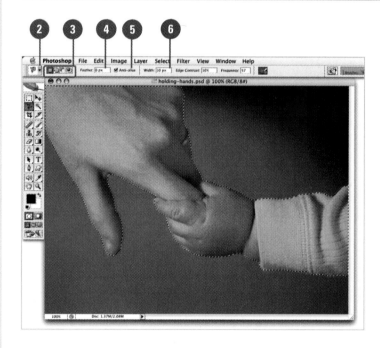

7 Enter an Edge Contrast value (0 to 100) to instruct the Magnetic Lasso how much of a shift in the brightness values to use in determining the edge.

8 Enter a Frequency value (0 to 100) to instruct the Magnetic Lasso where points are added to the selection line.

9 Click once to create an anchor point, and then move the pointer along the edge you want to trace.

10 If the border doesn't snap to the desired edge, click once to add a anchor point manually. Continue to trace the edge, and add anchor points as needed.

11 Double-click or click the starting point to complete the selection.

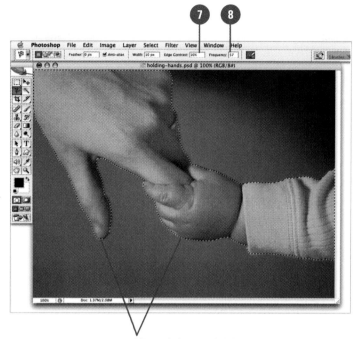

Magnetic Lasso selection

Did You Know?

You can remove anchor points. When you're using the Magnetic Lasso and you want to reverse the selection, simply back track the mouse all the way back to the last anchor point. To move even farther backwards, press the Backspace (Win) or Delete (Mac) key to remove the last anchor.

You can temporally use the Magnetic Lasso tool as a freeform Lasso tool. Hold down the Alt (Win) or Option (Mac) key, and then drag to draw. Release the mouse to return to the Magnetic Lasso tool.

4

Selecting by Color Range

PS 4.1

Photoshop makes selection easy by giving you ways to draw selection borders in any shape, size, or form. However, selection is more than dragging your mouse across the screen to create a selection. In addition to standard drawing tools, Photoshop lets you select image information based on channel color information. Maybe it's that bright red car in your background, or the white stucco finish adorning an adobe house, it doesn't matter because Photoshop lets you choose the color and select the maximum range to select. When you work with the Color Range option, the image displayed in the dialog box becomes a mix of black and white. The white areas represent the selected portions of the image, while the black areas represent the masked portions of the image.

Selection by Color Range

① Click the **Select** menu, click **Color Range**, and then select an option:

◆ **Select.** Lets you choose Sampled Colors, a specific color, or Out-of-Gamut colors.

  If you select Sampled Colors, choose the select color eyedropper, and then click in the visible image to select a color range.

◆ **Selection or Image.** Lets you view the Selection Mask or the Image.

◆ **Selection Preview.** Changes the view of the image in the document window. You can select None, Grayscale, Black Matte, White Matte, or Quick Mask.

② Click the **eyedroppers** to add or subtract colors from the selection, and then click within the image.

③ Click the **Fuzziness** slider to increase or decrease the color values selected (0 to 200).

④ Select the **Invert** check box to reverse the Selection Mask.

⑤ Click **OK** to transfer the color range mask to the selection.

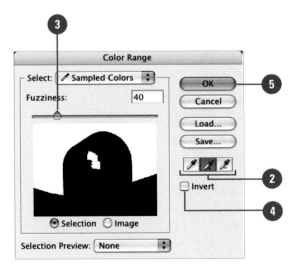

Modifying an Existing Selection

PS 4.1

Selections can be as simple as dragging a circle or square with one of the marquee tools to a more complicated freeform selection. Whatever the case, Photoshop allows you to enhance any selection with its useful modification tools. After creating a selection, you can modify it with the various options that Photoshop offers in order to make complex selections easier to use. With selection being an important part of Photoshop process, practice is the key to success.

Selection

Modify an Existing Selection

1. With a selection, click the **Select** menu, and then select an option:

   ◆ **All**. Selects all pixels within the active document.

   ◆ **Deselect or Reselect**. Removes any pixels from the active document.

   ◆ **Reselect or Inverse**. Lets you select or reverse the previous selection.

   ◆ **All Layers**. Lets you select all the layers in the Layers palette (excluding the Background).

   ◆ **Deselect Layers**. Deselects all layers in the Layers palette.

   ◆ **Similar Layers**. Selects similar layers such as: all type layers, or all shape layers.

   ◆ **Color Range**. Creates a selection based on a color or colors within the active document.

   ◆ **Feather**. Creates a visually softer selection edge.

   ◆ **Modify**. Lets you Modify the border, Expand, Contract, or Smooth the selection in the active document.

   ◆ **Grow**. Lets you increase a selection by adding pixels.

   ◆ **Similar**. Lets you increase a selection by adding non-contiguous pixels.

   ◆ **Transform Selection**. Creates a bounding box around the active selection which you can modify.

   ◆ **Load and Save Selection**. Lets you load or save a previously saved channel mask selection.

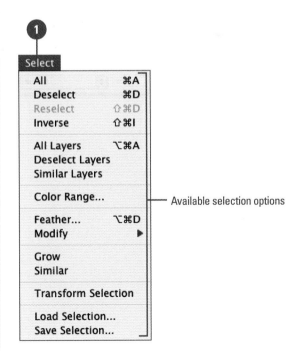

Available selection options

4

Using Free Transform and Transform

Once a selection is made, the next step is to get to work. Selections are not just to control color correction, or image enhancement. It's possible you may need to use some of Photoshop's transform commands. The transform commands let you move, modify, or resize the area enclosed within the selection area. Unlike the Free Transform command, Transform gives you several options, such as Scale, Distort, Perspective, and Warp (**New!**), which you can use to modify an existing selection. The selection area is visually defined by a bounding box with nodes, or anchor points, in the four corners and the center of each axis.

Use the Free Transform Command

① Select an area of an image using any of Photoshop's selection tools.

② Click the **Edit** menu, and then click **Free Transform**.

③ Move to any of the four corners, and then drag to expand or contract the size of the selection.

Move outside the bounding box selection until you cursor resembles a bent arrow, and then drag to rotate the selection.

Move to the horizontal or vertical center nodes to expand the image.

④ Press Enter (Win) or Return (Mac), or double click inside the bounding box to apply the transformation.

Selection enlarged and rotated

Did You Know?

You can create proportional transform boundaries. Hold down the Shift key while dragging a corner handle maintains the proportions of the original image.

You can use the Free Transform command to create distorted images. Hold down the Ctrl (Win) or ⌘ (Mac) key, while dragging a corner handle to create a distorted selection.

Use the Transform Command

1 Select an area of an image using any of Photoshop's selection tools.

2 Click the **Edit** menu, point to **Transform**, and then select an option:

- ◆ **Again.** Lets you repeat the previous Transform command.

- ◆ **Scale.** Lets you increase or decrease the size of the selected area.

- ◆ **Rotate.** Lets you rotate the selection area 0 to 360 degrees.

- ◆ **Skew.** Lets you select a node and drag it in vertical or horizontal direction without affecting the other nodes.

- ◆ **Distort.** Lets you select a node and drag it in any direction desired without affecting the other nodes.

- ◆ **Perspective.** Lets you change the perspective of a selection.

- ◆ **Warp.** Lets you wrap an image around any shape using a modifiable grid (**New!**). To warp an image using a specific shape, click the Warp Style list arrow on the Option bar, and then select a shape, such as Twist, Flag, Fisheye, or Inflate.

TIMESAVER *To show or hide the warp grid and anchor points, click the View menu, and then click Extras.*

3 Select any settings you want on the Options bar and modify the transformed image as desired using the anchor points, a segment of the bounding box or grid, or an area within the grid.

Additional transform commands

Warp

Grid

4

Adding, Subtracting, and Cropping a Selection

To say that Photoshop will help you make selections easy would be an understatement. Not only can you modify selections in any number of ways, Photoshop gives you the option to change your mind by adding and subtracting to an existing selection or even using the selection tools to crop the image. Since most selections are not perfect the first time around, knowing how to modify a selection marquee gives you the control you need to make perfect selections. Adding and subtracting to an image is accomplished by simple keyboard shortcuts, or items on the Options bar. Either way you can create complex selections with ease.

Add to an Existing Selection

① Create a selection using any of Photoshop's selection tools.

② Add to the selection by holding down the Shift key, and then use a selection tool to add to the existing selection (the selected areas do not need to be contiguous).

③ Release the mouse and the Shift key to complete the addition.

Two separate selections

Subtract from an Existing Selection

① Create a selection using any of Photoshop's selection tools.

② Subtract from the selection by holding down the Alt (Win) or Option (Mac) key.

③ Create a selection that intersects with the existing selection.

④ Release the mouse and the Shift key to complete the subtraction.

Crop an Image

① Create a selection using any of Photoshop's selection tools.

The selection area does not have to be a rectangle.

② Click the **Image** menu, and then click **Crop** to crop the image.

Did You Know?

Once a selection is made, it's possible to modify the selection using standard transform tools. To transform a selection, click the Selection menu, and then click Transform Selection. You will now be able to expand, contract, and even rotate the selection marquee. To exit Transform Selection, simply double-click in the middle of the selection marquee, or press the Enter (Win) or Return (Mac) key.

Image cropped

4

For Your Information

Cropping an Image to Bring Focus

Cropping a document brings focus to the information contained within the image. For example, if you take a photograph of someone standing in front of a building, is the focus the building or the person? If the focus is the person, then crop out the building. Cropping eliminates distractions, which would otherwise take away from the message of the image. A picture may be worth a thousand words; however, sometimes a picture can say too much.

Using Channels to Create and Store Selections

Photoshop's primary method of creating selections is through the use of tools on the toolbox, such as the Marquee, Lasso, and Magic Wand, and while they create impressive and complex selections, Photoshop has other ways to capture that tricky selection using the Channels palette. The Channels palette primarily holds color information, but that's not all it can hold. You can use the Channels palette to create and store complex selections. Photoshop holds selection information using black (mask), white (selection), and shades of gray (percentages of selection). In addition, channels are saved with the image file.

Create Selections with Channels

1. Select the **Channels** palette.

2. Click the individual color channels.

3. Look for a channel that represents a brightness difference between what you want to select and what you want to mask.

4. Make a copy of the channel by dragging it down over the New Channel button on the Channels palette.

5. Select the new channel.

6. Click the **Image** menu, point to **Adjustments**, and then **Threshold**.

7. Drag the **Threshold** slider left or right until the visible image represents a black and white mask of your selection.

8. Click **OK**.

Did You Know?

Selection masks created from color channels will not always be perfect. For example, you may see unwanted spots of white or black. When that happens, do the best you can using the Threshold command, and then use you Paintbrush with white or black to clean up the mask.

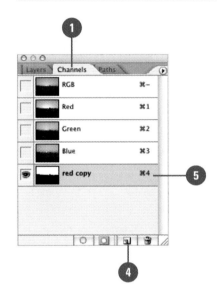

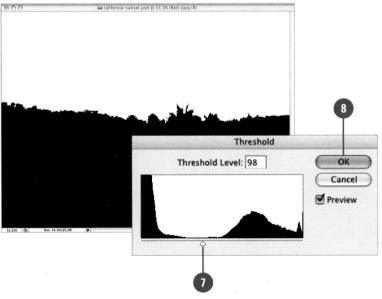

Apply Selection Masks to an Image

1. Click the **Select** menu, and then click **Load Selection**.

2. Click the **Channel** list arrow, and then select the newly created channel.

3. Click **OK**.

See Also

See "Creating Channel Masks from Selections" on page 243 for more information on using channel masks as selections.

Selection

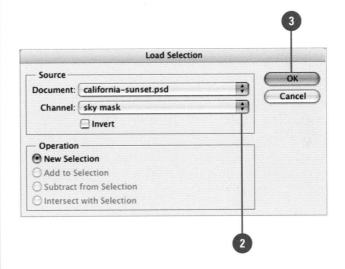

4

Using Smart Guides

Photoshop gives you the ability to use Smart Guides (**New!**) to help align shapes, slices, and selections as you draw. They appear automatically as you draw a shape, or create a selection or slide, and then disappear after the shape is drawn. They give you ability to visually align one object to another object with a minimum of effort. The default for Smart Guides is on. Smart Guides are also available in ImageReady; they work and function exactly the same way as they do in Photoshop.

Use Smart Guides

1 Open or create a multi-layered document.

2 Select a layer that contains an object.

3 Select the **Move** tool, and drag the object.

As you move the object, smart guides appear to help you align the objects.

4 Release the mouse and the guides disappear.

> ### Did You Know?
>
> *You can turn smart guides on and off.*
> Click the View menu, point to Show, and then click Smart Guides.

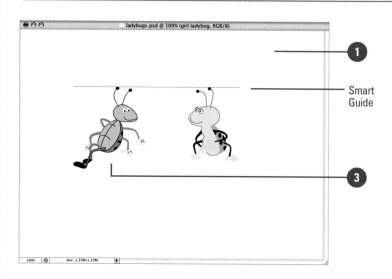

Smart Guide

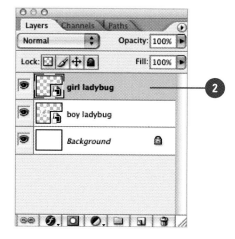

Organizing with Multi-Level Groups

Grouping layers in ImageReady helps to organize multiple layers. Layer groups are similar to layer sets, but allow for different kinds of quick manipulation. Layer groups let you move, drag, resize and physically manipulate multiple layers as one. For example, if you're creating a tabbed navigation bar, having all the tabs in one group helps to move and position the objects as one. When you create a layer group, the layers included in the group appear in the Layers palette indented under a heading of Group ending with a number representing a unique value for the group. Using the Layer Select tool you can click on any layer in the group to move the entire group.

Organize with Multi-Level Groups

1 Open a document in ImageReady.

2 Select the **Layers** palette.

3 Hold down the Shift key, and then click to select the layers you want to add to the group.

4 Click the **Layer** menu, point to **New**, and then click **Layer Group From Selected**.

ImageReady creates a Group based on the selected layers.

5 To separate the layers from a group, click the group, click the **Layer** menu, and then click **Delete Layer Group**.

6 Click **Set Only** or **Set And Contents**.

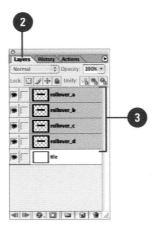

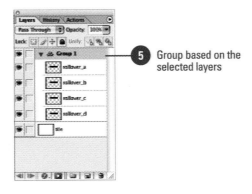

5 Group based on the selected layers

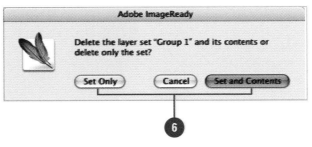

> ### Did You Know?
>
> **You can nest ImageReady groups.**
> Select one or more layers within a group. Click the Layer menu, point to New, and then click Layer Group From Selected. ImageReady lets you create nested groups up to five levels deep.

Using the Quick Mask Option

 PS 4.3

Photoshop represents selection using an animated single-pixel wide marquee, sometimes referred to as a crawling or marching ant marquee. Typically the enclosed or "marquee" area represents the working area of the document. Unfortunately, when selections become complicated you wind up with crawling ants marching all over the screen. While complicated selections are a part of the Photoshop designer's life, they shouldn't have to be hard to visualize or modify. Photoshop knows this and created the Quick Mask option. When you're using Quick Mask, Photoshop displays the selected areas with a user-defined color and opacity. Then by using your painting tools, you can make quick work of modifying the selection.

Modify Selections with Quick Mask

1. Create a selection using any of Photoshop's selection tools.

2. Click the **Default Colors** button to default your foreground and background painting colors to black and white.

3. Click the **Quick Mask** button to enter Quick Mask mode.

   By default the selected area remains clear and the unselected area becomes masked with a 50 percent red.

4. Select the **Paintbrush** tool.

5. Add to the selection by painting the Quick Mask with white and black. In Quick Mask mode, painting with black produces 50 percent red, and painting with white opens up the original image.

6. Click the **Edit In Standard Mode** button to revert the image back to a normal selection marquee.

7. Continue using the **Edit In Quick Mask** and **Edit In Standard Mode** buttons until you achieve the desired selection.

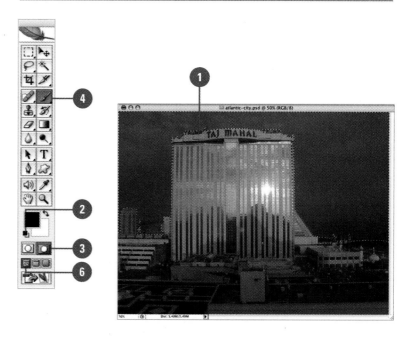

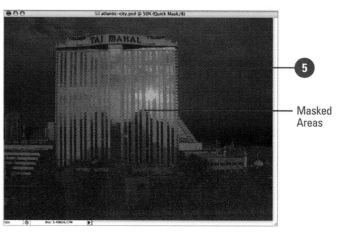

Masked Areas

96

Working with Layers

Introduction

To be successful with Adobe Photoshop, the single most important item you will need is control. You need control over color, control over the elements of the design, even control over what order design elements appear. If control is what you crave, then Layers, more than any other single Photoshop feature helps you gain control. Layers give you the ability to separate individual elements of your design, and then let you control how those elements appear. You can think of layers as transparency sheets one on top of the other. You can blend the elements of two or more layers, and even create layers to adjust and control contrast, brightness, and color balance. You can group layers together to help organize and manage your design.

Layers are the digital designers canvas, and they are just as real as a stretched canvas is to a natural media designer. The strokes you apply to a real canvas, using a brush, appear as strokes in a Photoshop layer when you use any of the painting tools. The natural artist uses oils, and watercolors; the Photoshop artist uses electronic inks. The Layers palette gives us the ability to view the image almost as if we were actually painting or designing. However, we don't work in the world of natural media, and our canvas—the Layers palette—goes far beyond anything possible in the "real" world.

In Photoshop, multiple layers are how you control the information within a document. There are times when you will create several layers, each with a piece of the document design. The multiple layers give you the ability to adjust and move each element. Eventually, during the course of the design, the multiple layers are no longer necessary. You don't want to link them together, or even place them within a folder; you'll want to combine them into a single unit. Once again, Photoshop comes to the rescue by giving you several options for combining layers without flattening the entire document.

Understanding the Layers Palette

PS 2.5

With the Layers palette, you can control elements of a Photoshop design by assigning separate layers to each individual object. In addition, Layer effects control the application of everything from drop shadows to gradient overlays, and adjustment layers let you control color overlays and image corrections. To access the Layers palette, select the Layers palette or, if the Layers palette is not visible, click the Windows menu, and then click Layers.

Blending Modes. Select this option to change how two or more layers interact or "blend" together.

Opacity. Select a value from 0 to 100 percent to change the opacity of the active layer.

Fill. Select a value from 0 to 100 percent to change the opacity of the active layer without changing the opacity of any applied layer styles.

Lock options. Click the Lock Transparent Pixels, Lock Image Pixels, Lock Position, or Lock All button.

Link Layers. Hold down the Shift key and click to select two or more layers, and then click this button to link the layers (**New!**).

Add Layer Style. Click this button, and then select from the available layer styles.

Add Layer Mask. Click this button to apply a layer mask to the active layer, click this a second time to add a vector mask to the active layer.

Create New Fill Or Adjustment Layer. Click this button, and then select from the available fill or adjustment layers.

Create New Group. Click this button to create a new set. A set is a folder where you can drag, store, and organize layers.

Create New Layer. Click this button to create a new layer in the active document.

Delete Layer. Click this button to delete the active layer.

Layers Options. Click this button to access a menu of layer specific commands.

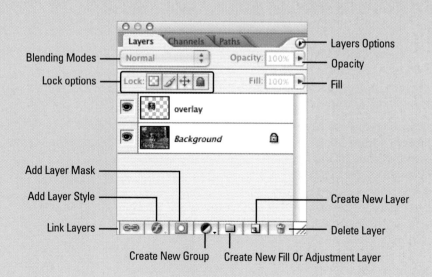

Defining Layer Designations and Attributes

 PS 2.5

Not only does Photoshop give you the ability to generate layers, it gives you the ability to generate layers with different designations. The **designation** of a layer determines the type of information the layer contains. For example, type layers hold editable text, and a mask layer holds image masks. The ability to control the designation of a layer helps to organize the different elements that typically make up a Photoshop image.

Background. The Background is a unique type of layer element (technically, it's not called the Background layer; just the Background). Backgrounds are always positioned at the bottom of the layer stack and they cannot be moved. In addition, the Background does not support transparency.

Layer. Clicking the Create New Layer button creates Photoshop layers. New layers are always inserted directly above the active layer. Traditional layers support all of Photoshop's drawing and shape tools, opacity and fill and blending mode options, but do not support type. Traditional layers can be moved up and down in the layer stack by dragging.

Type. To create a Type layer, select one of Photoshop's Type tools, click in the active document and begin typing. Photoshop automatically creates the Type layer directly above the active layer in the Layers palette.

Mask. Masks are applied to a layer by clicking the Add Layer Mask button on the Layers palette. Masks serve a function; they create transparent areas in the visible image. Use masks to remove elements of an image without physically erasing them.

Shape. Shape layers control vector data by the use of a vector mask. You can create a shape layer in one of several ways: Select the Pen tool from the toolbox, click the Shape Layer button (located on the Options bar, and then begin drawing, or select any of Photoshop's shape tools using the Shape layer option.

Adjustment. Adjustment layers let you control everything from contrast to color. To create an Adjustment layer, click the Create New Fill Or Adjustment Layer button, and then select from the available options. The adjustment layer is placed directly above the active layer, and controls the information in all the underlying layers.

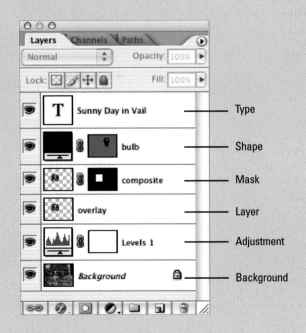

5

Creating a New Layer

PS 3.1

Layers give you control over the design elements of your document, so Adobe's Photoshop makes sure you have plenty of them. You have the ability to create up to 8,000 layers. While that may be more layers than you would ever use in one single document, it guarantees that you have the creative options to carry your designs to any level you desire. To create a new layer, you must first have an open document. A new image in Photoshop has a single layer. If you have more than one document open, make sure the active image is the one you want to add a layer. You can quickly add a layer using a menu or button or add a layer and select options using a dialog box. You can select options to name the layer, designate it as a clipping group, or even change its color Blending mode, and Opacity.

Add Layers to an Active Document

1 Select the **Layers** palette.

2 Click the **Layers Options** button, and then click **New Layer**.

> **TIMESAVER** *Click the Create New Layer button on the Layers palette to quickly add a layer.*

The new layer is inserted directly above the active layer.

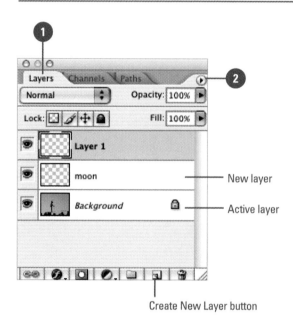

New layer

Active layer

Create New Layer button

Did You Know?

You can move a layer in the stacking order. Press the Ctrl (Win) or ⌘ (Mac) key, and then use the Left/Right Bracket keys ([ ]). The Left Bracket key moves the layer down and the Right Bracket moves the layer up.

You can hide all layers except the clipping mask layer and the layer it is clipped to. Press the Alt (Win) or ⌘ (Mac) key, and then click the layer's visibility icon (**New!**).

Add Layers and Select Options

1 Select the **Layers** palette.

2 Hold down the Alt (Win) or Option (Mac) key, and then click the **Create New Layer** button to open the New Layer dialog box.

3 Select the layer options you want:

◆ **Name.** Enter the name of the layer into the Name box.

◆ **Use Previous Layer To Create Clipping Mask.** Select this check box to use the image information in the previous layer to mask the elements of the new layer.

◆ **Color.** This option lets you color-code your layers. Click the Color list arrow, and then select from the available colors.

◆ **Mode.** Click the Mode list arrow, and then select from the available blending modes.

◆ **Opacity.** This option controls the visibility of the new layer. Select a value from 0 to 100 percent.

4 Click **OK**.

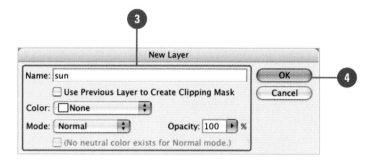

Did You Know?

You can control what layers the adjustment is applied. To confine the effects of an adjustment layer to the layer immediately below, hold down the Alt (Win) or Option (Mac) key, and then click on the visible line separating the adjustment layer from the next lower layer.

For Your Information

Selecting Layer Options

When you create a new layer in Photoshop, the size of the file does not increase. It's only when you begin painting, or adding information to the layer that the size of the Photoshop document will begin to grow. For example, creating a blank layer in a document with a file size of 10 MB does nothing to increase the size of the file. However, opening a 10 MB file, and creating a copy of the original document layer, will create a file size of 20 MB. Layers are great creative tools, but you only want to use them when you need them. Remember, performance is directly related to the size of the active document file, and the bigger the file size, the slower Photoshop performs.

5

Selecting Layers

Photoshop CS2 now lets you select multiple layers (**New!**) either in the Layers palette, or directly in the document window, using the Move tool. Say, for example, you want to quickly move two or more layers but you don't want to spend the time linking, and then unlinking, you could quickly select the layers, and then perform the move. Or, perhaps you want to delete several layers and you don't delete them one at a time. The ability to select multiple layers gives you the ability to exert more control over Photoshop, and that control quickly changes into creative energy. A single selected layer is called the **active layer**.

Select Layers

1 Open a multiple layered document.

2 Select multiple layers in the Layers palette using the following options:

- ◆ **Contiguous Layers.** Click on the first layer, and then Shift+click the last layer to select first, last, and all layer in-between.

- ◆ **Non-Contiguous Layers.** Click on a layer, hold down the Ctrl (Win) or ⌘ (Mac) key, and then click on another layer.

3 Select layers in the document window using the following options:

- ◆ **Single and Multiple Layers.** Select the Move tool, select the Auto Select Layer check box in the Options bar, and then click on an object in the document window. The layer holding that object is selected. To add or subtract layers from the selection, Shift+click (or drag).

  TIMESAVER *Select the Move tool, hold down the Ctrl (Win) or ⌘ (Mac) key, and then click on an object. Hold down the Shift+Ctrl (Win) or Shift+⌘ (Mac), and click on another object to add that object's layer to the selection.*

4 To deselect all layers, click the Select menu, and then click Deselect Layers.

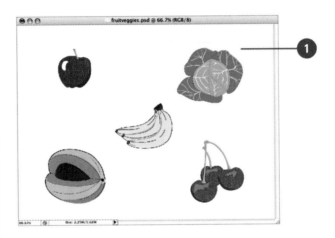

Contiguous Multiple
Layers selected

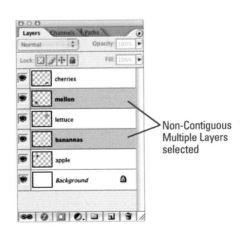

Non-Contiguous
Multiple Layers
selected

Creating a Layer Group

Layer groups help to bring organization to large multi-layered documents. Photoshop layer groups give you control over all the layers within the group. For example, multiple layers within a group can all be hidden or locked with one click of a button. In addition, if you click on the Group name, you can transform or move all the layer objects within the set as one unit. To further help organize your Layers palette, Photoshop lets you create nested groups. Nested groups are groups that are held within another groups. When you nest groups, you control all of the groups by clicking on the main group's name, or control the individual groups by selecting the nested group name.

Create a Layer Group or Nested Layer Group

1. Open a document.

2. Select the **Layers** palette.

3. If the document contains a layer group, click the **triangle** to expand the group, and then select one of the layers within the group to create a nested group.

4. Click the **Create New Group** button on the Layers palette, or press Ctrl+G (Win) or ⌘+G (Mac) (**New!**).

   Photoshop creates a layer group.

   TIMESAVER *To quickly create a Layer Group, hold down the Shift key and click the layers you want in the group, click the Layers Options button, and then click the New Group from Layers.*

5. To add layers to the group, drag layers from the Layers palette onto the folder icon of the group.

6. To remove layers from the group, drag them from the group back into the Layers palette.

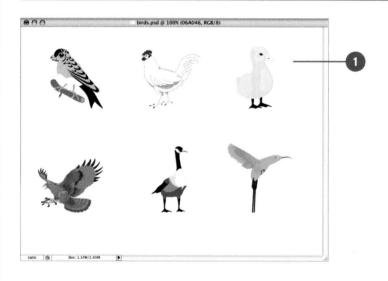

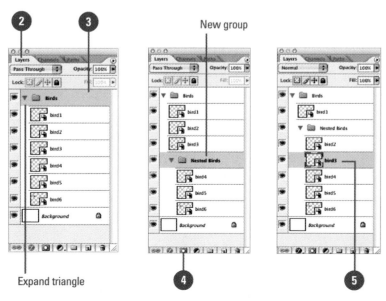

New group

Expand triangle

Creating a Selection from a Layer

Photoshop's traditional layers are basically sheets of transparent acetate or clear plastic. Once created they support all of Photoshop's painting tools, as well shape and gradient tools. While traditional layers may start out as transparent pieces of plastic, they don't remain that way for long. In fact, a layer can, over time, be a complicated mix of non-transparent (the image), and transparent areas. It's also possible you might want to make a selection out of that complicated image. Photoshop knows this and gives you an easy way to convert an image on a layer into a selection.

Create a Selection from a Layer

1. Click the **Layers** palette.

2. Hold down the Ctrl (Win) or ⌘ (Mac) key, and then click on the image thumbnail of the layer you want converted into a selection. Be sure you click on the image thumbnail (**New!**), not the layer name like previous versions.

   The visible portions of the image on the layer are converted into a selection.

   IMPORTANT *Since Photoshop creates the selection based on the image information, there must be transparent and non-transparent areas within the image or the command selects the entire layer as if you had clicked the Select menu, and then clicked All.*

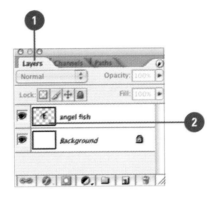

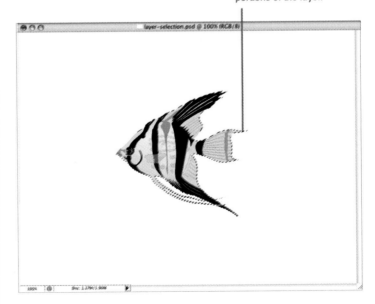

Selection based on the visible portions of the layer.

Creating a Layer from a Selection

On the previous page, you learned how to create a selection based on the image information within a layer. In addition to creating a selection from a layer, Photoshop gives you the ability to instantly create a layer from a selection. Creating layers from selections opens up all kinds of opportunities for generating special effects. For example, selecting an object from one layer, and then making a layer with that selection, or making a selection of a portion of a image, creating the layer, and applying a layer style to the copy. The possibilities are endless, and the fun of using Photoshop is exploring those possibilities.

Create a Layer from a Selection

1 Select the **Layers** palette.

2 Click on the layer containing the information you want to convert into a layer.

3 Select an area of an image using any of Photoshop's selection tools.

4 Press Ctrl+J (Win) or press ⌘+J (Mac) to make a copy.

Photoshop converts the selected area into a new layer, and places that layer directly above the active layer.

Did You Know?

You can make a copy of all elements within a layer. Select the layer in the Layers palette, and then click Ctrl+J (Win), ⌘+J (Mac). Since there are no selections, Photoshop creates a copy of the entire layer.

You can make copies of layer objects without selection. To make a copy of a layer that contains an object, select the layer in the Layers palette, select the Move tool, hold down the Alt (Win) or Option (Mac) key, and then click and drag (in the document window).

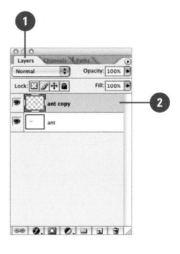

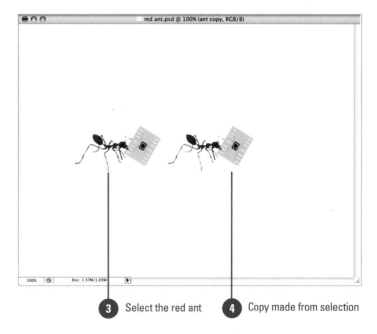

3 Select the red ant   **4** Copy made from selection

Converting a Background into a Layer

The Background serves a unique function in Photoshop. Since some layout programs do not support Photoshop's multiple layers, and transparency; in a process called flattening, a final image must sometimes be converted into a background. When an image is flattened, all of the documents layers are compressed into a single element in the Layers palette designated as the Background. That means no more layers, no more transparency, and no more control. Backgrounds are a necessary evil because Photoshop does not stand alone, and it's sometimes necessary to move images from Photoshop into other applications. However, there are times you start with an image that's on a background—images from a digital camera, scanned images, or images from a photo CD—and you want to apply transparency, blending modes, or other adjustments that cannot be applied to a background. In that case you will need to convert the Background into a Photoshop traditional layer.

Convert a Background

1. Select the **Layers** palette.

2. Double-click on the Background to open the New Layer dialog box.

3. Rename the layer in the Name box (leave the other options at their default values).

4. Click **OK**.

   The Background is converted into a traditional layer.

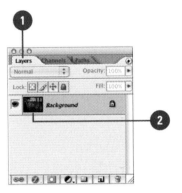

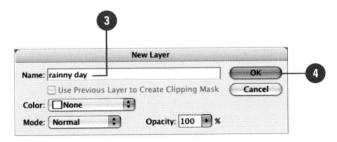

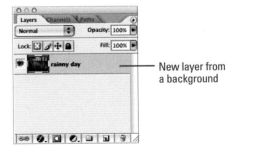

New layer from a background

Convert a Multi-Layered Document into a Background

1. Select the **Layers** palette.

2. Click the **Layers Options** button, and then click **Flatten Image**.

   The multi-layer document is compressed into a single-layer Background.

Did You Know?

You can create a composite image of a multi-layered document without flattening the image. Create and select a new layer, and then hold down the Alt (Win) or Option (Mac) key. Now, go to the Layers palette, click the Layers Options button, and then click Merge Visible. Photoshop creates a composite of all the visible layers in the new layer. You now have the control and flexibility of a multiple-layered document, along with a separate composite layer and control gives you the confidence to be more creative.

See Also

See "Using the Merge Layer Options" on page 110 for more information on how to merge two or more layers without flattening all the layers.

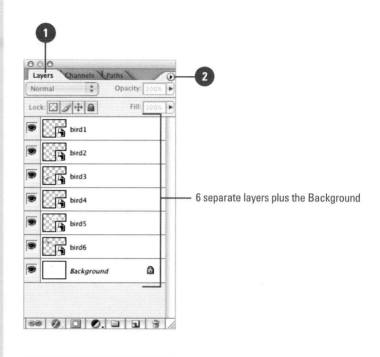

6 separate layers plus the Background

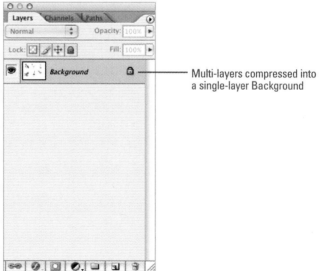

Multi-layers compressed into a single-layer Background

5

Controlling Image Information Using the Layers Palette

PS 3.6

When you work on multi-layered documents, it's important to understand the ways Photoshop gives you to control image information. For example, working on a document that contains 20 layers is a difficult proposition. Fortunately, Photoshop gives you control over the document, everything from layer names to locking pixel information is available in Photoshop's bag of image-control tricks. When linking two layers together, you can move or resize the layers at the same time, thus saving valuable time. Let's explore some of the ways you can control image information on the Layers palette.

Control Image Information

1 Select the **Layers** palette, and then use one of the following options:

- ◆ **Layer Name.** To name a layer, double-click on the current layer name, type a new name, and then press Enter (Win) or Return (Mac).

- ◆ **Show/Hide.** To temporally hide or show a layer (make its contents invisible or visible in the document window), click the Eyeball button, located in the Show/Hide box.

- ◆ **Linking.** To link two or more layers, hold the Shift key and click the layers you want to link, and then click the **Link Layers** button (**New!**) (located at the bottom left of the Layers palette). The link icon indicates the layers are linked. Linking lets you move or resize the layers as a unit.

- ◆ **Locking.** The four available locking options are Lock Transparent Pixels, Lock Image Pixels, Lock Position, and Lock All.

- ◆ **Stacking Order.** To change the position of a layer in the stack, drag the layer up or down. A dark line appears as a visual cue to indicate the new layer location.

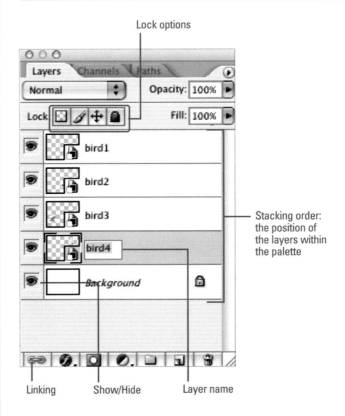

Moving Layers Between Documents

 PS 3.6

Photoshop documents typically contain multiple layers. One Web survey concluded that the Photoshop designer creates documents with an average of 14 layers. Controlling layers is an important aspect of design, because the more control you maintain, the more organized you are, and the better your designs will be. But what about controlling layers across multiple documents? For example, you're working on a Photoshop design, and you need access to some additional image information. The only problem is that the additional information is located in another Photoshop document. Photoshop gives you the ability to move layers between open documents.

Move Layers Between Documents

1. Open the documents in which you want to move layers.

2. To have more than one document in view, click the **Window** menu, point to **Arrange**, and then click **Tile** or **Cascade**.

3. Click on the document containing the layer you want to move.

4. Drag the layer from the Layers palette into the window of the receiving document.

   Photoshop creates a new layer with a copy of the image information from the other document.

Did You Know?

You can control the position of the moved layer. Hold down the Shift key while dragging the layer into the other document. Photoshop aligns the new layer to the center of the receiving document.

You can move selected portions of a layer. Select the area you want to move, click the Move tool, and then drag the selected area directly from the document window into the window of the receiving document.

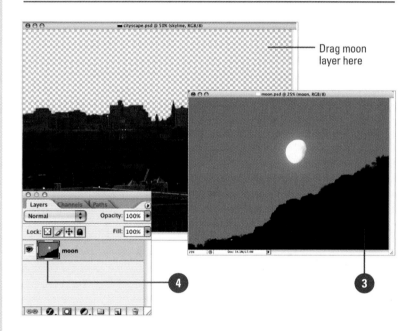

Drag moon layer here

Moon layer

New layer from donor document

Using Merge Layer Options

 PS 3.6

The Merge Down option lets you merge one selected layer into the layer directly below. Merged layers take on the characteristics of the layer they are being merged into. For example, merging a layer into a layer that uses the Darken blending mode. The two merged layers will still use Darken, or if you merge a layer into the background, the merged layer becomes a part of the background. The Merge Visible option gives you the ability with one click to merge all of the layers that have the Show option enabled.

Merge Down

1 Select the **Layers** palette.

2 Click the **Layers Options** button, and then click **Merge Down**.

The selected layers merge into the next layer down.

When you use the Merge Down command, the top layer will take on the name and characteristics of the bottom layer.

TIMESAVER *Press Ctrl+E (Win) or ⌘+E (Mac) to merge layers down.*

Merge Visible

1 Select the **Layers** palette.

2 Click the **Show** option for all layers you want to merge.

3 Click the **Layers Options** button, and then click **Merge Visible**.

All layers with the Show option enabled are merged together.

TIMESAVER *Press Alt (Win) or Option (Mac), click the Layer menu, and then click Merge Visible to merge all visible layers into a new layer (New!).*

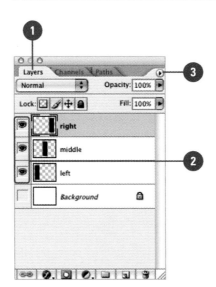

Linking and Unlinking Layers

If you're currently looking at the Layers palette, and wondered where the linking button is, don't worry; it's not missing, it's just been moved. Linking multiple layers is a snap, simply select one or more layers and then click the Link Layers button (**New!**) at the bottom of the Layers palette. You can link two or more layers or groups. Unlike selected multiple layers, linked layers retain their relationship (stay together) until you unlink them, which allows you to move or resize the layers as a unit.

Link Layers

1. Open a multiple layered document.
2. Select the **Layers** palette.
3. Select two or more layers.
4. Click the **Link Layers** button, located at the bottom of the Layers palette.

   The selected layers are now linked. A link icon appears next to the linked layers.

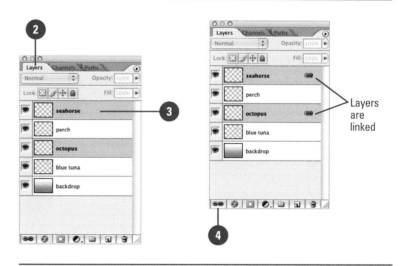

Unlink Layers

1. Open a multiple layered document that contains links.
2. Select the **Layers** palette.
3. Select a layer that contains the link icon.

   TIMESAVER *To unlink several linked layers, select them before continuing.*

4. Click the **Link Layers** button, located at the bottom of the Layers palette.

   TIMESAVER *To temporarily disable a linked layer, Shift+click the link icon for the linked. A red X appears. Shift+click the link icon to enable it.*

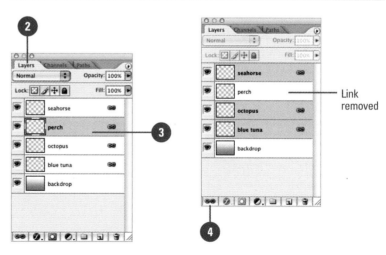

5

Working with Layer Blending Modes

PS 2.5

Layer Blending Modes are one of the most creative areas in the Layers palette. With blending modes you can instruct Photoshop to mix the image information between two or more layers. For example, the Multiply blending mode instructs Photoshop to mix the image information of two or more layers together. Blending modes give you control over Photoshop images up and over that what you would expect to find in the real world.

Mix Layer Information with Blending Modes

1. Open a multiple layered document.

2. Select the **Layers** palette.

3. Select a layer.

   Since blending modes work downward, select the layer directly above the layer you want to blend.

4. Click the **Blending Mode** list arrow, and then select a blending mode.

   Photoshop uses the selected blending mode to visually blend the image through all the layers below the blending mode layer.

Did You Know?

You can control the number of layers a blending mode is applied. Hold down the Alt (Win) or Option (Mac) key, and then click on the visible line separating the adjustment layer from the next lower layer.

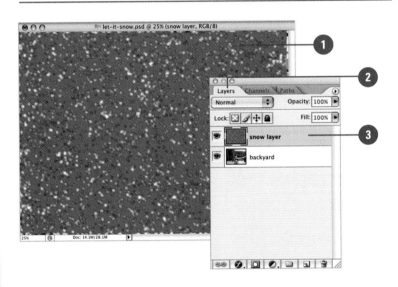

The snow layer blended with the backyard layer

Duplicating a Layer

There are times when you will need a copy of a Photoshop layer. Duplicating a layer is a simple process which creates a pixel-to-pixel copy of the selected layer. Once the copied layer is created, it becomes a separate image within the document. You can then begin to make any additions to the new layer. Duplicating a layer gives you the ability to control each layer separately and to create any desired effect.

Duplicate a Layer

1. Select the **Layers** palette.

2. Select the layer you want to duplicate.

3. Click the **Layers Options** button, and then click **Duplicate Layer**.

4. Enter a name for the new layer.

5. To place the layer in another open document, click the **Document** list arrow, and then select a document.

6. Click **OK**.

Did You Know?

You can duplicate a layer with the Create New Layer button. Drag the layer over the Create New Layer button and Photoshop creates an exact copy of the layer and appends the word copy at the end of the original layer name.

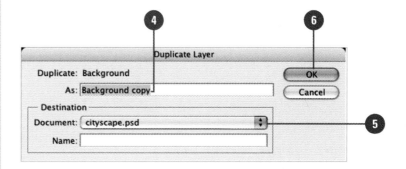

Deleting Layers

 PS 3.6

Photoshop lets you add layers to a document (up to 8,000), and it lets you delete layers. Remember that once you've deleted a layer, and saved the document, there is no way to recover the deleted layer. However, while the document is open, there is always the chance of recovering the deleted layer through the History palette.

Delete Layers

1. Select the **Layers** palette, and then select the layer you want to delete.

2. Hold down the Alt (Win) or Option (Mac) key, and then click the **Delete Layer** button.

> ### Did You Know?
>
> *You can delete a layer from the layers palette using the drag motion.* Click the layer you want to delete, and then drag it to the Delete Layer button.

The select layer has been removed from the Layers palette.

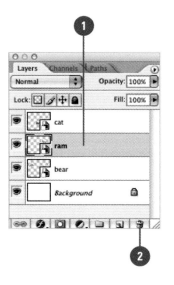

Delete Linked Layers

1. Select the **Layers** palette, and then hold down the Shift key and click on the layers you want to delete.

2. Hold down the Alt (Win) or Option (Mac) key, and then click the **Delete Layer** button.

   Photoshop deletes all the linked layers.

> ### Did You Know?
>
> *You can delete hidden layers from the layers palette.* Click the Layers Options button, and then click Delete Hidden Layers.

Selected layers are removed from the Layers palette.

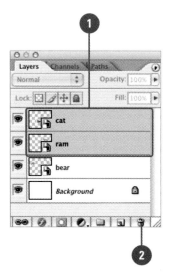

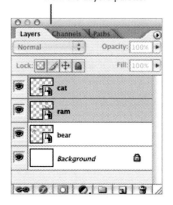

Changing Layer Properties

PS 3.7

The Layer Properties dialog box gives you control over the layer's name and its identifying color, two very important control items. For example, if you're working on a 20 layer document, and you're not naming the layers, after a while you'll loose track of what each layer contains. When you name the layers, you have a visual identifier of the information contained with that specific layer (assuming you name the layer correctly). In addition, you can use the colorize option to apply a color to a specific group of layers—coloring all the type layers red, for example. Layer properties may not seem like much, but they go a long way to helping you organize a complex, multi-layered document.

Change Layer Properties

1. Select the **Layers** palette.

2. Click the **Layers Options** button, and then click **Layer Properties**.

   TIMESAVER *Hold down the Alt (Win) or Option (Mac) key and double-click a layer name to open Layer Properties.*

3. Change the name of the layer.

4. Click the **Color** list arrow, and then click a layer color.

5. Click **OK**.

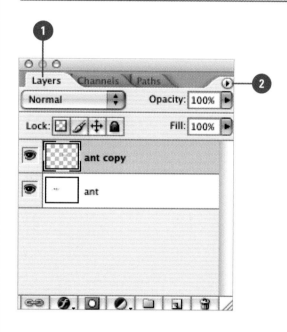

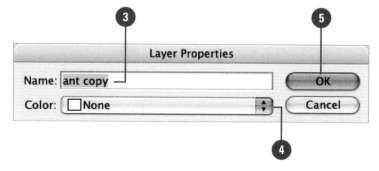

5

Working with the Layer Comps Palette

PS 3.2

Layer Comps are an image or snapshot of the current state of the Layers palette. When you create a layer comp, you're recording layer visibility, a layer's position within the document, and any layer styles applied to the image. Making changes to the layers in your document and updating the Layer Comps palette create comps. Any time you want to view a layer comp you can apply them to the existing image by selecting the appropriate comp from the Layer Comps palette. Layer comps give you the advantage of creating different versions of your document, and saving them with your document. In addition, they give you the option of printing the document using different layer comps.

Work with the Layer Comps Palette

1. Open a document.

2. Click the **Window** menu, and then click **Layers Comps** to open the Layer Comps palette.

3. Click the **Create New Layer Comp** button to create a snapshot of the current state of the image.

4. Select check boxes to adjust a layer's visibility, position, or appearance (layer style).

5. Click **OK**.

6. Click the **Create New Layer Comp** button to create another snapshot of the current state of the image.

7. Repeat steps 4 and 5 to create as many layer comps as you need.

8. Click the left and right arrows to cycle through the current layer comps.

9. Click the **Update Layer Comp** button to update the selected layer comp to the current state of the image.

10. Click the **Layer Comp** icon to change the active image to the selected layer comp state.

11. To remove a layer comp, click the **Delete Layer Comp** button.

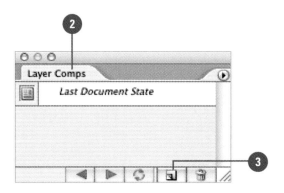

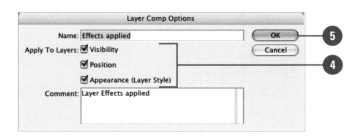

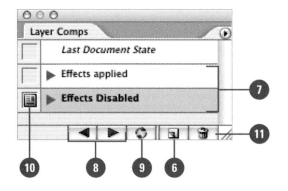

Exporting Layers as Files

ImageReady and now Photoshop (**New!**) give you the option of exporting and saving layers as individual files using a variety of formats. With ImageReady the formats include PSD, JPEG, GIF, WBMP, PNG, and even SWF. When exporting a layer as a file, different format settings can be assigned to individual layers, or one format can be applied to all exported layers. The Export Layers As Files option gives you the ability to create Web graphics and then select individual layers to save in a variety of formats.

Export Layers as Files

1 Open a document in ImageReady.

2 Select the **Layers** palette.

3 Select the layer you want to export.

4 Click the **File** menu, point to **Export**, and then click **Layers As Files**.

5 Click the **Export** list arrow, and then click **Selected Layers** or **All Layers**.

6 Click the **Format** list arrow, and then select an output option.

7 Click **OK**.

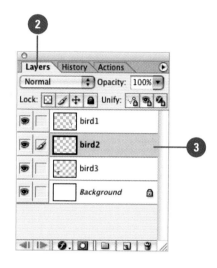

Did You Know?

You can export layers to files in Photoshop (**New!**). Click the File menu, point to Scripts, and then click Export Layers To Files. In the dialog box, click Browse to specify a destination for the files, enter a name for the files, select the Visible Layers Only check box to export only visible layers, click the File Type list arrow, select a file format (PSD, BMP, JPEG, PDF, Targa, and TIFF), select the Include ICC Profile check box to embed a color profile, and then click Run.

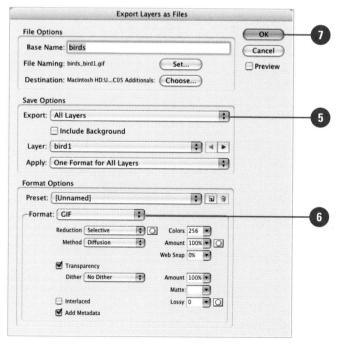

Setting Layers Palette Options

Adobe Certified Expert PS 3.7

Photoshop doesn't have a lot of options for controlling the palette; in fact, there is only one—changing the size of the thumbnail. Thumbnail size options come in three sizes, or you can select to have no thumbnail shown. When you change the size of the thumbnail, you're instructing Photoshop to spend more, or less processing time on the display of the image. The larger the thumbnail, the easier it is to see, but the longer it takes for Photoshop to draw the images in the Layers palette. If you're experiencing performance issues with Photoshop, and you're using a large thumbnail, you might consider downsizing the thumbnail image.

Set Layers Palette Options

1. Select the **Layers** palette.

2. Click the **Layers Options** button, and then click **Palette Options**.

3. Click a thumbnail size or the **None** option.

4. Click the **Layer Bounds** or **Entire Document** option.

5. Select the **Use Default Masks on Adjustments** check box to automatically insert a mask when creating a new Adjustment layer.

6. Click **OK**.

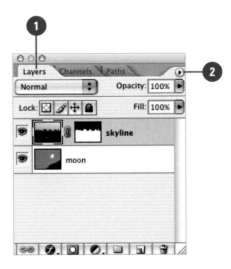

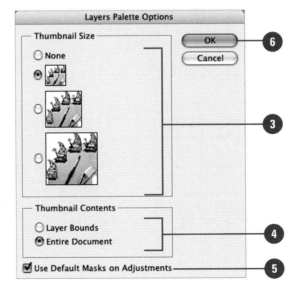

Working with the History Palette

Introduction

Adobe introduced the History palette in Photoshop 5, and the graphic design world hasn't been the same since. On an elementary level, the History palette gives you the ability to perform multiple undos. Think of History as having a magical mistake correction tool, which never wears out. However, the History palette does much more than give you the ability to go back in time and correct your mistakes. The History palette is simply a tool, but when you combine the power of the History palette with the History brush, and Art History brush, you have a trio of tools that can take your creative designs to the next level and beyond.

Adobe Photoshop gives you two options for using the History palette—linear and non-linear. The **linear** state helps you keep track of your recent steps, and erases and steps that interfere with a linear flow to the palette. The **non-linear** state preserves all the steps (linear or non), and is useful when you need to think outside the linear box.

Photoshop raises the bar on the History palette by giving you the ability to record and save the commands performed to a document in a History text document. Now, you can finally know exactly what you did to an image. And since the document can be printed, you can create history text documents of your favorite restoration and manipulation techniques, and save them as customized help topics.

In addition, when you combine the History brush with the History palette you have an awesome creative tool that can't be beat. In fact, it's even possible to convert the Eraser tool into a History brush.

Setting History Palette Options

Working with the History palette requires a firm understanding of how the palette functions, and what you can and cannot do with History. The History palette records your steps as you work through a document. A step is defined as a specific action, such as creating a layer, or adding a brush stroke. Every time you perform an action, a step is recorded in the History palette. The History palette gives you the ability to go back to a previous history state, which is the same as performing an undo command. You can perform multiple undo commands up to the number set in Photoshop preferences for the History States. In addition, the History palette creates snapshots of the document. **Snapshots** are images of the current state of the document. Snapshots are used in conjunction with the History and Art History Brushes to create special effects.

Set Number of History States

① Click the **Edit** (Win), or **Photoshop** (Mac) menu, point to **Preferences**, and then click **General**.

② Enter a value from 0 to 1000 for the number of steps recorded in the History States box.

③ Click **OK**.

Did You Know?

You can duplicate a History State. Hold down the Alt (Win) or Option (Mac) key, and then click the History State you want to duplicate.

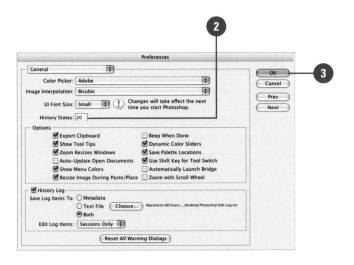

For Your Information

Performing Multiple Undos

The History palette represents the ability to perform multiple undo commands as many as you choose for your History States. However when you press Ctrl+Z (Win), or ⌘+ Z (Mac) you only move back and forth between the last command, just like a normal undo. To perform multiple undo commands press Ctrl+Shift+Z (Win) or ⌘+Shift+Z (Mac) to move forward through all your History steps, or press Alt+Shift+Z (Win) or Option+Shift+Z (Mac) to move backwards through the available History steps.

Set History Options

1. Select the **History** palette.

2. Click the **History Options** button, and then click **History Options**.

3. Select the check boxes for the History Options you want to use:

   ◆ **Automatically Create First Snapshot.** Creates a snapshot (image) when the document first opens.

   ◆ **Automatically Create New Snapshot When Saving.** Creates a snapshot every time you save the document.

   This is useful for keeping track of the changes made to a document.

   ◆ **Allow Non-Linear History.** Allows you to operate History in a non-linear state.

   ◆ **Show New Snapshot Dialog By Default.** Opens a dialog box with options each time you create a new snapshot.

   ◆ **Make Layer Visibility Changes Undoable.** Instructs Photoshop to make changes made to a layer's visibility undoable (**New!**).

4. Click **OK**.

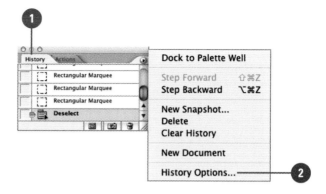

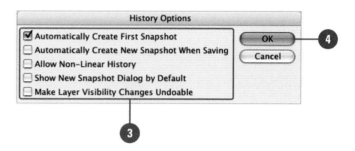

6

Working with Linear and Non-Linear History

The History palette records each step performed on a Photoshop document in a linear fashion from top to bottom. However, the purpose of the History palette is not to simply record your progress through a document, it's there to help you make changes and go back in time to correct mistakes. Photoshop handles the History palette in two ways-linear and non-linear. When you work in a linear History palette, clicking on a previous step causes all steps underneath to gray out. If you then add a step, the grayed out steps are removed and the new step is added to the bottom of the list. A linear palette is organized and is very RAM efficient, however, once a History Step is removed, it cannot be retrieved. When you work in a non-linear History palette, clicking on a previous step does not cause the steps underneath to gray out. If you then add a step, the new step is added to the bottom of the History palette. The new step represents the characteristics of the step you selected, plus any added actions. A non-linear palette is not organized and consumes more RAM memory. It's advantage lies in the fact that History steps are not deleted; they are simply reorganized.

Work with Linear History

1. Select the **History** palette.

2. Click the **History Options** button, and then click **History Options**.

3. Clear the **Allow Non-Linear History** check box, and then click **OK**.

4. Work in the document until you have generated ten or fifteen steps in the History palette.

5. Move halfway up the History palette, and then click on a step.

   The steps below the selected step turn gray.

6. Perform another action to the image.

   The grayed steps are removed, replaced by the latest action applied to the image.

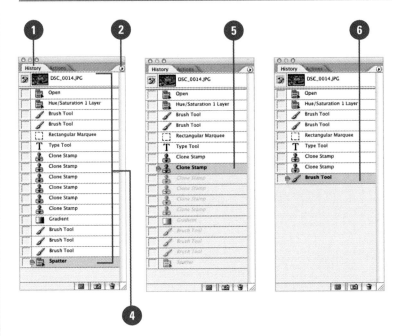

Work with Non-Linear History

1. Select the **History** palette.

2. Click the **History Options** button, and then click **History Options**.

3. Select the **Allow Non-Linear History** check box, and then click **OK**.

4. Work in the document until you have generated ten or fifteen steps in the History palette.

5. Move halfway up the History palette, and then click on a step.

   The steps below the selected step do not change.

6. Perform another action to the image.

   The new step is added to the bottom of the History steps.

Did You Know?

You can quickly purge the History States, and therefore recoup RAM memory. Hold down the Alt (Win) or Option (Mac) key, click the History Options button, and then click Clear History. But be warned, if you change your mind there is no undo available, you are stuck.

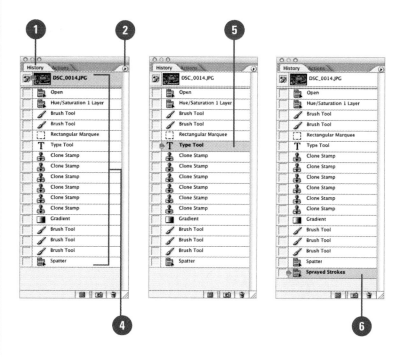

6

Controlling the Creative Process with Snapshots

The History palette contains more than just steps, it also holds snapshots. A History snapshot is an image of the document, as it exists at the time the snapshot was taken. The History palette can hold as many snapshots as needed, and they are not subject to the number of History States. That means they stay with the document throughout the creative process. By default, Photoshop takes a snapshot of the image when it first opens. This snapshot represents the original state of the image, before any adjustments or modifications are applied, and is identified with the file name of the image. It's a good idea to create a Snapshot every time you make a major change to the image. That way if you want to start all over, all you have to do is click on the snapshot, and Photoshop returns you to the moment in time the snapshot was created. It's like having your own personal time machine.

Create Snapshots

1. Select the **History** palette.

2. Click the **History Options** button, and then click **History Options**.

3. Select the **Show New Snapshot Dialog By Default** check box, and then click **OK**.

4. Perform several actions to the image.

5. Click the **Create New Snapshot** button.

6. Type a name for the new snapshot.

7. Click the **From** list arrow, and then click a save image information option:

    ◆ **Full Document.** Saves the entire visible image and all layers.

    ◆ **Merged Layers.** Saves only the merged layers.

    ◆ **Current Layer.** Saves only the active layer.

8. Click **OK**.

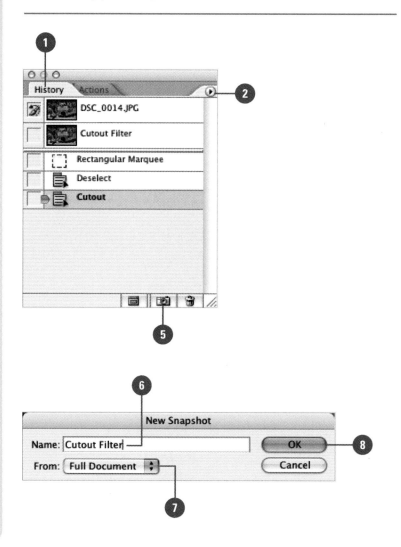

Duplicating a History State in Another Document

Here's a tool to help you gain control over the creative process, and save you a lot of time and effort as well. The History palette lets you create new documents, based on a specific History step or snapshot. For example, you're working on a complicated image, and you want to isolate a portion of the image in another document. This will not only help you reduce the clutter, but working on a portion of the image in a separate document creates a document with a much smaller file size, and that will help Photoshop work faster.

Create Another Document

1 Select the **History** palette.

2 Click on the snapshot or History State you want to use for the new document.

3 Click the **Create New Document From Current State** button.

Photoshop creates a new document based on the selected snapshot or state. The new document's History palette contains one snapshot, and one state.

IMPORTANT *Snapshots are not saved with the Photoshop document. When you reopen a document the History palette will display one snapshot of the current state of the image, and one History step.*

Did You Know?

You can save RAM by using the History palette. When you create a new document using the History palette, it's very RAM efficient, as opposed to the traditional copy and paste method.

New document based on the selected snapshot or state

6

Saving the History State of a Document

Photoshop gives you the ability to save the History states of a document as a separate text document, or as embedded metadata. Saving History is an excellent way to revive the steps you took to produce a particular design. Not only does the saved data record the steps you took; it also records the date and time each step was performed. This gives you a running record of the time spent on a document, which is useful for client billing purposes. Photoshop saves the history files as a standard text document, which can be opened in any text-editing program you choose.

Set Up to Save History

1 Click the **Edit** (Win) or **Photoshop** (Mac) menu, point to **Preferences**, and then click **General**.

2 Select the **History Log** check box.

3 Select the file type option you want to save log items:

◆ **Metadata**. Records the data as embedded metadata.

◆ **Text File**. Records the data to a text file.

◆ **Both**. Records the information as both metadata and text.

4 Click **Choose**, and then select location where you want to store the files.

5 Click the **Edit Log Items** list arrow, and then select the type of data you want to save:

◆ **Sessions Only**. Only records basic information, such as when the file was opened or closed.

◆ **Concise**. More information on actions taken.

◆ **Detailed**. The most data, including dates and times for actions, and each individual stet.

6 Click **OK**.

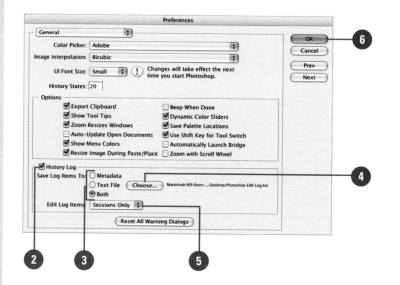

Reviewing the History State Text File

Photoshop creates the History State file on the fly, as you work each step precisely recorded. Photoshop does not create a separate data file for each working session, but a single file recording all work sessions. If you delete the original history data file, Photoshop will create a new file, and place it in the same location with the same name. Have you ever worked on a document, performing command after command and suddenly you step back, and really like the end result? Then you immediately grab a notepad and attempt to jot down all the steps—it's always the most important step that you forget. Not with Photoshop and the History text file. The text document faithfully records each and every step. Later, after the project is finished, you can access the file and all your commands and steps will be listed.

Open the History State Text File

① Close Photoshop.

② Open the folder where the History text file is saved.

The default name is Photoshop Edit Log.txt, and the default location is the desktop.

③ Double-click to open the document with the default text editor.

NotePad (Win), TextEdit (Mac), or use a Word Processor, such as Microsoft Word.

◆ The date and time the file was opened is recorded at the top of the document.

◆ The steps performed are listed, one at a time.

◆ The date and time the file was closed is recorded at the bottom of the document.

④ Close your text editor program.

Date and time file was opened

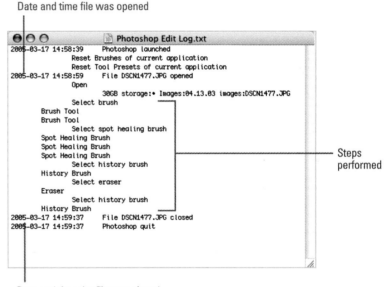

Steps performed

Date and time the file was closed

6

Controlling History States

The History palette is a fantastic tool! It can help you go back in time and correct errors, and even take snapshots of the image, which you can use to create new documents. But all great tools come with a price. The History palettes price is consumption of RAM memory. The more you use the History palette the more RAM memory it needs. If you find Photoshop slowing down on you, or if you get warning message stating that Photoshop is running low on RAM, you might want to try a few things to help gain back some of that lost efficiency. Photoshop lets you choose between 0 and 1,000 History states. That's 1,000 undos, and while that might seem like a great thing to have, History states take up memory. You can also check on your settings. Non-Linear History requires more RAM memory to maintain. If you don't require a non-linear history, then you can turn it off. Since Photoshop uses a lot of RAM memory (64MB just to open), it makes sense that Adobe would give you a way to manage the use of that memory.

Reset to Linear History

1. Select the **History** palette.

2. Click the **History Options** button, and then click **History Options**.

3. Clear the **Allow Non-Linear History** check box.

4. Click **OK**.

See Also

See "Setting History Palette Options" on page 120 for more information on setting the number of history states.

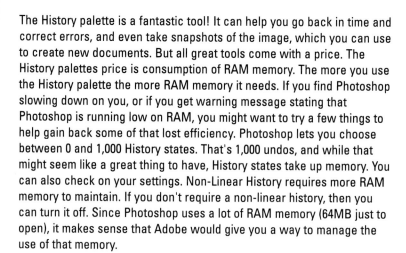

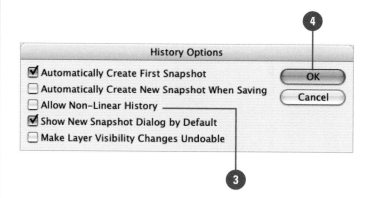

Purge RAM Memory

1 Click the **Edit** (Win) or **Photoshop** (Mac) menu, point to **Purge**, and then select from the following options:

◆ **Undo.** Removes the Undo states from History.

◆ **Clipboard.** If you have used the Edit menu, Copy and Paste commands, that information is still contained in RAM memory. Use this option to purge Clipboard memory.

◆ **Histories.** Select this option to purge all the states from the History palette.

◆ **All**. Wipe all RAM memory clean.

IMPORTANT *The purge option has no undo. If you select any of the purge options, there is no going back, so make sure you want to purge memory.*

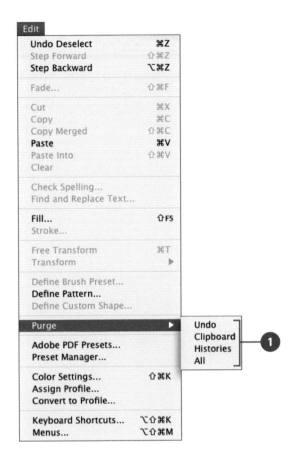

Combining the History Brush with a History State

When Adobe created History, they advertised the fact that Photoshop now had more than one undo. Multiple undos are a great thing, however if all you use the History palette for is to correct your mistakes, you're missing the whole idea of the History palette. The History palette does not stand by itself. It's linked to the History brush. The History brush receives its information from a selected state or snapshot. For example, the History palette holds a snapshot of the way the image looked when first opened, and by default the History brush is linked to that snapshot. Think of the History brush as a photo restoration tool that always remembers the original state of the image. As you work on a document you will make changes. If during the current work session, you wish to restore the document back to its original (first opened) state, the History brush is your tool. The History brush is not just for correcting mistakes, but also for creating awesome special effects. All you need is a bit of imagination and a couple of additional snapshots.

Correct Mistakes with the History Brush

1. Select the **History Brush** tool on the toolbox.

2. Click the **Brushes** palette, and then click a size brush.

3. Drag the History brush across the image.

   The places you drag are restored to their original (first opened) state.

Did You Know?

When you use the History brush on an image layer, you're changing the information based on the chosen History state or snapshot. However, you will gain more control if you use the History brush in a separate layer. Just create and select a new layer, and when you use the History brush, paint in the layer. Not only does the separate layer isolate the original image from damage, but you can utilize blending modes, and opacity settings for even greater creative control.

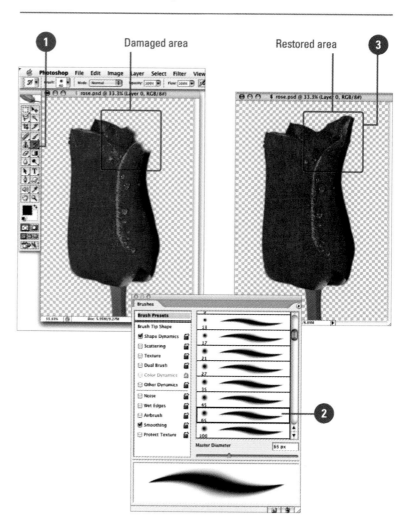

Damaged area   Restored area

Get Fancy with the History Brush

1. Apply a major change to a document (possibility a Brush Stroke filter).

2. Select the **History** palette.

3. Click the **Create New Snapshot** button to take a snapshot of the image in its current state.

4. Click on the original snapshot to return it back to its first-opened state.

5. Click in the History source box of the snapshot you created in step 3 to change the designation of the History brush.

   This instructs the History brush to paint using the special filter-effect image.

6. Drag your mouse over the image to replace the original image with the image information contained in the selected snapshot.

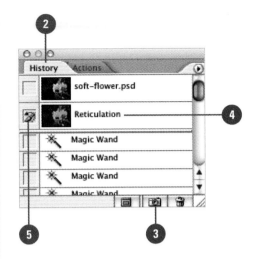

Using the Art History Brush

The History Palette comes equipped with two History brushes—the History and Art History brushes. The History brush paints whatever state or snapshot is selected. The Art History brush gives you the ability to create some painted effects, using information from one or more snapshots or History states. In effect, the Art History brush gives you the power to combine image information (based on the active snapshot or history state) with artistic brush strokes.

Use the Art History Brush

1. Click and hold the **History Brush** tool on the toolbox, and then click the **Art History Brush** tool.

2. Select from the following options on the Options bar:

   ◆ **Brush.** Select a brush tip and style.

   ◆ **Mode.** Select a blending mode from the list. The blending modes, when applied to a brush, control how the colors blend with the colors in the document.

   ◆ **Opacity.** Enter or select a value from 1 to 100 percent.

   ◆ **Style.** Select a style for the Art History brush.

   ◆ **Area.** Enter a value from 0 to 500 pixels to define the painting area.

   ◆ **Tolerance.** Select a value from 0 to 100 percent. Higher values limits paint strokes to areas in the image that differ from the color used by the Art History brush. Lower values lets the Art History brush use unlimited strokes, regardless of the color values in the image.

3. Drag your mouse over the image, using small controlled strokes.

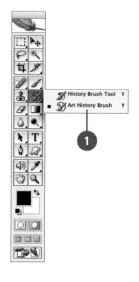

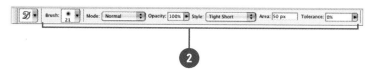

Original image

Effect applied with the Art History Brush

Changing the Eraser Tool into the History Brush

Photoshop has one more tool that works with the History palette—the Eraser tool. By changing a preference on the Options bar, you can turn the Eraser tool into a History brush. Using the Eraser tool to restore the image is just another way to get the same result as the History brush. And if you know anything about Adobe, they give you at least three ways for everything. Consider multiple ways to perform the same function as a control advantage. No two Photoshop users will create the same design, and no two Photoshop users will ever tackle a problem in the same way. Adobe gives you choices; so choose the best way to accomplish a task based on the available options. And remember, if you change the color mode, resolution, or canvas size of the active image, the History brush tools will not work.

Change the Eraser Tool into the History Brush

1 Select the **Eraser** tool on the toolbox.

2 Select the **Erase To History** check box on the Options bar.

3 Select a history state or snapshot from the History palette.

4 Drag the Eraser tool in the image.

The eraser tool does not erase the image, instead it paints the image, based on the current History selection.

Did You Know?

You can use multiple layers with the History brush. When you use any of the History brush tools, it's a smart idea to create a new layer, and do your History painting in the new layer. That way, if you don't like what you see, you can always delete the layer. In addition, placing the History information in a separate layer gives you the creative control of using layer transparency and blending mode settings to achieve greater creative results.

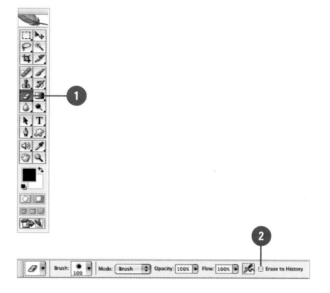

Working with Adjustment Layers, Filters, and Tools

7

Introduction

If you want to visually control an Adobe Photoshop document, then adjustment layers are the ultimate tool. The purpose of an adjustment layer is to visually illustrate how a specific adjustment, such as Hue & Saturation, is applied to the image. Since the adjustment is contained within a separate layer, the original image never changes. This gives you the ability to experiment with different settings, and since adjustment layers are saved with the document, you can save and return at a later time to make further adjustments.

Another advantage of adjustment layers is size. Adjustment layers do not increase the size of a Photoshop document. Most Photoshop layers are composed of pixels, so adding traditional layers to a document increases the size of the file. Since adjustment layers are simply a set of mathematical information, they do not increase the size of the file.

Photoshop has two ways to apply adjustments to an image. The first is going through the Image menu, and choosing Adjustments, however, when you apply the adjustment it's permanent. The other is using an adjustment layer—the very definition of control over time. When working with adjustment layers, you can modify, merge, or even create a temporary composite image, all while your original image stays in tact. With all of their advantages, you may never perform adjustments using the Image menu again.

In addition to letting you apply adjustments to an image without changing the original data, adjustment layers, because they are separate layers, give you the ability to apply standard layer controls, such as blending modes, opacity, and fill. Layer masks come with their own built-in masks, and allow you to control how and where the adjustment is applied to the image.

Creating an Adjustment Layer

Adjustment layers are applied within the Layers palette. By default, all layers beneath the adjustment layer are changed. In addition, adjustment layers will work on any type of Photoshop layer, including the Background. You can have as many adjustment layers as needed. For example, you might create a Levels adjustment layer to control the contrast of an image, and add a Curves adjustment layer to correct image color. When you create more than one adjustment layer, each adjustment is applied to the image based on its stacking order in the Layers palette.

Create an Adjustment Layer

1. Select the **Layers** palette.

2. Click the layer you want to adjust.

3. Click the **Create New Fill Or Adjustment Layer** button, and then select from the available adjustment options.

4. If a dialog box opens, make changes to the adjustment, and then click **OK**.

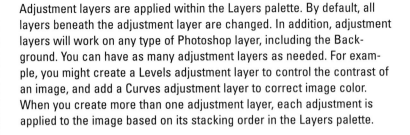

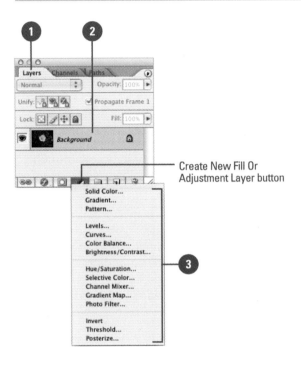

Create New Fill Or Adjustment Layer button

Modifying an Adjustment Layer

The beauty of adjustment layers is in the control they offer to the Photoshop user. When you work using the Image menu, and click Adjustments, any changes made to the image are permanent, as soon as you click OK. But that's not true of adjustment layers. Adjustment layers keep the changes isolated in a separate layer, and this allows you to modify the adjustment minutes, or even days later. With this type of creative control at your fingertips, you can experiment with different settings until the image is exactly what you want.

Modify an Adjustment Layer

1. Select the **Layers** palette.

2. Double-click on the thumbnail of the Adjustment layer you want to modify.

   The dialog box for that specific adjustment reopens. Options for each adjustment dialog box vary.

3. Make the changes you want for the specific adjustment.

4. Click **OK**.

Did You Know?

You can move adjustment layers up and down in the layer stack. Since each adjustment layer interacts with other adjustment layers, changing the order of the layers creates a totally different image.

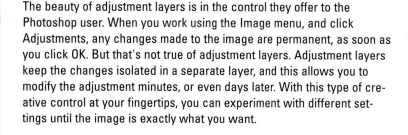

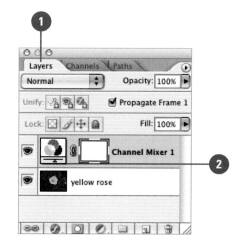

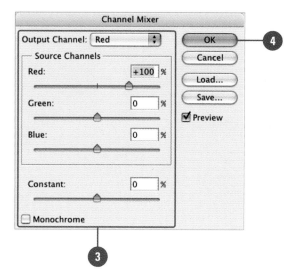

Merging Adjustment Layers

Photoshop lets you create as many adjustment layers as needed. For example, you might create a Levels adjustment layer to balance image contrast, Curves to correct color, and a Photo Filter, to create an overall warming effect to the image. Each adjustment layer works with the other adjustment layers to produce the final image. It's not unusual to have three, four, or even five adjustment layers controlling a single image. At some point in the design, you might decide to save space by merging some or all of the adjustment layers. However, when you merge the adjustment layers, the image looses the effect produced by the adjustments. The reason lies in how Photoshop works with adjustment layers. Each adjustment layer controls one part of the adjustment. The layers themselves do not hold an image; they hold mathematical data on how to change an image. Each adjustment layer holds data relating to a specific adjustment, such as Curves or Levels. A single adjustment layer cannot hold more than one set of adjustments. That's why you have multiple adjustment layers. Merging two or more adjustment layers together forces Photoshop to discard all of the adjustment data and the merged adjustment layers turn into a plain old transparent layer. To solve the problem, try merging the adjustment and the image layers into a single layer.

Merge Adjustments with Images

1. Open a document containing an image layer, and two or more adjustment layers.

2. Select the **Layers** palette.

3. Click the **Layers Options** button, and then select from the following merge options:

   ◆ **Merge Layers.** Merges only the layers selected in the Layers palette into a single layer (**New!**).

   ◆ **Merge Visible.** Merges only the layers that are visible, leaving the hidden layers untouched.

   ◆ **Flatten Image.** Merges all layers into a flattened background. If you have one or more layers hidden, Photoshop will open a warning dialog box and ask if you want to discard the hidden layers.

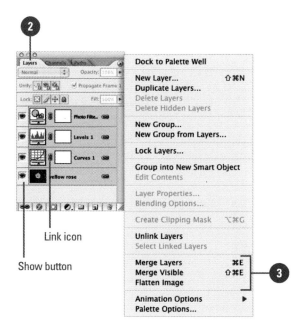

Link icon

Show button

138

Creating a Temporary Composite Image

PS 3.2

When you merge adjustment layers into the image, you wind up with a single layer, which contains all of the adjustments. By merging the adjustment layers, you do lose control over the individual adjustment layers. It's basically a trade off of smaller files sizes, less layers to contend with, but less control over the image. Let's say you want the best of both worlds — a single layer that contains the image, all of the adjustments, and the original image with separate adjustment layers. It's possible, all you have to do is create a composite layer.

Create a Temporary Composite Image

1. Open a document that contains an image, and two or more visible adjustment layers.

2. Select the **Layers** palette, create a new layer at the top of the layer stack, and then select it.

3. Hold down the Alt (Win) or Option (Mac) key, click the **Layers Options** button, and then click **Merge Visible**.

   Photoshop combines all of the visible layers into the new layer; while leaving the original layers untouched.

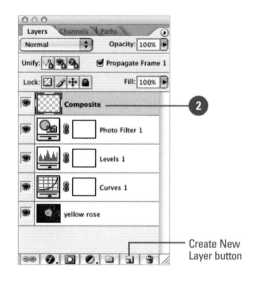

Create New Layer button

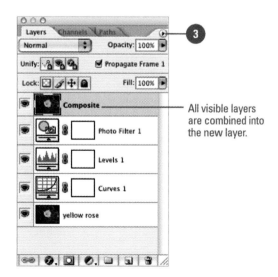

All visible layers are combined into the new layer.

Did You Know?

You can use the composite layer option on any multi-layered Photoshop document. Once you've created the composite layer, you can perform other adjustments without impacting the original images, or even drag and move the composite into another Photoshop document.

You can use the link option to control the composite image. Create a new layer, and then link the layers you want included in the composite. Follow the steps for creating a composite, except click Merge Linked.

Grouping Adjustment Layers

When you work with adjustment layers, the effects of the adjustment are applied to all the layers below the adjustment layer, including any additional adjustment layers. However, there are times when you only want the adjustment applied to a specific layer. For example, you're working on a multi-layered document and you create a Curves Adjustment layer for the purpose of adjusting the color in the next layer down. Unfortunately, the Curves adjustment is applied to all the layers. The answer is simple, group the adjustment layer to the layer you want to correct.

Control Adjustment Layers with the Group Option

① Select the **Layers** palette, and then click the layer you want to adjust.

② Move your cursor down until the fingertip of the hand pointer touches the line separating the adjustment layer from the next layer down.

③ Hold down the Alt (Win) or Option (Mac) key.

The cursor changes from a hand pointer to a double-circle button (the group button).

④ Click your mouse to group the two layers together.

The thumbnail of the adjustment layer indents to indicate the two layers are grouped. The effect of the adjustment layer impacts the grouped layer and no others.

Did You Know?

You can group more than one layer together. Hold down the Alt (Win) or Option (Mac) key, and then click on the line separating the next layer to add a layer to the group. To remove a layer from the group, hold down the Alt (Win) or Option (Mac) key, and then click on the line separating two grouped items.

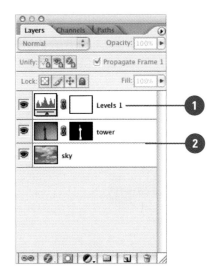

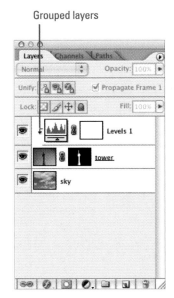

Grouped layers

Deleting an Adjustment Layer

When you delete an adjustment layer you are simply deleting the adjustment, not the image. Adjustment layers do not contain image data; they only manipulate the information contained within the image layer. Deleting an adjustment layer is as easy as deleting any other layer type. The effect is the same; the function of the layer is removed from the document. For example, if you delete a curves adjustment layer, the effects are removed and the image returns to its original state. When you delete an Adjustment layer, the change to the image induced by the adjustment layer is removed, and the image returns to normal.

Delete an Adjustment Layer

1. Select the **Layers** palette.

2. Click the adjustment layer you want to delete.

3. Drag the adjustment layer on the Delete Layer button.

Did You Know?

You can convert an adjustment layer into a regular layer. By default, adjustment layers come with a built-in mask. To remove the mask, and preserve the adjustment layer, select the adjustment layer in the Layers palette, hold down the Alt (Win) or Option (Mac) key, and then click the Delete Layer button.

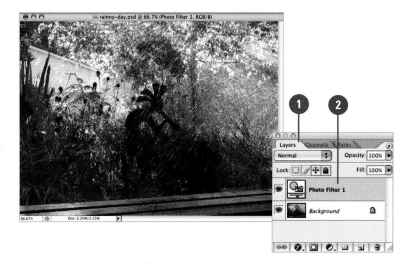

The adjustment layer is removed from the document.

Using Blending Modes and Opacity with Layers

Adobe Certified Expert PS 2.5

Adjustment layers perform two functions—they adjust the image and they give you control. Since an adjustment is held in a separate layer, you have the advantage of isolating the adjustment, and all the options that apply to normal a layer. Combine that with an adjustment layers ability to manipulate pixel information and you have a very powerful image-editing tool. Blending Modes change how two or more layers interact. For example, the multiply blending mode instructs Photoshop to mix the pixels of two or more layers, thus creating an entirely new image from the mix. With that in mind, the five modes that produce the most stunning results are Multiply, Screen, Hard Mix, Difference, and Exclusion. The opacity of an adjustment layer controls the intensity of the selected adjustment. You can reduce the opacity of the Hue & Saturation adjustment to 50 percent, and it would reduce its effect on the image. Since each adjustment layer has its own opacity settings, multiple adjustment layers can be fine-tuned to create the desired impact on the image.

Use Blending Modes with Adjustment Layers

1. Select the **Layers** palette.

2. Click the layer you want to adjust.

3. Click the **Blending Mode** list arrow, and then select from the available options.

   The results of the blend are visible in the document window.

Blending Mode changed applied to image

Control Through Opacity

1. Select the **Layers** palette.

2. Click the layer you want to adjust.

3. Click the **Opacity** list arrow, and then drag the slider to lower the opacity of the layer.

   The results of the change appear in the document window.

   TIMESAVER *Click inside the Opacity box, and then use the Up and Down Arrow keys to increase or decrease the opacity 1 percentage point at a time. Hold the Shift key, and then use the Up and Down Arrow keys to increase or decrease the opacity 10 percentage points at a time. You can also select the percentage in the box and enter a value.*

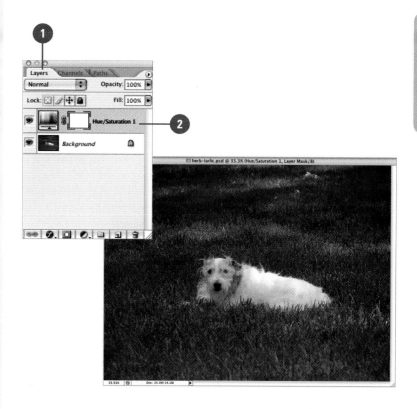

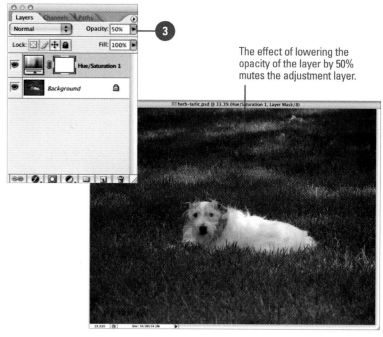

The effect of lowering the opacity of the layer by 50% mutes the adjustment layer.

Using Masks with Adjustment Layers

When you create an adjustment layer, the effects of the adjustment are applied to the entire image. For example, if you use the Curves adjustment, the entire image receives the effects of the adjustment. It's true you can modify the adjustment with the use of layer blending modes, and opacity settings but, the effects are applied equally to the entire image. The problem is that many times you don't want the adjustment applied to the entire image. For example, color correcting a portion of the image, or lightening the shadows of an image without applying the same lightening adjustment to the highlights. Photoshop handles this problem with the use of masks. When you create an adjustment layer, Photoshop creates a mask with the image. The mask controls how the adjustment is applied to the image, and you control the effect by painting in the mask with black, white, or a shade of gray. When you paint the mask with black, it will mask the adjustment, painting with white fully applies the adjustment. If you paint with 50 percent gray, then 50 percent of the adjustment is applied to the image.

Paint on an Adjustment Mask

1. Select the **Layers** palette.

2. Click the layer mask thumbnail in which you want to paint a mask.

3. Select a **Paintbrush** tool.

4. Select a brush size on the Options bar.

5. Set the **Foreground Color** box on the toolbox to black as the painting color.

6. Paint the areas of the image in the document window you want to mask. The adjustment layer must be selected.

   The areas painted black mask the adjustment, and return the image to normal.

7. To restore the masked areas, switch to white and drag across the image in the areas previous painted black.

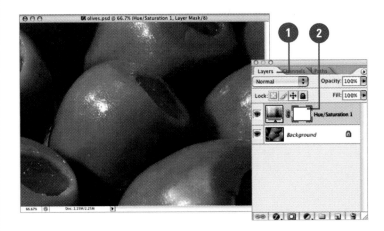

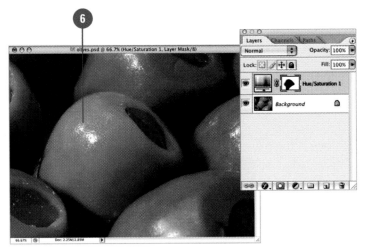

Creating Masks with Selection

You can create an instant mask using traditional selection techniques. Before creating the adjustment layer, select the area of the image you want the adjustment applied. Use any of Photoshop's selection tools for this purpose. When you create the adjustment layer, Photoshop converts the selection into a mask, and only the selected areas of the image receive the adjustment.

Create Masks with Selection

1. Use any of Photoshop's selection tools to create a selection around the area of the image you want the adjustment applied.

2. Select the **Layers** palette.

3. Click the **Create New Fill Or Adjustment Layer** button, and then select from the available adjustments.

   Photoshop creates a mask based on your selection with the selected areas receiving the adjustment and the non-selected areas masked.

> ### Did You Know?
>
> **You can use any of Photoshop's filters on an adjustment layer mask.**
> For example, you could use the Gaussian Blur filter to soften the edge between adjustment and mask. Experiment with different filters for different creative effects.

Mask from selection

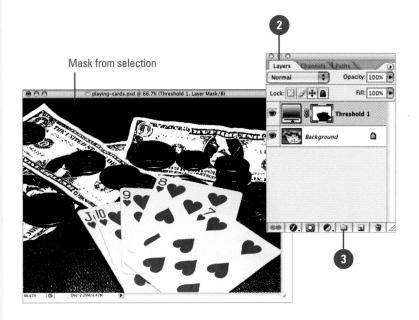

Using the Add Noise Filter

When wanting to retouch an image, you can apply the Add Noise filter. The Add Noise filter applies random pixels to an image, simulating a grainy effect. For example, you would use the Add Noise filter to make an image look like it was taken using high-speed film. In addition, the Add Noise filter can be used to reduce banding in feathered selections or graduated fills or even give a more realistic look to heavily retouched areas. Experiment with the Add Noise filter in combination with other filters, such as Motion Blur filters, to create eye-catching special effects.

Use the Add Noise Filter

① Select the **Layers** palette.

② Select the layer in which you want to apply the Add Noise filter.

③ Click the **Filter** menu, point to **Noise**, and then click **Add Noise**.

④ Select from the following options:

◆ **Amount.** Drag the slider, or enter a value (0.10 to 400) to increase or decrease the amount of noise added to the image.

◆ **Distribution.** Click the Uniform option to created a more ordered appearance, or click the Gaussian option to create a more random noise pattern.

◆ **Monochromatic.** Select this check box to apply the filter to the tonal elements in the image without changing the colors.

TIMESAVER *The plus and minus signs, located directly under the image preview, let you increase or decrease the viewable area of the image.*

⑤ Click **OK**.

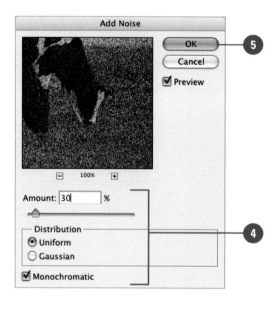

Using the Reduce Noise Filter

The Reduce Noise Filter (**New!**) helps to remove the random noise that crops up in digital images. It's called noise, but in reality is a pattern of distracting color or grayscale information that lays on the original image information. Noise can be generated by the Add Noise filter, but it typically comes from scanners and even digital cameras. Since there is a mathematical pattern to most noise, the Reduce Noise filter is designed to seek out and reduce the amount of noise in an image. The Reduce Noise filter works on individual layers, not the entire document. After applying the filter, you can use other restoration tools, such as the Healing Brush and Patch tool, to further clean up image problem areas.

Use the Add Noise Filter

1. Click the **Filter** menu, point to **Noise**, and then click **Reduce Noise**.

2. Select the **Preview** check box to view the changes to the image.

3. Select the **Basic** or **Advanced** option. Advanced allows you to adjust the noise on individual channels.

4. Select from the following options:

   ◆ **Settings.** Click the setting arrow and select a user-defined preset.

   ◆ **Strength.** Drag the slider to determine how strong to apply the reduce noise filter.

   ◆ **Preserve Details.** Drag the slider to determine a balance between blurring the noise and preserving details.

   ◆ **Reduce Color Noise.** Drag the slider to convert noise composed of colors into shades of gray (this may desaturate other areas of the image).

   ◆ **Sharpen Details.** Drag the slider to determine where the details of the image exist, in terms of shift of brightness.

   ◆ **Remove JPEG Artifact.** Check to help remove artifacts (typically noise within shadows) from severely compressed JPEG images.

5. Click **OK**.

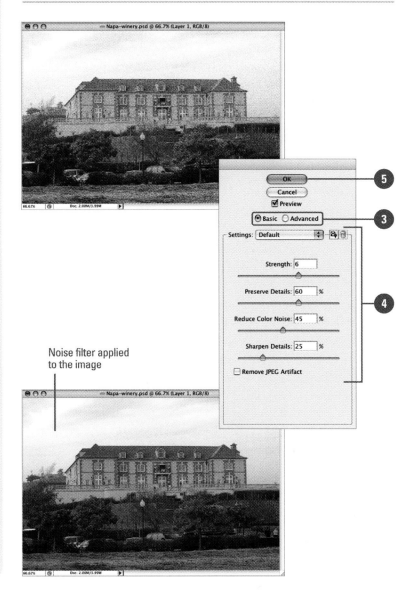

Noise filter applied to the image

Keeping Proper Perspective with Vanishing Point

Photoshop's Vanishing Point (**New!**) is what I like to call one of those why-didn't-you-think-of-this-sooner options. It gives you the ability to move and/or copy objects within the document window and maintain the same visual perspective of the original. Let's say that you shoot an image of a roadway disappearing into the distance, and along the there's a billboard. Unfortunately, you want the billboard to appear as if it is further away. With Vanishing Point you simply create a framework that identifies the depth of the image, and then move the billboard (using the Move or Stamp tools). Wherever you move the sign, it will appear within the proper perspective. Or maybe you have an image with a damaged area, and you want to fix it with a repetitive area from somewhere else in the image. That's not a problem with Vanishing Point.

Use the Vanishing Point Tool

1. Open an image.

2. Click the **Filter** menu, and then click **Vanishing Point**.

3. The following tools are available:

   - **Edit Plane.** Adjusts the grid to match the perspective of the image.

   - **Create Plane.** First tool to use; it creates the initial perspective grid plane.

   - **Marquee Tool.** Makes selections in the grid and then changes their perspective as you move them to match the perspective of the grid.

   - **Stamp Tool.** Lets you make copies of areas and then stamp them onto other areas using the perspective of the grid.

   - **Brush Tool.** Lets you paint with color, within the grid. If you click the Heal button and then click Luminance, Vanishing Point will adapt the color to the shadows or textures of the areas being painted.

   - **Transform Tool.** Lets you rotate, resize or flip a selection created with the Marquee tool.

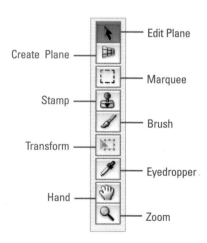

- ◆ **Eyedropper Tool.** Click to select a specific color from the image.
- ◆ **Hand Tool.** Click to move the image within the Vanishing Point window.
- ◆ **Zoom Tool.** Click to Zoom in, or Alt+click (Win) or Option+click (Mac) to zoom out.

④ Select the **Create Plane** tool.

⑤ Click on the image to create the first point of the perspective grid, and then click three more times to create the box shape of the grid.

⑥ Use the **Edit Plane** tool to change the perspective of the plane, and to extend the plane over the area you want fix, and the area you want to fix it with.

The plane should follow the perspective of the image. The grid should be blue; however, if the grid goes red or yellow, that means Vanishing Point believes you have a bad grid.

⑦ Select the **Zoom** tool, and zoom in on the working areas of the image.

⑧ Select the **Stamp** tool.

⑨ Position the Stamp tool directly over the image area you want to use to fix the offending portions of the image, and then Alt+click (Win) or Option+click (Mac) to confirm the selection.

⑩ Move to the area you want to fix and then click and drag with the Stamp tool. Not only will the Stamp tool replace the original information; the perspective will change to match the grid (bigger or smaller).

⑪ Click **OK**.

Edit Plane

7

Working with the Lens Correction Filter

The Lens Correction filter (**New!**) fixes flaws when shooting images, such as barrel and pincushion distortion, vignetting; even chromatic aberration. **Barrel** distortion causes straight lines to bow out toward the edges of the image. On the other hand, **Pincushion** distortion has the opposite effect (straight lines bend inward). **Vignetting** is a defect where edges of an image are darker than the center. **Chromatic** aberration appears as a fringe of color along the edges of objects caused by the lens focusing on different colors of light in different planes. In addition, you can use the Lens Correction filter to rotate an image or fix perspective caused by tilting the camera. Although some of these corrections can be made with the Transform command, the image grid makes adjustments easier.

Use the Lens Correction Filter

1 Open an image.

2 Click the **Filter** menu, point to **Distort**, and then click **Lens Correction**.

3 Select from the following tools:

- ◆ **Remove Distortion Tool.** Click in the grid and then drag left or right to remove barrel or pincushion distortion.

- ◆ **Straighten Tool.** Click in the grid and drag to draw a new horizon line (image will shift to the new horizon).

- ◆ **Move Grid Tool.** Drag to reposition the visible grid.

- ◆ **Hand Tool.** Select the tool, then click and drag to move the image within the view window.

- ◆ **Zoom Tool.** Select the tool, and then click in the view window to zoom in, or Alt+click (Win) or Option+click (Mac) to zoom out.

4 Select from the following tools:

- ◆ **Settings.** Click and choose from user-defined settings, or to apply the previous settings to the current image.

- ◆ **Remove Distortion.** Drag the slider left or right to precisely remove pincushion or barrel distortion.

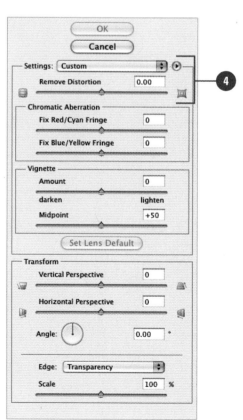

⑤ Select from the following Chromatic Aberration options:

◆ **Fix Red/Cyan Fringe.** Drag left or right to remove a red or cyan fringe from the image.

◆ **Fix Blue/Yellow Fringe.** Drag left or right to remove a blue or yellow fringe from the image.

⑥ Select from the following Vignette options:

◆ **Amount.** Drag left or right to create a light or dark vignette around the image.

◆ **Midpoint.** Drag left or right to select the midpoint for the vignette.

⑦ Click **Set Lens Default** to change the setting to default values.

⑧ Select from the following Transform options:

◆ **Vertical Perspective.** Drag left or right to change the image's vertical perspective.

◆ **Horizontal Perspective.** Drag left or right to change the image's horizontal perspective.

◆ **Angle.** Drag the angle option to rotate the image clockwise, or counter clockwise.

◆ **Edge.** Click and select to fill in transparent areas of the image with the background color, Edge Extension, or Transparent.

◆ **Scale.** Drag left or right to change the scale (size) of the image.

⑨ Select the **Preview** check box to view changes as they are made.

⑩ Select the **Show Grid** check box to view or hide the visible grid.

⑪ Click the **Size** list arrow to change the size of the grid boxes.

⑫ Click the **Color** box to change the color of the grid.

⑬ Click **OK**.

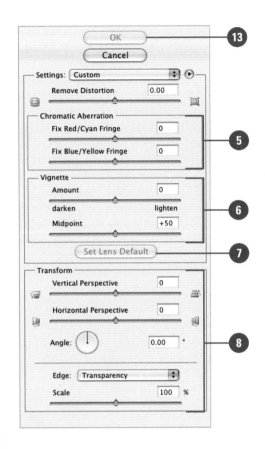

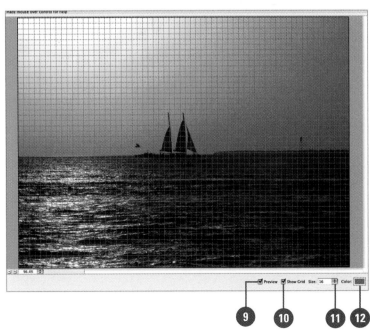

Using the Box, Surface, and Shape Blur Filters

Photoshop introduces three new blur filters (**New!**): Box, Surface, and Shape. The Box Blur filter blurs an image based on the average color value of neighboring pixels. Its primary function is in the creation of special effects. You can adjust the size of the area used to calculate the average value for a given pixel; a larger radius results in greater blurring. The Surface Blur filter blurs an image while saving the visible edges; useful for creating special effects or removing that pesky noise or graininess. The Radius option specifies the size of the area sampled for the blur. The Threshold option controls how much the tonal values of neighboring pixels must diverge from the center pixel value before being part of the blur. Pixels with tonal value differences less than the Threshold value are excluded from the blur. The Shape Blur filter uses a specified shape to create the blur. Choose a kernel from the list of custom shape presets, and use the radius slider to adjust its size. You can load different shape libraries by clicking the triangle and choosing from the list. Radius determines the size of the shape; the larger the shape, the greater the blur.

Use the Box Blur Filter

1. Open an image.

2. Click the **Filter** menu, point to **Blur**, and then click **Box Blur**.

3. Drag the **Radius** slider left or right to decrease or increase the amount of blur applied to the image.

4. Click **OK**.

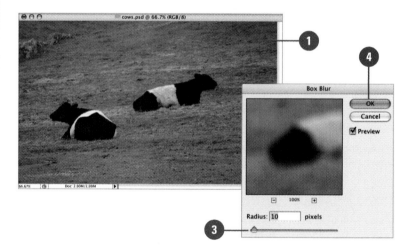

Results of Box Blur

Use the Surface Blur Filter

1. Open an image.

2. Click the **Filter** menu, point to **Blur**, and then click **Surface Blur**.

3. Drag the **Radius** slider left or right to decrease or increase the amount of blur applied to the image.

4. Drag the **Threshold** slider left or right to decrease of increase the acceptance of the shift in brightness of the image information (the edges).

5. Click **OK**.

Use the Shape Blur Filter

1. Open an image.

2. Click the **Filter** menu, point to **Blur**, and then click **Shape Blur**.

3. Select a shape (called a kernel) from the available options.

4. Drag the **Radius** slider left or right to decrease or increase the amount of blur applied to the image.

5. Click **OK**.

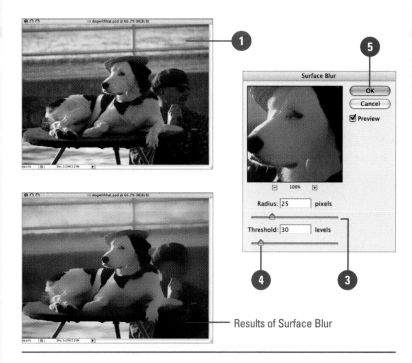

Results of Surface Blur

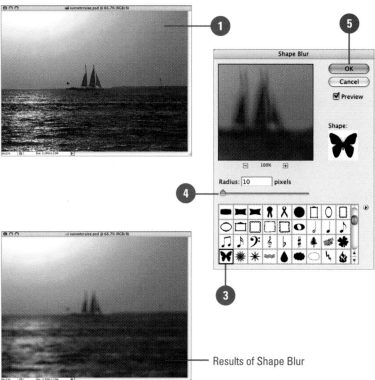

Results of Shape Blur

Using the Gaussian Blur and Despeckle Filters

You can also apply the Gaussian Blur filter which blurs an image, or a selection by a controllable amount. While not strictly a restoration tool, the Gaussian Blur filter can be used to add a sense of depth to the image. For example, you could select and blur the background of an image, while leaving the foreground object in focus. The outcome of the filter is to create a hazy, out-of-focus effect to the image. Another filter, the Despeckle filter, detects the edges in an image and blurs the entire image except those edges. Of course, there are no real edges in a Photoshop document—the Despeckle filter works along areas where there is a significant shift in the brightness of the pixels. Since a shift in brightness usually signifies an edge, the Despeckle filter performs a very accurate blurring of the image, while preserving detail.

Use the Gaussian Blur Filter

1. Select the portions of the image you want to blur or leave the image unselected to apply the filter to the entire image.

2. Click the **Filter** menu, point to **Blur**, and then click **Gaussian Blur**.

3. Select the **Preview** check box to view the results.

4. Drag the **Radius** slider or enter a pixel value to increase or decrease the amount of Gaussian blur applied to the image.

5. Click **OK**.

Use the Despeckle Filter

1. Select the **Layers** palette.

2. Select the layer in which you want to apply the Despeckle filter.

3. Click the **Filter** menu, point to **Noise**, and then click **Despeckle**.

   Photoshop applies the Despeckle filter to the image.

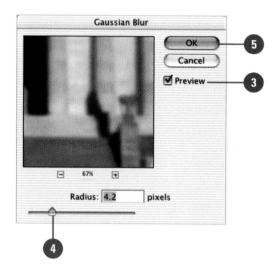

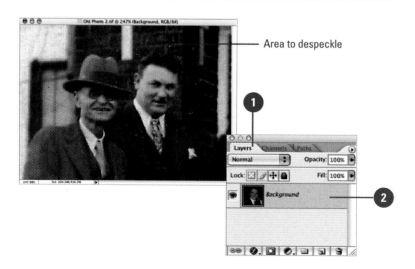

Area to despeckle

Using the Unsharp Mask Filter

The Unsharp Mask filter creates a visually sharper image by locating pixels that differ in value from surrounding pixels. When the filter is applied to the image, the bordering pixels specified by the threshold option get lighter and the darker pixels get darker. It's important to understand that the Unsharp Mask does not actually sharpen the image; it only attempts to create the illusion of sharpness. Be careful, an over application of this filter creates harsh images with ragged edges and shadows. Also, the effects of the Unsharp Mask filter appear more severe on a monitor with its low resolution, then when the document is output to a printer.

Use the Unsharp Mask Filter

1. Select the **Layers** palette.

2. Select the layer you want to sharpen.

3. Click the **Filter** menu, point to **Sharpen**, and then click **Unsharp Mask**.

4. Select from the following options:

    ◆ **Preview.** Select the option to view changes to the image directly in the active document window.

    ◆ **Amount.** Drag the slider or enter a value to determine how much to increase the contrast of pixels.

    ◆ **Radius.** Drag the slider or enter a value to determine the number of pixels surrounding the edge pixels that affect the sharpening.

    ◆ **Threshold.** Drag the slider or enter a value to determine how different the sharpened pixels must be from the surrounding area before they are considered edge pixels and sharpened by the filter.

5. Click **OK**.

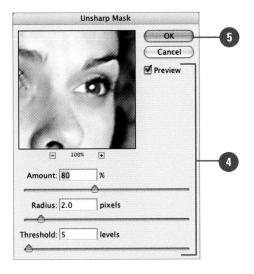

The Unsharp Mask filter applied to the image.

Using the Smart Sharpen Filter

PS 9.2

The Smart Sharpen filter (**New!**) attempts to sharpen the pixels of an out-of-focus image in much the same way as Unsharp Mask. The major difference is the ability of Smart Sharpen to remove previously applied Gaussian, Lens, and Motion Blur filters. For example, you've applied a Lens blur to an image, but later decide to reduce the effect. The problem is that Unsharp Mask will attempt to sharpen what it assumes to be an out-of-focus image. Unfortunately, an image taken with an out-of-focus lens, and a Gaussian blur are two different things, and that's where the Smart Sharpen filter comes to the rescue.

Use the Smart Sharpen Filter

1. Select the **Layers** palette.

2. Select the layer you want to sharpen.

3. Click the **Filter** menu, point to **Sharpen**, and then click **Smart Sharpen**.

4. Select the **Preview** check box to view the results.

5. Select the **Basic** or **Advanced** option.

6. Click the **Settings** list arrow, and then select from a list of user-defined settings.

7. Select from the following Sharpen options:

   ◆ **Amount.** Drag the slider to determine the amount of sharpness applied to the image.

   ◆ **Radius.** Drag the slider to determine the width of the sharpening effect.

   ◆ **Remove.** Click the list arrow and then select what type of blur effect you are removing from the image.

   ◆ **Angle.** Enter the angle of the Motion Blur filter to remove.

   ◆ **More Accurate.** Select for a more accurate (slower) sharpening effect.

Original image

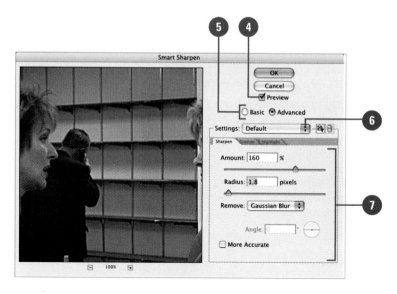

8 Select the **Shadow** palette and then select from the following Shadow options:

   ◆ **Fade Amount.** Drag the slider to determine the amount of shadow correction applied to the image.

   ◆ **Tonal Width.** Drag the slider to set the width of the tonal values in the image shadows.

   ◆ **Radius.** Drag the slider to choose the scale size for the shadows.

9 Select the **Highlight** palette, and then select from the following Highlight options:

   ◆ **Fade Amount.** Drag the slider to determine the amount of highlight correction applied to the image.

   ◆ **Tonal Width.** Drag the slider to set the width of the tonal values in the image highlights.

   ◆ **Radius.** Drag the slider to choose the scale size for the highlights.

10 To save a copy of the current Smart Sharpen settings, click the **Save** button.

11 To delete the active saved Smart Sharpen settings, click the **Delete** button.

12 Click **OK**.

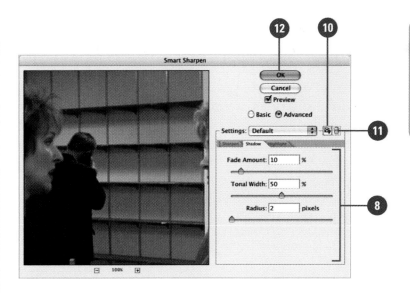

Image using Smart Sharpen

Using the Clone Stamp Tool

One of Photoshop's most powerful features is its ability to retouch a photographic image. When wanting to manipulate an image, you can apply the Clone Stamp tool. The Clone Stamp tool allows you to sample the image, and then apply that sample over another same image, or another open document. When you use the Clone Stamp tool, by selecting Aligned In The Options bar, you can reuse the most current sampling point, no matter how many times you stop and resume painting. When Aligned is deselected, you'll reuse the same sampled pixels each time you paint. For example, you could use the Clone Stamp tool to repair damage to an image, remove a tree, even remove or add someone from an image.

Use the Clone Stamp Tool

1. Select the **Clone Stamp** tool on the toolbox.

2. Select a brush tip, and then select brush options, such as blending mode, opacity, and flow, on the Options bar.

3. Select the **Aligned** check box on the Options bar to sample pixels continuously without losing the current sampling point.

   Clear the check box to continue to use the sampled pixels from the initial sampling point each time you stop and resume painting.

4. Select the **Sample All Layers** check box on the Options bar to sample data from all visible layers or clear the check box to sample only from the active layer.

5. Hold down the Alt (Win) or Option (Mac) key, and then click an area to sample the portion of the image you want to use for your sample.

6. Drag over the area of the image you want to restore or modify.

7. Repeat steps 5 and 6, until you've modified the image.

Clone Stamp tool

Joshua tree removed using the Clone Stamp tool

Using the Dodge and Burn Tools

You can also use the Dodge and Burn tools to lighten or darken specific areas of an image. If you wanted to lighten the shadow areas of an image, you would use the Dodge tool, and conversely, if you wanted to darken the highlight areas of an image, you would select the Burn tool. While there are other ways to control the highlights and shadows of an image, such as the Levels adjustment, the Dodge and Burn tools are controlled by using a brush and dragging in the image. That kind of control gives you the option to choose exactly what you want to modify.

Use the Dodge and Burn Tools

1. Select the **Dodge** or **Burn** tool on the toolbox.

2. Select a brush tip, and then select brush options on the Options bar.

3. Click the **Range** list arrow on the Options bar, and then select from the following options:

   ◆ **Midtones.** Changes the middle range of grays.

   ◆ **Shadows.** Changes the dark areas.

   ◆ **Highlights.** Changes the light areas.

4. Specify the Exposure value for the stroke.

5. To use the brush as an airbrush, click the **Airbrush** button. Alternately, select the Airbrush option in the Brushes palette.

6. Drag over the part of the image you want to lighten or darken.

Did You Know?

The Sponge tool does not lighten or darken an image. It saturates or desaturates color values as you drag over portions of the image. Since over or under exposed images have a tendency to lose some tonal values and appear flat, you can use the Sponge tool (with Saturate) to return some of the color values back to the image.

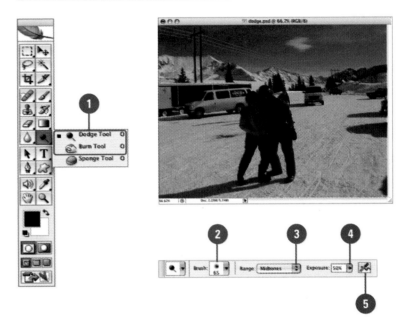

Dark areas restored using the Burn tool

Using the Healing Brush and Patch Tools

PS 2.2

Since these tools have become my favorite tools for working and correcting problems with digital images. The Healing Brush tool allows you to correct small imperfections, making them disappear into the surrounding image. This tool works from a sample of the original image, and then matches the texture, lighting, transparency, and shading of the sampled pixels into the source pixels. If an image contains a lot of random noise, before working with the Healing brush try lowering the amount of noise with the new Reduce Noise filter. Once applied you can use the Healing brush to clean up the rest of the troubled areas. The Patch tool works with the Healing Brush tool. It takes a sample and matches the texture, lighting, transparency, and shading of the sample to the source, creating an almost seamless repair of the image. You can also use the Patch tool to clone isolated areas of an image. When you use healing operations in a separate layer, you gain control over the process; you can even use the opacity and blending mode settings to further control the healing process. Always use the Healing brush in a separate layer... always.

Use the Healing Brush Tool

1. Select the **Healing Brush** tool.

2. Select a soft round brush on the Options bar.

3. Create a new layer above the layer you want to modify.

4. Select the **Sample All Layers** option.

5. Hold the Alt (Win) or Option (Mac) key, and then click on the area of the image for a sample.

   This area should represent the texture (not color) of the areas you want to heal.

6. Use small short strokes and carefully drag over the areas you want to change, then release your mouse and move to the next area.

   The Healing brush works to match the sample to the source.

7. If the texture of the area you are healing changes, repeat step 4, and sample a different area of the image.

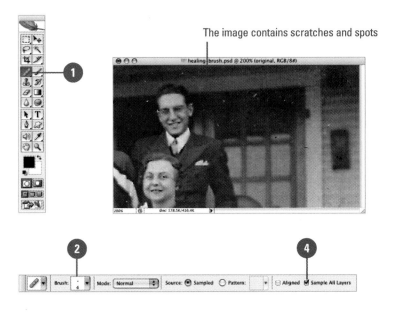

The image contains scratches and spots

The Healing Brush makes short work of correcting damaged images.

Use the Patch Tool

① Select the **Patch** tool.

② Select the layer you want to modify.

③ Using the Patch tool, select the damaged area of the image you want to repair (the Patch tool functions just like the Lasso selection tool).

④ Click the **Source** option on the Options bar.

⑤ Move into the middle of the selection marquee, and drag the selection over the area you want to repair and release. As you drag you will see a copy of the area you are moving over appear in the original selection.

⑥ Release your mouse when you see the best match.

The Patch tool corrects the damaged area of the image.

⑦ Repeat steps 2 through 6 to patch any other damaged areas of the image.

Did You Know?

The Patch tool options on the Option bar provide power. On the Options bar, use the Source option with the Patch tool if you are selecting the damaged area and dragging it over the good area, and use the Destination option if you would rather select a good area to drag over the damaged area. The Transparent option preserves transparent areas during the patching process.

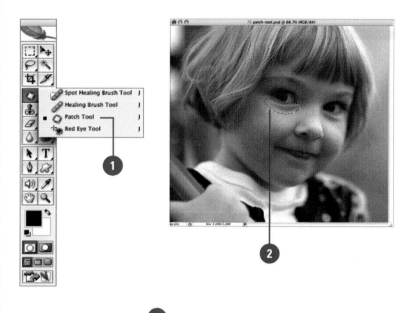

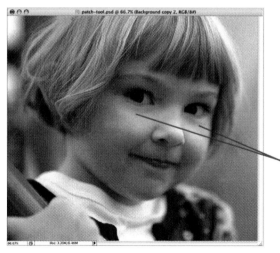

The Patch tool removed the rings under the models eyes

Working with the Spot Healing Brush

A new tool in Photoshop's formidable arsenal of restoration and correction tools is the Spot Healing Brush (**New!**). With a name similar to the Healing brush, you might expect that the tools have similar features, and you would be correct. The main difference between the two tools is that the Spot Healing Brush does not require you take a sample of the area to heal. The Spot Healing Brush tool takes the area sample as you work by sampling the surrounding pixels. The Spot Healing brush, as its name implies, works best on small spots and imperfections. To heal larger areas, the standard Healing Brush, Patch tool, and even the good old Clone Stamp tool are your best bets.

Use the Spot Healing Brush

1. Select the **Spot Healing Brush** tool.

2. Select a soft round brush on the Options bar.

3. Create a new layer above the layer you want to modify.

4. Select the **Sample All Layers** option.

5. Using small short strokes, carefully drag over the areas you want to change, then release your mouse and move to the next area.

   The Spot Healing brush works to match the sample to the source.

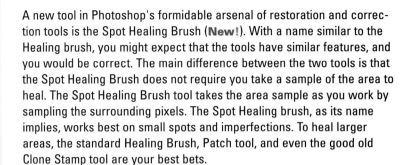

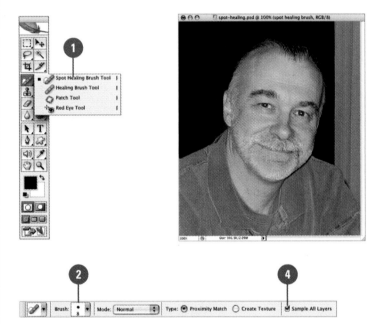

The Spot Healing Brush smoothed out some of the wrinkles

Working with the Red Eye Tool

The new Red Eye tool (**New!**) not only gives the digital restorer an excellent tool for removing pesky red eye, it will also remove the green and white reflections in pet's eyes. The biggest generator of red eye is the onboard flash on your camera. Actually, if they would simply rename a camera's built-in flash, red-eye generator, it might help amateur photographers pay more attention. However, until that day comes, designers will still have to deal with images that contain red eye. The Red Eye tool performs two operations: it desaturates the red values, and darkens the pupil.

Use the Red Eye Tool

1 Select the **Red Eye** tool.

2 Select from the following options on the Options bar:

   ◆ **Pupil Size.** Select the size of the pupil in relation to the amount of red eye.

   ◆ **Darken Amount.** Select how much you want to darken the pupil area of the eye.

3 Click in the middle of the red portion of the eye, and release.

   The red is removed, and the pupil is darkened.

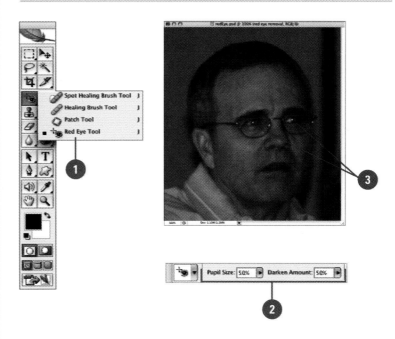

The red eye is removed with the click of your mouse.

Controlling Tonal Range

Control Tonal Range

① Open a document in which you want to change the tonal range.

② Select the **Layers** palette, and then select the layer in which you want to apply the Levels adjustment.

③ Click the **Create New Fill Or Adjustment Layer** button, and then click **Levels**.

④ Select the **Preview** check box to view the adjustments directly in the active document window.

⑤ Click the **Channel** list arrow to select whether to work on the entire image, or just one of the images default color channels (useful for color correction).

⑥ Drag the **Shadow** input slider to the right to adjust the balance of black in the image.

⑦ Drag the **Midtone** input slider left or right to lighten or darken the midtones of the image.

⑧ Drag the **Highlight** input slider to the left to adjust the balance of white in the image.

⑨ Drag the **Black** and **White Output Levels** sliders left and right to adjust the percentage of ink used in printing the image.

The Levels adjustment lets you adjust the tonal range of an image by giving you three sliders—shadows, midtones, and highlights. Dragging the sliders precisely adjusts the tonal ranges of an image. In addition, the Output sliders lets you adjust the ink percentages used for the output to print. By adjusting the output ink levels, you avoid the overly black images that sometimes accompany printing images using high dot-gain papers.

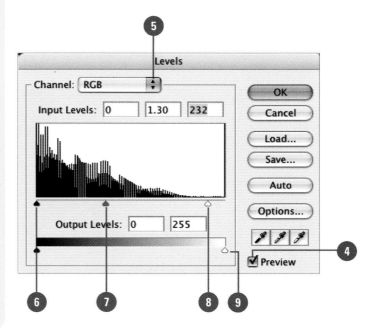

10 To load a previously saved Levels adjustment, click **Load**, and then select and load the file.

11 Click **Save** to save the current Levels adjustment.

12 Use the eyedropper tools to select black, white, and midtone points directly within the active image.

13 Click **OK**.

Photoshop uses the Levels adjustment layer to apply the tonal changes to the image.

Did You Know?

You can apply the same Levels adjustments to an image without an adjustment layer. Click the Image menu, point to Adjustments, and then click Levels. Make your adjustments using the Levels options, and then click OK.

You can view the Levels Histogram anytime. Click the Window menu, and then click Histogram. Photoshop opens a Histogram palette that lets you view tonal changes to the image as you make them.

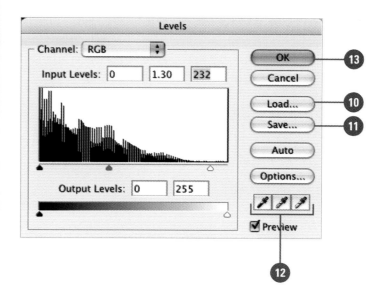

Tonal changes applied

Working with the Histogram Palette

Photoshop's Histogram palette gives you many options for viewing tonal and color information about the active image. The Histograms default display is the tonal range of the entire image. However, you can use any of Photoshop's selection tools, select a portion of the active document, and display a histogram for that portion of the image. You can also view a specific color channel or view all the channels at once. The tonal range and color values for an image are vitally important to generating great graphics, and the Histogram palette is a great resource for instant up-to-date information.

Work with the Histogram Palette

1. Select the **Histogram** palette.

   TROUBLE? *Click the Window menu, and then click Histogram.*

2. Click the **Histogram Options** button, and then select from the following options:

   ◆ **Dock To Palette Well.** Click to place the History palette into the Palette Well on the Options bar.

   ◆ **Uncached Refresh.** Click to refresh the image cache (rescans the image).

   ◆ **Compact View.** Click to create a small palette-size view of the Histogram palette.

   ◆ **Expanded View.** Click to create an expanded view of the Histogram palette. Includes options to view specific channels, luminosity settings or color.

   ◆ **All Channels View.** Click to view all the color channels.

   ◆ **Show Statistics.** Click to show history statistics.

   ◆ **Show Channels In Color.** Click to show the channels using specific colors, such as red, green, and blue.

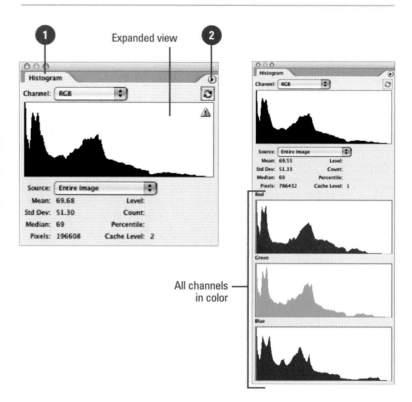

Expanded view

All channels in color

For Your Information

Viewing Information Using Histogram Palette

You can view information about a specific pixel or range using the Histogram palette. Make sure the Expanded View option is selected, and then place the pointer in the histogram to view information about a specific pixel value. To view information about a range of values, drag in the histogram to highlight the range.

Understanding Colors and Channels

Introduction

In the world of design, color is one of the most important elements. When you're creating a brochure, advertisement, or banner using Adobe Photoshop, good use of color attracts the attention of the viewer. It also helps draw the elements of your design into one cohesive unit. Color is a strong motivator and is used in all aspects of our daily life.

Since color is so important to design, Photoshop lets you use industry-standard color sets, or you can create and save your own customized color palettes. You can also color correct a photograph by removing the color entirely or selectively remove colors from portions of the image. In addition, Photoshop gives you ways to select areas based on color, and then fill those areas with any color you choose.

Not only is it important to understand how color is used, it's also important to understand how Photoshop manages color information and that's where the Channels palette comes into the picture. **Channels** are where color information is stored. The number of channels in an image is based on its **color mode**, or color model, such as RGB (Red, Green, Blue) or CMYK (Cyan, Magenta, Yellow, and Black). A firm understanding of channels and color modes, and their function in Photoshop will go a long way in helping you control and manage color.

When adjusting your image, you can use various commands—Auto Contrast and Color, Curves, Color Balance, and Brightness/Contrast, Saturate and Desaturate, just to name a few. You can also use the Match and Selective Color adjustments to further fine-tune your image. Photoshop also provides a photo filters adjustment, as well as a shadow and highlight adjustment to correct those over or under-exposed images. With all of the commands and adjustments available, the real dilemma will be where do you begin?

Working with 8, 16, and 32 Bit Images

PS 6.3, 6.4

It's all about the numbers, and that's a fact. The number of colors available for displaying or printing each pixel in an image is called **bit depth**—also known as pixel depth or color depth. A higher bit depth means more available colors and more accurate color representation in an image. A bit depth setting of 2-bit displays 4 colors; 4-bit displays 16 colors; 8-bit displays 256 colors; 16-bit displays 32,768 colors; and 24-bit and 32-bit, both of which display 16.7 million colors. Normal digital images have 8-bits of data per channel. For example, an RGB image with 8-bit channels is capable of producing 16.7 million colors (a 24-bit RGB image: 8 bits x 3 channels) possible colors per pixel. While that may seem like a lot of color information, when it comes to color correction and adjustment, it isn't.

In response to needing more control, Photoshop supports 16-bit and now 32-bit—known as **High Dynamic Range (HDR)** (New!)—images. High Dynamic Range works with images in 32-bits-per-channel, extended dynamic range. It's all about dynamic range. **Dynamic Range** is the ability of a channel to capture information from black to white, dark and bright areas of an image. An 8-bit channel image has a dynamic range of 250:1 (per channel), similar to the dynamic range of printed paper or a computer display. A 16-bit channel image has a dynamic range of 65,000:1, and a 32-bit channel image has a dynamic range of over 200,000:1. The greater dynamic range translates into better control over an image, when making fine color, and contrast adjustments using Levels and Curves (shown below). Working with HDR images is very similar to using camera RAW files and applying exposure changes after the fact. Photographers can capture the full dynamic range of a scene with multiple exposures and merge the files into a single image.

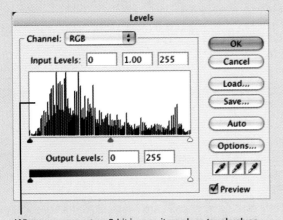

When you correct an 8-bit image, it can lose tonal values.

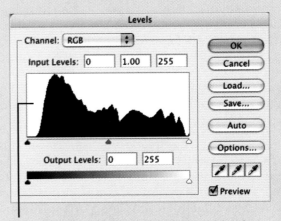

16 and 32-bit images hold more image data and therefore hold more data during correction operations.

Changing Bits Per Channel

The ability of working with 32-bit images is new to this version of Photoshop, so you have a limited use of adjustments and filters. However, when you convert an image from 32-bits into 16-bits, all of your adjustments are available even though you lose some filters.

Therefore, when color or contrast adjusting an image, first convert a standard 8-bit image to 16-bits, and do all the corrections. This helps prevent loss of color information, and banding between light and dark shades. Once all the color/contrast adjustments have been made, you can (if necessary) convert the image back to 8-bit. It's that simple. When you convert a 16-bit image to 32-bits, you need to use the Flatten Image command on the Layers menu on the image first. You can change an image's bits by displaying the image, clicking the Image menu, pointing to Mode, and then clicking 8 Bits/Channels, 16 Bits/Channels, or 32 Bits/Channels.

When you convert a 32-bit image to 8- or 16-bits per channel, Photoshop opens the HDR Conversion dialog box to let you make exposure and contrast corrections, so the image retains the dynamic range you want. The Exposure And Gamma option lets you manually adjust brightness and contrast. Drag the Exposure slider to adjust the gain and drag the Gamma slide to adjust the contrast. The

Highlight Compression option automatically adjusts highlight values to fit within the range for 8- or 16-bit images. The Equalize Histogram option automatically preserves image contrast. The Local Adaption option adjusts the tonality (local brightness regions) in the image. Drag the Radius slider to specify the size of the local brightness regions and then drag the Threshold slider to specify the distance between tonal values before they are not included in the brightness region. If you want to reuse these settings in the future, you can save them, and then load them again as needed.

Viewing 32-Bit Images

The dynamic range of HDR images exceeds the display capabilities of standard monitors. When you view a 32-bit HDR image, the high-lights and shadows may look dark or washed out. To correct the problem, Photoshop allows you to adjust 32-bit preview options, so 32-bit images display properly on your monitor. The preview options are stored in the image file, so each file retains its own settings. To set pre-view options, open a 32-bit HDR image, click the View menu, and then click 32-Bit Preview Options. In the 32-bit Preview Options dialog box, select the preview settings (described ear-lier in this topic) you want, and then click OK.

8

Working with the Channels Palette

The Channels palette is Photoshop's storage locker for color and selection information. For example, when you open an RGB image, the Channels palette displays color channels of red, green, and blue. When you open a CMYK image, the color channels are cyan, magenta, yellow, and black. These primary color channels are defined as the native color channels of the image. The Channels palette can also contain spot-color channels and selection masks. In addition, to color information and selection masks, the Channels palette contains a composite channel. The composite, when selected, lets you view the full-color image in the document window. Selecting any of the individual native color channels changes the active view of the image to display the selected color channel. The Channels palette stores color information using shades of gray, and each color channel is capable of displaying 256 steps from black to white. A zero value pixel displays as black, and a 255-value pixel displays as white. The darker the shade of gray, the less of the selected ink color is used to create the visible colors within the image.

Work with the Channels Palette

1. Open a color document.

2. Select the **Channels** palette.

3. Click on the individual channels to view the native color channels of the active document.

4. Click the composite channel to view the full-color image.

See Also

See "Creating Spot Color Channels" on page 188 for more information on using the Channels palette.

See "Using Channels to Create and Store Selections" on page 92 for more information on using Channels.

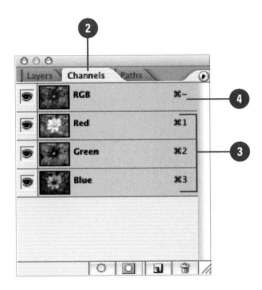

Working with Color Modes

 PS 6.1

Color modes define the colors represented in the active document. Although you can change the color mode of a document, it is best to select the correct color mode at the start of the project. Photoshop's color modes are Bitmap, Grayscale, Duotone, Indexed Color, RGB (Red, Green, and Blue), CMYK (Cyan, Magenta, Yellow, and Black), Lab, and Multichannel. See "Selecting Color Modes and Resolution" on page 15 for information on best use for each color mode. The number of channels in an image depends on its color mode. For example, CMYK image contains at least four channels, one for each color.

Color modes determine the number of colors, the number of channels, and the file size of an image. For example, a RGB image has at least three channels (like a printing plate), one for each red, green, and blue color information. Color modes not only define the working color space of the active document, they also represent the color space of the output document. It's the document output (print, press, or monitor), which ultimately determines the document color mode. Color modes do not just determine what colors the eye sees; they represent how the colors are mixed, and that's very important because different output devices use different color mixes.

Therefore, when selecting a color mode, know the file format of the document, and where it will be used. An image taken with a digital camera, and then opened in Photoshop would most likely be in the RGB color mode. An image displayed on a monitor would be RGB, or possibly Indexed Color. A photograph scanned on a high-end drum scanner would most likely be in the CMYK color mode. An image being sent to a 4-color press would be CMYK too. If you were creating a Photoshop document from scratch, the color mode chosen would represent the eventual output of the document, such as a Web page, inkjet printer, or a 4-color press.

Switching Between Color Modes

Unfortunately, images do not always arrive in the correct format. For example, you take several photographs with your digital (RGB) camera, but the images are being printed on a 4-color (CMYK) press, or you want to colorize a grayscale image. Changing color modes is a snap, but changing the color mode of an image isn't the problem. The problem is what happens to the digital color information when you change color modes. For example, if you open an RGB image with the intent of sending it out to a 4-color press (CMYK), the smartest course of action is to remain in the RGB color mode through the processing of the image, and then convert the image into the CMYK mode. The reason is in how Photoshop moves between those two color spaces. For example, if you move a color-corrected CMYK image into the RGB color mode, and then back to CMYK, the colors shift because Photoshop rounds color values during the change process. Not to mention that a CMYK image is 25% larger than an RGB image, and the RGB color mode represents the color space of your monitor, not CMYK. It is impossible to view a subtractive CMYK color on an RGB device. If, however, the image originally came to you as a color-corrected CMYK image, then stay and work in that color mode. See topics in this chapter for specific steps to switch between color modes.

Understanding the RGB Color Mode

PS 6.1

The RGB color mode is probably the most widely used of all the color modes. RGB generates color using three 8-bit channels: 1 red, 1 green, and 1 blue. Since each channel is capable of generating 256 steps of color; mathematically that translates into 16,777,216 possible colors per image pixel. The RGB color mode (sometimes referred to as Additive RGB) is the color space of computer monitors, televisions, and any electronic display. This also includes PDA's (Personal Digital Assistants), and cellular phones. RGB is considered a device-dependent color mode. Device dependent means that the colors in images created in the RGB color mode will appear different on various devices. In the world of computer monitors and the Web, what you see is very seldom what someone else sees; however, understanding how Photoshop manages color information goes a long way to gaining consistency over color.

Convert an Image to RGB Color

1. Open an image.

2. Click the **Image** menu, point to **Mode**, and then click **RGB Color**.

Photoshop converts the image into the RGB color mode.

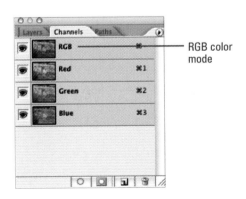

RGB color mode

Understanding the CMYK Color Mode

The CMYK color mode is the color mode of paper and press. Printing presses (sometimes referred to a 4-color press) convert an image's colors into percentages of CMYK (cyan, magenta, yellow, black), which eventually become the color plates on the press. One at a time, the plates apply color to a sheet of paper, and when all 4 colors have been applied, the paper contains an image similar to the CMYK image created in Photoshop. The CMYK color mode successfully takes an image from a monitor to paper. Before converting an image into the CMYK mode, it's important to understand that you will lose some color saturation during the conversion, known as **out of gamut**. To view the areas of an RGB image that will lose saturation values, click the View menu, and then click Gamut Warning. Photoshop will mask all the areas of the image that are out of gamut.

Convert an Image to CMYK Color

1. Open an image.

2. Click the **Image** menu, point to **Mode**, and then click **CMYK Color**.

   Photoshop converts the image into the CYMK color mode.

See Also

See "Using Curves and Color Adjustments" on pages 192 for more information on adjusting the color of an image.

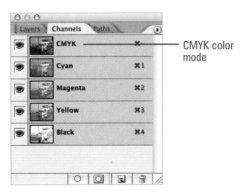

CMYK color mode

Understanding the Grayscale Color Mode

 PS 6.1

The grayscale color mode utilizes an 8-bit pixel (8 on/off light switches) to generate 1 black, 1 white, and 254 shades of gray. Although scanning and working on old black and white images might seem the obvious reason for using the grayscale color mode; the speed and power of Photoshop, combined with faster computer systems, has prompted most photo restorers to switch to the RGB color space because of its greater versatility, and it's ability to generate millions of colors (or shades of gray). Yet despite the move to RGB, the grayscale color mode is still used extensively on black and white images, where file size is a consideration (grayscale images are 2/3^{rds} smaller than RGB), and where output to rag style papers, such as newsprint, lack the ability to produce the detailed information available with RGB.

Convert an Image to Grayscale

1. Open an image.

2. Click the **Image** menu, point to **Mode**, and then click **Grayscale**.

   The image is automatically converted into the grayscale color mode.

Grayscale color mode

Did You Know?

You can colorize a grayscale image. Convert the image into the RGB mode, and then select a color, brush, and brush size on the Options bar. The trick is to change the blending mode of the brush on the Options bar to Color. Then, as you paint on the image, the selected color will replace the original grays.

For Your Information

Colorizing a Grayscale Image

If you're planning on colorizing a grayscale image, you can increase your control of the image by creating a layer directly above the image layer, and painting in the new layer. Leave the blending mode of the brush at Normal, and change the blending mode of the new layer to Color. When you paint, the color is applied and controlled in the new layer, and you have the additional option of using layer opacity to control the intensity of the effect.

Understanding the Bitmap Color Mode

 PS 6.1

Convert an Image to Bitmap

1. Open an image.

2. Click the **Image** menu, point to **Mode**, and then click **Bitmap**.

   IMPORTANT *Before converting an image into a bitmap, it must first be in the grayscale color mode.*

3. Enter a value for Output Resolution.

4. Click the **Use** list arrow, and then select from the available options:

   ◆ **50% Threshold.** Converts pixels with gray values above the middle gray level (128) to white and below to black. The result is a high-contrast, black-and-white image.

   ◆ **Pattern Dither.** Converts an image by organizing the gray levels into geometric patterns of black and white dots.

   ◆ **Diffusion Dither.** Converts pixels with gray values above the middle gray level (128) to white and below to black using an error-diffusion process. The result is a grainy, film like texture.

   ◆ **Halftone Screen.** Simulates the effect of printing a grayscale image through a halftone screen.

   ◆ **Custom Pattern.** Simulates the effect of printing a grayscale image through a custom halftone screen. This method lets you apply a screen texture, such as a wood grain, to an image.

5. Click **OK**.

Bitmap images consist of two colors: black and white. Bitmap images are sometimes referred to as 1-bit images. Think of a bitmap as a light switch with two positions, on and off. Each pixel in a bitmap image is either on or off, black or white. Because they are only 1-bit, the file size of a bitmap image is typically very small. Bitmap image have limited use, but are employed for black and white ink drawings, line art, sketches, and for creating halftone screens.

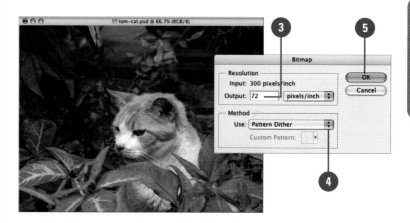

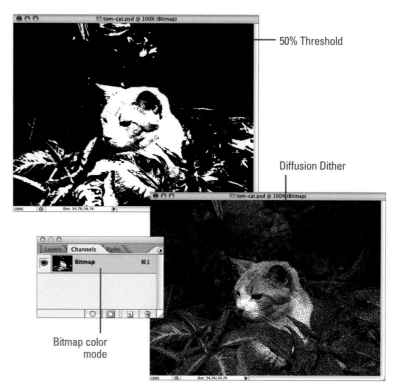

50% Threshold

Diffusion Dither

Bitmap color mode

Understanding the Indexed Color Mode

 PS 6.1

The indexed color mode gives you two advantages. You can create images as small as grayscale (8-bit pixels), and you get color instead of shades of gray. Its small file size, and its ability to generate color make is a winning color mode for images displayed on Web pages, as well as graphics used in computer-generated presentations. Its one drawback is the number of colors generated, indexed images generate a maximum of 256 colors (the same as the steps of gray in a grayscale image). The good news is you get to choose the colors. When you convert an image into the indexed color mode, Photoshop creates a color lookup table (CLUT) to store the images color information. When a color in the image cannot be found in the lookup table, Photoshop substitutes the closest available color.

Convert an Image to Indexed Color

1. Open an image.

2. Click the **Image** menu, point to **Mode**, and then click **Indexed Color**.

3. Select from the following Indexed Color Mode options:

   ◆ **Palette.** Click the list arrow to choose from the available color palettes, or click Custom and create your own palette.

   ◆ **Colors.** Select the number of colors for the lookup table (9 to 256).

   ◆ **Forced.** Force the lookup table to hold specific colors. Black And White adds a pure black and a pure white to the color table; Primaries adds red, green, blue, cyan, magenta, yellow, black, and white; Web adds the 216 web-safe colors; and Custom allows you to specify your own colors.

   ◆ **Transparency.** Select the check box to preserve transparent areas of the image (if there are no transparent areas, this option is disabled).

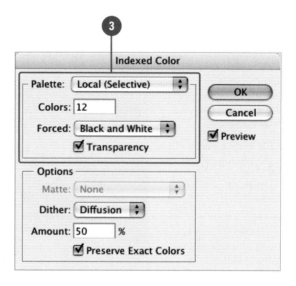

④ Select from the following options:

◆ **Matte.** Click the list arrow to fill transparent areas of the original image with a specific color.

◆ **Dither.** Click the list arrow, and then select a pixel-mixing (dither) scheme. Dithering helps transitional areas of the image (shadows, light to dark) appear more natural.

◆ **Amount.** If the Dither option is selected, the Amount instructs Photoshop how much color information to use in the dithering process (0 to 100).

◆ **Preserve Exact Colors.** Select the check box to hold exact color measurements in the lookup table.

⑤ Click **OK**.

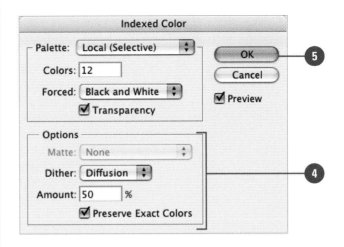

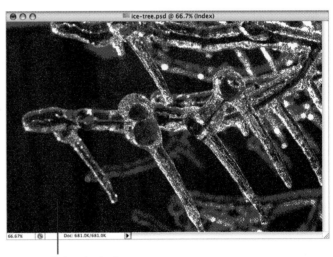

Indexed color image

Did You Know?

You can adjust the color lookup table (CLUT) of an indexed image.
Click the Image menu, and then click Color Table. Click the Table button, click Custom, and then click on one of the colors in the table. Photoshop opens a color picker dialog box, and lets you change the selected image color.

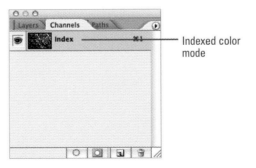

Indexed color mode

Understanding the Lab Color Mode

The Lab color mode is an old color measuring system. Created in France in 1939, its purpose was to measure color based on visual perception. Since computers were not around in 1939, the Lab model is not based on a particular computer or operating system, and so Lab color is device independent. Lab measures color using a lightness channel, an "a" channel (red to green), and a "b" channel (blue to yellow). Lab works well for editing images obtained from Photo CD's, moving images between operating systems (Photoshop Mac to Photoshop Win), and for printing color images to PostScript Level 2 or 3 devices. Because of its ability to separate the gray tones of an image into an individual channel (lightness), the Lab color mode is excellent to sharpening, or increasing the contrast of an image without changing its colors. Just convert the original RGB image to Lab color, select the Lightness channel, and perform sharpening, or Levels and curves adjustments directly to the channel.

Convert an Image to Lab Color

1. Open an image.

2. Click the **Image** menu, point to **Mode**, and then click **Lab Color**.

   Photoshop converts the image into the Lab color mode.

Did You Know?

You can use the Lab color mode to archive RGB color images. Since the Lab space is device independent, and RGB is device dependent, archiving RGB images in the Lab color mode, stabilizes the image's color information and insures color accuracy, no matter what editing application used.

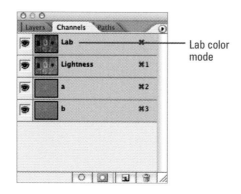

Lab color mode

Understanding the Duotone Color Mode

PS 6.1

The duotone color mode, converts a grayscale image into duotone (2-color), tritone (3-color), and quadtone (4-color) image using 2 to 4 custom inks. Duotones are frequently used to increase the tonal depth of a grayscale image. For example, most printing presses produce 50 levels of gray per color. By converting an image into a duotone, and using black and a mid gray, the press can produce a grayscale image with more dynamic range. A more common method for employing the duotone color mode is to create an image with an overall colorcast. For example, converting the grays in the image to sepia tone. If you're uncertain how to create the proper color mix for a duotone image, Photoshop comes equipped with dozens of sample duotone color values.

Convert an Image to Duotone

1 Open an image.

2 Click the **Image** menu, point to **Mode**, and then click **Duotone**.

> **IMPORTANT** *Before converting an image into a duotone, it must first be in the grayscale color mode.*

3 Click the **Type** list arrow, and then select from the following options:

◆ **Monotone.** Uses one color to generate image tone (limited dynamic range).

◆ **Duotone.** Uses two colors to generate image tone (better dynamic range for B&W images).

◆ **Tritone.** Uses three colors to generate image tone (great dynamic range, with a variety of color combinations).

◆ **Quadtone.** Uses four colors to generate image tone (best dynamic range, practically unlimited color choices).

4 Click the **Overprint Colors** button to adjust how the colors will display when the inks are printed.

5 Click **OK**.

Duotone color mode

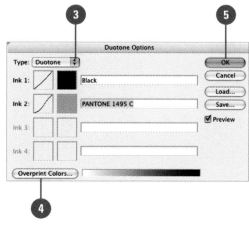

Using Multi-Channel Color Mode

PS 6.1

The Multi-Channel color mode is a specialized mode. Images converted into multi-channel color mode, converts the original color channels into shades of gray, with the grays based on the original luminosity values of the original image, and the original channels are converted into spot colors. Since multi-channel mode is used almost exclusively by the printing industry, converting a CMYK image into multi-channel color mode, produces Cyan, Magenta, Yellow, and Black spot channels, and converting an RGB image produces Cyan, Magenta, and Yellow spot channels, minus the Black channel. In both instances, converting to Multi-channel causes the loss of the mixing, or Composite channel.

Use the Multi-Channel Color Mode

1. Open an image.

2. Click the **Image** menu, point to **Mode**, and then click **Multi-Channel**.

   Photoshop converts the image into the Multi-Channel mode.

   IMPORTANT *Images converted to the multi-channel mode, must be saved in the DCS 2.0 format (Digital Color Separation). The DCS 2.0 format generates a separate file for each of the multi-channel's spot colors.*

See Also

See "Preparing an Image for the Press" on page 392 for more information on saving an image in the DCS 2.0 format.

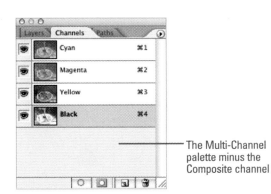

The Multi-Channel palette minus the Composite channel

Using the Replace Color Adjustment

Photoshop's Replace Color command lets you create a selection, based on image color, and replace that color selection with any other color. The Replace Color adjustment accomplishes this by giving you access to the three items that control color: Hue, Saturation, and Brightness. Hue gives you the ability to change the images physical color, Saturation controls the amount of color, and Brightness determines how bright the color is, based on its Hue and Saturation.

Use the Replace Color Adjustment

1. Open a color document.

2. Click the **Image** menu, point to **Adjustments**, and then click **Replace Color**.

3. Click on the active document using the Selection eyedroppers to select, add, or subtract colors.

4. Click the **Color** box to select a specific color for the selection.

5. Drag the **Fuzziness** slider to increase or decrease the sensitivity of the eyedropper tools.

6. Click the **Selection** or **Image** option to toggle between a view of the selection mask and the active image (white areas of the mask represent selection).

7. Drag the **Hue**, **Saturation**, and **Lightness** sliders to change the selected areas.

8. Select the **Preview** check box to view the changes in the active document.

9. Click **OK**.

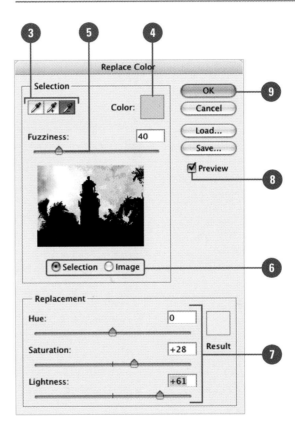

Working with the Color Palette

Photoshop not only lets you select virtually any colors you desire, it also lets you store those colors for future use. For example, you create a color scheme for a recurring brochure and you want a way to save those colors, or you're working on an Internet graphic and you need a Web-safe color palette. Whatever your color needs, Photoshop stands ready to meet them. The Color palette gives you access to Photoshop's color generation tools. This single palette lets you create colors using 6 different sliders sets, 2 spectrum color selectors, a grayscale ramp, and an option that lets you create a color ramp for the current foreground and background colors.

Work with the Color Palette

① Select the **Color** palette.

② Click the **Color Options** button.

③ Select from the following Color Sliders:

- **Grayscale.** Creates a single slider going from white (0) to black (100).

- **RGB.** Creates three sliders (red, green, and blue). Each slider has a possible value from 0 to 255.

- **HSB.** Creates three additive sliders (hue, saturation, and brightness). Each slider has a possible value from 0 to 255.

- **CMYK.** Creates four subtractive sliders (cyan, magenta, yellow, and black). Each slider has a possible value from 0 to 100.

- **Lab.** Creates three sliders (L, a, and b). The L slider has a possible value from 0 to 120, and the a, b sliders have a possible value from -120 to 100.

- **Web Color.** Creates three sliders (red, green, and blue). Each slider has a possible hexadecimal value from 00 to FF.

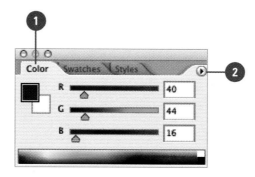

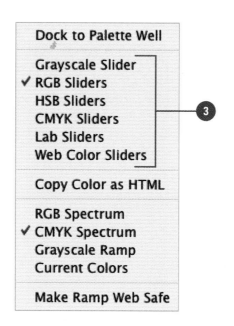

4 Click the **Color Options** button, and then select from the following Spectrums or Ramps:

◆ **RGB.** Converts the lower portion of the Color palette to the RGB spectrum. Clicking anywhere in the spectrum changes the active color.

◆ **CMYK.** Converts the lower portion of the Color palette to the CMYK spectrum. Clicking anywhere in the spectrum changes the active color.

◆ **Grayscale.** Converts the lower portion of the Color palette to grayscale ramp. Clicking anywhere in the ramp changes the active color.

◆ **Current Colors.** Converts the lower portion of the Color palette to a color ramp, using the current foreground and background colors. Clicking anywhere in the ramp changes the active color.

5 To conform the color ramp to the Web safe palette, click the **Color Options** button, and then click **Make Ramp Web Safe**.

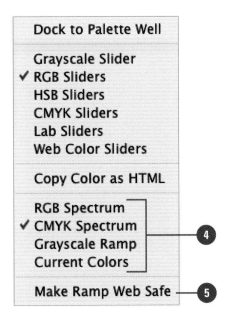

Working with the Swatches Palette

Photoshop not only lets you select virtually any colors you desire, it also lets you store those colors for future use. Where the Color palette lets you select virtually any color you need, the Swatches palette, lets you save and use swatch palettes. By default, the Swatches palette holds 31 pre-defined color palettes, and has the ability to hold as many user-defined palettes as you desire.

Add a Color Swatch to the Swatches Palette

1 Select the **Swatches** palette.

2 Click the **Swatches Options** button, and then choose from the 31 predefined color palettes.

3 Click the **Append** button to add the selected color palette.

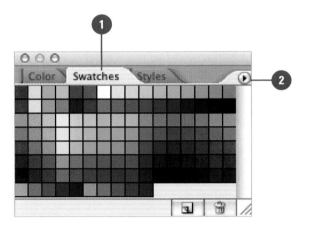

Change and Delete Colors on the Swatches Palette

1 Select the **Swatches** palette.

2 Select a color, and then change the following:

◆ **Foreground.** Change the color by clicking on any color in the Swatches palette.

◆ **Background.** Change the color by holding down the Ctrl (Win) or ⌘ (Mac) key, and then clicking on any color in the Swatches palette.

◆ **Delete.** Hold down the Alt (Win) or Option (Mac) key, and then click the color in the Swatches palette.

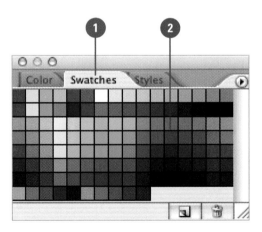

Add Colors to the Swatch Palette

1. Select the **Color** palette, and then drag the sliders or enter values to create a new color swatch.

2. Select the **Swatches** palette, and then drag the lower-right corner to expand its size beyond the range of the available colors.

3. Move the cursor just below the last swatch color until it resembles a paint bucket.

4. Click once, name the color, and then click **OK**.

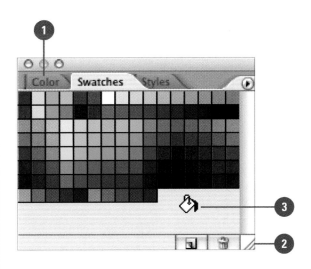

Save Customized Swatch Palettes

1. Select the **Swatches** palette.

2. Create a customized swatch palette by adding and/or deleting colors from an existing palette.

3. Click the **Swatches Options** button, and then click **Save Swatches**.

4. Enter a name in the Save As box.

5. Click the **Where** (Mac) or **Save In** (Win) list arrow, and then select a location to store the swatch.

6. Click **Save**.

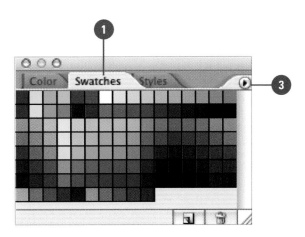

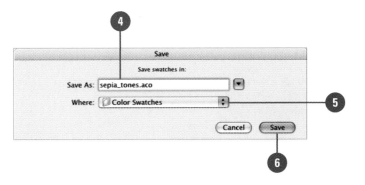

Did You Know?

You can access your customized swatch palettes from the Swatches Options button. When you save Swatch Palettes in the Color Swatches folder (default location), your customized swatch palettes appear at the bottom of the Swatches Options menu.

Using the Stroke and Fill Commands

Photoshop gives you many choices when it comes time to add or modify the colors of a document—paint brushes, airbrushes, and drawing tools, just to name a few. Two little used but powerful tools are the Stroke and Fill Commands. Both the Stroke and Fill commands work with selection tools. For example, you may want to create a unique stoke around an object, or fill a specific area of a document with a color or pattern. If that's the case, then the Stroke and Fill commands are the best and quickest ways to perform those operations.

Create a Stroke

1 Create a selection using any of Photoshop's selection tools, or really get fancy and make a selection from one of Photoshop's Shape drawing tools.

TIMESAVER *To further control the process, perform the stroke (or fill) operations within a new layer.*

2 Click the **Edit** menu, and then click **Stroke**.

3 Enter a Width value (1 to 250) for the stroke.

4 Click the **Color** box, and then select a color (the color box defaults to the foreground color).

5 Select a location option (Inside, Center, or Outside) for the stroke of the selection marquee.

6 Click the **Mode** list arrow, and then select a blending mode.

7 Enter an Opacity percentage value (0 to 100) for the stroke.

8 Select the **Preserve Transparency** check box to protect any transparent image areas (if there are no transparent areas, this option is disabled).

9 Click **OK**.

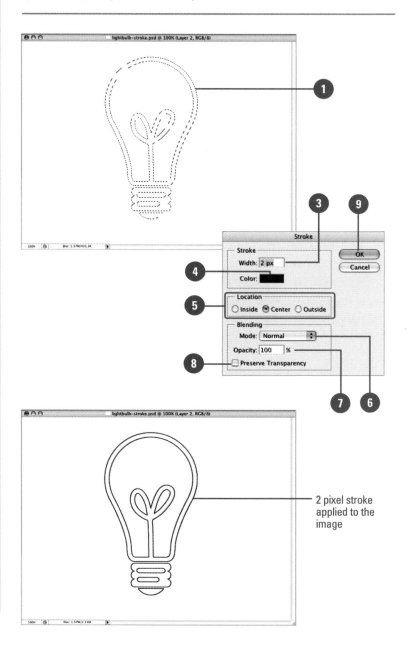

2 pixel stroke applied to the image

Create a Fill

① Create a selection using any of Photoshop's selection tools.

② Click the **Edit** menu, and then click **Fill**.

③ Click the **Use** list arrow, and then select a fill option:

- ◆ Foreground Color
- ◆ Background Color
- ◆ Color
- ◆ Pattern
- ◆ History
- ◆ Black
- ◆ 50% Gray
- ◆ White

④ Click the **Mode** list arrow, and then select a blending mode.

⑤ Enter an Opacity value (0 to 100) for the stroke.

⑥ Select the **Preserve Transparency** check box to protect any transparent image areas (if there are no transparent areas, this option is disabled).

⑦ Click **OK**.

Did You Know?

You can use the Fill command for more than filling an area with a solid color or unique pattern. For example, selecting a sepia color, and changing the Fill Blending mode to Color, tints the selected area with sepia, creating an old-style, sepia-toned image. Experiment with the Fill blending modes to create unique image effects.

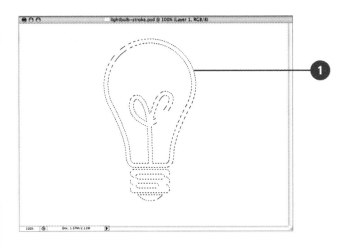

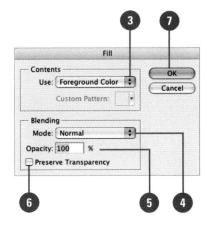

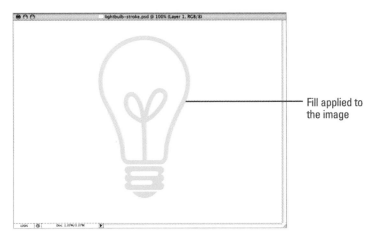

Fill applied to the image

Creating Spot Color Channels

When you work in the world of service bureaus and press machines, there are certain things you must do to create a printable document. The color mode of the image will be CMYK, and the output of the document will most likely be in a format designed to create color plates such as DCS 2.0 (Digital Color Separation). In addition, you may want to apply a spot color to the image. **Spot colors** instruct a press to apply a specific color to a specific portion of a document. For example, you may want to create a book cover jacket, and you want the author's name in a specific Pantone Blue, or want to apply a varnish to a portion of a brochure. Whatever the case, you will need to create a spot color channel.

Create a Spot Color Channel

1. Open a document.

2. If the document is not in the CMYK format, click the **Image** menu, point to **Mode**, and then click **CMYK** to convert it.

3. Create a selection, defining the area for the spot color. Use any of Photoshop's selection tools, including the Type Mask tool.

4. Select the **Channels** palette.

5. Click the **Channels Options** button, and then click **New Spot Channel**.

6. Click the **Color** box, and then select a color.

   If you need a specific press color, such as the Pantone Color Matching System, click the **Custom** button in the Color Picker, select from the available color sets, and then click **OK**.

   The Name box displays the name of the selected color.

7. Enter a Solidity value (0 to 100) to view the spot color at a specific opacity (Solidity does not affect press output).

8. Click **OK**.

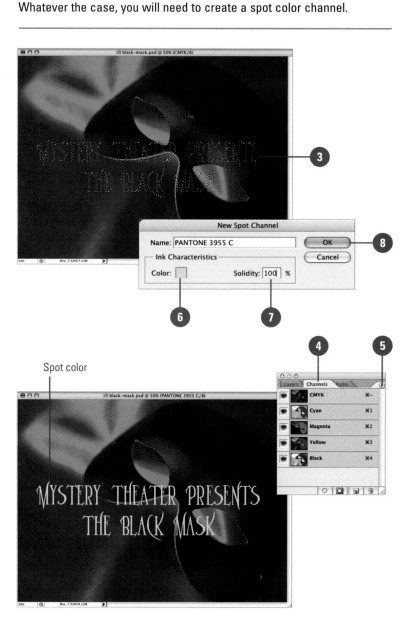

Spot color

Using the Variations Adjustment

Photoshop's Variations adjustment gives you a look at how working with analogous and complimentary colors impacts the color in a Photoshop document. For example, if an image has an overall green cast, it needs additional magenta. Understanding how colors interact and work to produce different colors helps you decide the correct course of action to take, and the Variations adjustment is an excellent teacher.

Use the Variations Adjustment

1. Open a document.

2. Click the **Image** menu, point to **Adjustments**, and then click **Variations**.

   The Original and Current Pick are displayed in the upper-left portions of the Variations dialog box.

3. To restore the image, click **Original** any time during the adjustment process.

4. Click the **Shadows**, **Midtones**, **Highlights**, or **Saturation** options to apply a color shift.

5. Drag the **Fine/Coarse** slider to determine how much change occurs with each adjustment.

6. Select the **Show Clipping** check box to display a mask over areas of the image outside of the CMYK printable color space.

7. Click the color thumbnails surrounding the image to add specific colors to the Current Pick.

8. Click Lighter or Darker to change the brightness of the image.

9. Click **OK**.

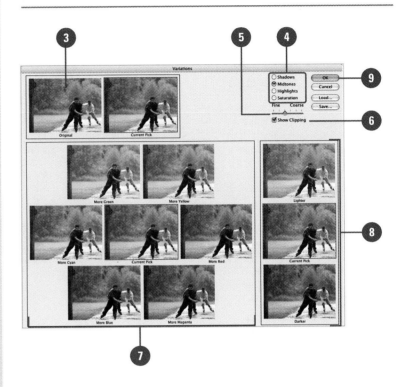

Using the Levels Adjustment and Command

 PS 2.3

Through interactive feedback using a Histogram, the Levels adjustment gives you live information about the tonal values in the active image. It's an excellent tool to perform overall tonal adjustments, and some color correction. Auto Levels is considered a quick fix color adjustment which, in some cases, works just as well as manually correcting color. However, with all the problems that exist in the average photo, it's always best to manually adjust an image. Since the Auto Levels command relies on information contained within the image—information that is sometimes inaccurate—it's usually best to correct the image manually using the Levels Adjustment command.

Use the Levels Adjustment

1. Open an image.

2. Click the **Image** menu, point to **Adjustments**, and then click **Levels**.

3. Click the **Channel** list arrow, and then select the composite channel.

4. Drag the **Input Level** sliders to adjust the brightness level.

5. Drag the **Output Level** sliders to adjust the level of ink sent to the output device (printer).

6. Click **OK**.

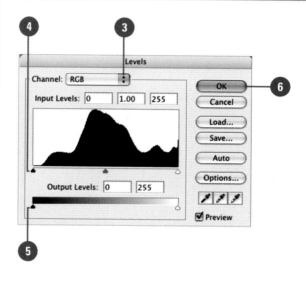

Use the Auto Levels Command

1. Open an image.

2. Click the **Image** menu, point to **Adjustments**, and then click **Auto Levels**.

   If you don't like what you see, don't forget you have the ability to use undo.

Using the Auto Contrast and Color Commands

PS 2.3, 2.4

The Auto Contrast command adjusts the tonality of the image without impacting color. The Auto Color command adjusts the tonality and color of the image by ignoring channels and looking directly at the image. The automatic color commands receive their adjustment queues from information within the active image, including any erroneous color information. For example, if the image contains a large border (typically white), the auto commands will factor that information into the correction of the image. It's best to correct any dust, and scratch problems, and crop out any borders before applying the auto contrast and color commands.

Use the Auto Contrast Command

1. Open an image.

2. Click the **Image** menu, point to **Adjustments**, and then click **Auto Contrast**.

   IMPORTANT *Use the Auto buttons (Levels, Contrast, Color) buttons only if you do not understand how to manually control the image using powerful adjustments, such as Levels and Curves.*

Use the Auto Color Command

1. Open an image.

2. Click the **Image** menu, point to **Adjustments**, and then click **Auto Color**.

Did You Know?

You can use a selection to define how the Auto Contrast and Auto Color commands work. If the image contains a border, and you don't want the Auto command using the border to influence the correction, simply select the Rectangular marquee and draw a border around the image. When the Auto command is applied, only the selected areas will be adjusted.

8

Using Curves and Color Adjustments

 PS 2.4

The Curves adjustment lets you adjust tonal ranges in the image without changing image exposure. Curves is an excellent adjustment for lightening the dark shadows of an image to bring out detail, or for creating special effects like solarization. The Color Balance adjustment lets you change the highlight, shadows, and midtones of an image separately. The Color Balance dialog box performs linear adjustments to color; therefore, it's a good tool for correcting common tonal adjustments, such as using traditional outdoor film, indoors and getting a green cast to the image. The Brightness/Contrast adjustment changes an image by an overall lightning or darkening of the image pixels. While good for special effects, its linear way of changing an image's brightness and contrast do not lend themselves to photo restoration. Curves and Levels are much better for this type of work.

Use the Curves Adjustment

1 Open an image.

2 Click the **Image** menu, point to **Adjustments**, and then click **Curves**.

3 Click the **Channel** list arrow, and then select the composite channel.

4 Click the **Tonal Input** bar to reverse the Curves tonal values.

5 Click on the diagonal line to add an edit point, and then drag up or down to increase or decrease the tonal values of the active image.

6 Use the Eyedropper tools to select tonal values directly in the active image window.

7 Select the **Preview** check box to view changes to the image.

8 Click the curve or pencil option to change how edit points are added to the Curves graph window.

9 Click the **Enlarge** button to get a larger Curves dialog box.

10 Click **OK**.

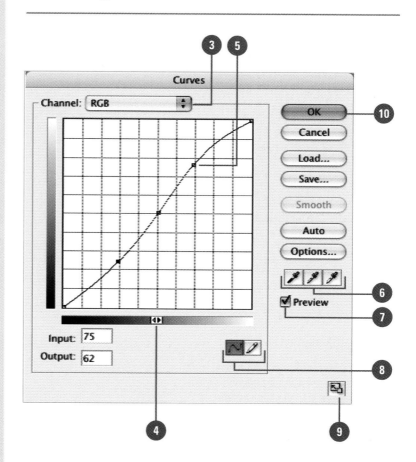

Use the Color Balance Adjustment

1 Open an image.

2 Click the **Image** menu, point to **Adjustments**, and then click **Color Balance**.

3 Drag the **CYMK** to **RGB** sliders to adjust the color.

4 Click a Tone Balance option.

5 Click **OK**.

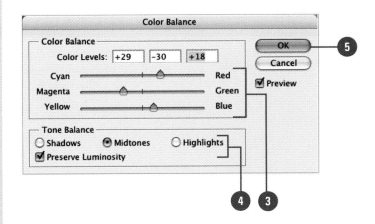

Use the Brightness/Contrast Adjustment

1 Open an image.

2 Click the **Image** menu, point to **Adjustments**, and then click **Brightness/Contrast**.

3 Drag the **Brightness** slider left to decrease the brightness values or right to increase the values of the colors in the active image.

4 Drag the **Contrast** slider to the left to decrease the color steps or left to increase the steps in the image.

5 Click **OK**.

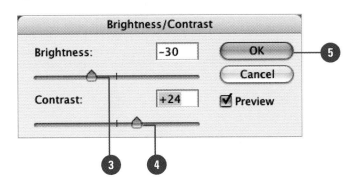

Did You Know?

You can use selection to control the Brightness/Contrast adjustment. Use any of Photoshop's selection tools to isolate a portion of the image before using the Brightness/Contrast adjustment, and then only the selected areas will be adjusted.

For Your Information

Understanding Brightness and Contrast

The Brightness/Contrast adjustment performs linear adjustment to an image. For example, moving the brightness slider to the right will increase the brightness values of all the pixels in the image equally. Since photographs are not linear in nature, the Brightness/Contrast adjustment is not recommended for use on images. For images, use the Levels, and Curves (non-linear) adjustments, and use Brightness/Contrast for clipart, text, and non-photographic images.

Using the Hue/ Saturation and Desaturate Commands

The Hue/Saturation adjustment gives you separate control over an image's Hue, Saturation, and Brightness, and it's Colorize option lets you apply a color cast to an image that's similar to a duotone effect. The Desaturate command removes all the color from an image, which preserves the Hue and Brightness values of the pixels, and changes the Saturation value to zero. The result is a grayscale image.

Use the Hue/Saturation Adjustment

1. Open an image.

2. Click the **Image** menu, point to **Adjustments**, and then click **Hue/Saturation**.

3. Drag the **Hue**, **Saturation**, and **Lightness** sliders to the level you want for your image.

4. Click the **Edit** list arrow, select a color, and then click inside the active image with the eyedropper tools to adjust the Hue/Saturation.

5. Select the **Preview** check box to see how your image looks.

6. Select the **Colorize** check box to color tint the image with the current foreground color.

7. Click **OK**.

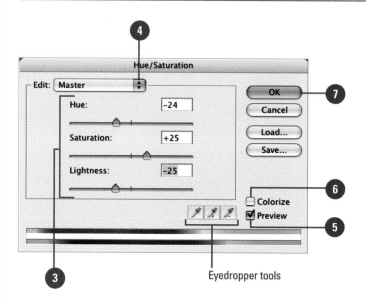

Eyedropper tools

Use the Desaturate Command

1. Open an image.

2. Click the **Image** menu, point to **Adjustments**, and then click **Desaturate**.

Did You Know?

You can Desaturate selected areas of an image using the Sponge tool. Click the Sponge tool, click Desaturate on the Options bar, and then drag to slowly remove color from the image.

Using the Match Color Adjustment

The Match Color adjustment lets you select colors in the image, and then match and change them—using Luminance, Color Intensity, and Fade sliders—to another image. The Match Color adjustment will only work on images in the RGB color mode. Match Color is a great tool to help you get that consistent look you'll need when you need to match colors with your images.

Use the Match Color Adjustment

1. Open an image.

2. Click the **Image** menu, point to **Adjustments**, and then click **Match Color**.

3. Drag the various sliders (Luminance, Color Intensity, and Fade) to adjust the image.

4. Select the **Neutralize** check box to automatically remove the color case in the active image.

5. Click the **Image Statistics Source** list arrow, and then select another image or layer for matching the color in the Destination Image.

   If you select a portion of an image before entering the Match Color dialog box, you can choose whether to use the selection in the source or target document calculate the color match.

6. Click **Save Statistics** to save the current adjustment, or click **Load Statistics** to load adjustments made to other images.

7. Select the **Preview** check box to view changes to the active image.

8. Click **OK**.

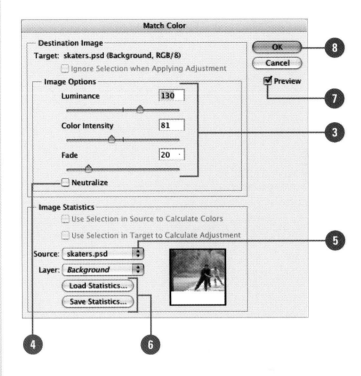

Using the Selective Color Adjustment

The Selective Color adjustment is designed to give you the ability to add or subtract specific amounts of cyan, magenta, yellow, and black inks. An excellent tool for making adjustments to an image based on a color proof, or for adding/subtracting certain primary colors; based on information supplied by your printer.

Use the Selective Color Adjustment

1. Open an image.

2. Click the **Image** menu, point to **Adjustments**, and then click **Selective Color**.

3. Click the **Colors** list arrow, and then click the specific color to adjust.

4. Drag the **Cyan**, **Magenta**, **Yellow**, and **Black** sliders to the right or left to decrease or increase the color values.

5. Click the **Relative** option to change the selected color using a percentage of the color's total ink.

6. Click the **Absolute** option to change the existing color using an absolute value of 1 to 100 percent.

7. Select the **Preview** check box to view changes to the active image.

8. Click **OK**.

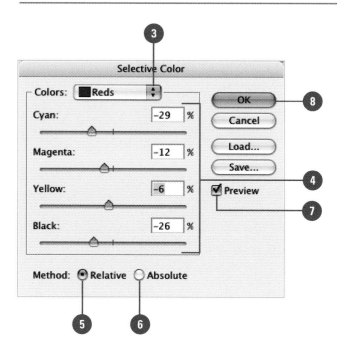

Using the Channel Mixer Adjustment

The Channel Mixer adjustment is the tool of choice for adjusting individual color channels, or for making an image conversion to black and white. The Channel Mixer adjustment modifies the selected output channel by blending it with a mix of the existing image color channels. Since color channels record information using shades of gray, you're essentially adding or subtracting grayscale information, not color information like the Selective Color adjustment. That's what makes the Channel Mixer adjustment ideal for converting images into grayscale.

Use the Channel Mixer Adjustment

1. Open an image.

2. Click the **Image** menu, point to **Adjustments**, and then click **Channel Mixer**.

3. Click the **Output Channel** list arrow, and then select from the available output channels.

4. Drag the **Source Channel** sliders right or left to increase or decrease the colors in the active image.

5. Drag the **Constant** slider left or right to adjust the grayscale output of the active image.

   Dragging to the left adds more black to the image; dragging to the right adds more white.

6. Select the **Monochrome** check box to convert the colors of the image into shades of gray.

7. Select the **Preview** check box to view changes to the active image.

8. Click **OK**.

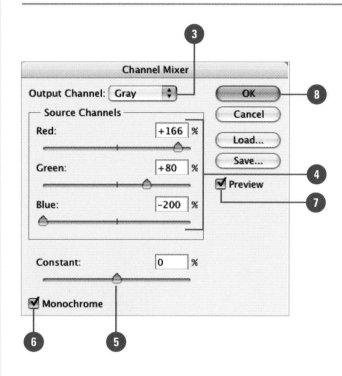

Using the Gradient Map Adjustment

 PS 2.7

The Gradient Map adjustment replaces the tonal values of the image with the colors supplied by a gradient. It's a great tool for generating special color effects. In addition, the Gradient Map adjusts the active image's colors to the colors of the selected gradient; taking the shadows of the image and mapping them to one endpoint of the gradient, and the highlights to the other point.

Use the Gradient Map Adjustment

1 Open an image.

2 Click the **Image** menu, point to **Adjustments**, and then click **Gradient Map**.

3 Click the **Gradient Used For Grayscale Mapping** list arrow to adjust the gradient.

4 Select or clear the **Dither** or **Reverse** check boxes for the Gradient Options.

5 Select the **Preview** check box to view changes to the active image.

6 Click **OK**.

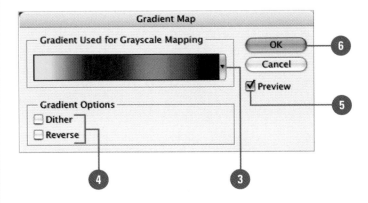

Gradient map applied to the image

Using the Photo Filter Adjustment

The Photo Filter adjustment lets you apply a specific filter or color to an image. Applying the Photo Filter adjustment to an image is similar to placing a colored filter in front of a camera lens. Photographers use filters to help correct color problems associated with unique lighting conditions—early morning sunlight or indoor florescent lighting—you can use Photoshop's Photo Filter adjustments to get the same results.

Use the Photo Filter Adjustment

1 Open an image.

2 Click the **Image** menu, point to **Adjustments**, and then click **Photo Filter**.

3 Click the **Filter** option, click the **Filter** list arrow, and then select from the available color filter options.

4 Click the **Color** option to select a user-defined color filter.

5 Drag the **Density** slider left or right to adjust the intensity of the filter effect on the active image.

The higher the value, the greater the effect.

6 Select the **Preserve Luminosity** check box to preserve the color of the image highlights.

7 Select the **Preview** check box to view changes to the active image.

8 Click **OK**.

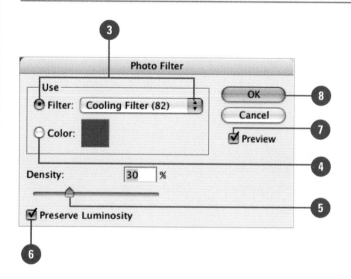

Cooling Photo Filter applied to the image

Using the Shadow/ Highlight Adjustment

The Shadow/Highlight adjustment lets you quickly correct the problems associated with the over and under-exposed areas of an image such as deep shadows or bright highlights. In addition, the Shadow/Highlight adjustment makes quick work out of images that have really dark shadows or overexposed areas by adjusting the problem areas without changing the middle range of the image. The Shadow/Highlight adjustments will not work on images in the CMYK color mode.

Use the Shadow/Highlight Adjustment

1 Open an image.

2 Click the **Image** menu, point to **Adjustments**, and then click **Shadow/Highlight**.

3 If necessary, select the **Show More Options** check box to display Highlights and Adjustments options.

4 Drag the **Shadows Amount**, **Tonal Width**, and **Radius** sliders right or left to adjust the shadow areas of the active image.

5 Drag the **Highlights Amount**, **Tonal Width**, and **Radius** sliders right or left to adjust the highlight areas of the active image.

6 Drag the **Adjustments Color Correction** and **Midtone Contrast** sliders left or right to decrease or increase the color saturation values of the adjusted areas of the image.

7 Enter values from 0 to 50 percent in the Black Clip and White Clip boxes to indicate how much of the shadow and highlight values will be clipped in the new image. Greater values produce images with more contrast.

8 Select the **Preview** check box to view changes to the active image.

9 Click **OK**.

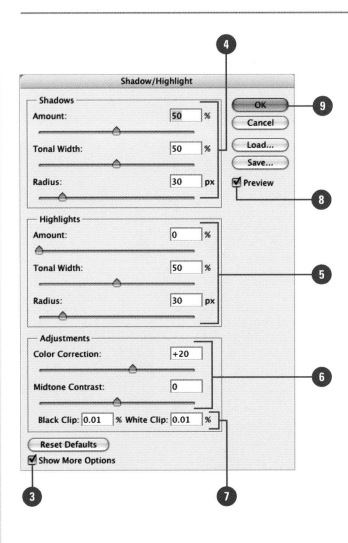

Using the Exposure Adjustment

Photoshop's Exposure adjustment (New!) is primarily designed for performing tonal adjustments to 32-bit High Dynamic Range (HDR) images, but it works with 8-bit and 16-bit images as well. Exposure works by changing an image using a linear color space (gamma 1.0) not the image's current color space. When used with HDR images, it gives you the ability to draw out details of the image that otherwise might be completely lost within the shadows and highlights.

Use the Exposure Adjustment

1. Click the **Image** menu, point to **Adjustments**, and then click **Exposure**.

2. Select from the following options:

   ◆ **Exposure.** Adjusts the highlight end of the image's tonal scale with little effect in the extreme shadows.

   ◆ **Offset.** Darkens the shadows and midtones with little affect on the highlights.

   ◆ **Gamma.** Adjusts the image gamma, using a simple power function. Similar to adjusting the mid points in an image's brightness.

3. Use the eyedroppers to adjust the image's luminance values only; not all the color channels, such as Levels, or Curves.

   ◆ **Black.** Sets the Offset, shifting the pixel you click to zero, or pure black.

   ◆ **White.** Sets the Exposure, shifting the point you click to pure white.

   ◆ **Midtone.** Sets the Exposure, making the value you click middle gray.

4. Select the **Preview** check box to view changes to the active image.

5. Click **OK**.

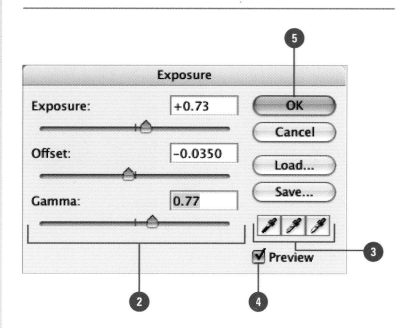

Using the Invert and Equalize Commands

The Invert command reverses the colors and tonal values to their opposite values; in effect creating a negative. The Equalize command exaggerates the contrast between similar color values. It's useful in finding stray pixels in a seemingly solid color area, or for a special color effect.

Use the Invert Command

1 Open an image.

2 Click the **Image** menu, point to **Adjustments**, and then click **Invert**.

The brightness values of each image channel are reversed, creating a negative color or grayscale image.

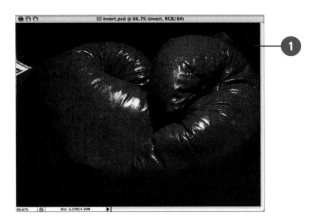

Invert adjustment applied to the image

Use the Equalize Command

1. Open an image.

2. Click the **Image** menu, point to **Adjustments**, and then click **Equalize**.

   The brightness values of the image pixels are distributed in a way that more accurately represents the entire range of brightness levels from white to black.

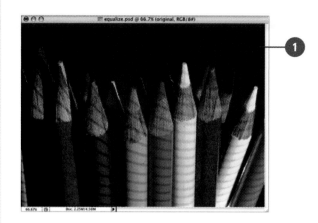

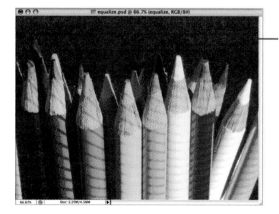

Equalize adjustment applied to the image

Using the Threshold and Posterize Adjustments

The Threshold adjustment splits an image into black and white, based on the original brightness levels of the pixels. It's useful for locating the darkest and lightest pixels in an image, or for creating some great looking black and white special effects. The Posterize adjustment creates a simpler image by reducing the number of colors. It's useful for creating an image with a clipart look, or for reducing the number of colors in preparation for the Web.

Use the Threshold Adjustment

1. Open an image.

2. Click the **Image** menu, point to **Adjustments**, and then click **Threshold**.

3. Drag the **Threshold** slider to the right or left to change the point in which black and white are defined.

   For example, setting the threshold slider to a value of 75 creates an image where all pixels with a brightness value of 75 or less are black, and all pixels with a value of 76 or higher are white.

4. Click **OK**.

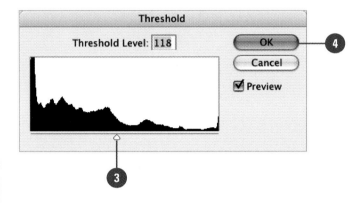

Use the Posterize Adjustment

1. Open an image.

2. Click the **Image** menu, point to **Adjustments**, and then click **Posterize**.

3. Enter a Levels value (2 to 255) to define the number of colors used.

   Lower values produce less colors, and more visual contrast.

4. Click **OK**.

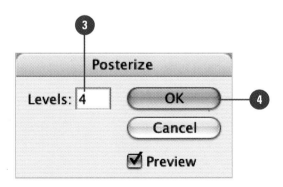

Using the Paint, Shape Drawing, and Eraser Tools

9

Introduction

Adobe Photoshop supplies you with all types of adjustment and manipulation tools. In addition to image enhancement, Photoshop can also be considered a powerful design from scratch application. With the vast array of brushes, tips, and shape drawing tools that are supplied, Photoshop helps you produce the images, either enhanced or developed from scratch, which you might need for virtually any conceivable project.

Brushes come in all sizes and shapes, and can be controlled with a mouse or drawing tablet. Since the shape of the tip controls brushes, Photoshop gives you access to several sets of pre-defined brush tip shapes, or you can create you own customized sets. As for shape drawing tools, Photoshop doesn't limit your creativity to just drawing circles and squares; it gives you instant access to dozens of pre-defined shapes. You can even create and save your own custom shapes. When it comes to Photoshop's paint and drawing tools, your choices are limitless, based only on your knowledge of the available tools, and a creative imagination—the more you know, the more you can do with Photoshop.

And, when all the drawing is said and done, there will be a need for cleaning up. With the various Eraser tools that Photoshop provides, you can make quick work of touching up those small problem areas. Photoshop provides straight eraser tools, eraser tools that erase to a definable edge, and even eraser tools that target specific color values.

When enhancing an image, you might want to apply a gradient. Gradients can be something as simple as black and white, or as complex as one that contains the colors of the rainbow. Gradients can be applied to an image; completely covering the original image information, or they can be controlled through targeted selection, and creative uses of blending modes.

Understanding Foreground and Background Colors

 Adobe Certified Expert **PS 13.1**

The Foreground and Background colors, located near the bottom of the toolbox, are Photoshop's way of identifying your primary painting color, as well as the color Photoshop uses in conjunction with the Background layer. When you select any of Photoshop's painting or drawing tools, the color applied to the document will be the foreground color—that's its purpose. Hence, it's sometimes referred to as Photoshop's active color. The Background color serves several functions—its primary purpose is to instruct Photoshop how to handle erasing on the Background layer. When you use an eraser tool on a Photoshop layer, by default, the pixels are converted to transparent. However, when you use an eraser tool on the Background something different happens. Since the Background does not support transparency, it replaces the erased pixels with the current background color.

Change the Active Foreground and Background Colors

Use any of the following methods to change the active foreground or background colors:

◆ Select the **Eyedropper** tool on the toolbox, and then click anywhere in the active document to change the foreground color.

Hold down the Alt (Win) or Option (Mac) key, and then click to change the background color.

◆ Click on a color swatch in the Swatches palette to change the foreground color.

Hold down the Ctrl (Win) or Option (Mac) key, and then click to change the background color.

◆ Create a color in the Color palette. Click the **Foreground** or **Background** thumbnail to choose the color's destination.

◆ Click the **Foreground** or **Background** Color box to open the Color Picker dialog box, select a color or enter color values, and then click **OK**.

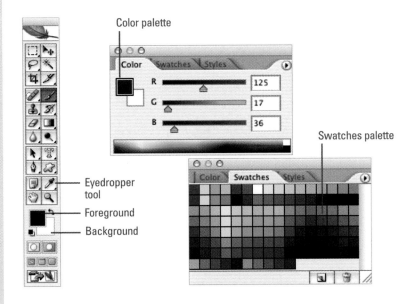

Color palette

Eyedropper tool

Foreground

Background

Swatches palette

Color Picker dialog box

Default and Switch the Foreground and Background Colors

1 Click the **Default Foreground And Background Colors** button to revert the foreground and background colors to their default values of black and white.

2 Click the **Switch Foreground And Background Colors** button to switch current colors.

TIMESAVER *Press D to change the foreground and background colors to their default values of black and white, and press X to switch the current colors.*

For Your Information

Selecting Colors

In Windows, you can use the Color dialog box, which displays basic and custom color squares and a color matrix with the full range of colors in the color spectrum, to help you select a color. You can enter RGB values or hue, saturation, and luminosity (also known as brightness) values to specify a color. Hue is the color created by mixing primary colors (Red, Blue, and Yellow). Saturation is a measure of how much white is mixed in with the color. A fully saturated color is vivid; a less saturated color is washed-out pastel. Luminosity is a measure of how much black is mixed with the color. A very bright color contains little or no black. You can also change the hue by moving the pointer in the color matrix box horizontally, the saturation by moving the pointer vertically, and the luminosity by adjusting the slider to the right of the color matrix box. On the Macintosh, you click one of the color modes and select a color, using its controls. You can select RGB values by selecting the color sliders at the top of the dialog box; by choosing RGB Sliders from the pop-up menu, then dragging Red, Green, and Blue sliders; or by entering values (color numbers) to select a color. You can select hue, saturation, and brightness (or luminosity) values by selecting Color Sliders, choosing HSB Sliders, then dragging sliders or entering values.

Using the Painting Engine

Photoshop's painting engine (released in version 7) changed forever how Photoshop designers use brushes. Previously, Photoshop gave you the ability to create a brush in any size and shape, and then use the brush in a traditional manner. However, with the exception of changing the brush's spacing, it wasn't more than a glorified paintbrush. The painting engine with options, such as Shape Dynamics, Scattering, Texture, Dual Brush, and Color Dynamics, gives you control over brushes in ways that once were only available in programs like Corel Painter and Adobe Illustrator.

An Overview of the Brushes Palette

Photoshop's painting engine is, by default, located in the Dock on the Options bar. To access the painting engine you will first need to have a brush tool, or a tool that requires the use of a brush, such as the Eraser tool, and then click the Brushes palette. If you do not see the Brushes palette, click the Window menu, and then click Brushes.

Brushes palette

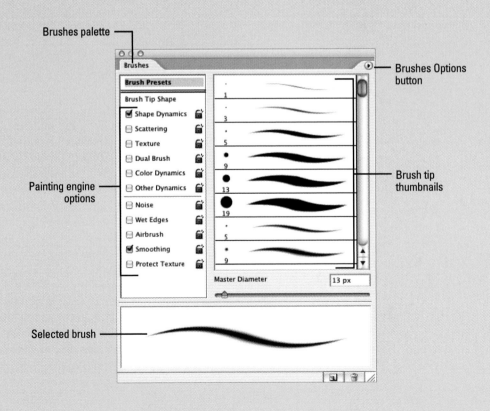

Brushes Options button

Painting engine options

Brush tip thumbnails

Selected brush

Modifying the Brushes Palette

The Brushes palette comes in many forms; you can view brushes as strokes, or you can choose thumbnails, or even text descriptions. The form of the Brushes palette does not impact its performance, only how you view the available brush tips. Choose the version that best suits your current design needs, and then change the view as needed. When you select a brush, it becomes the default for that tool only. This gives you the ability to choose a default brush for each of the brush-specific tools.

Change the Brushes Palette View

1 Select a Brush tool on the toolbox, and then select the **Brushes** palette.

2 Click the **Brushes Options** button, and then select from the available View options:

◆ **Expanded View.** Click Expanded View to gain access to painting engine options: Brush Tips, Shape Dynamics, Scattering, Texture, Dual Brush, Color Dynamics, and Other Dynamics.

◆ **Text Only.** Select this option to display all brush tips by their names.

◆ **Small Thumbnail.** Select this option to display all brush tips using a small thumbnail.

◆ **Large Thumbnail.** Select this option to display all brush tips using a large thumbnail.

◆ **Small List.** Select this option to display all brush tips by their names and small thumbnail.

◆ **Large List.** Select this option to display all brush tips by their names and large thumbnail.

◆ **Stroke Thumbnail.** Select this option to display all brush tips with a stroke. (This is useful in determining how the brush will look when applied in the document).

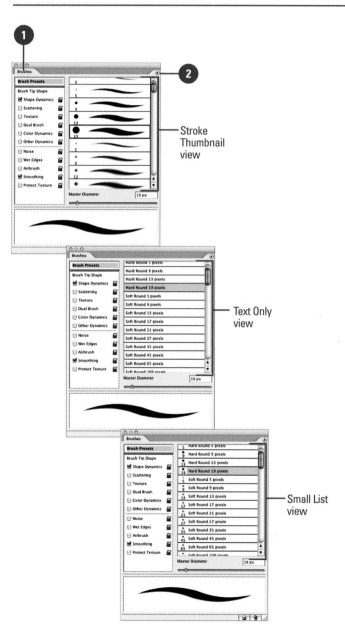

Stroke Thumbnail view

Text Only view

Small List view

Selecting Brush Tip Sets

The Brushes palette comes with 12 pre-defined sets. Each set, organizes specific brush tips by name. Since more than the paintbrush tool uses brush tips, it's important to have the right tool (brush tip) for the right job. Using or making do with the wrong brush tip is akin to digging a swimming pool with a teaspoon. You wouldn't paint a portrait with a house-painting brush, so don't settle for anything less than the exact brush tip you need to get the job done.

Select Brush Tip Sets

1. Select a Brush tool on the toolbox, and then select the **Brushes** palette.

2. Click the **Brushes Options** button.

3. Click any of the pre-defined brush palettes.

4. Click **OK**.

   This replaces the current brush tips with the selected set, or you can click Append to add them to the current set.

Did You Know?

You can draw straight lines using Photoshop's brush tools. Holding the Shift key while dragging, constrains the brush to a 90-degree line. To draw a straight line between two points, click once in the document window, move the mouse to another position, hold down the Shift key, and then click a second time. A straight line will be drawn between the first and last mouse clicks.

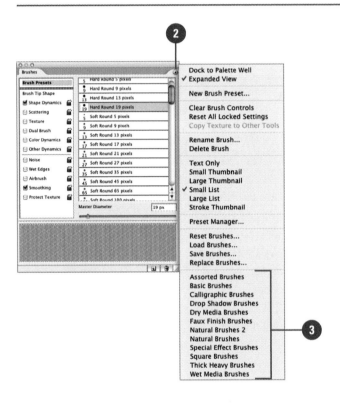

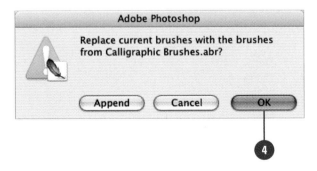

Creating Customized Brush Tips

PS 2.9

Photoshop's painting engine gives you many choices for brush tips. Any good designer will tell you that no matter how many brush tips you have, you'll always want more. For example, you're working on a 100-year-old photograph, and you need a specific brush to add hair details to the blown-out areas of the image. It's a special type of brush that literally creates the illusion of wavy hair. Photoshop, in an effort to help keep you organized, gives you the ability to create your very own customized brush tips, and then save them later in organized sets.

Create a New Brush Tip

1. Open an image, scan an item, or select any of Photoshop's painting tools and create a shape for a new brush tip.

   IMPORTANT *Since the color of a brush is determined when the brush tip is selected, create the brush tip using black or in shades of gray.*

2. Select the brush tip using any of Photoshop's selection tools.

   IMPORTANT *Photoshop picks up any pixel information in the underlying layers, even white. If you want the brush to have a transparent background, make sure the areas surrounding the image show as transparent.*

3. Click the **Edit** menu, and then click **Define Brush Preset.**

4. Enter a name for the new brush preset.

5. Click **OK**.

   Open the Brushes palette, and then scroll to the bottom of the list to access your newly created brush tip.

   Since the Define Brush Preset button picks up any background colors within the selection area, always create the brush tip in a black layer.

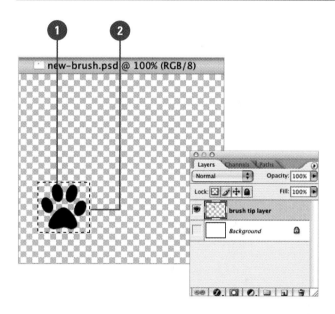

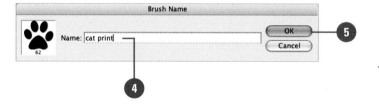

Saving Customized Brush Tips

 PS 2.9

Once a brush tip is created, it becomes a part of the current set. However, the brush has not yet been permanently saved in Photoshop. Although the new brush tip will reappear every time you access the Brushes palette, if you choose the option to reset the palette, the new brush will be lost. To keep brushes you must save them into customized sets.

Save a Customized Brush Tip

1 Select a **Brush** tool on the toolbox, and then select the **Brushes** palette.

2 Create a set of customized brushes.

3 Click the **Brushes Options** button, and then click **Save Brushes**.

4 Type the name of the set (with a .abr extension) in the Save As box.

5 Click the **Where** (Mac) or **Save In** (Win) list arrow, and then select where you want to save the brush.

6 Click **New Folder** or **Add To Favorites** to add your customized brush tip.

7 Click **Save**.

Did You Know?

You can access your customized sets directly from the Brushes Options menu. When you save your customized brush set, click the Brushes folder, located in the Adobe Photoshop CS2/Presets folder. Brush sets saved here appear in the Brushes Options menu along with the other Photoshop presets.

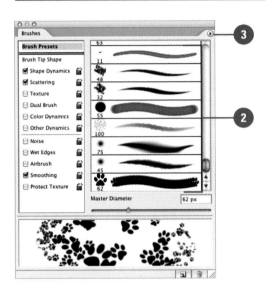

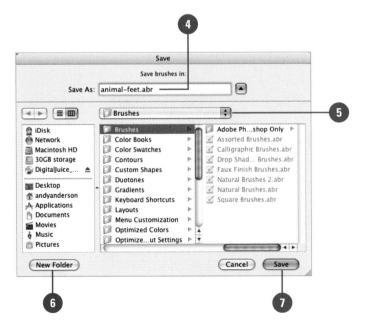

Working with the Painting Engine

The Painting Engine is a series of controls that let you define how a brush tip is applied to the active image. Features, such as Scattering and Color Dynamics let you further customize your brush tips so you can create that specialized brush for your image enhancement needs.

Work with the Painting Engine

1. Select a **Brush** tool on the toolbox, and then select the **Brushes** palette.

2. Click the **Brushes Options** button, and then click **Expanded View**.

3. Click to select a specific brush tip.

4. Select from the various Painting Engine options:

   ◆ **Brush Tip Shape.** Lets you modify the angle, roundness, and spacing of the brush tip. In addition, you can flip the brush shape along its x (left to right), or y (top to bottom) axis.

   ◆ **Shape Dynamics.** Lets you randomly (jitter) generate different sizes, angles, and roundness for the brush tip.

   ◆ **Scattering.** Lets you randomly scatter the shape. Options include the ability to distribute (Scatter) the shape, as you draw, choose how many to use (Count), and randomly change the number (Count Jitter), as you draw.

   ◆ **Texture.** Lets you select a predefined or custom texture, in place of a solid color.

   ◆ **Dual Brush.** Lets you select a second brush.

   ◆ **Color Dynamics.** Lets you key off of the active foreground and background colors.

   ◆ **Other Dynamics.** See Table.

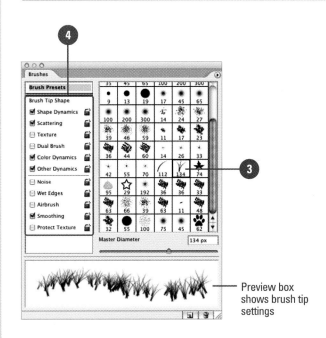

Preview box shows brush tip settings

Other Dynamics

Dynamic	Purpose
Noise	Generates random noise in the brush tip as you draw.
Wet Edges	Fades the edges of the drawn shape, similar to running a watercolor brush over a wet canvas.
Airbrush	Change the Paintbrush tool into an Airbrush.
Smoothing	Applies anti-aliasing to the drawn shapes, creating a smoother shape.
Protect Texture	Preserves texture pattern when applying brush presets.

Working with the Paintbrush and Airbrush Tools

 PS 2.1

Photoshop's Paintbrush and Airbrush tools were designed to reproduce the visual effect of applying paint to a canvas. You have full control over the brush tip, color, size, opacity, and even the brush's blending mode. Control over the image is achieved by using additional layers to hold the brush strokes—adding additional layers increases the file size of a Photoshop document. Since layers have their own control systems, such as opacity, fill, and blending modes, you achieve even greater control over the final design, and once the brush stroke is correct, you can always merge the brush-stroke layer into the image to conserve file size.

Work with the Paintbrush and Airbrush Tools

1 Select the **Paintbrush** tool on the toolbox.

2 Select a brush tip on the Options bar or from the Brushes palette.

3 Specify Paint Engine options for the brush on the Brushes palette.

4 Select from the following Paintbrush options on the Options bar:

◆ **Mode.** Click the list arrow to choose from the available blending modes. The blending mode option controls how the active paintbrush color blends with the colors in the active image.

◆ **Opacity.** Enter an opacity percent (1 to 100), or click the list arrow, and then drag the slider left or right.

◆ **Flow.** Enter a flow percentage (1 to 100), or click the list arrow, and then drag the slider left or right. When you apply the brush, flow controls the amount of ink supplied to the brush.

◆ **Airbrush.** Click the button to change the Paintbrush into an Airbrush.

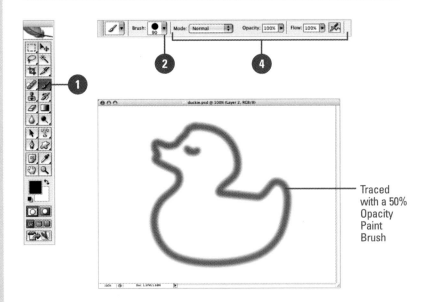

Traced with a 50% Opacity Paint Brush

Working with the Pencil Tool

Adobe Certified Expert   PS 2.1

Work with the Pencil Tool

① Select the **Pencil** tool on the toolbox.

② Click the **Brush Preset Picker** list arrow, and then click a brush tip.

③ Click the **Mode** list arrow, and then select a blending mode.

④ Enter an Opacity percentage value (1 to 100).

⑤ Drag the **Pencil** tool across the active document.

Did You Know?

You can use the Pencil tool to create calligraphy lettering. Select the Pencil tool, click black as your painting color, and then click one of the oblong brush tips on the Options bar. If you own a drawing tablet, use the tablet with the Pencil tool to create beautifully formed calligraphy letters.

The Pencil tool is exactly what its name implies... a pencil. The Pencil tool is limited to hard brush tips of any size or shape, and creates freeform lines using the current foreground color. In fact, the major difference between the Pencil and Paintbrush tools, is the Pencil tool's inability to draw anything but a hard edge line. A unique feature of the Pencil tool is its ability to switch between the current foreground and background colors using the Auto Erase feature.

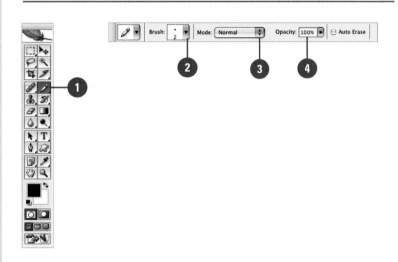

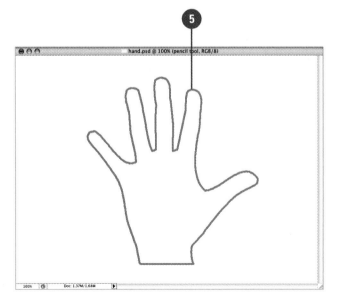

Working with Auto Erase

The Auto Erase feature lets you automatically switch the Pencil tool's painting color using the current foreground and background color swatches. The trick is where you start drawing the line. If you start dragging the brush tip from a new location in the document, the Pencil tool creates a line in the active foreground color. If you then place the brush tip on a previously drawn line and drag, the Pencil tool creates a new line in the active background color. Since the Auto Erase feature doesn't really erase anything, it will perform exactly the same way on a transparent layer as it does on the background layer.

Work with Auto Erase

1 Select the **Pencil** tool on the toolbox.

2 Select the **Auto Erase** check box on the Options bar.

3 Drag the **Pencil** tool across the active document to create a line in the active foreground color.

4 Click anywhere in the background and the Pencil tool will use foreground color.

5 Move the brush tip over one of the previous lines, and then drag to create a line in the active background color.

Did You Know?

You can draw straight lines with the Pencil tool. Click once in the document to create a black dot, move to another position, hold down the Shift key, and then click again. When you hold down the Shift key, the Pencil tool creates a straight line between the two mouse clicks.

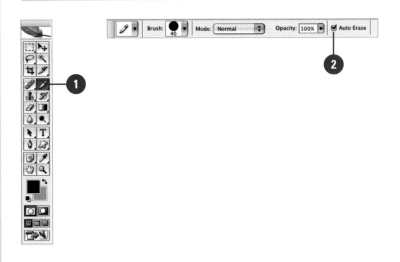

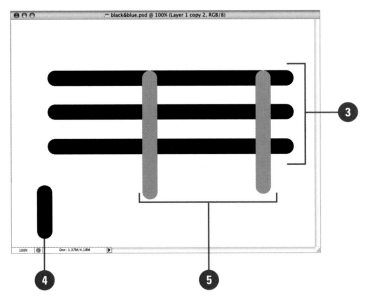

Working with the Line Tool

The Line tool lets you draw lines by dragging from one point in the active document and releasing in another. Lines drawn at precise 90- or 45-degree angles are achieved by holding down the Shift key as you drag. Select the Line tool, or if you have any drawing tool selected, you can choose the Line tool from the Options bar. Then configure the Line tool, using the Options bar. It's also a good idea to create the lines in a separate layer. That way once the line has been drawn, it's as easy as selecting the Move tool, and repositioning the line to the desired position.

Work with the Line Tool

1. Select the **Line** tool on the toolbox.

2. Click the **Fill Pixels** button to create raster shapes in the active foreground color.

3. Click the **Geometry** list arrow, and then select from the following options:

   ◆ **Arrowheads.** Select the Start and/or End check boxes to create arrowheads on the line.

   ◆ **Width.** Enter a percentage (10 to 1000), to determine the width of the arrowhead in relation to the width of the line.

   ◆ **Length.** Enter a percentage (10 to 5000), to determine the length of the arrowhead.

   ◆ **Concavity.** Enter a percentage (-50 to +50) to determine the concavity of the arrowhead.

4. Enter a value (1 to 1000 pixels) to determine the weight of the line.

5. Click the **Mode** list arrow, and then select a blending mode.

6. Enter an Opacity percentage value (1 to 100).

7. Select the **Anti-alias** check box to create a visually smoother line.

8. Drag in the document window to create the line.

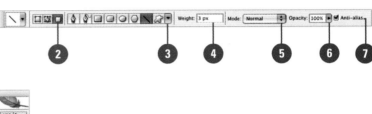

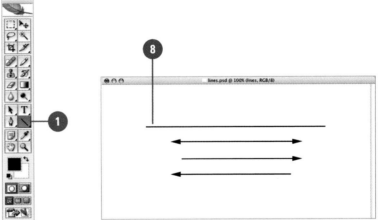

For Your Information

Using the Line Tool

The Line tool can be used to create customized guidelines for those projects that require something other than guidelines that are vertical or horizontal. Just create a new layer, and then select the line tool. Choose a line width of one or two pixels, select a drawing color that contrasts with the image, and then draw the required guides. When you're finished, lock the layer, and use the visual guides to complete your project. Hide the layer when it's not needed, and finally, delete the layer when your done with the job. One more thing, remember to turn off the arrowhead option.

Using the Standard Shape Tool

Creating standard shapes, such as polygons or rectangles with rounded corners used to be a hassle. That is until Photoshop released its standard shape drawing tools. Now, it's a simple matter of selecting the correct tool, choosing a color, and then drawing the shape. As with any of Photoshop's drawing functions, control is maintained with the use of additional layers. Photoshop's standard shapes consist of rectangles, rounded rectangles, ellipses, polygons; and each one of the shape tools comes with additional options to control exactly how the shape appears when drawn.

Work with the Standard Shape Tool

1. Select the **Rectangle** tool on the toolbox.

2. Click the **Fill Pixels** button to create raster shapes in the active foreground color.

3. Click the **Rectangle**, **Rounded Rectangle**, **Ellipse**, or **Polygon** tool buttons.

4. Click the **Geometry** list arrow, and then select from the following drawing options or check boxes:

    ◆ **Unconstrained.** (Rectangle, Rounded Rectangle, Ellipse)

    ◆ **Square.** (Rectangle, Rounded Rectangle)

    ◆ **Circle.** (Ellipse)

    ◆ **Fixed Size.** (Rectangle, Rounded Rectangle, Ellipse)

    ◆ **Proportional.** (Rectangle, Rounded Rectangle, Ellipse)

    ◆ **From Center.** (Rectangle, Rounded Rectangle, Ellipse)

    ◆ **Snap to Pixels.** (Rectangle, Rounded Rectangle)

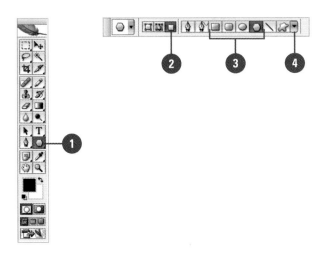

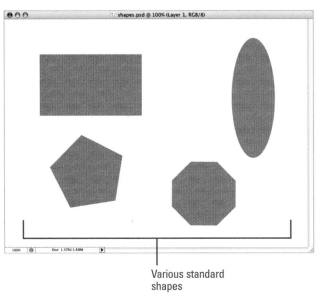

Various standard shapes

- ◆ **Radius.** (Polygon)

- ◆ **Smooth Corners.** (Polygon)

- ◆ **Star.** (Polygon)

- ◆ **Indent Sides By.** (Polygon)

- ◆ **Smooth Indents.** (Polygon)

5 Click the **Mode** list arrow, and then select a blending mode.

6 Enter an Opacity percentage value (1 to 100).

7 Select the **Anti-alias** check box to create a visually smoother image.

Useful when drawing shapes with curved edges.

8 Drag in the document window to create the shape.

IMPORTANT *Maintain control over your design by drawing shapes in separate layers.*

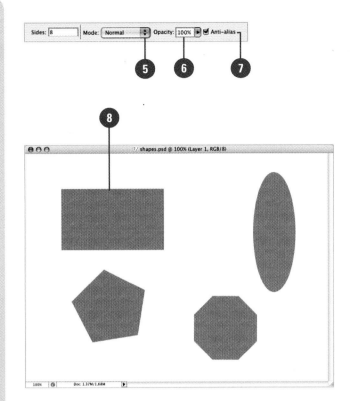

9

Working with the Custom Shape Tool

Having the ability to draw a perfect polygon or rounded-corner rectangle is nice, however, Photoshop went way beyond standard shapes when it introduced the Custom Shape tool. Photoshop now comes packaged with dozens of pre-designed shapes, or you can even create your own. User-defined shapes can be literally any vector objects. For example, a company logo can be converted to a custom shape. Custom shapes have many timesaving applications. As previously mentioned, a company logo, if used frequently, is only a mouse click away. Any vector form, outline, or shape used on a recurring basis, can be converted to a custom shape and saved for future use. Select the Custom Shape tool or, if you have any shape drawing tool selected, click the Custom Shape button from the Options bar, and then configure the shape using the options on the Option bar.

Work with the Custom Shape Tool

1 Select the **Custom Shape** tool on the toolbox.

2 Click the **Fill Pixels** button to create raster shapes, using the active foreground color.

3 Click the **Geometry** list arrow, and then select from the available options: Unconstrained, Defined Proportions, Defined Size, Fixed Size, or From Center.

4 Click the **Shape** list arrow, and then select a shape from the available options.

5 Click the **Mode** list arrow, and then select a blending mode.

6 Enter an Opacity percentage value (1 to 100).

7 Select the **Anti-alias** check box to create a visually smoother line.

8 Drag in the document window to create the customized shape.

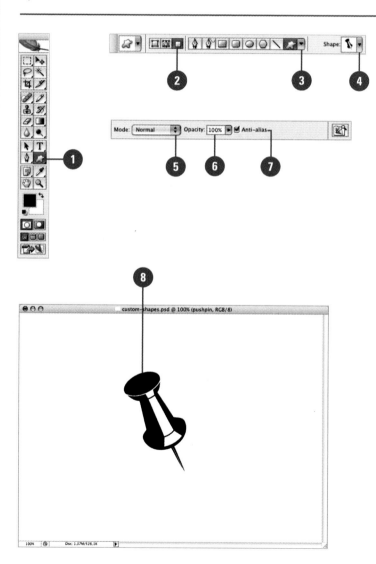

Creating a Custom Shape

Custom shapes can be created from anything you choose, and the process is quick and simple. You just create the shape, select the shape, and name the shape; that's it. Since shapes are vector images, they're resolution independent, which means you can draw them at any size without impacting image quality. Once custom shapes are saved, they can be accessed by opening a document, selecting the Shape tool, and choosing your new shape from the Custom Shapes palette.

Create a Custom Shape

1. Open a document that contains the vector image you want to convert into a shape, or create a shape using any of Photoshop's vector drawing tools.

2. Click the **Edit** menu, and then click **Define Custom Shape**.

3. Enter a name for the new shape.

4. Click **OK**.

   The shape appears as a thumbnail at the bottom of the active custom shapes palette.

Did You Know?

You can move Photoshop shapes into other vector programs, such as Illustrator, FreeHand, and even Flash. Click the File menu, point to Export, and then click Paths To Illustrator. Name the new document, and then click Save.

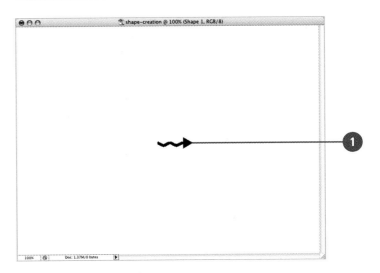

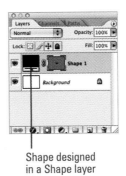

Shape designed
in a Shape layer

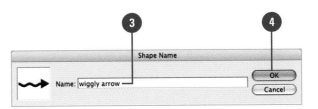

9

Saving Custom Shape Sets

Creating customized sets of shapes is an excellent way to get organized. The next time you need a specific shape all you have to do is select the shape from your organized sets. Organization can save you time, but it also lends a sense of consistency to design. Using customized shapes over again, helps to tie the elements of a design together, and Photoshop gives you the perfect way to maintain that consistency with customized shape sets.

Save Custom Shape Sets

1. Select the **Custom Shape** tool on the toolbox.

2. Click the **Shape** list arrow to see a list of the current shapes.

3. Create new shapes, and then add them to the current list.

   IMPORTANT *As you create new shapes, if there are some you don't like, delete them. Right-click the shape, and then click Delete Shape.*

4. To add pre-existing shapes, click the **Options** button, and then click **Load Shapes**, or choose from the available pre-defined shape lists.

5. Click the **Options** button, and then click **Save Shapes**.

6. Enter a descriptive name for the new set in the **Save As** (Mac) or the **File Name** (Win) box.

7. Click the **Where** (Mac) or **Save In** (Win) list arrow, and then select a location to save the new set.

   IMPORTANT *If you save the new set in the Custom Shapes folder, located in the Adobe Photoshop CS2 application folder, the new set will appear as a pre-defined set when you click the Shapes Options button.*

8. Click **Save**.

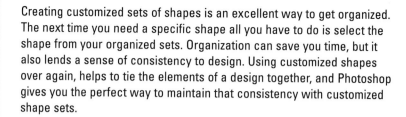

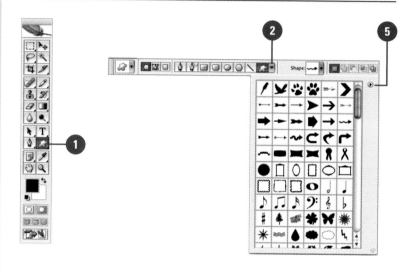

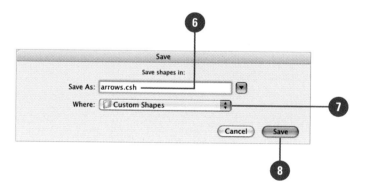

Using the Paint Bucket Tool

The Paint Bucket tool is not new, in fact it's been around almost as long as Photoshop. The paint bucket's primary function is to fill an area with the active foreground color, but that's not all it's capable of doing. The Paint Bucket tool can fill areas with a selected pattern and, much in the same way that the Magic Wand tool selects image information, the fill area can be controlled by the shift in brightness of image pixels. Combine those features with the ability to change the paint bucket's blending mode, opacity, and you have a tool with a lot of horsepower.

Use the Paint Bucket Tool

1. Select the **Paint Bucket** tool on the toolbox.

2. Click the **Fill** list arrow, and then select an option:

   ◆ **Foreground.** Fills a selected area with the current foreground color.

   ◆ **Pattern.** Fills a selected area with a pattern.

3. Click the **Pattern** list arrow, and then select a pre-defined fill pattern. This option is available if you select Pattern as a fill option.

4. Click the **Mode** list arrow, and then select a blending mode.

5. Enter an Opacity percentage value (1 to 100).

6. Select a Tolerance value (0 to 255). The Tolerance value influences the range of the Paint Bucket uses to fill a given area.

7. Select the **Anti-alias** check box to create a visually smoother line.

8. Select the **Contiguous** check box to restrict the fill to the selected area.

9. Select the **All Layers** check box to fill all the color range information from the image's layers.

10. Click the **Paint Bucket** tool cursor on the area to be changed.

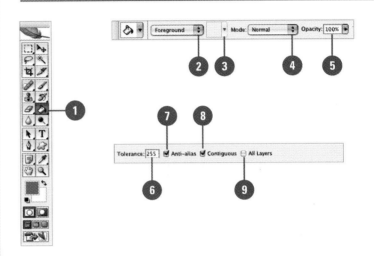

9

Working with the Eraser Tools

 PS 2.1

Photoshop's basic Eraser tool converts image pixels in a layer to transparent pixels. While the primary function of the eraser tool has not changed, it has been greatly improved upon. For example, you can use the eraser tool to remove a specific color or to erase around the edge of an image object. You can instruct the Eraser tool to remove a specific color while protecting another color and at the same time, increase or decrease the tools' tolerance (the range of selection). If you use the Eraser tool on a layered document, the tool will erase to transparency. If the Eraser tool is used on a flattened document (flattened documents do not support transparency), the Eraser tool will use the active background color to perform the eraser. As you can see, the eraser tools do more than blindly erase image information. As you master the eraser tools, you just may find those complicated image eraser jobs becoming easier and easier. The Background Eraser tool lets you select specific colors within an image and erase just those colors.

Use the Basic Eraser Tool

1. Select the **Eraser** tool on the toolbox.

2. Click the **Brush** list arrow, and then select a brush tip.

3. Click the **Mode** list arrow, and then select a blending mode.

4. Enter an Opacity percentage value (1 to 100) to determine how much the eraser removes from the image.

5. Enter a Flow percentage value (1 to 100) to determine the length of the eraser stroke.

6. Click the **Airbrush** button to change the solid eraser stroke of the eraser to that of an airbrush.

7. Select the **Erase To History** check box to temporarily turn the Eraser into a History Brush.

8. Drag the Eraser over an image layer to convert the image pixels to transparent.

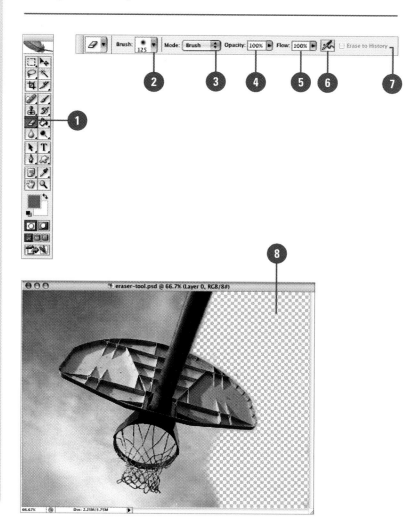

Use the Background Eraser Tool

1. Select the **Background Eraser** tool on the toolbox.

2. Click the **Brush** list arrow, and then select a brush tip.

3. Click one of the Sampling buttons (how the Background Erase selects the color range):

   ◆ **Continuous.** Continually selects a color range as you drag the Eraser tool across the image.

   ◆ **Once.** Sample a color range when you first click your mouse.

   ◆ **Background Swatch.** Only erases the active background color.

4. Click the **Limits** list arrow, and then click how far you want the erasing to spread:

   ◆ **Discontiguous.** Lets the Eraser tool work with all similar color range pixels throughout the image.

   ◆ **Contiguous.** Restricts the Eraser tool to the selected color range, without moving outside the originally sampled area.

   ◆ **Find Edges.** Looks for a shift in color range and attempts to erase to the visual edge of the image.

5. Select a Tolerance percentage value (1 to 100). The higher the tolerance, the greater the range.

6. Select the **Protect Foreground Color** check box to prevent that color from being erased.

7. Drag the image to erase.

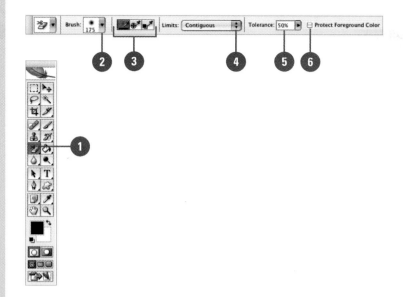

9

For Your Information

Using the Background Eraser Tool

The Background Eraser tool erases an image by converting the image pixels to transparent. If you attempt to use the Background Eraser tool on a flattened image, the tool will automatically convert the flattened background into a layer. Photoshop is actually making an assumption, that if you're using the Background Eraser tool, you obviously need the image to be on a layer not a background.

Working with the Magic Eraser Tool

The Magic Eraser tool functions the same way the Magic Wand selection tool functions, except instead of selecting an area it erases it. The Magic Eraser tool works on any traditional Photoshop layer, including the Background. Clicking with the Magic Eraser tool converts image pixels into transparent pixels. Since the Background layer does not support transparency, using the Magic Eraser tool causes Photoshop to convert the Background into a traditional layer.

Work with the Magic Eraser Tool

1 Select the **Eraser** tool on the toolbox.

2 Enter a Tolerance percentage value (0 to 255). The higher the value the greater the range the Magic Eraser erases.

3 Select the **Anti-alias** check box to create a visually softer eraser (useful when dealing with intensely rounded or curved selections).

4 Select the **Contiguous** check box to select adjacent pixels within the active document.

5 Select the **Sample All Layers** check box to sample image information from all layers (Photoshop treats the visual image as a composite).

6 Click within the active document.

The Magic Eraser tool, depending on options, samples the pixel directly under the tool and uses that to create a range for erasing image information.

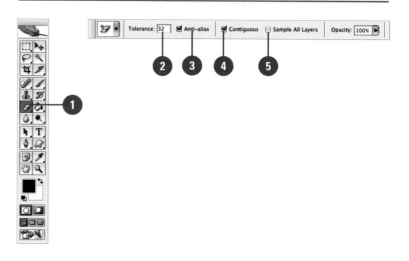

Creating and Applying Gradients

 PS 2.7

While most of Photoshop's paint and drawing tools let you select and paint with a single color, the gradient tool lets you paint with a veritable rainbow of colors. The gradient tool comes packaged with several sets of pre-designed gradients, or you can create and save your own customized gradient sets. The process of creating a gradient is simple; you select a gradient along with a specific type, and then drag in the document window. The length and angle of the drag, determines how the gradient is applied. Since gradients, by default, overwrite the image, it's a good idea to create gradients in separate layers.

Create a Standard Gradient

1. Select the **Gradient** tool on the toolbox.

2. Click the **Gradient** list arrow, and then select from the available gradients.

3. Click the **Gradient** list arrow, and then select one of the following:

   ◆ Linear, Radial, Angle, Reflected or Diamond.

4. Click the **Mode** list arrow, and then select a blending mode.

5. Enter an Opacity percentage value (1 to 100).

6. Select the **Reverse** check box to reverse the color order of the selected gradient.

7. Select the **Dither** check box to visually create a smoother transition between gradient colors.

8. Select the **Transparency** check box to create gradients using a gradient mask (allows for transparency in the gradient).

9. Drag in the image to create a gradient.

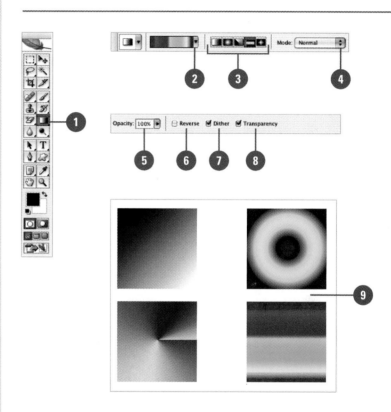

9

For Your Information

Adding Pre-Defined Gradients

To add a pre-defined gradient, you must first select the Gradient tool. Click the Gradient Picker button, located on the Options bar to use one of the available gradient sets. Choose to append the new gradients to the existing list, or click OK to replace the existing gradients with the new list.

Creating and Saving Customized Gradients

 PS 2.7

Customized gradients are easy to create and essential when you just can't find what you want in Photoshop's predefined sets. It doesn't matter how many gradients Photoshop provides for you, there will always be that one instance where they just don't do the required job. With just a few clicks of your mouse, you can create your own customized gradients. You can start with one of Photoshop's gradients, and modify it to your needs. You can also start completely from scratch; the choice is yours, and so are the rewards of creating that one-of-a-kind stunning gradient you can use for your current project and in the future.

Create and Save a Customized Gradient

1. Select the **Gradient** tool on the toolbox.

2. Click the thumbnail of the active gradient on the Options bar to open the Gradient dialog box.

3. Select a gradient from the available options that is close to what you want to create.

4. Enter a name for the new gradient.

5. Click **New**.

   A thumbnail (copy of the selected gradient) appears at the bottom of the list.

6. Click the **Gradient Type** list arrow, and then select one of the following:

   ◆ **Solid.** Uses solid colors for the gradient.

   ◆ **Noise.** Uses noise to distribute the colors.

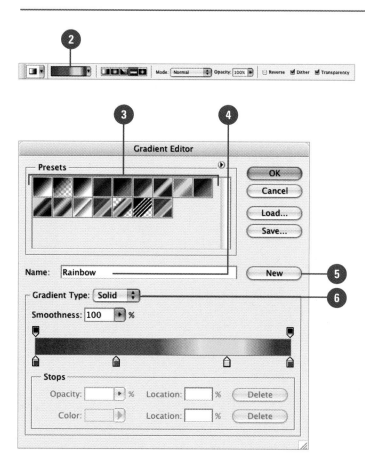

7 Click the **Smoothness** list arrow, and then select one of the following:

◆ **Smoothness.** A percentage value (0 to 100) that determines how smoothly the colors of the gradient blend together (available when the Solid option is selected).

◆ **Roughness.** A percentage value (0 to 100) that determines how much noise to introduce into the gradient colors (available when the Noise option is selected).

8 To add Opacity Stops, click above the gradient line; to remove Opacity Stops, drag a stop away from the line.

9 To add Color Stops, click below the gradient line; to remove Color Stops, drag a stop away from the line.

10 Click on an Opacity Stop, and then enter an Opacity percentage (0 to 100), and a Location percentage (0 to 100) for the stop to rest on the line.

11 Click on a Color stop, and then select a color, and a Location percentage (0 to 100) for the color stop to rest on the line.

12 Click **Delete** to delete the selected opacity or color stop.

13 Click **Save** to save the new gradient set.

The set will include the new gradients, and all the gradients that appear in the Presets panel.

14 Click **OK**.

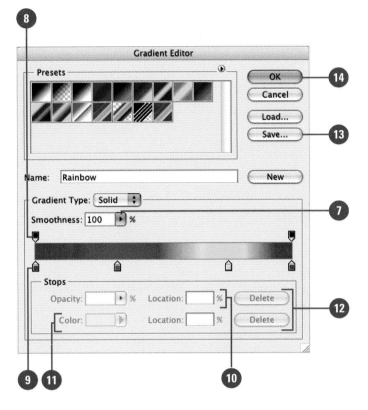

For Your Information

Creating a Customized Gradient

Gradient Gradients serve many purposes. They can be used to jazz up a shape drawn with Photoshop's drawing tools or they can be applied to an entire document and used as a background on a Web page, brochure or newsletter. Whatever you use gradients for, remember that they are powerful image elements. Use gradients to attract attention to a document, but don't use them if they draw people's eyes away from the main elements of the image. It will be a small consolation to know that your fantastic marketing graphic attracted attention, but everyone was so focused on your special effects and gradients, that they forgot to buy what you were selling. Remember, it's always about the message. An image is worth a thousand words… let the image tell its story.

9

Using the Color Replacement Tool

PS 2.2

The Color Replacement tool lets you replace a specific color in your image. For best results use soft brushes with this tool, to help blend the colors into the original image. Have you ever captured that perfect picture of a family member or friend, only to see the resulting image with red eyes? Or maybe there's a part of your image where the color draws attention away from the focal point. Either way, the Color Replacement tool is a great feature that allows you to take control of the image output.

Use the Color Replacement Tool

1. Select the **Color Replacement** tool on the toolbox.

2. Select a Brush tip on the Options bar.

3. Select from the available Sampling options:

   ◆ **Continuous.** Samples colors continuously as you drag.

   ◆ **Once.** Replaces the targeted color only in areas you click.

   ◆ **Background Swatch.** Erases areas matching the background.

4. Select from the available Limits options:

   ◆ **Discontiguous.** Replaces the sampled color under the pointer.

   ◆ **Contiguous.** Replaces connected areas containing the sampled color and preserves the sharpness of shape edges.

5. Enter a Tolerance percentage value (0 to 255).

6. Select the **Anti-alias** check box for a smoother edge on areas you correct.

7. Select a foreground color to use to replace the unwanted color.

8. Drag in the image the color you want to replace.

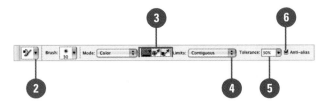

Creating Layer and Channel Masks

10

Introduction

When you work on documents in Adobe Photoshop, the application does its best to make the experience as similar to the real world as possible. When you select the Paintbrush tool and drag the document, you expect to see a swath of color using the pre-selected size and brush tip. That's what you expect to see when you drag a brush on a canvas, and that's what you see in Photoshop. Creating a realistic experience is what Photoshop is all about. Yet, as realistic as the Photoshop experience is, there are elements of digital design that go way beyond the real world. For example, something as simple as the ability to undo. Photoshop has an undo button, life does not. Layer masks give you the ability to remove elements of a layer without actually erasing the image pixels. Layer masks fall into the area of Photoshop called "controlling the image." If you can control what elements of an image are visible, without erasing, you have control. In addition, layer masks are editable, which means you can change your mind at any time during the creative process.

Imagine creating a complicated selection in Photoshop. You will probably use several of Photoshop's selection tools and by the time you're finished (or almost finished) you have selection marquees all over the document. Traditional selections are temporary; they last only as long as your document is open. But what if you want to save this selection for use later in the design? What you need is a channel mask. Channel masks hold simple, or complicated selections, and can be saved with the document. Channel masks are created from pre-existing selections, or can be created from scratch by painting the mask with black, white, or shades of gray. The process of creating a Channel mask is simple, but the results are powerful.

Understanding the Role of Layer Masks

 PS 3.4

Layer masks are not new; however, Photoshop designers find new ways to use them every day. A layer mask is an attachment to a layer that defines the visible elements of the layer. Each layer type in Photoshop, with the exception of the Background, has the ability to hold a layer mask. Imagine a layer mask as a piece of paper laying directly over the image, and then take a trimming blade and cut holes in the paper. The holes in the paper represent the visible elements of the image, while the other areas of the image become transparent. Each

layer in a multiple layered document has the ability to hold its own mask, and the mask only influences the image elements of the layer it's attached. Once a mask is created, it can be modified using any of Photoshop's painting or drawing tools. Black represents transparent elements, and white represents visible elements. Painting with a shade of gray introduces a level of transparency. For example, painting with 50 percent gray, makes the image pixels appear 50 percent transparent.

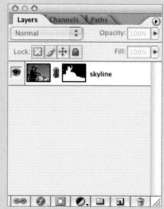

Creating a Layer Mask

 PS 3.4

Create a Layer Mask

1. Open a document.

2. Click the **Layers** palette.

3. Click the layer to contain the mask.

4. Click the **Add Layer Mask** button.

5. Click on the image thumbnail to modify or adjust the image.

   The active pointer resembles a paintbrush, indicating you are working on the image.

6. Click on the mask thumbnail to modify or paint the mask.

   The active pointer resembles the mask button, indicating you are working on the mask.

7. Click the **chain** button to separate the mask from the image.

   This allows you to move the mask, without moving the image, or vise versa.

8. Click the **chain** button again to reestablish the link between mask and image.

9. Shift+click on the mask button to temporarily disable or enable the mask.

10. Alt+click (Win) or Option+click (Mac) to view or hide the mask in the document window.

The creation of a layer mask requires two things: an open document and any Photoshop layer type with the exception of the Background. When you add the layer mask, you will be working with two layer elements—the image and the mask. It's important to know what element you're working on, or you might wind up painting on the image instead of the mask. When that occurs, it's good to remember the undo button. Once the mask is created, you can selectively control, without erasing, the visible portions of the image.

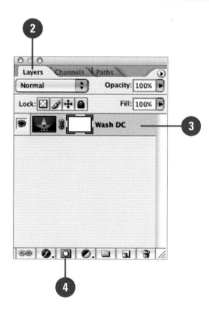

Working with the Paint Tools

Unless a mask is created using a selection, layer masks begin their lives as pure white. The reason a created layer mask does not appear to have any visible effect on the image, is that the color white indicates the visible areas of the image. It's only when you begin painting on the mask does the image change. You create transparency in the image by painting in shades of gray. The deeper the shade of gray, the more transparent the image. Painting the mask with pure black produces 100 percent image transparency. Any of Photoshop's drawing or painting tools can be employed to create the mask. In fact, you could even use the custom shape drawing tools and create a mask in the shape of a rubber duck. The trick is to use the right tools to create the right effect. For example, using a hard edge brush creates an image with sharp edges and using a soft-edge brush creates an image where the visible edges of the image blend smoothly with transparent elements.

Work with the Paint Tools

1. Open a document.

2. Create a layer mask on one of the active image layers.

3. Click the layer mask thumbnail.

4. Select the **Paintbrush** tool and brush tip.

5. Move into the document window and paint, and then use black to create transparency.

6. Use white to touch up the image.

7. Use shades of gray to create partial transparency.

See Also

See "Working with the Paintbrush and Airbrush Tools" on page 214 for more information on using the Paintbrush tool.

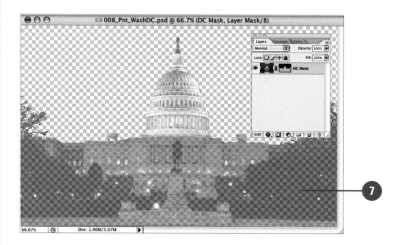

Using Selections to Generate Complex Layer Masks

Layer masks are easy to create, you select a layer and then click the Add Layer Mask button. Unfortunately, when you create a mask this way, it's up to you to define the transparent areas, using drawing or painting tools. There is another way to generate a mask, and that's through selection. When you click the Add Layer Mask button, Photoshop searches the document for any selected areas. If it doesn't find any, it creates a blank (all white) mask. However, if you first select an area or areas of the image, Photoshop interprets the selection as the area you want to remain visible.

Use Selections to Generate Masks

1. Open a document.

2. Select the areas of the image you want to preserve.

3. Click the **Add Layer Mask** button.

   Photoshop generates a layer mask based entirely on your selection.

Did You Know?

You can apply layer styles to a masked image. Create the mask, and then click the Add Layer Style button, located at the bottom of the Layers palette. Then use any of Photoshop's layer styles, such as Drop Shadow, or Bevel And Emboss. The layer style will only be applied to the visible portion of the image.

See Also

See Chapter 4, "Mastering the Art of Selection," on page 77 for information on selecting areas of an image using different tools.

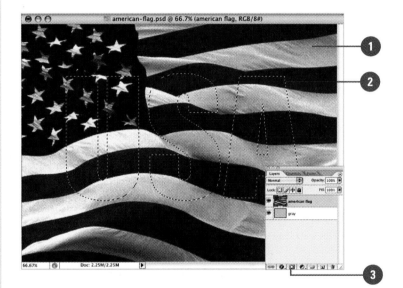

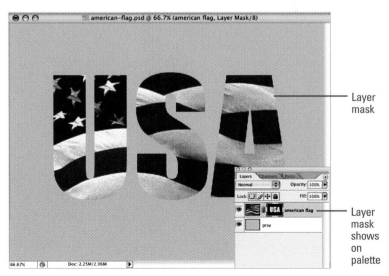

Layer mask

Layer mask shows on palette

10

Using Layer Masks to Generate Soft Transparency

When you create a layer mask using Photoshop's selection tools, the edges of the image where transparency occurs appear as if cut out with a knife. This occurs because selection tools create knife-edge selections, and then when you create the layer mask, the edges appear as ragged as the mask. You could click the Selection menu, and then click Feather to soften the effect of the selection; however you won't be able to determine the effects of your Feather option until you create the mask. Many times this technique turns into a guessing game, with you creating mask after mask, until you see what looks best. A better way to work is create the hard mask, and then visually create a softer mask using a Photoshop filter named Gaussian Blur. Since the Gaussian Blur filter has the ability to preview the blur before applying, you have the perfect tool to create visually pleasing results.

Use Layer Masks for Transparency

1. Open a document.

2. Create a selection around the area you want to preserve.

3. Click the **Select** menu, and then click **Feather**.

4. Select a Feather Radius value (1 to 250). The greater the value, the greater the feathering effect.

5. Click **OK**.

6. Click the **Add Layer Mask** button.

    The Layer mask uses the Feather option to soften the visual effect of the mask.

See Also

See Chapter 14, " Manipulating Images with Filters," on page 319 for more information on using filters.

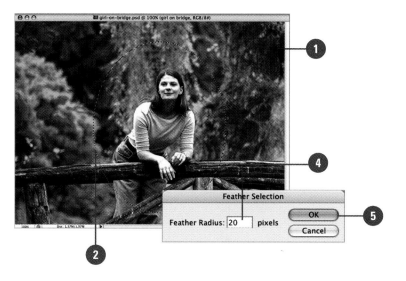

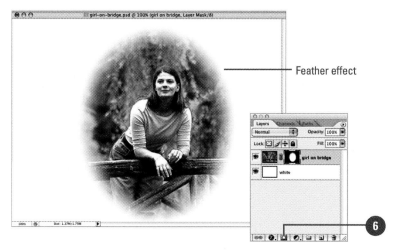

Feather effect

Blending Images with Layer Masks

Layer masks make areas of an image appear transparent by painting with black. Then just as quickly, you can make those areas reappear by painting with white. There are obvious applications to the use of layer masks—changing a sky, removing a tree, or even removing a person who was cut off in the photo. For example, you have an image, and you want the image to change from line art to a normal photograph. To accomplish this, you'll need a copy of the image in a separate layer, a layer mask, and the linear gradient tool.

Blend Images with Layer Masks

1 Open a document.

2 Select the layer you want to use for the effect in the Layers palette. If this is a multi-layered document, this layer should be at the top of the layer stack.

3 Drag the layer over the **Create New Layer** button to make a copy.

TIMESAVER *If making a copy of a layer is a common practice, press Ctrl+J (Win) or ⌘+J (Mac).*

4 Click the **Add Layer Mask** button, and then add a layer mask to the copy layer.

5 Use any of Photoshop's adjustment or filter effects to make changes to the copy.

6 Select black and white for the default foreground and background colors.

7 Select the **Gradient** tool, and then select a linear gradient using the foreground to background gradient option.

8 Click the layer mask thumbnail in the copy layer.

9 Drag the **Gradient** tool, left to right, across the document.

The image slowly goes transparent from left to right, exposing the original image.

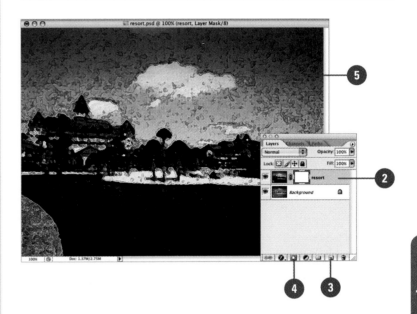

10

Using a Layer Mask to Create a Vignette

When you open a document in Photoshop, the image displays in a standard bounding-box format; a square or rectangle with 90-degree corners. Bounding boxes serve a purpose, and many times a nice square or rectangle box is exactly what you want. But let's face it, bounding boxes can be a bit boring, especially when you want to spice up that image with a nice soft vignette. To create a soft vignette, you need four things—an image, a selection, a layer mask, and a Gaussian Blur filter.

Create a Vignette

1 Open a document.

2 Select the **Elliptical Marquee** tool, and then create an oval selection in the document. The Ellipse should contain the area you want to preserve.

3 Click the **Add Layer Mask** button in the Layers palette.

4 Click the layer mask thumbnail.

5 Click the **Filter** menu, point to **Blur**, and then click **Gaussian Blur**.

6 Drag the Radius slider right or left to increase or decrease the amount of blur applied to the mask.

7 Select the **Preview** check box, and then watch the live preview until you see the correct amount of blurring applied to the layer mask.

8 Click **OK**.

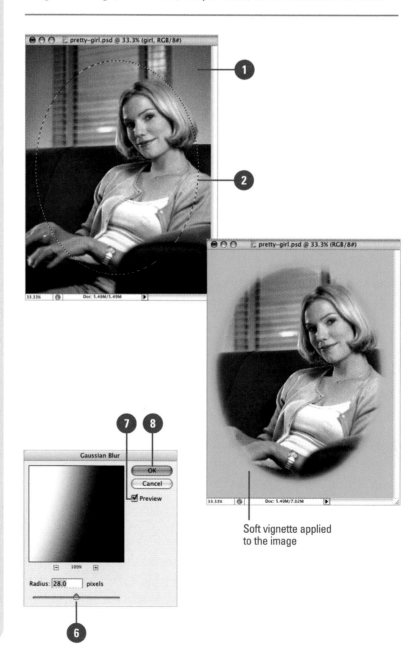

Soft vignette applied to the image

Creating Unique Layer Mask Borders

Layer masks can create more than simple vignettes around an image. In fact, with the right filters you can create some very interesting and fun-looking borders. For example, when you create a selection using one of Photoshop's standard selection tools—rectangle, ellipse, or lasso—the selection has a sharp, definable border. The secret to creating unique borders is to create a general selection around a portion of the image you want to preserve, create the layer mask, and then use some of Photoshop's creative filter effects, such as the Artistic or Distort filters on the mask. Using filters on the image mask creates eye-catching borders, and it's only a filter away.

Create a Layer Mask Border

1. Open a document.

2. Click the layer you want to use in the Layers palette to apply a unique border.

3. Create a rectangular selection around a portion of the image.

4. Click the **Add Layer Mask** button.

5. Click the layer mask thumbnail.

6. Click the **Filters** menu, point to **Brush Strokes**, and then click the **Sprayed Strokes** filter.

7. Adjust the filter options to change the edge of the layer mask.

8. Click **OK**.

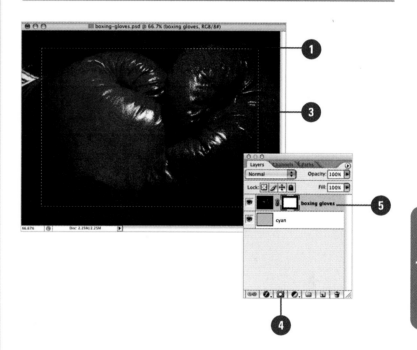

Did You Know?

You can apply more than one filter to a layer mask border. For example, using the Spatter filter creates a ragged edge to the layer mask. Applying a small amount of Gaussian Blur to the mask softens the effect and creates a more pleasing visual transition between the mask and the background.

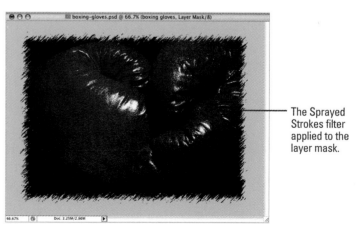

The Sprayed Strokes filter applied to the layer mask.

10

Understanding Channel Masks

The Channels palette serves three purposes—to hold color information, to hold spot color information, and to hold selections (channel masks). Creating channel masks can be as easy as clicking the Create New Channel button, and then using any painting or drawing tools to create the mask, or by making a selection, and converting the selection into a mask, by clicking the Convert To Mask button. When you paint the channel mask, the defaults are—black for masked areas, white for selected areas, and shades of gray for percentages of selection.

Use Channel Masks

1 Open an image.

2 Select the **Channels** palette.

3 Click the **Create New Channel** button.

4 Select the new channel.

5 Select the **Brush** tool on the toolbox, and then select a brush tip on the Options bar.

6 Paint areas of the mask white to create a selection.

7 Paint areas of the mask black to mask the image.

Did You Know?

You can quickly convert a Channel mask into a selection. To view a Channel mask as a selection, open the Channels palette, and then Ctrl+click (Win) or ⌘+click (Mac) on the channel. Photoshop instantly translates the black, white, and gray areas of the mask into a visible selection in the document window.

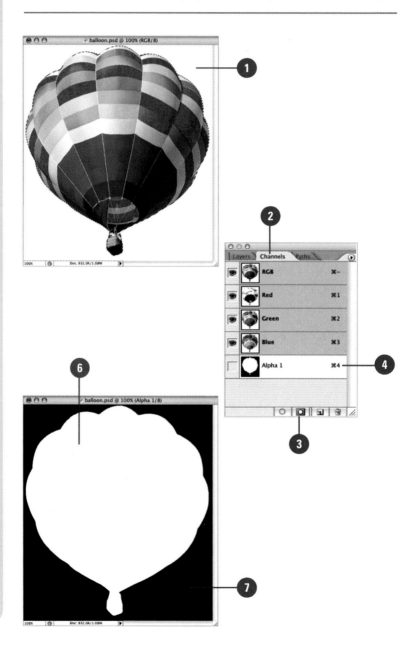

Creating Channel Masks from Scratch

Channel masks are easy to create and once created, are just as easy to modify. All you need is an open document, and access to the Channels palette. By selecting a painting or drawing tool, you paint the mask to define the selection area. The problem is you can't see the image, you only see the mask. What you need is the ability to view the mask and the image, almost like a piece of tracing paper, and then use the drawing tools to paint (trace) the portions of the image you want to select. The secret to viewing the image as you create the mask is to temporarily enable or show, the composite channel. In fact, the composite channel acts like a toggle switch—when it's showing, you see the image and the mask like tracing paper, when it's hidden you only view the mask.

Create Channel Masks

1. Open an image.

2. Select the **Channels** palette.

3. Click the **Create New Channel** button.

4. Click the **Show/Hide** button on the composite channel. The image is revealed in the document window (the new Alpha channel should still be selected). You will use the image to guide the creation of the mask.

5. Select the **Brush** tool on the toolbox.

6. Paint areas of the image using white to create a selection (painting with white, exposes the original image).

7. Paint areas of the image black to mask the image (painting with black, masks the image with a default color of red).

8. Click the **Show/Hide** button on the composite channel. The image is hidden revealing just the mask.

9. Repeat steps 6-8 until the mask is complete.

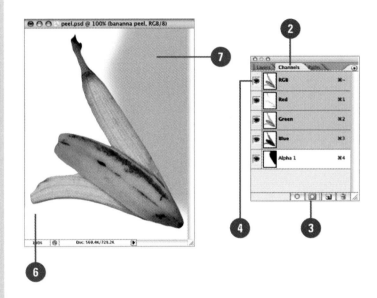

10

Modifying Channel Mask Options

Channel masks have default options that control how the mask looks and functions. Photoshop gives you the ability to change the default options of a channel mask. For example, you could change the default color from red to blue, or you could change the function of the channel mask from selection to spot color. Knowing you can change the mask options gives you more control over the final results.

Modify Channel Mask Options

1 Open a document.

2 Select the **Channels** palette.

3 Click the **Channels Options** button, and then click **New Channel**.

4 Enter a name for the new channel.

5 Click the option to define the mask color as the Masked Areas, Selected Areas, or Spot Color.

6 Click the **Color** box, and then select a color from the Color Picker.

7 Enter an Opacity percentage value (1 to 100) for the color.

8 Click **OK**.

Did You Know?

You can change the Channel options for a pre-existing channel. Double-click on the channel, and Photoshop will open the Channel options dialog box.

You can set Channel options for each channel. Changing the Channel options only impacts that specific channel. Each channel can have its own individual settings.

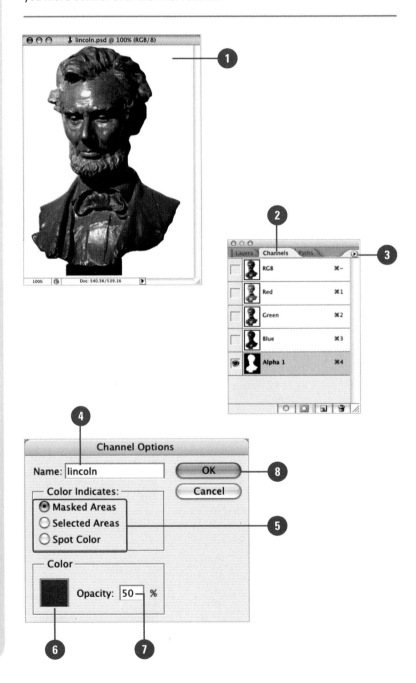

Creating Channel Masks from Selections

PS 4.2

Creating Channel masks from scratch (using paintbrush and drawing tools) is a useful feature, and gives you the ability to create a mask in any desired size or shape. However, there are times when it would be easier to first define the areas you want to save, and then create the mask. When you create a Channel mask from an existing selection, Photoshop uses the selected areas to create the mask. For example, you have an image of a woman wearing a red dress, and you want to change the color of the dress to green. The first step would be to select the red dress. Rather than create a new mask, and paint out the area representing the dress, it would easier to first use a tool like the Magic Wand, select the dress, and then convert the selected area (the dress) into a Channel mask. Once the mask is created, you could fine-tune the mask, using Photoshop's painting tools, and then change the dress color. Whether you create a mask from scratch or choose to create one through a pre-defined selection depends on the image, and what you're trying to accomplish.

Create Channel Masks from Selections

1 Open a document.

2 Create a selection using any of Photoshop's traditional selection tools.

3 Select the **Channels** palette.

4 Click the **Save Selection As Channel** button.

Photoshop creates a new channel mask based on the selected areas of the document.

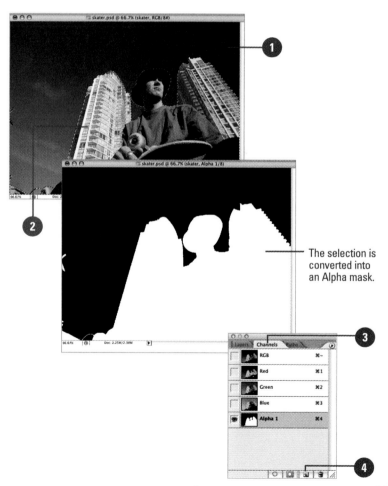

The selection is converted into an Alpha mask.

10

Making Channel Masks from Native Color Channels

Creating a channel mask from a native color channel, takes a few steps; however, if you're successful the effort spent making the selection is well worth it. The trick to creating a mask with a native color channel is to use the shifts of gray in one specific color channel to create the black and white areas characteristic of a typical channel mask. For example, you have an image of a model, and you want to remove the model from the background. Unfortunately, that requires selecting around the model's hair, a difficult thing to accomplish, even in the best of circumstances. To make the channel mask, open the Channels palette and examine the native color channels, one at a time. You're looking for a color channel that displays a significant shift of gray between the model's hair, and the background. For example, you click on the red channel of an RGB image, and the models hair appears dark gray, while the background appears light gray. The difference is so pronounced you can actually see individual strands of hair, standing out against the background. If you can find such a contrast, you can quickly make a channel mask.

Make Channel Masks from Native Color Channels

1. Open a document.

2. Click the **Channels** palette.

3. Click and view the individual native color channels one at a time.

4. Click the channel that best represents a visual difference between what you want to select and what you want to mask.

5. Drag the selected channel over the **Create New Channel** button.

   Photoshop makes a copy of the selected native color channel.

6. Click the native color channel copy.

7 Click the **Image** menu, point to **Adjustments**, and then click **Threshold**.

8 Move the **Threshold** slider left or right until you see a sharp black and white image with the black and white representing the selected and masked areas of the image.

9 Click **OK**.

10 Use Photoshop's painting tools with black and white to touch up the new mask.

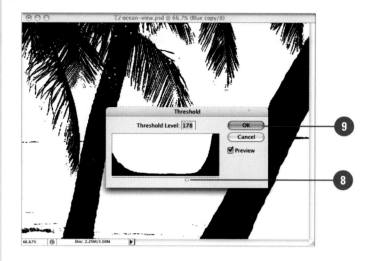

Did You Know?

You can use native color channel masks to perform image correction. Channel masks created from native color channels can be used for more than creating a mask. For example, you have a photo where the shadow portions of the image are too dark. Correct the problem by creating a channel mask that selects just the darker portions of the image, and then use the mask to control the Levels or Curves adjustments to lighten the overexposed areas of the image.

10

Loading Channel Masks

PS 4.2

Once you create a channel mask, and you can have up to 28 separate masks in one document, the next step is to use the masks. To save the channel mask all you have to do is save the document in a format that supports channels, such as Photoshop's native .psd format, or even the .tif format. The next time you open the document, your channel masks will be there. Deleting a channel mask is simple; just drag the channel mask over the Delete button, located at the bottom of the Channels palette, or select the channel mask you want to delete, and click the Delete button. However sooner or later, you're going to want to do more than just save or delete—you're going to want to use a channel mask. Using a channel mask involves a process of converting the mask back into a selection. It's an easy step, but necessary to complete the process from mask to selection.

Load Channel Masks

1. Open a document that contains a channel mask, or create a new channel mask.

2. Click the **Select** menu, and then click **Load Selection**.

3. If more than one document is open, click the **Document** list arrow, and then select the document you want to use.

4. Click the **Channel** list arrow, and then click the channel you want to convert into a selection (native color channels do not appear in this list).

5. Select the **Invert** check box to instruct Photoshop to use the black areas of the mask (instead of the white areas) for the selection.

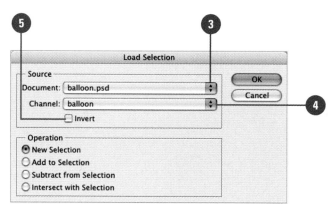

6 Select the Operation option you want to perform:

- ◆ **New Selection.** Creates a new selection.

- ◆ **Add To Selection.** Adds the channel mask to an existing selection.

- ◆ **Subtract From Selection.** Uses the channel mask to subtract from an existing selection.

- ◆ **Intersect With Selection.** Uses the channel mask to intersect, based on an existing selection.

7 Click **OK**.

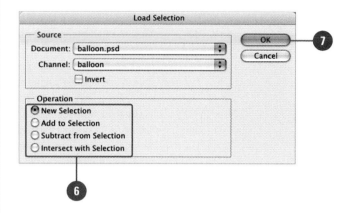

For Your Information

Working with Channel Masks

Channel masks provide controls over the selected areas of an image. By default, the white areas of the mask represent the selected areas, and the black areas represent the masked areas. When a mask is applied to an image, the sharp black and white of the mask create a very sharp-edged selection. To soften the effect of the mask, click the Filters menu, point to Blur, and then click Gaussian Blur. Apply a small amount of blur (one or two pixels) to the mask. Now, when the mask is applied to the image, the Gaussian blur will soften the effects of the selection and create a visually softer transition.

10

Moving Channel Masks Between Documents

Once you create a channel mask in one document, it is possible to move that channel mask from document to document. While most channel masks are so specific to a particular document, it wouldn't be practical to move them—a channel mask defining a selection of a tree line against a blue sky—many channel masks can be used over and over again. For example, a series of channel masks that create unique selection borders around an image. You spent a lot of time creating the borders, and you would like to apply those same border selections to other images. If that's the case, then increase your efficiency by saving them as layer masks and moving them between documents. Not only will it save you a lot of time, but using selections more than once can add a sense of cohesiveness to a design.

Move Channel Masks Between Documents

1. Open a document that contains a channel mask.

2. Open a second document (this is the document you will move the mask into).

3. Position the two document windows side-by-side.

4. Click the document containing the channel mask.

5. Select the **Channels** palette.

6. Drag the channel mask from the Channels palette into the open document window of the second document.

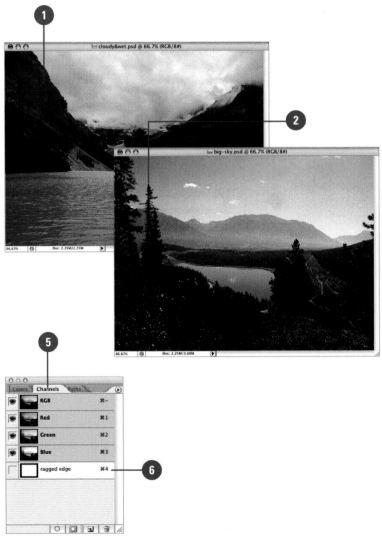

Combining Channel Masks

Channel masks are simply selections, which are defined with black, white, and shades of gray. Once a channel mask is placed in the Channels palette, you can use Photoshop's vast array of drawing and painting tools or filters. The Gaussian Blur filter can make a great enhancement to a channel mask. It's even possible to combine the selection elements of two or more channels together, and in doing so, create an even more complicated mask.

Combine Channel Masks

1 Open a document that contains two or more channel masks.

2 Click the **Channels** palette.

3 Press Ctrl+click (Win) or ⌘+click (Mac) on one of the channel masks.

The white areas of the channel become a selection.

4 Press Shift+Ctrl+click (Win) or Shift+⌘+click (Mac) a second channel mask.

The white areas of the second channel mask are added to the previous selection.

5 Click the **Save Selection As Channel** button.

Photoshop takes the combined areas of the two channels and creates a new channel mask.

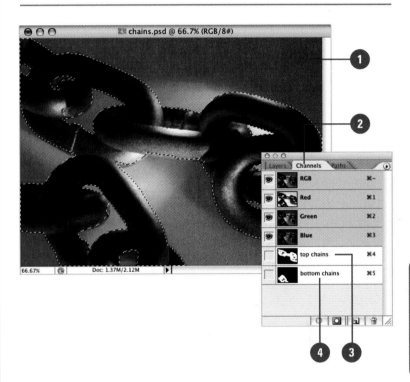

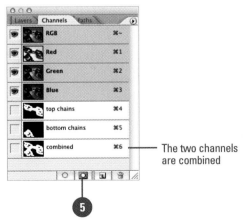

The two channels are combined

Using the Quick Mask Mode

Quick Mask Mode gives you the ability to create a selection using Photoshop's painting and drawing tools, without creating a channel mask. For example, you're creating a selection using traditional selection tools, and there's a portion of the image you're having difficulty selecting. Since this is a one-time selection, you don't want to go to the trouble of creating a channel mask. The solution is to move into the Quick Mask Mode. Quick Mask Mode toggles between a selection and quick mask. When you enter Quick Mask Mode, any pre-existing selections are converted into a red mask, and changes to the mask are performed using painting tools. When you return to Standard Mode, the masked (painted) areas are converted into a selection. While quick masks are created the same way as channel masks, they're temporary. It's a quick way to create a one-time selection.

Use the Quick Mask Mode

1. Open a document.

2. Create a selection using any of Photoshop's selection tools.

3. Click the **Edit In Quick Mask Mode** button to convert the selection into a red overlay mask.

4. Select the **Brush** tool.

5. Paint with white to open up more selection areas.

6. Paint with black to mask the image, which by default is red.

7. Click the **Edit In Standard Mode** button to return to a standard selection.

8. Toggle between Quick Mask and Standard modes until you create the perfect selection.

> ### Did You Know?
>
> ***You can convert a quick mask into a permanent channel mask.*** Create the quick mask, return to Standard Mode, select the Channels palette, and then click the Create Channel From Selection button.

Working with Quick Mask Options

 PS 4.3

Work with Quick Mask Options

1. Double-click the **Quick Mask Mode** or **Standard Mode** buttons.

2. Click the **Masked Areas** or **Selected Areas** option to instruct Photoshop whether to create a mask or a selection from the color areas of the mask.

3. Click the **Color** box, and then select a color from the Color Picker.

4. Enter an Opacity percentage value (0 to 100).

5. Click **OK**.

IMPORTANT *Quick Mask options are program, not document specific. The changes made to the Quick Mask options remain set until you change them.*

Did You Know?

Once you've created a Quick Mask selection, you can save it as a permanent Channel mask. Just return the screen to Standard mode, open the Channels palette, and then click the Save Selection As Channel button.

When you work in the Quick Mask Mode, the color for the mask is red, the opacity of the mask is 50 percent, and the red mask represents the masked areas of the document. Photoshop set up the Quick Mask options as a default, but they can be modified. For example, it would be very difficult to view a red mask if you were working on a primarily red image, or you might want to increase or decrease the opacity of the mask. Photoshop lets you do this through mask options.

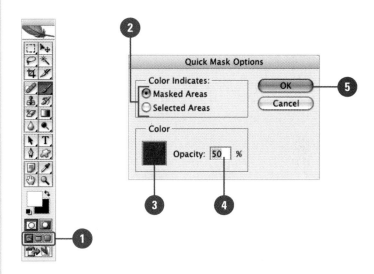

For Your Information

Using Quick Masks

One of the powerful features of a Quick Mask is you can use filters directly on the mask. Create a selection in the Quick Mask Mode, and then click the Filter menu and choose from Photoshop's many filters, such as Brush Strokes, Blur, or Distort. When you click OK, the filter is applied directly to the Quick Mask. Then, when you return to Standard Mode, the effect of the filter is applied to the selection. Working with filters and quick masks gives you the option of creating highly complicated masks, without every using the Channels palette.

10

Using the Paths Palette

Introduction

Adobe Photoshop is a hybrid application, not only can it handle raster information (pixels), it can also hold path information (vector). Photoshop stores raster information in the Layers palette, and stores vector information in the Paths palette. When you use Photoshop's vector drawing, or pen tools, Photoshop creates a path in the Paths palette to store that information. In addition, it is possible to create a selection with Photoshop's traditional selection tools, and convert that selection into a path. Paths are defined mathematically using anchor points and segments. Once created, they can be precisely modified to fit any design situation. In many ways, paths serve a function similar to channel masks—they can define selections, but because they're vector and not raster, they are much more precise. When paths are saved they take up far less room than channels.

Working with the various Pen tools, it's possible to create precise paths, and even create complicated selections around virtually any shape. Once the path is created it's a simple matter to subtract anchor points, and add new or modify existing anchor points to produce complex paths. It's even possible to convert straight segments (the visible line that connects two anchor points together) into elegantly curved segments, or you can remove the curve from a segment with a single click of the Convert Curve tool. Paths can be used to precisely guide a brush stroke, or the interior of a path can be filled with any color, pattern, or gradient available in Photoshop using the Stroke and Fill Commands. Paths can even be used to create a clipping path around an image. When moving an image into a layout program, such as InDesign, a clipping path lets you define certain areas of an image as transparent. In addition, you can create paths in Photoshop, then export and open them in Adobe Illustrator. Using Photoshop paths give you precise, mathematical control over the creation of complex shapes, selections, and even transparency.

Understanding Vector and Raster Images

 PS 7.2

Photoshop is a hybrid application that gives you great control over photographic (raster) images, and seamlessly combines that with the elegance and form of artistic (vector) shapes. When you work on the raster side of Photoshop, you're dealing with an image that is a visual brick wall with each brick (or pixel) identifying one piece of color information. The reason raster images are considered resolution dependent is that once the image is created or scanned, any enlargement of the image forces Photoshop to enlarge and average the existing color information in the document.

This process, called **interpolation**, is what causes enlarged raster images to become blurred, or pixilated. Vector images are created using mathematical shapes, not pixels, and that's why vector shapes are considered resolution independent. For example, if you enlarge a vector image to 100 times its original size, Photoshop merely changes the mathematical formulas to coincide with the new size, and since vector shapes are constructed of math not pixels, file sizes are extremely small.

Raster Image

Close up shows pixels

Vector Image

Close up shows lines

Converting a Selection into a Path

Selection marquees are Photoshop's way of identifying the work areas within the active document. Since selections are created in the raster format, the accuracy of the selection is based on the resolution of the active image. This can be a problem when you're working with low-resolution images such as, Web and presentation graphics. However, when you convert a selection into a path, you can precisely reshape it, using Photoshop's vector tools, and this gives you more control over the final results.

Convert a Selection into a Path

1. Open a document.

2. Select an area of the image, using any of Photoshop's traditional selection tools.

3. Select the **Paths** palette.

4. Hold down the Alt (Win) or Option (Mac) key, and then click the **Make Work Path** button.

5. Enter a Tolerance value (0.5 to 10).

   Low tolerance values create a path with many anchor points, and the path conforms precisely to the selection marquee, but low tolerances can cause printing errors (too much information). Higher tolerance values create a path with fewer anchor points, and the path will be smoother.

6. Click **OK**.

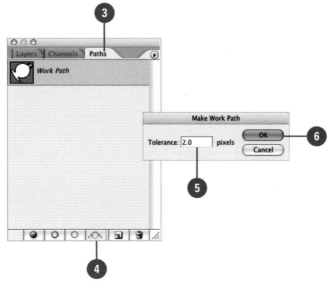

11

Working with Pen Tools

When you work with Photoshop's Pen tools, you're creating a path with-out the conversion from selection (raster) to path (vector). Vector paths are mathematical and are therefore not hampered by problems with image resolution. For example, a path created in a low-resolution image (72ppi) would function the same as a path created in a high-resolution (300ppi) image. An added benefit of paths is that they take up less room than selections saved as channel masks. When you create a path using the Pen tools, Photoshop automatically creates a path in the Paths palette. If you have an existing path selected, Photoshop adds the new path to the selected path.

Work with Pen Tools

1. Open a document.

2. Select the **Standard Pen** tool on the toolbox.

3. Click the **Paths** button on the Options bar.

   IMPORTANT *To view the segments as you draw, click the Geometry Options list arrow on the Pen Options bar, and then select the Rubber Band check box.*

4. Create an anchor point (or node) by clicking once in the open document.

5. To create a straight segment (two anchor points connected by a line), move and click again.

6. To create a curved segment (two anchor points connected by a curved line), move and drag.

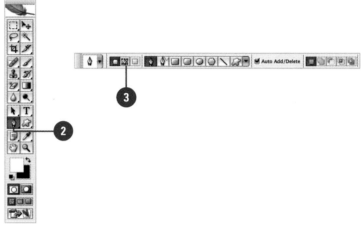

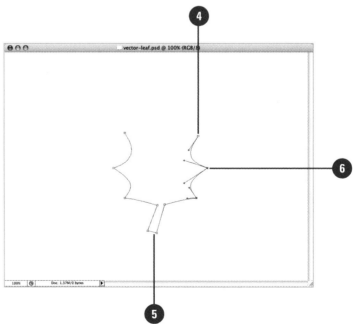

7 Continue to move through the document, clicking or dragging until the shape is complete.

8 Create a closed shape by moving the Pen tool over the original anchor point and clicking when you see a small circle appear underneath the Pen tool.

IMPORTANT *As with any tool, control is gained through practice. Work with the Pen tool until you can make a path around any shape. The more time you spend practicing, the better your paths will be, and the better your designs.*

Did You Know?

You can create an open shape.
Move somewhere away from the last anchor point, and then press Ctrl+click (Win) or ⌘+click (Mac).

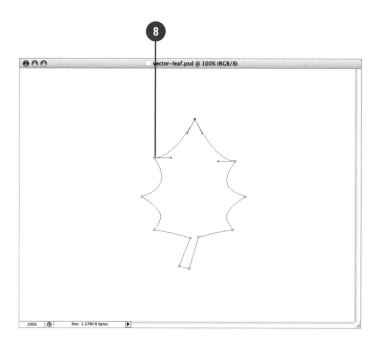

For Your Information

Using the Pen Tools

The Pen tools in Photoshop perform the same way they do in all vector-based applications, such as Adobe Illustrator. If you have any experience using vector-based applications, you should have no trouble working with Photoshop's vector tools. The good news is that Adobe Illustrator and Adobe Photoshop let you move seamlessly between the two programs. In fact, if you have both programs open, you can drag a Photoshop document directly into Illustrator.

11

Creating Paths Using the Freeform Pen Tool

 Adobe Certified Expert PS 7.1, 7.4

Use the Freeform Pen Tool

1. Open a document.

2. Select the **Freeform Pen** tool on the toolbox.

3. Click the **Paths** button on the Options bar.

4. Drag in the document window using your mouse or drawing tablet to create a unique shape.

5. Close the shape by dragging the Freeform Pen tool over the shape's starting point, and then releasing when you see a small circle appear underneath the tool.

6. Create an open shape by dragging and releasing anywhere but over the starting point.

Did You Know?

You can control the complexity of a path. Click the Geometry button on the Options bar, and then enter a Curved Fit value from 0.5 to 10. The higher the value the less complex the path (less anchor points), and the lower the value, the more precise, but more complex the path.

Where the Pen tool requires you to click and move your mouse, the Freeform Pen tool lets you drag on the screen to create any desired path. When you create a path with the Freeform tool, Photoshop adds anchor points to the line at predefined intervals. The distance between anchor points is determined by a value called a Curved Fit. The more complicated the design, the more anchor points the Freeform Pen Tool must create to support the path. Once created, you can always modify the path or even add or subtract anchor points.

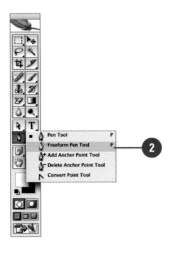

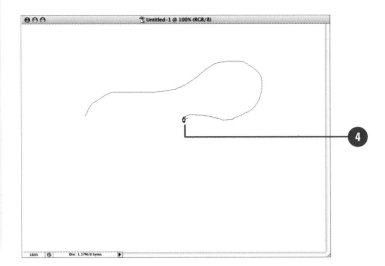

Using the Magnetic Option with the Freeform Pen Tool

 PS 7.1

Use the Magnetic Option with the Freeform Pen Tool

1. Open a document.

2. Select the **Freeform Pen** tool on the toolbox.

3. Select the **Magnetic** check box on the Options bar.

   IMPORTANT *When using the Magnetic option with the Freeform Pen tool, you cannot create an open shape.*

4. Click the **Shape Layers** or **Paths** button.

5. Position the **Freeform Pen** tool over the edge of a shape, and then click and release the mouse.

6. Drag in the document window using your mouse or drawing tablet to follow the visible edge.

   The magnetic option helps you stay on the edge.

7. Close the shape by dragging the Freeform (magnetic) Pen tool over the shape's starting point, and then releasing when you see a small circle appear underneath the tool, or by double-clicking.

The Magnetic option changes the Freeform Pen tool into a magnetic vector drawing tool. For example, selecting the Magnetic option forces the tool to follow the visible edge of an object in the document window. The Magnetic option instructs the Freeform Pen tool to key to the shift in brightness between an object and its background. It's a great way to make a difficult path. Once you click to define the starting point, it's not necessary to hold down the mouse, just move while closely following the visible edge of the image. If you get to a tricky point where the Magnetic lasso doesn't know what to do, just click your mouse to add a user-defined anchor point.

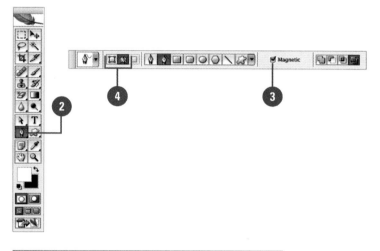

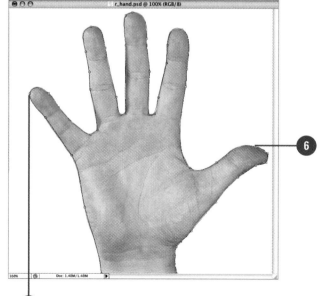

7 Starting point

11

Adding and Deleting Anchor Points

Creating a path is not the end of the task, in fact, there are many ways you can modify a path once it's been created. For example, you can add, subtract, or delete anchor points to an existing path. You can also modify those points to conform to any desired shape. In addition, existing anchor points can be modified, and in so doing, change the segments connecting the points. Just like anything else in Photoshop, paths are flexible, they can be modified to meet whatever design considerations are needed to make the job successful.

Add Anchor Points

1. Open a document that contains an existing path, or create a new path.

2. Select the **Paths** palette.

3. Select a path.

4. Select the **Add Anchor Point** tool on the toolbox.

5. Click once on the path to add, not modify, a new anchor point.

6. Click and drag on the path to add, and modify the segment.

Did You Know?

You can move anchor points using your arrow tools. Select the Direct Selection tool, and then click on an anchor point. Click your arrow keys to move the anchor point up, down, left or right one pixel at a time. To move 10 pixels at a time, hold down the Shift key while using the arrow keys.

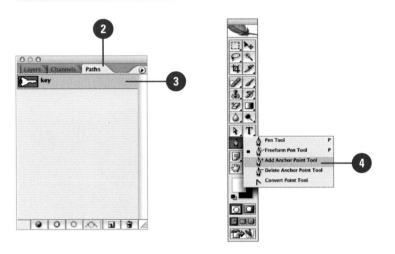

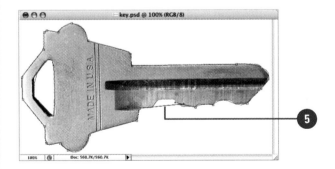

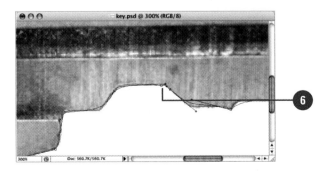

Delete Anchor Points

① Open a document that contains an existing path, or create a new path.

② Select the **Paths** palette.

③ Select a path.

④ Select the **Delete Anchor Point** tool on the toolbox.

There are no additional options for the Delete Anchor Point tool.

⑤ Click once on an existing anchor point to remove it from the path.

The anchor points on either side of the deleted point are now used to define the segment.

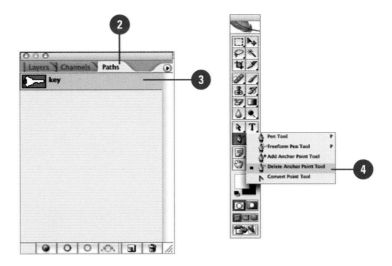

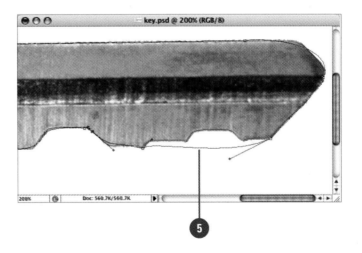

Modifying Anchor Points

PS 7.1, 7.4

Anchor points can be added or deleted, and existing anchor points can be modified. In reality, the anchor points are used to define the length and curve of the segments, or lines that connect the anchor points together. Just think of a farmer that strings a line of barbed wire to protect his cattle, he places posts in the ground and strings the wire between the posts. The more posts he uses, the more complex the path of the barbed wire. In Photoshop, the posts are the anchor points, and the barbed wire, the segments. However, we have one advantage over the barbed wire, we can cause a segment line to curve between the anchor points, while the farmer must stretch the barbed wire in a straight line between posts.

Modify Anchor Points

1. Open a document that contains an existing path, or create a new path.

2. Select the **Paths** palette.

3. Select the path you want to modify.

4. Select the **Path Selection** tool on the toolbox.

5. Click on the path to move, without modifying, the entire path.

Did You Know?

You can move a path using the keyboard. Click the path and then use the arrows on the keyboard to move it.

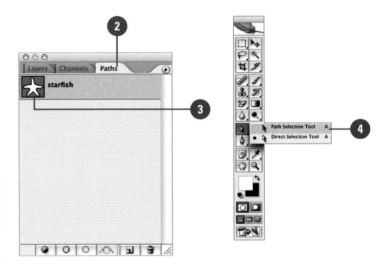

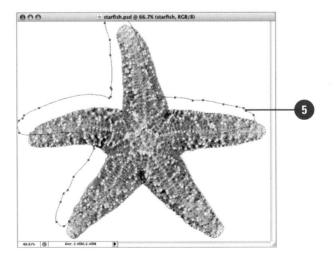

6 Select the **Direct Selection** tool on the toolbox.

7 Drag an individual anchor point to move the anchor to another location.

Did You Know?

You can use one tool to add or delete anchor points. Press the Alt (Win) or Option (Mac) key when using the Add or Delete Anchor Point tool. This reverses the display, The Add tool becomes the Delete tool.

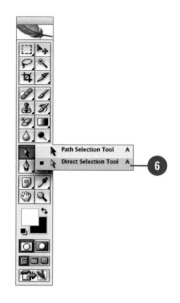

Path Selection Tool   A

Direct Selection Tool   A   6

7

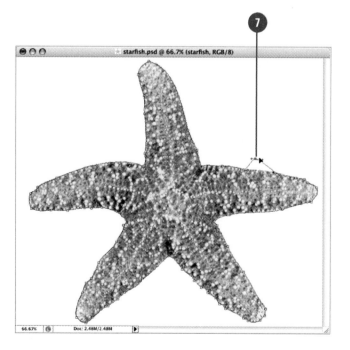

starfish.psd @ 66.7% (starfish, RGB/8)

66.67%   Doc: 2.48M/2.48M

11

Modifying Existing Direction Lines

Anchor points are composed of two elements—the anchor point and direction lines. The anchor point is the fence post that connects segments together. The direction lines influence the amount of curve applied to the segment. The further away a direction point lays from the anchor, the more aggressive the curve. Conversely, the closer the direction lines lay to the anchor point, the less the curve. If an anchor point does not have any direction lines, it is said to be a straight anchor point.

Modify Existing Direction Lines

1. Open a document that contains a path, or create a new path.

2. Select the **Paths** palette, and then select the path you want to modify.

3. Select the **Direct Selection** tool on the toolbox.

   There are no additional options for the Direct Selection tool.

4. Click the very end of the direction line, and then drag to change the curve of the segment.

5. Hold down the Alt (Win) or Option (Mac) key, and then click at the very end of the direction line to break the line at the anchor point.

   This lets you independently control each end of the direction line, as it extends out from the anchor point.

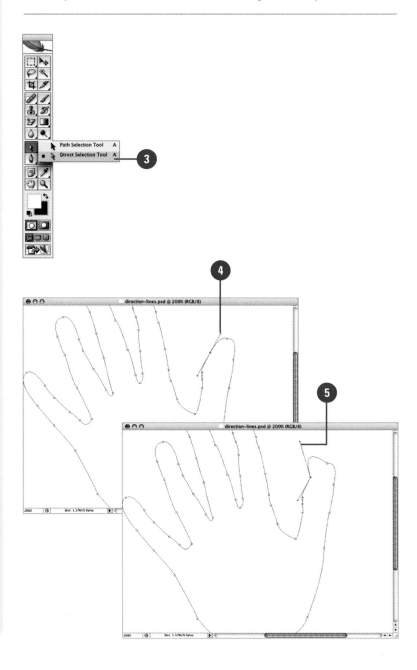

Converting Straight Points and Curved Points

 PS 7.1, 7.4

Sooner or later you'll encounter a situation where you want to convert an anchor point from curved to straight or straight to curved. Rather than try to collapse the direction lines into the anchor point (a difficult task), or try to drag non-existent direction lines from a straight anchor point, Photoshop gives you a useful conversion tool called, the Convert Point tool. The Convert Point tool lets you convert existing points on a path. For example, to convert a curved point into a straight point click once on the curved anchor point, and it's instantly converted into a straight point. To convert a straight point to curved, simply drag on the anchor point, and the line converts to curved.

Convert Points

1. Open a document that contains a path, or create a new path.

2. Select the **Paths** palette, and then select the path you want to modify.

3. Select the **Convert Point** tool on the toolbox.

4. Click on a curved anchor point to convert it into a straight point.

5. Click and drag a straight anchor point to convert it into a curved point.

Did You Know?

You can change the curve of a segment line with a click and drag. Click the Direct Selection tool, and then drag directly on the line, not the anchor point.

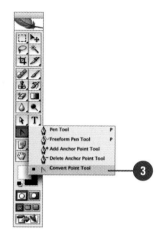

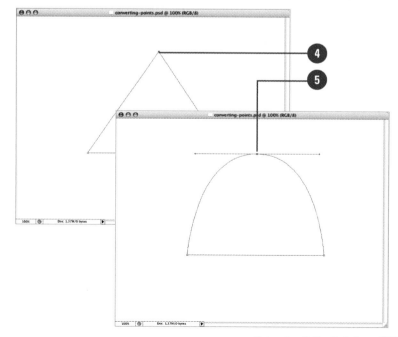

11

Working with Clipping Paths

Photoshop documents are an image contained within a bounding box. A bounding box consists of a square or rectangle with 4, 90-degree corners. Unfortunately, most images are not shaped like a bounding box. Clipping Paths let you place non-rectangular images onto a transparent background, and then save and use them in other applications, such as Quark Xpress, without having a big white box surrounding the image. The trick is to create a well-defined path, and then convert the path into what Photoshop calls a Clipping Path.

Work with Clipping Paths

1. Open a document.

2. Select the **Pen** or **Freeform Pen** tool on the toolbox.

3. Click the **Paths** button on the Options bar.

4. Create a path around the portion of the image you want to keep.

5. Select the **Paths** palette.

6. Double-click on the new Work Path, enter a Name for the path, and then click **OK**.

7. Click the **Paths Options** button, and then click **Clipping Path**.

Did You Know?

Clipping paths allow you to move objects with transparent backgrounds into other applications. However, the edges of clipping paths appear as if they were cut out with a pair of scissors. That makes it difficult to move objects with soft edges.

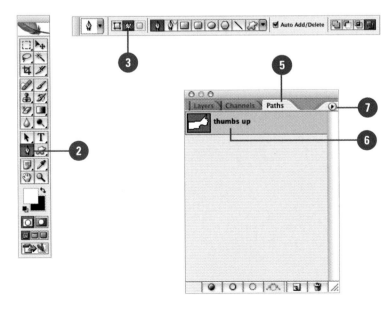

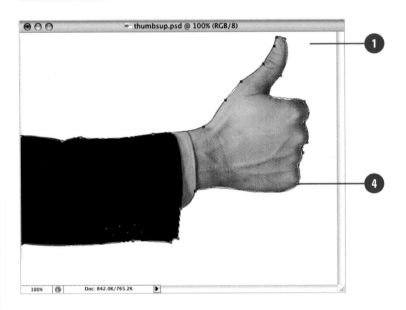

8 Click the **Path** list arrow, and then select the new path.

9 Enter a Flatness value (0 to 100) or leave it blank to use the printer's default settings (recommended).

10 Click **OK**.

11 Click the **File** menu, and then click **Save As**.

12 Click the **Format** list arrow, and then select the **Photoshop EPS** format.

13 Click **Save**.

The image, when placed in a layout program, appears with a transparent background.

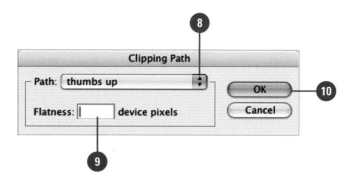

Did You Know?

Working with clipping paths is becoming a part of the past. You can move transparent Photoshop objects (including soft drop shadows) directly into Adobe InDesign CS without using any clipping paths.

For Your Information

Clipping Paths

Clipping paths work to create a transparent area without the sacrifice of the actual image information. Therefore it is not necessary to delete any of the image information when creating the clipping path. If you want to restore the original image without transparency, just open the Paths palette, and then delete the clipping path.

Filling an Area of an Image Using Paths

Paths are easy to create and versatile. Once you create a path, it has many applications—you can convert a path into a clipping path, or you can even convert a path into a standard selection, and use it to define a work area. In addition to some of the more common applications, paths can be used to define an area to be filled, or you can use the Stroke command to control any of Photoshop's drawing tools.

Fill an Area of an Image Using Paths

1. Open a document that contains a path, or create a new path.

2. Select the **Paths** palette, and then select one of the paths.

    IMPORTANT *When you select a path from the Paths palette, the path becomes visible in the document window.*

3. Select the **Paths Options** button, and then click **Fill Path**.

4. Click the **Use** list arrow, and then select from the available fill options.

5. Click the **Mode** list arrow, and then select a blending mode.

6. Select an Opacity percentage value (0 to 100) for the blending mode.

7. Select the **Preserve Transparency** check box to protect any transparent areas in the active image.

8. Enter a Feather Radius value (0 to 250) to feather the edge of the fill.

9. Select the **Anti-alias** check box to visually soften the fill.

10. Click **OK**.

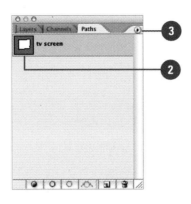

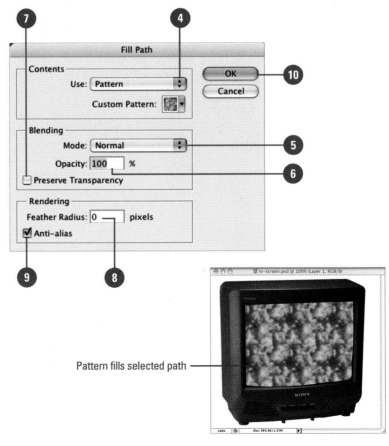

Pattern fills selected path

Stroking an Area of an Image Using Paths

The Stroke Path option is an excellent way to control any of Photoshop's drawing or image-editing tools. When you select the Stroke Path options, you're essentially giving Photoshop control of the tool, and using a pre-existing path to control the shape of the stroke. The important thing to remember is that the tool selected for the Stroke Path option will perform the way it was last used. For example, if the last time you used the Paintbrush tool you selected a star-shaped, 40-pixel brush; selecting the Paintbrush as the Stroke tool will cause it to stroke the path using a star-shaped, 40-pixel brush.

Stroke an Area of an Image Using Paths

1. Open a document that contains a path, or create a new path.

2. Select the **Paths** palette, and then select one of the paths.

3. Click the **Paths Options** button, and then click **Stroke Path**.

4. Click the **Tool** list arrow, and then select from the available tools.

5. Select the **Simulate Pressure** check box to mimic the pressure variables experienced when using a drawing tablet.

6. Click **OK**.

The Stroke Path command applies the stroke using the original path to guide the brush.

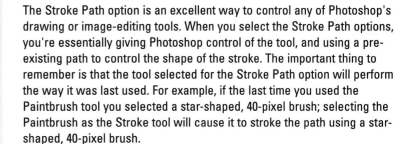

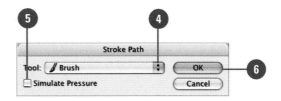

Stroke applied using the original path to guide the brush.

11

Creating Shapes as Paths

PS 7.4

Paths can be created using any of Photoshop's traditional Pen tools, or you can use shape tools to create a unique path. For example, you want to create a unique stroke border around an image, and you find the perfect shape in Photoshop's custom shapes palette. Rather than create the shape, select it, and then convert it into a path, Photoshop lets you draw any shape and place it directly into the Paths palette. Once the shape is placed in the Paths palette, you can modify or change it, just like any other path.

Create Shapes as Paths

1. Open a document.

2. Select the **Custom Shape** tool (or any of Photoshop's drawing tools) on the toolbox.

3. Click the **Shape Layers** button.

4. Click the **Shape** list arrow, and then select a pre-defined shape.

5. Select the **Paths** palette.

6. Draw the shape in the document window.

   Photoshop creates a Work Path, containing the custom shape.

See Also

See "Modifying Anchor Points" on page 262 for information on reshaping a path.

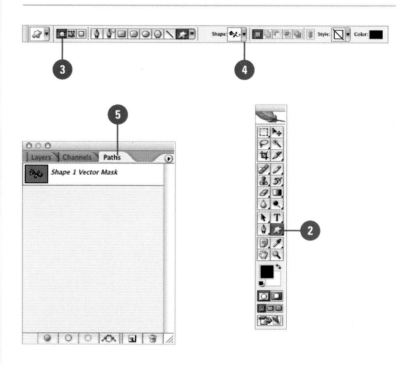

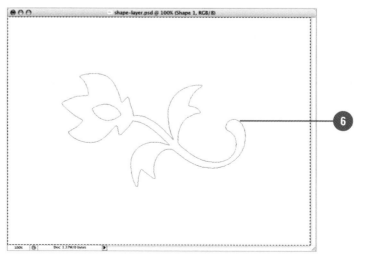

Exporting Paths to Adobe Illustrator

Paths are vector shapes, and programs such as Adobe Illustrator support Paths created in Photoshop. You want to create a unique path in Photoshop, and then use Illustrator's creative vector controls to further enhance the image. If that's the case, Photoshop gives you several ways to move the image out of Photoshop and into Illustrator. Remember, when you export a path into Adobe Illustrator, you're not moving an image, you're moving stroke and fill vector data.

Export Photoshop Paths Using the Save As Method

1. Open a document that contains a path, or create a new path.

2. Click the **File** menu, and then click **Save As**.

3. Enter a file name.

4. Click the **Format** list arrow, and then select the **Photoshop EPS** format.

5. Click the **Where** (Mac) or **Save In** (Win) list arrow, and then select a location for the file.

6. Click **Save** to open the EPS Options dialog box.

7. Click **OK**.

8. Open the image in Adobe Illustrator.

   Illustrator gives you full access to the path, including the ability to manipulate, add, and delete anchor points.

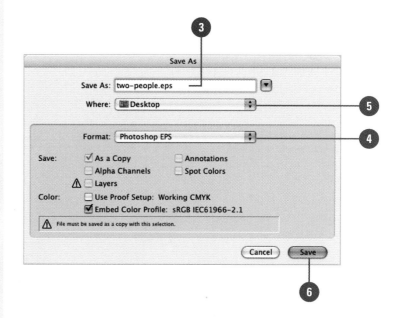

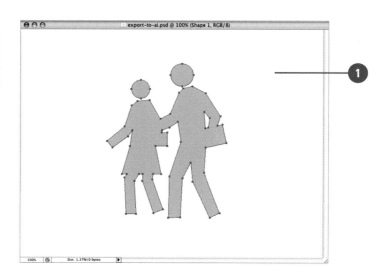

Exporting Paths Using the Export Method

The Paths To Illustrator command lets you quickly export a Photoshop path into a format acceptable to Adobe Illustrator. This makes the process of working with Photoshop and Illustrator artwork much more efficient. For example, you could create a path in Photoshop, and then export the path to Illustrator for use in another piece of artwork. In addition, exported Photoshop paths can also be used to help align elements of an Illustrator document, to that of its Photoshop counterpart. Then, later the two documents can be combined to produce one piece of artwork. Two pieces of artwork, created in separate applications, precisely combined with the use of an exported path. In other words, paths give you control, which you can use to your advantage.

Export Photoshop Paths Using the Export Method

1. Open a document that contains a path or create a new path.

2. Click the **File** menu, point to **Export**, and then click **Paths To Illustrator**.

3. Enter a file name.

   The files extension is .ai (Adobe Illustrator).

4. Click the **Where** (Mac) or **Save In** (Win) list arrow, and then select a location for the file.

5. Click the **Write** list arrow, and then select which path or paths to export.

6. Click **Save**.

   Photoshop creates an Adobe Illustrator document containing only the paths (not images) in the document.

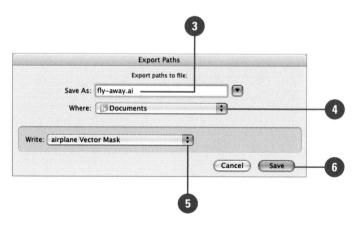

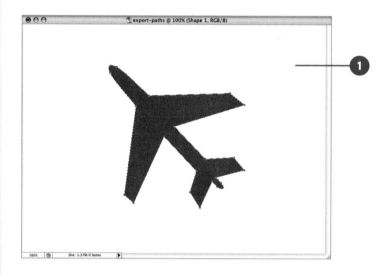

Working with Layer Styles

Introduction

Layer styles are the very definition of creativity and control when using Adobe Photoshop. Using styles, such as Bevel and Emboss or Drop Shadow, you can move from two-dimensional into the world of three-dimensional. You can effortlessly change the look of a document with Gradient Overlay, Color Overlay, and Pattern Overlay, and you can do it all without ever changing the original image. That means you can apply a style to an image, and at any time in the creative process, change your mind. This level of control gives you the power you need to take your designs to the creative edge and beyond.

When you create a customized layer style, you can move that style to another layer, save the style in the Styles palette, even move the style between two open documents. That kind of flexibility gives you the ability to add consistency to your designs with a minimum of effort, and since layer styles do not change the original image, you can modify or remove the style at any time during the creative process. Not only do layer styles let you create special effects, but they give you the control you need over the image to experiment until you see exactly what you want.

Understanding Layer Styles

 PS 3.5

Layer styles are applied to the layers in the active document. When you add a style to a layer, the results of the style are only displayed in that layer. Each layer can have it's own style, and you can apply more than one style to a single layer. Layer styles can be applied to any layer, except the Background.

Two of Photoshop's layer styles require transparent and non-transparent layer elements (Drop Shadow and Outer Glow). For example, to apply a Drop Shadow to a layer, it would require a transparent area within the image to hold the shadow.

Layer Styles

Drop Shadow

Satin

Inner Shadow

Color Overlay

Outer Glow

Gradient Overlay

Inner Glow

Pattern Overlay

Bevel & Emboss

Stroke

Adding a Layer Style

PS 3.5

To add a layer style to the active layer, select the layer, and apply one or more of the styles by clicking the Add Layer Style button. Once selected, the layer style appears as a sub-element of the active layer. Once applied, layer styles are easy to modify. Each of Photoshop's layer styles has options to control exactly how the style appears in the active document. To modify a style, just reopen the Layer Style dialog box, and make your changes. In addition, each layer style has its own Show/Hide button. The Show/Hide button is a toggle that lets you temporarily hide the layer styles in the document.

Add a Layer Style

1. Select the **Layers** palette.

2. Select a layer.

3. Click the **Add Layer Style** button, and then select from the available style options.

4. Make changes to the layer style in the dialog box using the options; options vary depending on the layer style.

5. Click **OK**.

   The selected layer style appears as a sub-element of the active layer.

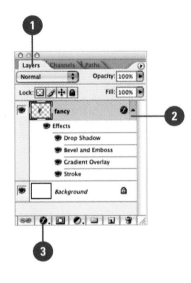

Modify an Existing Layer Style

1. Select the **Layers** palette.

2. Double-click on the attached name of the layer style.

3. Make changes to the layer style using the options; options vary depending on the layer style.

4. Click **OK**.

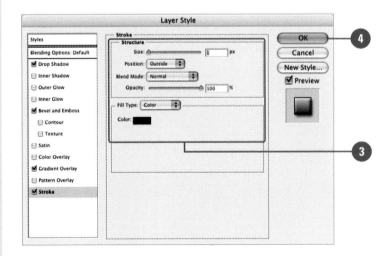

12

Creating and Modifying a Drop Shadow

 PS 3.5

The Drop Shadow style is probably the most common layer style used (next to Bevel and Emboss). Since Photoshop needs somewhere to apply the drop shadow, you will need a layer that contains an object surrounded by a transparent Background. For example, you could create a type layer or use the shape drawing tools to create a unique object, add a drop shadow with the click of the mouse, and then use the layer style options to controls the color, shape, and direction of the shadow. Once the shadow is created, it can be transferred to other objects in other layers—not only making the process easy, but consistent.

Work with a Drop Shadow

1. Select the **Layers** palette.

2. Click the layer you want to apply the Drop Shadow style.

3. Click the **Add Layer Style** button, and then click **Drop Shadow**.

4. Select from the following Drop Shadow options:

   ◆ **Blend Mode.** Click the list arrow, and then select how you want the color of the shadow to blend with underlying layers (default: Multiply).

   ◆ **Color.** Click the Color Swatch, and then select a color for the shadow (default: Black).

   ◆ **Opacity.** Specify an Opacity percentage value for the shadow, or drag the slider left or right (default: 75 percent).

   ◆ **Angle.** Enter a value from 0 to 360 degrees, or drag the radius slider left or right to set the angle of the shadow (default: 30).

   ◆ **Use Global Light.** Select the check box to conform the angle of the drop shadow to any other effects applied to other layers.

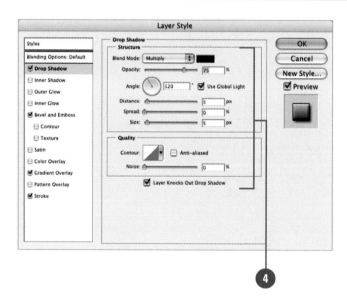

For Your Information

Using Global Light and Shadow Angles

You can control the direction of a light source across multiple layers. The Global Light option is very important because it ties the light sources used in multiple layers together. For example, if you create multiple layers with drop shadows, and you change the direction of the shadow in one of the layers, the Global Light option will ensure that all the layers maintain the same direction. The most common shadow angle used is 125 degrees; called the comfortable angle, it directs the shadow down and to the right. Studies show that most people expect the light source to be in the upper-right portion of the image.

- ◆ **Distance.** Enter a value from 0 to 30000 pixels, or drag the slider left or right. Distance determines the amount the shadow is offset from the original image (default: 5).

- ◆ **Spread.** Enter a value from 0 to 100 percent, or drag the slider left or right. Spread determines the amount of image used for the spread of the shadow (default: 0).

- ◆ **Size.** Enter a value from 0 to 250 pixels, or drag the slider left or right. Size determines the amount of blur applied to the shadow (default: 5).

- ◆ **Contour.** Click the list arrow, and then select from the available options. Contours are mathematical curves that determine the brightness of the shadow at different levels (default: null curve).

- ◆ **Anti-aliased.** Select the check box to create a visually smooth drop shadow.

- ◆ **Noise.** Enter a value from 0 to 100 percent, or drag the slider left or right. The noise option introduces a random shift to the colors of the Drop Shadow.

- ◆ **Layer Knocks Out Drop Shadow.** Select the check box to create a knock out in the underlying layers.

5 Click **OK**.

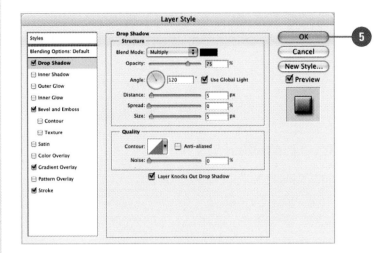

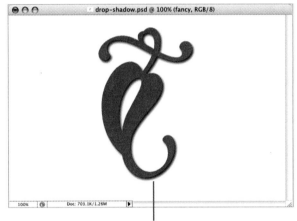

Drop Shadow style applied

12

Working with Bevel and Emboss

 PS 3.5

The Bevel and Emboss style, second only to Drop Shadow in popularity, creates the 3-D illusion of roundness to a flat surface. You can apply the Bevel layer style to text, to get the impression of 3-D text. If the layer you're applying the Bevel and Emboss to has no transparent areas, the style will be applied to the outer edge of the image, and if you want to move away from the standard rounded bevel, you can now use a Chisel Hard Technique, that makes a bevel appear as if it's carved out of stone.

Work with Bevel and Emboss

1 Select the **Layers** palette.

2 Select the layer you want to apply the Bevel and Emboss style.

3 Click the **Add Layer Style** button, and then click **Bevel And Emboss**.

4 Select from the available Bevel and Emboss options:

◆ **Style.** Click the list arrow, and then select from Outer Bevel, Inner Bevel (default), Emboss, Pillow Emboss, and Stroke Emboss.

◆ **Technique.** Click the list arrow, and then select from Smooth (default), Chisel Hard, and Chisel Soft.

◆ **Depth.** Enter 0 to 1000 percent. Higher Depth values increase the intensity of the bevel or emboss.

◆ **Direction.** Click the Up or Down option to reverse the highlight and shadows of the Bevel or Emboss.

◆ **Size.** Enter 0 to 250 pixels, or drag the slider left or right. Size determines how much of the image is used to create the Bevel/Emboss style.

◆ **Soften.** Enter 0 to 16 pixels. The higher the value, the softer the edge of the bevel (default: 5).

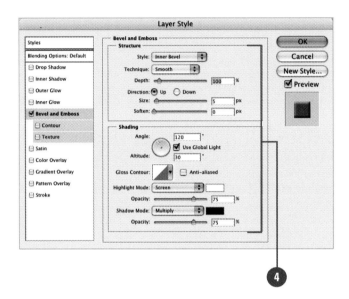

- ◆ **Angle.** Enter 0 to 360 degrees. Angle determines the angle of the light source in relation to the bevel/emboss (default: 30).

- ◆ **Use Global Light.** Select the check box to conform the angle of the bevel and emboss to any other styles applied to other layers.

- ◆ **Altitude.** Enter a value from 0 to 90 degrees. Altitude determines the height of the light source, in relationship to the image.

- ◆ **Gloss Contour.** Click the list arrow, and then select from the available options. Gloss Contours are mathematical curves that determine the brightness of the bevel/emboss at different levels.

- ◆ **Highlight Mode.** Click the list arrow and Color box, and then select a blending mode and color for the highlight (default: Screen, white).

- ◆ **Opacity for Highlight Mode.** Enter a value from 0 to 100 percent. Opacity determines the overall transparency of the highlight. Higher values equate to more aggressive highlights.

- ◆ **Shadow Mode.** Click the list arrow and Color box, and then select a blending mode and color for the shadow (default: Multiply, black).

- ◆ **Opacity for Shadow Mode.** Enter a value from 0 to 100 percent. Opacity determines the overall transparency of the shadow. Higher values equate to more aggressive shadows.

⑤ Click **OK**.

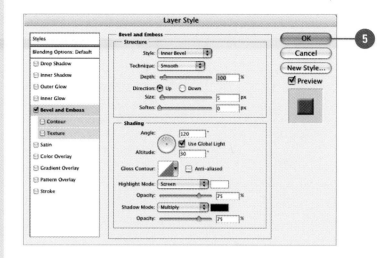

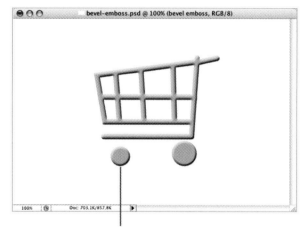

Bevel and Emboss style applied

For Your Information

Understanding the Contour Option

The Contour option redistributes the brightness levels of the shadow and highlights portions of the bevel and emboss. By experimenting with an alternate contour, you can enhance the realism of a bevel, or create a surrealistic emboss.

12

Working with Contour and Texture

 PS 3.5

The Bevel and Emboss layer styles have two powerful features, the ability to add a contour or texture to the active bevel or emboss. This lets you give your creative elements more of a realistic texture. When you apply the Contour and Texture options, the image takes on a three-dimensional texture, based on a selected pattern. Once applied, the relative depth and intensity of the texture can be precisely controlled to create rough rock-like surfaces, as well as brush metal. In addition, the Contour option lets you shape the appearance of the shadow areas of the texture style, creating even more realistic surfaces.

Work with Contour and Texture

1. Select the **Layers** palette.

2. Select the layer you want to apply the Bevel and Emboss style.

3. Click the **Add Layer Style** button, and then click **Bevel And Emboss**.

4. Select the appropriate bevel or emboss.

5. Click **Contour**, and then select from the available options:

   ◆ **Contour.** Click the list arrow, and then select from the available options. Contours are mathematical curves that determine the brightness of the bevel or emboss at different levels (default: null curve).

   ◆ **Anti-aliased.** Select the check box to create a visually smooth bevel or emboss.

   ◆ **Range.** Enter a value from 1 to 100, or drag the slider left or right. Range determines range of the contour as it is applied to the image (default: 50).

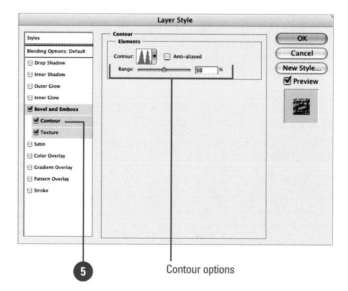

Contour options

See Also

See "Working with Bevel and Emboss" on page 278 for more information on using the contour option.

6 Click **Texture**, and then select from the available options:

◆ **Pattern.** Click the list arrow, and then select from the available Patterns. To add addition patterns from the Photoshop pattern library, click the Pattern Options button, located in the upper-right of the Pattern dialog box, and then select from the available pattern options.

◆ **Add To Presets.** Click the button to add the current pattern to Photoshop list of presets.

◆ **Snap To Origin.** Click the button to begin the pattern tiling from the upper left corner of the document layer.

◆ **Scale.** Enter a value from 1 to 1000 percent. Scale determines the size of the pattern as it applies to the active image (default: 100).

◆ **Depth.** Enter a value from -1000 to 1000 percent. Depth determines the intensity of the highlight and shadow areas in the texture. Negative numbers reverse the highlight and shadows (default: 100).

◆ **Invert.** Select the check box to reverse the color set of the pattern.

◆ **Link With Layer.** Select the check box to physically link the active pattern with the active layer (default: checked).

7 Click **OK**.

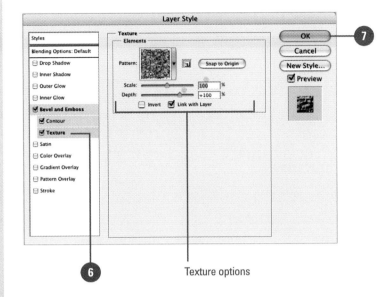

Texture options

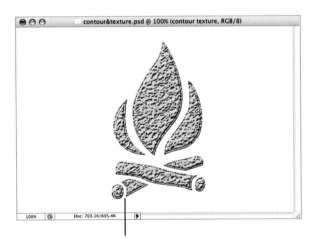

Contour and Texture style applied

Applying a Color Overlay

 PS 3.5

The Color Overlay style covers the elements of a layer with any color you choose. For example, you create some black text and you want to experiment with other colors, without changing the original color values of the text. Or, possibly apply the Blend Mode option, when you want to see how a specific color blends into the image. Whatever the case, Color Overlay temporarily masks the image with whatever color you choose. In addition, you can use the Color Overlay style with other layer styles to produce hundreds, if not thousands, of style combinations.

Apply a Color Overlay

1 Select the **Layers** palette.

2 Click the layer you want to apply the Color Overlay style.

3 Click the **Add Layer Style** button, and then click **Color Overlay**.

4 Select from the available Color Overlay options:

◆ **Blend Mode.** Click the list arrow, and then select from the available options. The Blend Mode option instructs Photoshop how to blend the selected Color Overlay with the colors of the active image (default: normal).

◆ **Color.** Click the Color swatch box, and then select any color from the Color Picker (default: red).

◆ **Opacity.** Enter a value from 0 to 100 percent. Opacity determines how much of the Color Overlay masks the original image pixels (default: 100).

5 Click **OK**.

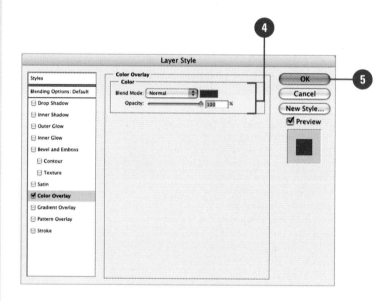

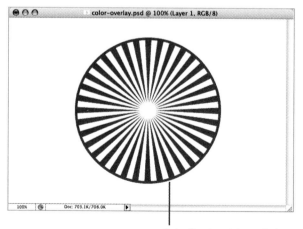

Color Overlay style applied

Using the Stroke Layer Style

Use the Stroke Layer Style

1. Select the **Layers** palette.

2. Select the layer you want to apply the Stroke Layer style.

3. Click the **Add Layer Style** button, and then click **Stroke**.

4. Select from the Stroke options:

   ◆ **Size.** Enter 1 to 250 pixels to define the width of the stroke.

   ◆ **Position.** Click the list arrow, and then select to place the stroke on the Outside, Inside, or Center of the layer object.

   ◆ **Blend Mode.** Click the list arrow, and then select from the available options. The Blend Mode option instructs Photoshop how to blend the selected Stroke color with the colors of the active image.

   ◆ **Opacity.** Enter an amount, or drag the slider left or right. Opacity determines how much of the Stroke masks the original image pixels (default: 100).

   ◆ **Fill Type.** Click the list arrow, and then select to create a stroke from a solid color, gradient or pattern.

   ◆ **Color.** Click the color box, and then select a color.

5. Click **OK**.

The Stroke Layer style lets you apply a stroke around any layer object. Since the stroke will be applied to the edge of the object, it must be surrounded by transparent pixels. For example, you could use the stroke feature to apply a solid color or gradient stroke to a group of text, or apply a stroke around an image. Strokes are not limited to solid colors, you can also use gradients, and even patterns as a stroke. The Stroke Layer style can provide you with many interesting styles.

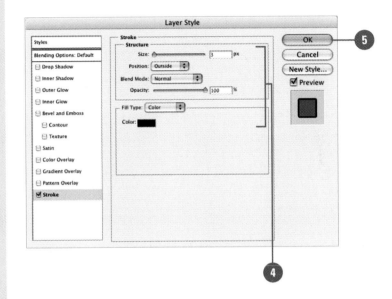

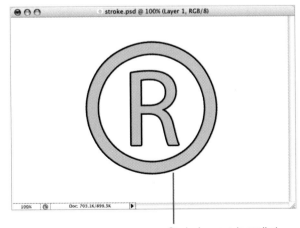

Stroke Layer style applied

Using Pattern Overlays

PS 3.5

Pattern Overlays replace the pixels in the active layer with a specific pattern. Photoshop comes equipped with dozens of pre-existing patterns, or you can create and save your own. Patterns can be used to spice up an otherwise dull area of an image—similar to covering a solid-color wall in your house with decorative wallpaper. When you apply a pattern, the original image is overlaid with the selected pattern, and once that's accomplished you can use blending modes and opacity to control the effect the pattern has over the original image.

Use Pattern Overlay

1. Select the **Layers** palette.

   IMPORTANT *Pattern Overlays, as all of Photoshop's layer styles, are applied to all the non-transparent pixels in the image. You cannot use selection to control what areas of the image are affected by the layer style.*

2. Click the layer you want to apply the Pattern Overlay style.

3. Click the **Add Layer Style** button, and then click **Pattern Overlay**.

4. Select from the available Pattern Overlay options:

   ◆ **Blend Mode.** Click the list arrow, and then select from the available options. The Blend Mode option instructs Photoshop how to blend the selected Pattern Overlay with the colors of the active image (default: Normal).

   ◆ **Opacity.** Enter a value from 0 to 100 percent. Opacity determines how much of the Pattern Overlay masks the original image pixels (default: 100). For example, 50 percent opacity would let 50 percent of the original image colors blend with the Pattern Overlay.

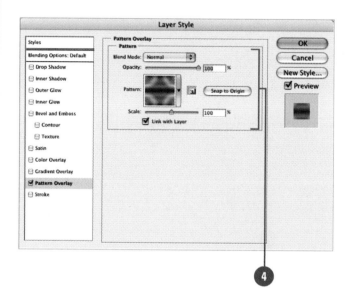

For Your Information

Using Pattern Overlays

You can use the pattern overlay on a photograph. Normally, a pattern completely covers the original image information; however, if you use the Blending Mode option when you apply the pattern, you can achieve some interesting results. Experiment with photographs and patterns using the Multiply, Screen, and Overlay blending modes to start. The style is a combination of the pattern, blending with the photograph.

◆ **Pattern.** Click the list arrow, and then select from the available Patterns. To add addition patterns from Photoshop pattern library, click the Pattern Options button, located in the upper-right of the pattern dialog box, and then choose from the available pattern options.

◆ **Add To Presets.** Click the button to add the current pattern to Photoshop list of presets.

◆ **Snap To Origin.** Click the button to begin the pattern tiling from the upper left corner of the document layer.

◆ **Scale.** Enter a value from 1 to 1000 percent. Scale determines the size of the pattern as it applies to the active image (default: 100).

◆ **Link With Layer.** Select the check box to physically link the active pattern with the active layer (default: checked).

⑤ Click **OK**.

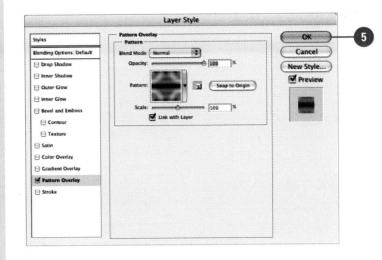

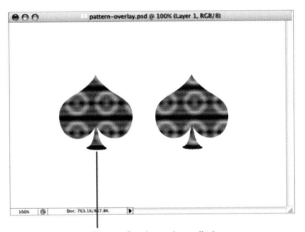

Pattern Overlay style applied

Did You Know?

You can reposition any Pattern Overlay. Click any pattern from the pattern library. However, before you click OK, move into the document window and drag. The pattern is repositioned as you drag. Click the Snap To Origin button to return the pattern to its default position.

12

Working with Outer Glow and Inner Shadow

 PS 3.5

Outer Glow applies a glow in any color you choose to all objects within the active layer. Since the Outer Glow style requires somewhere to work, the objects must be surrounded by transparent pixels. The Outer Glow style is an excellent way to create a neon effect to text. The Inner Shadow style applies a shadow to the inside of an object. Since the shadow is applied directly to the image, the Inner Shadow style does not require an image surrounded by transparent pixels. When you apply the Inner Shadow style, the shadow effect appears on the inside edges of the image—like a reverse drop shadow.

Apply an Outer Glow and Inner Shadow Style

1 Select the **Layers** palette.

2 Click the layer you want to apply the Outer Glow style.

3 Click the **Add Layer Style** button, and then click **Outer Glow**.

4 Select from the available Outer Glow options:

- ◆ **Structure.** Allows you to change Blending Mode and Opacity (determines how much of the Outer Glow masks the original image pixels), plus you can add a bit of Noise (introduces a random shift to the colors of the Outer Glow), and even change the Color or use a Gradient on the Outer Glow.

  For example, 50 percent opacity would let 50 percent of the original image colors blend with the Outer Glow.

- ◆ **Elements.** Allows you to change the Technique used (softer or more precise glow), as well as change the Spread and Size of the glow. The precise option creates a realistic, but more complex Outer Glow. Spread determines the amount of image is used for the spread of the glow.

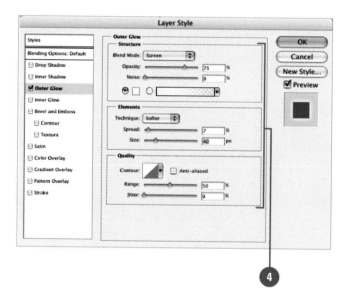

For Your Information

Creating Neon

You can create realistic neon using the outer glow layer style and text. Just create a text layer using a rounded font, such as Arial Rounded, or Brush, and then choose a neon color for the font, such as red or yellow. Apply an outer glow using a light yellow for the glow color. Place the text against a black Background layer (for effect), and then tweak the glow options until you see a realistic glow appear around the text. Add a Bevel and Emboss style to the text to complete the effect of a glowing neon sign.

◆ **Quality.** Allows you to access the Contour of the glow to create interesting special effects, select the Anti-aliased check box to visibly smooth the glow (or drop shadow), as well as change the Range of the contour and Jitter (random value of gradients) of the glow.

Contours are mathematical curves that determine the brightness of the glow at different levels.

⑤ Click **Inner Shadow** from the available styles.

⑥ Select from the available Inner Shadow options:

◆ **Structure.** Allows you to change Blending Mode and Opacity, as well as the Angle of the shadow. In addition, you can control the shadow's Distance, Choke and Size.

◆ **Quality.** Allows you to access the Contour of the shadow to create interesting special effects, select the Anti-aliased check box to visibly smooth the glow (or drop shadow), as well as add a bit of Noise to the final product.

⑦ Click **OK**.

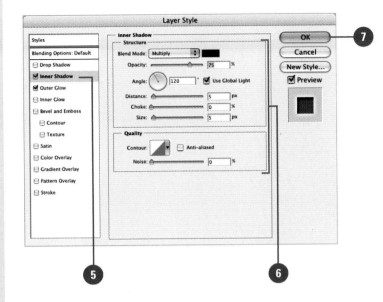

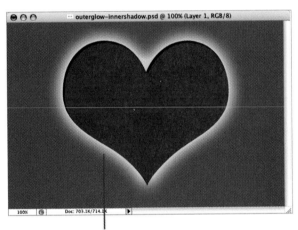

Outer Glow and Inner Shadow style applied

Applying an Inner Glow Style

The Inner Glow style creates the appearance of a glow on the inside of a layer object. For example, creating black text and applying an inner glow style, changes the object by lightening the edges of the text. Once you apply the inner glow, you can control the color size and intensity of the glow style to create the exact special effect you're after. You can also apply the Outer Glow style to the image, and the glow effect spreads out into the surrounding transparent areas of the layer.

Apply an Inner Glow Style

1. Select the **Layers** palette.

2. Click the layer you want to apply the Inner Glow style.

3. Click the **Add Layer Style** button, and then click **Inner Glow**.

4. Select from the available Inner Glow options:

   ◆ **Blend Mode.** Click the list arrow, and then select from the available options. The Blend Mode option instructs Photoshop how to blend the selected Inner Glow with the colors of the active image (default: Normal).

   ◆ **Opacity.** Enter a value from 0 to 100 percent, or drag the slider left or right. Opacity determines how much of the Inner Glow masks the original image pixels (default: 100).

   ◆ **Noise.** Enter a value from 0 to 100 percent, or drag the slider left or right. The noise option introduces a random shift to the colors of the Inner Glow (default: 0).

   ◆ **Solid Color.** Click the Solid Color swatch box, and then select a color from the Color Picker dialog box (default: light yellow).

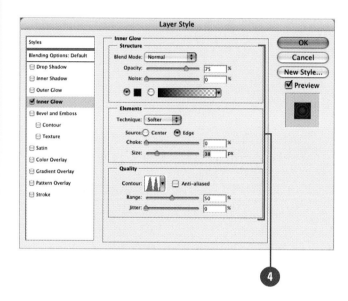

For Your Information

Creating Chiseled Text with Inner Glow

You can create realistic chiseled text using the Inner Glow style. Just create some white text, and apply an inner glow using a dark gray inner glow color. Add a dark Background layer, and the text appears as if it's chiseled into the background.

◆ **Gradient.** Click the Gradient list arrow, and then select a gradient (as opposed to a solid color) for the Inner Glow.

◆ **Technique.** Click the list arrow, and then select between a Softer, and a Precise Outer Glow. The precise option creates a realistic, but more complex Outer Glow.

◆ **Source.** Click the Center option to have the glow illuminate from center, or the Edge option to have the glow illuminate from the edge.

◆ **Choke.** Enter a value from 0 to 100 percent, or drag the slider left or right. Choke reduces the layer mask prior to blurring (default: 0).

◆ **Size.** Enter a value from 0 to 250 pixels, or drag the slider left or right. Size determines the size of the glow (default: 81)

◆ **Contour.** Click the list arrow, and then select from the available options.

◆ **Anti-aliased.** Select the check box to create a visually smooth Inner Glow.

◆ **Range.** Enter a value from 1 to 100, or drag the slider left or right. Range determines range of the contour as it is applied to the image (default: 50).

◆ **Jitter.** Enter a value from 1 to 100, or drag the slider left or right. Jitter increases or decreases the random value of gradients applied to the Inner Glow.

5 Click **OK**.

Gradient list arrow

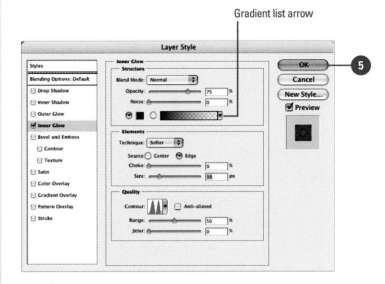

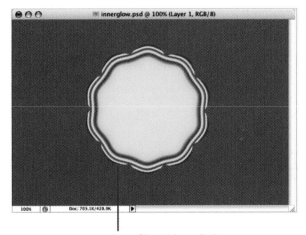

Inner Glow style applied

12

Creating Customized Layer Styles

Layer styles can be one or a combination of many styles. For example, you could create a layer style that includes a stroke, inner bevel, and gradient overlay. Once you create a layer style, its possible you might want to use it again. If that's the case, Photoshop gives you an easy way to create a layer style directly from the Layer Style dialog box, or using the Styles palette. Creating customized styles is a great time-saving feature, and not only speeds up the process of applying a style to a layer, but ensures that the style is applied in exactly the same way. That gives your designs a consistent look and feel.

Create Customized Layer Styles

1 Select the **Layers** palette.

2 Click the layer in which you want to apply a layer style.

3 Click the **Add Layer Style** button, and then click a style.

4 To add a style to an existing style, select the style from the styles list.

5 To modify an existing style, select from the various style options.

Did You Know?

You can combine elements of one layer style with another. Drag from one layer style into another. If you have two layers, both containing layer styles, and you want the drop shadow from one layer style added to the second layer, simply drag the drop shadow layer element to the other layer, to create a copy of the drop shadow. In addition, you can drag layer styles between two open documents.

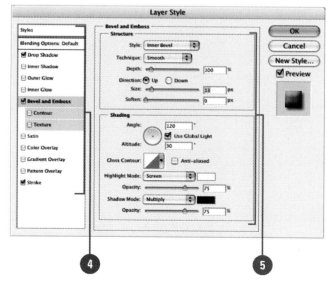

6 Click **New Style**, and then select from the following options:

◆ **Name.** Enter a name for the new layer style.

◆ **Include Layer Effects.** Select the check box to include any layer effects to the style.

◆ **Include Layer Blending Options.** Select the check box to include any blending mode options applied to the style.

7 Click **OK**.

8 Click **OK**.

If you open the Styles palette, you'll see the new style is added to the bottom of the current list.

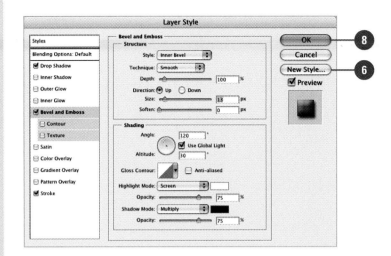

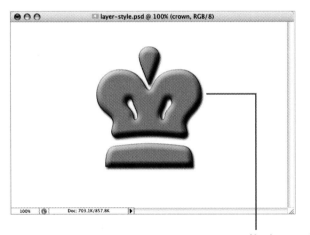

Newly created style applied

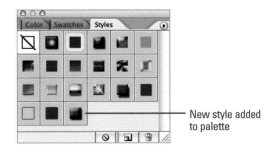

New style added to palette

12

Creating Customized Styles Using the Styles Palette

Creating customized styles using the Styles palette requires you have a layer with an applied style, and you want to save the style. If you do, you're only a button click away from saving the style into the Styles palette. When you create a layer style, the style appears as a sub-element of the layer. For example, creating a drop shadow, and inner glow layer style creates two sub-elements directly below the layer the styles were attached—one for the drop shadow and one for the inner glow. When you save a customized style, you select a layer, not an individual style, and save all the sub elements of that layer. To save a customized style with only the inner glow, you must first drag the drop shadow to the Delete Layer button.

Create Customized Styles

1. Select the **Layers** palette.

2. Select a layer that contains a layer style.

3. Select the **Styles** palette.

4. Move to the bottom of the Styles palette, and then click your mouse when you see the cursor change to a paint bucket.

Did You Know?

You can download additional styles from Adobe. In your Web browser, go to *www.adobe.com* and navigate to Adobe Studio Exchange for more styles.

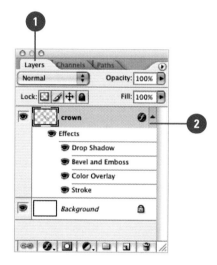

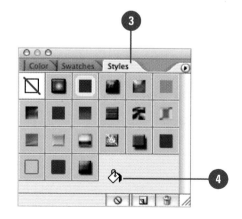

5 Select from the following options:

◆ **Name.** Enter a name for the new layer style.

◆ **Include Layer Effects.** Select the check box to include any layer effects to the style.

◆ **Include Layer Blending Options.** Select the check box to include any blending mode options applied to the style.

6 Click **OK**.

If you open the Styles palette, you'll see the new style is added to the bottom of the current list.

Did You Know?

You can share your styles with other Photoshop users. First click the Styles Options button, and then click Save Styles. The styles are now a file that can be e-mailed to any other Photoshop user. All the user has to do is click the Styles Options button, and then click the Load Styles option to load and use the new styles.

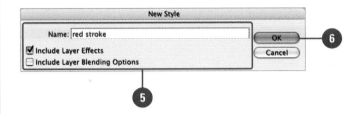

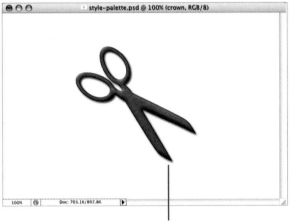

Customized style applied

Moving Existing Layer Styles

Once a layer style is applied to a layer, it can be moved to other layers, or into another document. This kind of flexibility and control lets you create specific layer styles and then apply them effortlessly to other layers or move them into other documents. In most cases it would make sense to save the style in the Styles palette. However, there are those times when you will only use the style once or twice. In that instance, a quick drag and drop is the most efficient way.

Move Existing Layer Styles

1. Select the **Layers** palette.

2. Click a layer that contains a layer style.

3. Click the **triangle** to expand the grouped layer styles.

4. Press the Alt (Win) or Option (Mac) key, and drag the grouped layer over another layer.

   Photoshop makes a copy of all the styles and applies them to the new layer.

Did You Know?

You can move individual styles between layers. Drag the named style, instead of the Effects group to move a single layer style instead of the entire group. When you release your mouse, the single layer style will be copied and applied to the new image.

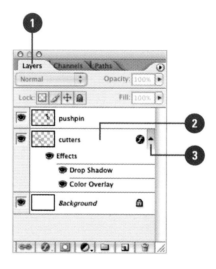

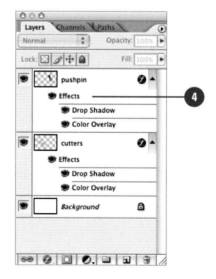

Getting Creative with Type

13

Introduction

The Type tool in Adobe Photoshop has advanced far beyond its humble beginnings. When Photoshop first appeared, the most you could expect from the Type tool was to enter text. Today it's a powerful and creative tool. Not only can you place text into any open Photoshop image, you can also use text as a mask, path, or even warp text into any shape you desire. In addition, Photoshop now preserves type without rastering. That means, that type created in Photoshop will print out as fine as type created in Adobe Illustrator, or InDesign; regardless of the image's resolution. When you work in Photoshop, type becomes as creative a design element as any other available feature.

Working with the Character palette gives you the ability to select a specific font, style, and size, as well as expand or contract the space between letters with leading and kerning, or you could simply increase or decrease the physical width of the text. Baseline shifting even gives you the ability to raise or lower text off the original line. In addition, the Paragraph palette lets you create automatic breaks between paragraphs, and align rows of text left, center, right, or force justify.

When you're working with large blocks of text, Photoshop's Spell Check command lets you identify and correct any misspelled words, and the Find and Replace feature makes quick work of identifying and replacing words or formats. You can isolate image pixels with a type mask to create words out of pictures. For example, you could type the phrase Fall is Coming, and use the image of leaves. The Type mask would make the words appear as if they were spelled out in colorful fall leaves. In addition, you could use a type mask in combination with Photoshop's layer styles to create text that almost leaps off the page. Working with text in Photoshop is more than typing words on paper, it's a process every bit as creative as working with graphic images.

Using Standard Type Tools

 PS 7.3

Photoshop comes with a set of standard typing tools, which are controlled in much the same way as any typing tools in any typing program. However, the creative possibilities go far beyond those of a standard typing program. When you work with the Type tools, you begin by typing some text, and then controlling the text, through the toolbox and the Options bar. Photoshop helps you maintain control over the text by automatically placing it in a separate type layer.

Use Standard Type Tools

1 Click and hold the **Type** tool on the toolbox, and then select the **Horizontal Type** tool.

2 Click in the document window and begin typing.

Photoshop creates a Type layer, and places the text in the layer.

IMPORTANT *When you work with the Type tools, the normal shortcut functions of the keyboard will not work. For example, holding down the Spacebar to access the Hand tool will only create a space at the insertion point of the text.*

3 Move your cursor to a point away from the text, and then drag to move the text.

Did You Know?

You can create type on a path.
Create a path using Photoshop's Pen tool, select the Type tool, and then click on the path. Photoshop creates an insertion point and when you type, the text follows the path.

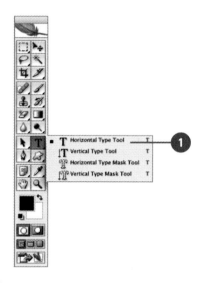

Text layer

4 Double-click to select a specific word, or drag across the text to select groups of words.

5 Change the text color by clicking the Options bar color swatch, and then choosing a new color from the Color Picker dialog box, or use the Swatches or Color palettes to select a new color.

6 Delete the text by clicking within the text and pressing the backspace key to erase one letter at a time, or select a group of text and press the Backspace (Win) or Delete (Mac) key.

7 Insert text by clicking within the text to create an insertion point, and then typing.

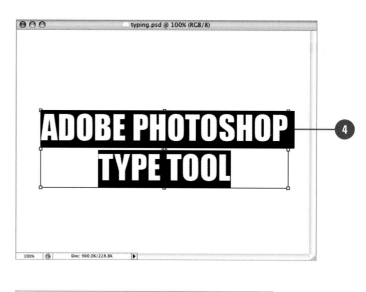

Did You Know?

You can edit type on a path.
To edit text at any time in the creative process, double-click on the Type layer thumbnail, or select the Type tool, and then click on the text.

See Also

See *"Creating a New Layer"* on page 100 for more information on creating layers.

For Your Information

Preserving Text to Print

Photoshop lets you preserve text to print. Photoshop's type options give you control over text in much the same way as high-end layout programs, and even allow you to save the vector nature of text. This allows you to print Photoshop images with crisp text that's not dependent on the resolution of the document.

To save a Photoshop document and preserve the text, click the File menu, point to Save As, and then choose the EPS (Encapsulated PostScript) format. Click the Include Vector Data option, and then save the file. The EPS document holds the type information and lets you print the document from any program including layout programs like InDesign, and Quark Xpress.

Working with Type Options

PS 7.3

Photoshop lets you control text through the type options, located on the Options bar. To access the Type options you must have one of Photoshop's Type tools selected. It is not necessary to change type options after typing. If you know what you're after, you can set the options, and then commence typing. However, if the need arises to change the text, Photoshop comes to the rescue with a host of type options, such as font family, size, color, justification, even high-end type processing controls like leading and kerning. You can preview font families and font styles directly in the Font menu (**New!**). Font names appear in the regular system font, and a sample word ("Sample") appears next to each font name, displayed in the font itself.

Work with Type Options

1. Open a document.

2. Select the **Type** tool on the toolbox.

3. To toggle between horizontal and vertical type, click the **Change Text Orientation** button on the Options bar.

   If this option is selected on a pre-existing type layer, the text switches between horizontal and vertical.

4. Click the **Font Family** list arrow, and then select from the fonts available on your computer.

5. Click the **Font Style** list arrow, and then select from the font styles available on your computer.

6. Click the **Font Size** list arrow, and then select from the pre-set font sizes, measured in points (6 to 72).

   Photoshop uses a standard Postscript measuring system of 72 points to the inch.

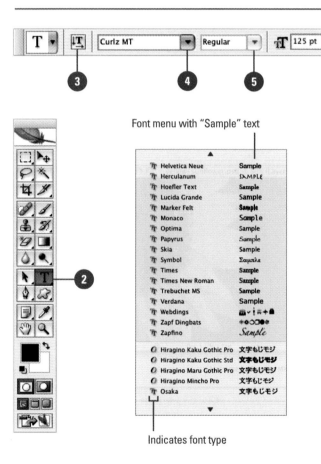

Font menu with "Sample" text

Indicates font type

7 Click the **Anti-aliasing** list arrow, and then select from the available options.

Anti-aliasing creates text that is visually smoother to the eye.

8 Click the **Left**, **Center**, or **Right Justification** button.

Justification balances text created on two or more vertical or horizontal lines.

9 Click the **Color Swatch** button, and then select a color from the Color Picker dialog box.

10 Click the **Warped Text** button to apply special warped text effects to text.

11 Click the **Toggle The Character And Paragraph Palettes** button to show the palettes or to turn them off.

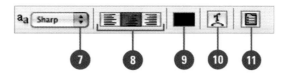

Anti Aliased - ON

Anti Aliased - OFF

Did You Know?

You can use non pre-set font sizes from the Options bar. Select the current point size on the Options bar, type a point size, and then press Enter (Win) or Return (Mac).

You can change font attributes with the Character palette. Click the Character palette, select the text you want to change, and then use the options on the Character palette.

See Also

See "Using the Warp Text Option" on page 304 for information on warping text in your document.

Frequently Asked Questions

What's the Difference Between the Fonts?

Everything you type appears in a font, a particular typeface design and size for letters, numbers, and other characters. Usually, each typeface, such as Times New Roman, is made available in four variations: normal, bold, italic, and bold italic. There are two basic types of fonts: scalable and bitmapped. A **scalable font** (also known as **outline font**) is based on a mathematical equation that creates character outlines to form letters and numbers of any size. The two major scalable fonts are Adobe's Type 1 PostScript and Apple/Microsoft's TrueType or OpenType. Scalable fonts are generated in any point size on the fly and require only four variations for each typeface. A **bitmapped font** consists of a set of dot patterns for each letter and number in a typeface for a specified type size. Bitmapped fonts are created or prepackaged ahead of time and require four variations for each point size used in each typeface. Although a bitmapped font designed for a particular font size will always look the best, scalable fonts eliminate storing hundreds of different sizes of fonts on a disk.

Working with the Character Palette

 PS 7.3

Each version of Photoshop brought it closer to becoming a true typesetting application, and with the ability to preserve text layers, and work through high-end type controls, that time has finally arrived. You can work through the Character options without having any Type layers. However, if you select the text in a Type layer, the changes made will impact the selected text. Changes made to the active type layer do not impact any other type layers, and only the text actually selected in the type layer will be changed.

Use the Character Palette

1 Open a document.

2 Select the **Type** tool on the toolbox.

3 Click the **Toggle The Character And Paragraph Palettes** button on the Options bar.

4 Select the **Character** palette.

5 Select from the following options:

◆ **Font Family.** Click the list arrow, and then select a font family from the fonts available on your computer.

◆ **Font Style.** Click the list arrow, and then select a font style, such as Regular, Bold, Oblique, and Italic. If the font family you select does not have any styles, this box will be grayed out.

◆ **Font Size.** Click the list arrow, and then select from the preset font sizes, measured in points (6 to 72). Photoshop uses a standard Postscript measuring system of 72 points to the inch.

◆ **Kerning.** Click the list arrow, and then select from the preset values for kerning. Kerning adds or subtracts space between two characters.

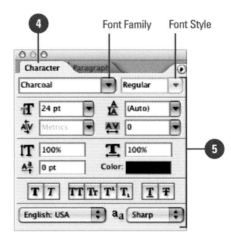

Font Family   Font Style

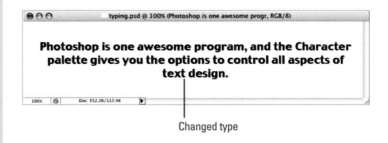

Changed type

◆ **Leading.** Click the list arrow, and then select from the pre-set values for leading. Leading adds or subtracts space vertically between lines of text.

◆ **Tracking.** Click the list arrow, and then select from the pre-set values for Tracking. Tracking adds or subtracts space between words.

◆ **Vertical Scale.** Enter a value to change the vertical scale. Vertical Scale increases or decreases the vertical height of the text.

◆ **Baseline Shift.** Enter a value to set the Baseline Shift. Baseline Shift raises or lowers selected text, using the baseline as a reference.

◆ **Horizontal Scale.** Enter a Value to change the Horizontal Scale. Horizontal Scale increases or decreases the width of the text.

◆ **Font Color.** Click the color swatch, and then select a color from Photoshop's Color Picker dialog box.

◆ **Font Attributes.** Click the buttons to select additional font attributes, such as Underline, and Strikethrough.

◆ **Spelling And Hyphenation.** Click the list arrow, and then select a language reference for Spelling And Hyphenation.

◆ **Anti-aliasing.** Click the list arrow, and then select from the available options. Anti-aliasing creates text that is visually smoother to the eye.

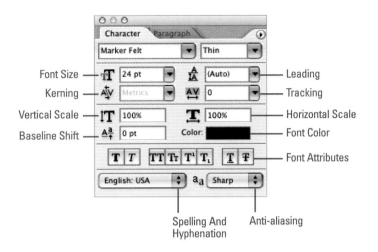

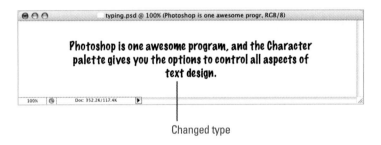

Changed type

13

For Your Information

Using the Character Palette

The function of the Character palette is to give you precise control over the elements of a paragraph. Unlike the Character palette, it is not necessary to select a paragraph to change it; you only need to have the insertion point of the cursor inside the paragraph you want to change. Photoshop as well as other type and layout programs, define a paragraph as the times between the pressing of the Enter (Win) or Return (Mac) key. For example, you press the Enter key and type several sentences, when you press the Enter key again, the cursor jumps to the next line and you continue typing. The pressing of the Enter (Win) or Return (Mac) key defined the end of one paragraph and the beginning of another.

Working with the Paragraph Palette

PS 7.3

Each version of Photoshop brought it closer to becoming a true typesetting application, and with the ability to preserve text layers, and work through high-end type controls, that time has finally arrived. You can work through the Paragraph options without having any Type layers. However, since paragraph styles are applied to paragraphs of type, not individual letters or words, if you select a Type layer, the changes made with the Paragraph palette will be applied to the text within the layer without the necessity of selection.

Use the Paragraph Palette

1 Open a document.

2 Select the **Type** tool on the toolbox.

3 Click the **Toggle The Character And Paragraph Palettes** button on the Options bar.

4 Select the **Paragraph** palette, and then select from the following options:

♦ **Justification.** Click to choose from the various Justification methods.

♦ **Indent Left Margin.** Enter a value to indent the left margin (values from -1296 to 1296).

♦ **Indent First Line.** Enter a value to indent the first line of the paragraph (-1296 to 1296).

♦ **Indent Right Margin.** Enter a value to indent the right margin (values from -1296 to 1296).

♦ **Space Before Paragraph.** Enter a value to increase or decrease the space before each new paragraph (-1296 to 1296).

♦ **Space After Paragraph.** Enter a value to increase or decrease the space after each paragraph (values from -1296 to 1296).

♦ **Hyphenate.** Select the check box to hyphenate long words at the end of text lines.

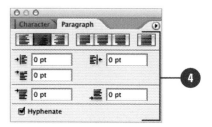

4

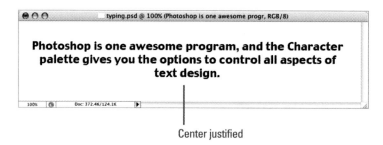

Photoshop is one awesome program, and the Character palette gives you the options to control all aspects of text design.

Center justified

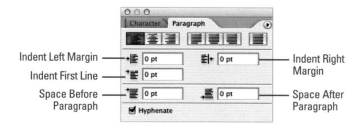

Indent Left Margin · Indent First Line · Space Before Paragraph · Indent Right Margin · Space After Paragraph

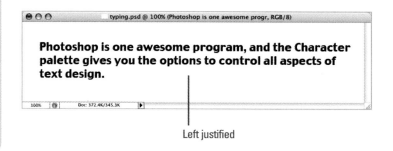

Photoshop is one awesome program, and the Character palette gives you the options to control all aspects of text design.

Left justified

Setting Anti-Aliasing Options

 PS 7.3

Photoshop's Anti-aliasing option helps to make text appear smoother by painting the edges of the text with semi-transparent colors. When text is displayed on a raster monitor, the text is built using pixels, and since pixels are essentially bricks, the edges of curved type have a tendency to look ragged. By painting the edges of the text with semi-transparent pixels, the type blends into the background, creating a smoother look. Unless you apply a gradient or mask, text is typically one color; activating anti-aliasing can increase the colors (at the edge) to 6 to 10. While this works to make the text smoother, it will also make small text (under 12 points) harder to read. The trick with anti-aliasing is to experiment with the various options to determine which one works the best, and that means occasionally turning anti-aliasing off.

Set Anti-Aliasing Options

1. Open a document that contains a type layer.

2. Select the **Type** tool on the toolbox.

3. Select the **Layers** palette, and then select the layer containing the text.

4. Click the **Anti-aliasing** list arrow on the Options bar, and then select from the following options:

   ◆ **None.** Turns off anti-aliasing.

   ◆ **Sharp.** Creates visually sharp type in the active layer.

   ◆ **Crisp.** Creates crisp type (not as sharp, as the Sharp option).

   ◆ **Strong.** Creates a heavier (bolder) type.

   ◆ **Smooth.** Creates type with a smooth appearance.

   IMPORTANT *The anti-aliasing option is only applied to the type in the active type layer.*

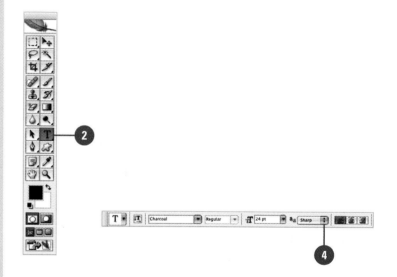

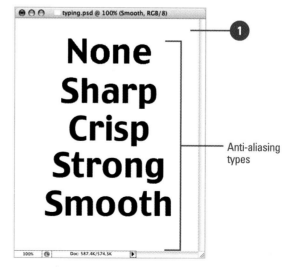

Anti-aliasing types

Using the Warp Text Option

Photoshop's Warp Text option gives you creative control over the look of text. No longer are you confined to straight vertical or horizontal text. In the Photoshop world, text can be created in almost any size and shape. As an additional bonus, warping text does not require converting the text into a raster. So days later, you can access the warped text, change its font family, size, and color. It's all about control… in this case, controlling text.

Use Warp Text

1 Open a document.

2 Select the **Type** tool on the toolbox, and then select a type layer in the Layers palette or create a new type.

3 Click the **Warp Text** button.

4 Click the **Styles** list arrow, and then select from the following style options:

- ◆ Arc
- ◆ Arc Lower
- ◆ Arc Upper
- ◆ Arch
- ◆ Bulge
- ◆ Shell Lower
- ◆ Shell Upper
- ◆ Flag
- ◆ Wave
- ◆ Fish
- ◆ Rise
- ◆ Fisheye
- ◆ Inflate
- ◆ Squeeze
- ◆ Twist

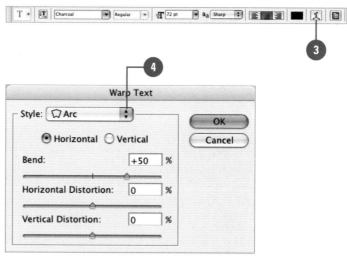

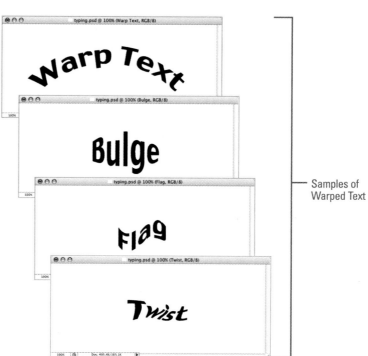

Samples of Warped Text

5 Click the **Horizontal** or **Vertical** option to warp the text in a horizontal or vertical direction.

6 Enter a percentage value in the Bend box, or drag the slider left or right (-100 to 100). Bend controls the physical amount of bend applied to the text, based on warp style.

7 Enter a percentage value in the Horizontal Distortion box, or drag the slider left or right (-100 to 100). Horizontal Distortion controls the amount of distortion on the horizontal axis applied to the text based, on warp style.

8 Enter a percentage value in the Vertical Distortion box, or drag the slider left or right (-100 to 100). Vertical Distortion controls the amount of distortion on the vertical axis applied to the text, based on warp style.

9 Click **OK**.

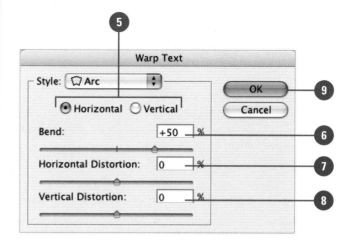

For Your Information

Designing with Warp Text

The Warp Text option is a great way to draw attention to a heading or word within a Photoshop document. However, warp text can be extremely hard to read, so use it sparingly. Think of the overall design of the image, and then ask yourself if the warp text supports the mood and message of the image. If it doesn't, then don't use it. Don't fall into the designer's trap of using every new feature you come across. If it doesn't support the message, use something else, like a layer style gradient, or bevel and emboss.

Using Spell Check

There's nothing more embarrassing than creating a document that contains misspelled words. Although you wouldn't use Photoshop to create a text document, Photoshop includes a fully functional spell checking system, which at least lets you make sure all of your words are spelled correctly.

Use Spell Check

1. Open a document that contains one or more Type layers.

   You do not need to have the Type tool selected to perform a spell check.

2. Click the **Edit** menu, and then click **Check Spelling**.

3. When Photoshop encounters a word not in its dictionary, it displays the word in the Not In Dictionary box, and gives you one of the following options:

   ◆ **Ignore.** Ignore this word one time.

   ◆ **Ignore All.** Ignore all instances of this word.

   ◆ **Change.** Photoshop will give you a list of possible alternative spellings. Select one from the Suggestions box, and then click Change.

   ◆ **Change All.** Change all occurrences of the word, based on the selected suggestion.

   ◆ **Add.** Add the word to Photoshop's dictionary.

   Photoshop continues to highlight misspelled words until the document is completely scanned.

4. When you're finished, click **Done**.

The highlighted word has been identified by spell checker.

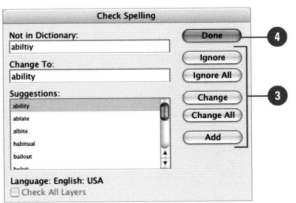

Finding and Replacing Text

In the editing process, it is sometimes helpful to find and replace a particular word or phrase because the text needs to be changed, either locally or globally, throughout the document. The Find and Replace Text command make it easy to locate or replace specific text in a document.

Use Find and Replace

1. Open a document that contains one or more type layers.

2. Click the **Edit** menu, and then click **Find and Replace Text**.

3. Enter the text to locate in the Find What box.

4. Select from the following Find and Replace Text options:

   ◆ **Search All Layers**. Select the check box to search all type layers.

   ◆ **Forward**. Select the check box to search forward through the document.

   ◆ **Case Sensitive**. Select the check box to search for the word in the same case as typed in the Find What box.

   ◆ **Whole Word Only**. Select the check box to search for whole words as typed in the Find What box.

5. Enter the text to replace the text in the Change To box.

6. Click **Find Next** to locate the next occurrence of the word:

   ◆ Click **Change** to change the word.

   ◆ Click **Change All** to change all occurrences of the word.

   ◆ Click **Change/Find** to automatically change the word and locate the next occurrence.

7. When you're finished, click **Done**.

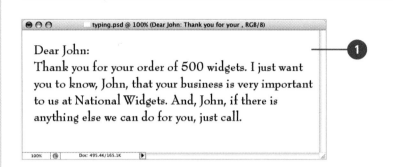

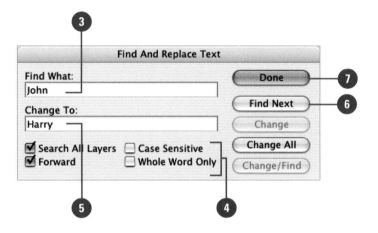

Using the Rasterize Type Command

When you are working with type, some commands, filters, and painting tools are not available. To continue working, you must first rasterize the type layer. When you rasterize a type layer, you're converting the type into pixels, and once the rasterize operation is complete, the text within the type layer is no longer a font. Therefore, make sure you like the font family, and it's spelled correctly before rastering. Once complete, you can now apply commands and filters normally reserved for non-text images.

Use Rasterize Type

① Open a document containing one or more type layers.

② Select the **Layers** palette, and then select one of the type layers.

③ Click the **Layer** menu, point to **Rasterize**, and then select from the following commands:

◆ **Type.** Click the command to rasterize the type in the active layer.

◆ **Layer.** Click the command to rasterize the contents of the active layer (does not have to be type).

The Type layer is converted into a standard layer, and all of Photoshop's painting tools, filters, and commands will work on the information in the layer.

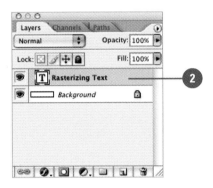

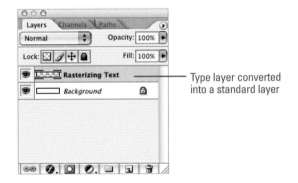

Type layer converted into a standard layer

Rasterize Type applied

Creating Work Paths and Shapes from Type Layers

When you work with type, there are certain restrictions to what you can do. You can't apply filter effects to type, and many of Photoshop's commands do not function with type. One solution is to rasterize the type layer. However, rasterized type is converted to pixels. What if you want the text converted into a vector path? Once type is saved as a path, you can manipulate it like any other vector path. The text path is no longer considered text; however the original type layer is intact, and editable. Creating a path and at the same time preserving the original type layer, gives you the best of both creative worlds.

Create Work Paths

1. Open a document containing a type layer.

2. Select the **Layers** palette, and then select one of the type layers.

3. Click the **Layer** menu, point to **Type**, and then click **Create Work Path**.

   IMPORTANT *Paths cannot be created from fonts that do not contain outline data, such as bitmap fonts.*

4. Select the **Paths** palette.

5. Select any of Photoshop's Pen tools to modify the path.

See Also

See Chapter 11, "Using the Paths Palette," on page 253 for more information on the Paths palette.

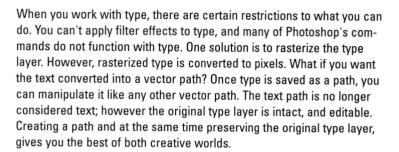

Work Path is created

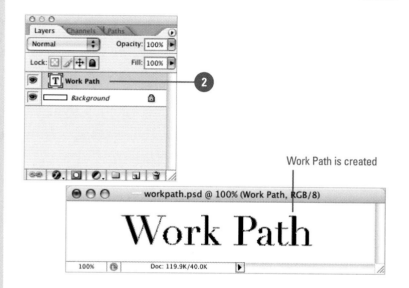

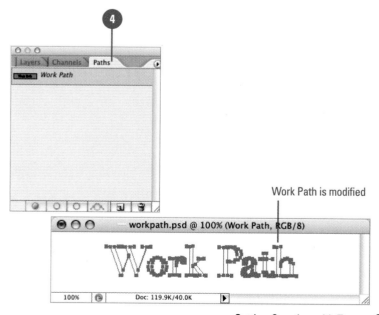

Work Path is modified

Creating Shape Layers

When you convert a type layer into a shape layer, the type layer is converted into a layer with a vector mask. In essence, Photoshop fills the layer with the color of the text, and then creates a vector mask to define the type. Once created, the vector mask can be edited just like any other vector shape.

Create Shape Layers

1. Open a document containing a type layer.

2. Select the **Layers** palette, and then select one of the type layers.

3. Click the **Layer** menu, point to **Type**, and then click **Convert To Shape**.

    IMPORTANT *When you convert a type layer into a shape layer, Photoshop removes the type layer and replaces it with the shape layer. You gain the ability of manipulating the image as a vector shape; however, you lose the ability to edit the type.*

4. Click the **Vector Mask** thumbnail in the Layers palette, and then edit the mask using any of Photoshop's Pen tools.

Did You Know?

You can change the fill color of the text in your document. Click the Image Thumbnail, and then fill the area with a color, pattern, or gradient.

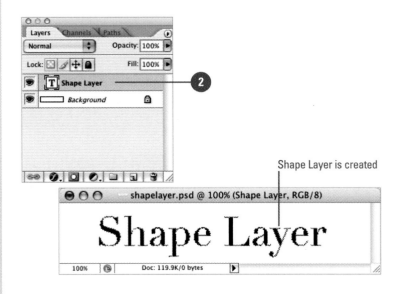

Shape Layer is created

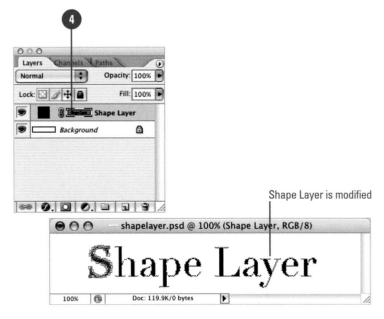

Shape Layer is modified

Creating a Type Mask ▶

Photoshop has two type tools—the Horizontal or Vertical type tools and the Horizontal or Vertical Mask tools. The former creates regular type, using the fonts available on your computer system, and when you add type to the screen, the color of the font defaults to the current foreground color. The latter is a masking tool. When you use the type mask tools, Photoshop creates a mask in the size and shape of the selected font with the mask appearing as a red overlay. Once the mask is created, you can modify it just like any normal text layer, by changing the font, size, or even use the Warp feature. Unlike the normal type tools, Photoshop does not create a type layer for the mask; the mask simply appears in the active layer. Being able to create a mask from a font opens up all kinds of creative possibilities. For example, you could use a mask in conjunction with a photograph to create a unique fill or you could use a mask to create a chiseled look to text.

Create a Type Mask

1. Open a document.

2. Select the **Horizontal Type Mask** tool on the toolbox.

3. Click in the document window to place an insertion point, and then type.

   As you type, Photoshop creates a mask in the size and shape of the current font.

4. Use the editing tools on the mask to change its font family, style, and size.

   IMPORTANT *Masks, like regular text, must be selected before any of the above changes are applied.*

5. Select the **Marquee** tool on the toolbox, or any other of Photoshop's selection tools.

   The mask converts from a red overlay into a traditional selection.

6. Move into the interior of one of the letters, and then drag to move the selection.

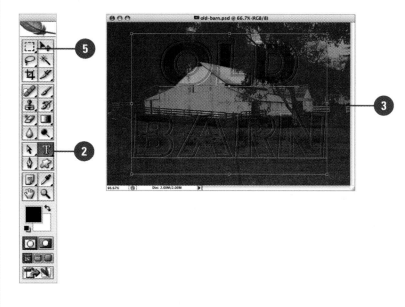

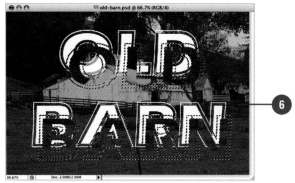

Isolating Image Pixels Using a Type Mask

One of the advantages to a mask is you can create type using any fill you desire. For example, you're doing an advertising piece for a real estate company in California, and you want something unique for the text, so you get an image of the plains, create a type mask with the words SUNSET and then use the image and mask to create a unique fill.

Isolate Image Pixels

1 Open a document containing the image you want to mask.

2 Select the **Layers palette**, and then select the layer containing the image.

3 Select the **Horizontal Type Mask** tool on the toolbox.

4 Click in the document window to place an insertion point, and then type.

As you type, Photoshop creates a mask in the size and shape of the current font.

IMPORTANT *If you want a lot of the image to show through the mask, use a large, thick mono-weight font, like Impact.*

5 Use the editing tools on the mask to change its font, style, and size.

Did You Know?

You can move the mask after you've converted it into a selection. Click any selection tool, and then drag from inside the selection. The selection area will move without modifying the actual image. In addition, you can use your arrow keys to gently nudge the selection left, right, up, or down.

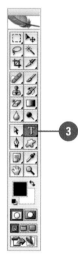

6 Select the **Marquee** tool on the toolbox, and then position the mask directly over the portion of the image you want inside the text.

7 Click the **Select** menu, and then click **Inverse**.

8 Press the Backspace (Win) or Delete (Mac) key to delete the inverse selection.

The Invert command reversed the selection and the deletion removed all the pixels outside the mask.

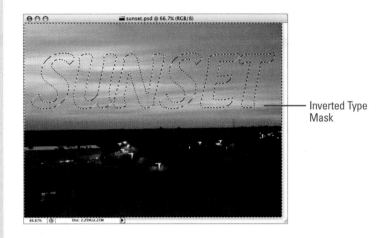

Inverted Type Mask

Did You Know?

You can use Photoshop's adjustment tools to control the selection. Instead of deleting the surrounding image, click the Image menu, point to Adjustments, and then click Levels. Move the middle gray slider left or right to increase or decrease the brightness of the surrounding pixels. That way the text will stand out against the original image background.

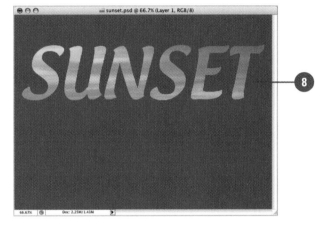

Creating Chiseled Type with a Type Mask

This technique is great for creating three-dimensional text on any image. For example, you could use this technique to create the extended text on a plastic credit card, or words chiseled in marble. The technique is simple, but the results are impressive. Using the Bevel and Emboss layer style generates the effect, and the trick is it darkens the upper-left portions of the selection, while lightening the lower-right portions. This creates the illusion of a light source falling across a concave or chiseled surface.

Create Chiseled Type

1. Open a document containing the image you want to use for the chisel effect.

2. Select the **Layers** palette, and then select the layer containing the image.

3. Select the **Horizontal Type Mask** tool on the toolbox.

4. Click in the document window to place an insertion point, and then type.

   As you type, Photoshop creates a mask in the size and shape of the current font.

5. Use the editing tools on the mask to change its font, style, and size.

   IMPORTANT *You'll need a thick sans serif font, like Arial Black, or Impact.*

6. Select the **Marquee** tool on the toolbox, and then position the mask directly over the portion of the image you want the words to appear.

7. Press Ctrl+J (Win) or ⌘+J (Mac).

   Photoshop creates a copy of the image pixels inside the type mask, and then places them in a layer directly above the active layer.

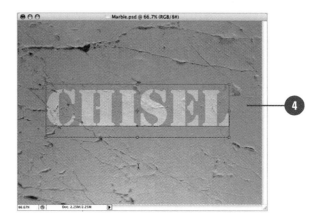

4

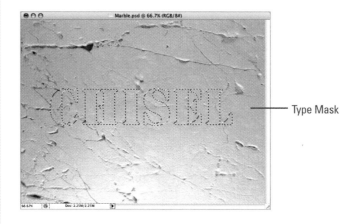

Type Mask

8 Click the layer containing the copied image pixels.

9 Click the **Add Layer Style** button, and then click **Bevel & Emboss**.

10 Select from the following options that will give the text the appearance of being chiseled:

+ **Style.** Inner Bevel

+ **Technique.** Chisel Hard

+ **Depth.** ~150%

+ **Direction.** Down

11 Click **OK**.

See Also

See Chapter 12, "Working with Layer Styles," on page 273 for more information on using layer styles.

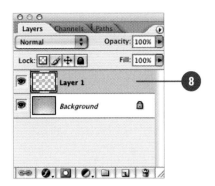

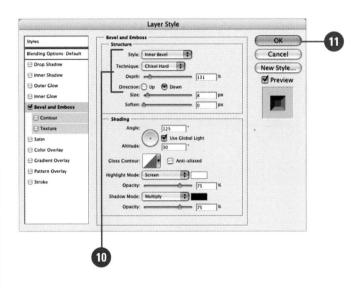

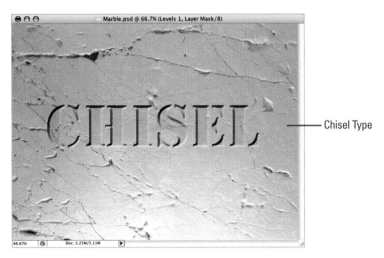

Chisel Type

Using Masks to Generate Special Effects

Using Type masks to generate unique fills or three-dimensional text are great features. However, one thing is always predictable, and that's the shape of the text. The mask created with the Type Mask tool will always follow the curve and shape of the font used to create the mask; but not if you combine a Type Mask with a Layer Mask. For example, you create a marketing piece where you are using the words RADICAL, and you want the edges of the word to be more dramatic. You've looked at some of Photoshop's Brush Stroke Filters, but you don't want to apply the filter to the image, just the edges of the word. That's where Type masks and Layer masks do their magic. By combining a Type and Layer mask, you can achieve exactly what you want using an image to fill type, and modifying the edges of the type without distorting the image.

Use Masks for Special Effects

1. Open a document containing the image you want to use for the type effect.

2. Select the **Layers** palette, and then select the layer containing the image.

3. Select the **Horizontal Type Mask** tool on the toolbox.

4. Click in the document window to place an insertion point, and then type.

   As you type, Photoshop creates a mask in the size and shape of the current font.

5. Use the editing tools on the mask to change its font, style, and size.

   IMPORTANT *Sans serif fonts, like Impact, always work best when you're using images to mask text; however, experiment with different fonts.*

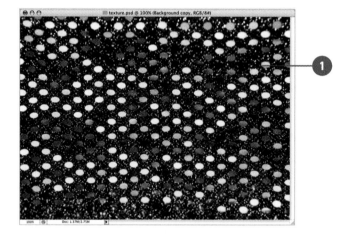

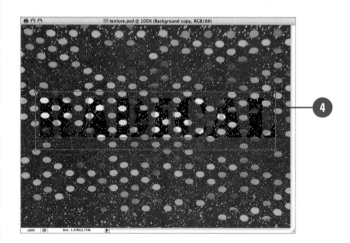

6 Select the **Marquee** tool on the toolbox, and then position the mask directly over the portion of the image you want inside the text.

7 Select the **Layers** palette.

8 Click the **Add Layer Mask** button.

Photoshop creates a layer mask from the type mask, and then selects the layer mask.

IMPORTANT *The Background cannot hold a layer mask. If the layer designated as the masking layer is background, move into the Layers palette and double-click on the Background thumbnail, give it a new name, and then click OK.*

9 Click the **Filters** menu, point to **Brush Strokes**, and then click **Spatter**.

10 Modify the Brush Stroke options until you see a good image.

- ◆ Sprayed Radius
- ◆ Smoothness

11 Click **OK**.

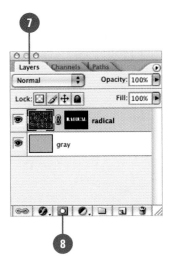

13

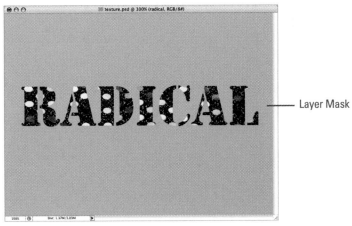

Layer Mask

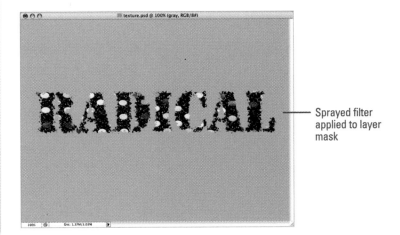

Sprayed filter applied to layer mask

Creating and Modifying Text on a Path

Using the type options, you can enter type that flows along the edge of a work path created by the Pen or Shape tool. When you enter type along a path, it flows in the direction in which anchor points were added to the path. For example, creating horizontal type on a path create type that are perpendicular to the baseline, and creating vertical type on a path creates type parallel to the baseline. Once the type is created, selecting the Direct Selection tool allows you to reshape the path, and the type will change to fit the new form of the path.

Create and Modify Text on a Path

1. Select a **Pen** or **Shape** tool on the toolbox, and then create a path.

2. Select a typing tool (horizontal, or vertical type or mask tools) on the toolbox.

3. Position the pointer directly over the path, and then click once.

   The path now has an insertion point added to the line.

4. Type the text you want. As you type, the words flow along the curve of the path.

5. Select the **Direct Selection** tool on the toolbox to access and modify the path by controlling the position and shape of the anchor points.

6. Select the **Path Selection** tool and click at the front of the text to move the text forward and backward on the path.

See Also

See Chapter 11, "Using the Paths Palette," on page 253 for more information on using and controlling the Pen and Shape tools.

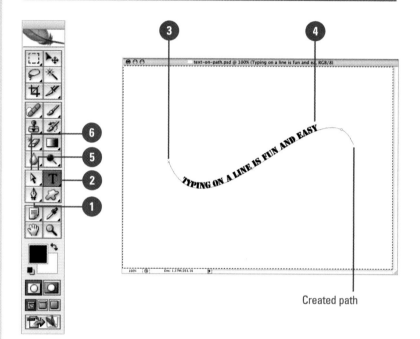

Created path

For Your Information

Printing Type on a Path

The path does not appear when the document is printed. If you want to see how the image will appear without the path, click the View menu, point to Show, and then click to uncheck the Target Path. To view the path, recheck the Target Path option.

Manipulating Images with Filters

Introduction

Adobe Photoshop filters are a designer's dream come true. With filters you can turn a photograph into an oil painting or a watercolor; even change night into day. Photoshop's Filter menu includes no less than 105 (6 **New!**) highly creative filters, which can be applied once, reapplied, or combined with other filters to create any effect your imagination can dream up.

In addition, the filter menu includes Extract, Liquify, and the Pattern Maker. The possible combination of filters and images literally runs into the millions. This means that Photoshop filters are truly an undiscovered territory. As a matter of fact, the Filter Gallery lets you view the effects of one or more filters on the active document. This level of power gives you unbelievable creative control over your images.

Other commands, such as the Fade command, let you reduce the effect of the applied filter, and even apply a blending mode to the final image. In addition, you can utilize a channel mask to control how the filter is applied to the image. You could use a black to white gradient channel mask to slowly fade the effects of the filter from left to right.

Photoshop even lets you protect you intellectual property by embedding a definable watermark into the image that is almost invisible to see, and virtually impossible to remove. In fact, you can print an image that contains a watermark, run it off on a copy machine and rescan, and the watermark is still there. Now that's protection.

Take a moment to view some of the various filter effects that Photoshop offers. Because there are 105 filters available, we can't show you all of them, but I think you'll enjoy viewing the selection at the end of the chapter.

What You'll Do

Work with the Filter Gallery

Apply Multiple Filters to an Image

Modify Images with Liquify

Work with Liquify Tool Options

Work with Liquify Mask Options

Work with Liquify View Options

Create a Liquify Mesh

Apply a Liquify Mesh

Use the Lens Blur Filter

Work with Photo Filters

Blend Modes and Filter Effects

Build Custom Patterns

Use the Fade Command

Control Filters Using Selection

Use a Channel Mask to Control Filter Effects

Protect Images with Watermarks

View Various Filter Effects

Working with the Filter Gallery

The Filter Gallery maintains complete and total control over Photoshop's filters. In essence, the Filter Gallery gives you access to all of Photoshop's filters and lets you apply the filters to any raster image, while viewing a large preview of the results. The Filter Gallery dialog box is composed of three sections—Image Preview, Filter Selection, and Filter Controls. When you use the Filter Gallery to modify the image, you see exactly how the image will look; there is no guesswork involved. When you apply a filter to an image you are physically remapping the pixel information within the image. Photoshop contains 105 filters and the combinations of those filters are astronomical. If you are a math wizard, there are over 100 million combinations available, and that means that no one has discovered all the ways you can manipulate an image in Photoshop... have fun trying.

Work with the Filter Gallery

1. Open a document.

2. Select the **Layers** palette, and then select the layer you want to modify with a filter effect.

3. Click the **Filters** menu, and then click **Filter Gallery**.

4. Change the image preview by clicking the plus or minus zoom buttons, or by clicking the black triangle and selecting from the pre-set zoom sizes.

5. If necessary, drag the lower-right corner in or out to resize the Filter Gallery dialog box.

6. Click the **expand triangle**, located to the left of the individual categories, to expand a filter category. Filter categories include:

   ◆ Artistic

   ◆ Brush Strokes

   ◆ Distort

   ◆ Sketch

   ◆ Stylize

   ◆ Texture

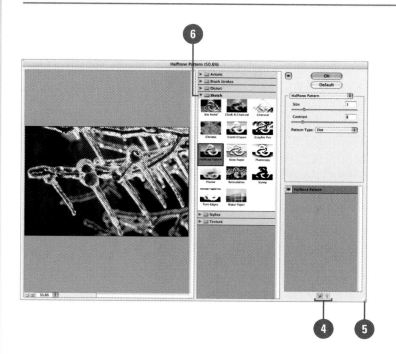

7 Click a filter from the expanded list to view its default effects to the image.

8 Modify the effects of the filter using the filter controls.

9 To temporarily hide the Filter Selections, click the **Hide Filter Section** button, located to the left of the OK button.

10 Click **OK**.

Did You Know?

You can reapply a specific filter effect using a shortcut. Press Ctrl+F (Win) or ⌘+F (Mac) to reapply the last filter to the image.

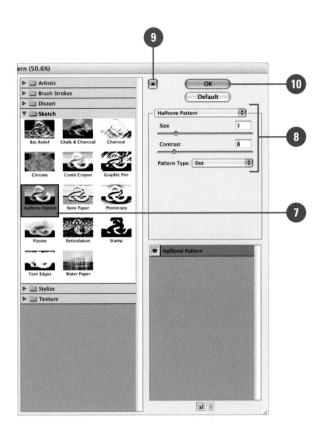

Applying Multiple Filters to an Image

 PS 9.3

Not only does Photoshop's Filter Gallery let you apply and view a filter effect, it lets you view the multiple effects of two or more filters. The Filter Gallery has its own Layers palette, and can have a lot of effect layers. The order of the filters influences their impact on the image. When you create a filter effect using more than one filter, drag the filter effect up or down in the effects stack. Changing the order of the filters changes their impact on the image, so experiment with different stacking orders to create eye-popping special effects.

Apply Multiple Filters to an Image

1 Open a document.

2 Select the **Layers** palette, and then select the layer you want to modify with a filter effect.

3 Click the **Filters** menu, and then click **Filter Gallery**.

4 Select the filter you want.

5 Adjust the filter as necessary.

6 Click the **New Layer Effect** button, located at the bottom of the Filter Adjustments section. You can add as many effects layers as needed.

7 Select and adjust a second filter (repeat steps 4 and 5).

TIMESAVER *If you want to give an image a second application of the last used filter, there's no need to repeat the filter process, simply select a layer, and press Ctrl+F (Win) or ⌘+F (Mac).*

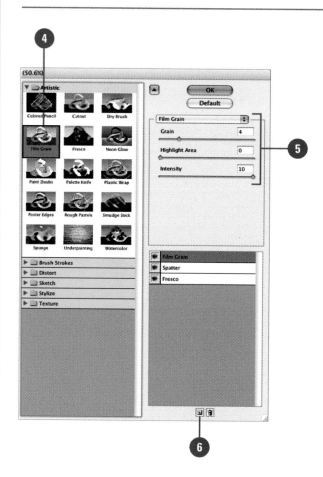

8 Adjust each individual effect by clicking on the effect layer you want to change.

9 To change filter influence on the image, drag an effect layer to another position in the stack.

10 To temporarily show or hide the effect on the image, click the **Show/Hide** button.

11 To delete a selected effect layer, click the **Delete** button.

12 Click **OK**.

IMPORTANT *Once you click the OK button, the effects are moved from the effects layers in the Filter Gallery and permanently applied to the active image.*

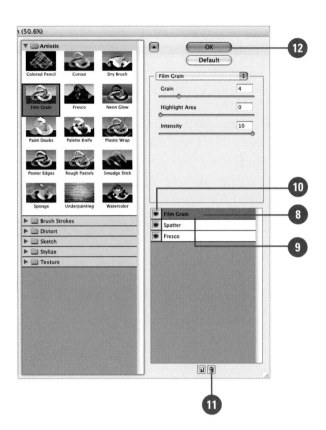

14

Modifying Images with Liquify

The Liquify filter gives you amazing control over an image. For example, you can distort the image pixels almost as if the image were an oil painting that had yet to dry. In addition, you can magnify specific areas of an image or reduce them in size. The Liquify filter lets you push, pull, rotate, reflect, pucker, and bloat any area of an image. The distortions you create can be subtle or drastic, which makes the Liquify command a powerful tool for retouching images as well as creating artistic effects.

Modify Images with Liquify

① Open a document.

② Select the **Layers** palette, and then select the layer you want to liquify.

③ Click the **Filters** menu, and then click **Liquify**.

④ Select from the following Liquify tools:

- ◆ **Forward Warp.** Pushes pixels in front of the brush as you drag.

- ◆ **Reconstruct.** Drag the image, using a specific brush size to restore previously modified areas of the image.

- ◆ **Twirl Clockwise.** Click in an area to twirl the pixels (contained inside the brush tip) clockwise. To twirl counter clockwise, hold down the Alt (Win) or Option (Mac) key.

- ◆ **Pucker.** Click and hold to move pixels towards the center of the brush tip.

- ◆ **Bloat.** Click and hold to move pixels away from the center of the brush tip.

- ◆ **Push Left.** Drag to push pixels to the left of the brush tip. For example, dragging straight up pushes pixels to the left, and moving to the right pushes pixels up.

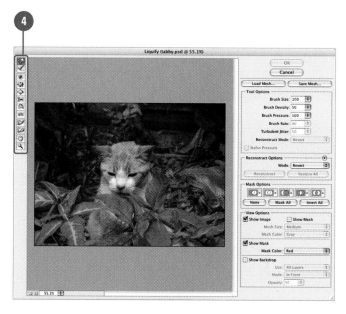

Forward Warp

Twirl Clockwise

- ◆ **Mirror.** Drag to copy pixels to the left of the stroke.

- ◆ **Turbulence.** Smoothly scrambles the pixels in an image. Creates realistic waves or fire.

- ◆ **Freeze.** Paints a mask over an area of the image, and then protects that area from change.

- ◆ **Thaw.** Erases the mask created with the Freeze tool.

- ◆ **Hand.** Drag to move the visible image. Useful if the image is larger than the physical document window.

- ◆ **Zoom.** Click to zoom in on a specific area of the image. Click and drag to define an area to zoom in on. Hold down the Alt (Win) or Option (Mac) key and click to zoom out.

5 Click **OK**.

Bloat

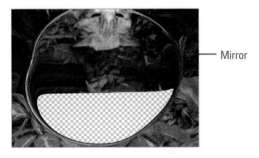

Mirror

Turbulence

Working with Liquify Tool Options

The Liquify Tool options control the brush tip. Since all the Liquify commands are executed with a brush, it's important to understand how you control the brush tip. When you apply the brush stroke the faster you drag the mouse the less effect is applied to the image; if you drag slowly, you gain more control and the effect is more intense. Practice dragging the cursor over the image to produce different effects, and if you make a mistake, don't forget the undo key—Ctrl+Z (Win), ⌘+Z (Mac).

Work with Liquify Tool Options

1. Open a document.

2. Select the **Layers** palette, and then select the layer you want to liquify.

3. Click the **Filters** menu, and then click **Liquify**.

4. Select from the following Liquify Tool options:

   ◆ **Brush Size.** Select a value (1 to 600).

   ◆ **Brush Density.** Select a value (0 to 100). Brush Density controls how much the brush feathers at the ends. Lower values equal increased feathering.

   ◆ **Brush Pressure.** Select a value (1 to 100). Determines how quickly a liquify effect is applied to the image, when the brush is moving. The lower the value, the slower the effect.

   ◆ **Brush Rate.** Select a value (0 to 100). Determines how quickly a liquify effect is applied to the image, when the brush is stationary. The lower the value, the slower the effect.

   ◆ **Turbulent Jitter.** Select a value (1 to 100). Controls how tightly the Turbulent Jitter tool distorts the image. The higher the value, the more distortion.

Liquify Tool options

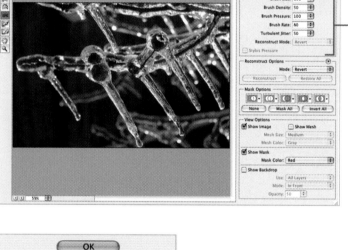

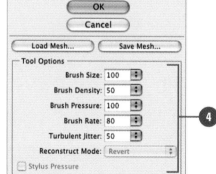

- **Reconstruct Mode.** Determines how the Reconstruct tool restores the image. Click the list arrow, and then select from the available options:

  - Revert
  - Rigid
  - Stiff
  - Smooth
  - Loose

- **Reconstruct.** Click the button to reconstruct the image stage by stage.

- **Reconstruct All.** Click the button to restore the image to its original state.

- **Stylus Pressure.** Select the check box if you're using a drawing table to allow pressure on the table to control pressure applied with the Liquify brush.

5 Click **OK**.

Working with Liquify Mask Options

When you work with an image that contains a selection or mask, you can use that information to control how the Liquify command adjusts the image. Think of the mask as a visual representation of the work areas of the image. Creating a mask gives you precise control over what portions of the image are modified.

Work with Liquify Mask Options

1. Open a document.

2. Select the **Layers** palette, and then select the layer containing a selection or mask.

3. Click the **Filters** menu, and then click **Liquify**.

4. Select from the following Liquify Mask options:

   ◆ **Replace Selection.** Shows the selection, mask, or transparency in the original image.

   ◆ **Add To Selection.** Shows the mask in the original image, so you can then add to the selection using the Freeze tool.

   ◆ **Subtract From Selection.** Subtracts pixels in channel from current freeze.

   ◆ **Intersect With Selection.** Uses only pixels that are selected and currently frozen.

   ◆ **Invert Selection.** Removes Image Information with Extract.

5. Click **OK**.

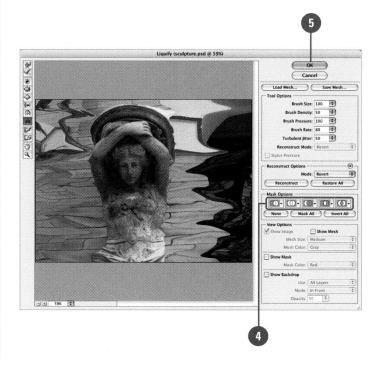

Working with Liquify View Options

The Liquify View Options control what you see in the preview window. For example, you can choose to view or hide a mask; even change its color. If the image you're working on is in a transparent layer you can even choose to view the image with or without the other image layers. How you view the image is up to you; however, having choices gives you greater control over the final results.

Work with Liquify View Options

1 Open a document.

2 Select the **Layers** palette, and then select the layer containing a selection or mask.

3 Click the **Filters** menu, and then click **Liquify**.

4 Select from the following Liquify View options:

- ◆ **Show Image.** Shows/hides the active image preview.

- ◆ **Show Mesh.** Displays a mesh (grid) over the image preview.

- ◆ **Mesh Size.** Select between a Small, Medium, or Large mesh.

- ◆ **Mesh Color.** Select a color for the mesh.

- ◆ **Show Mask.** Shows/hides the mask.

- ◆ **Mask Color.** Select a color for the mask.

- ◆ **Show Backdrop.** Shows/hides the backdrop.

- ◆ **Use.** Select what layers are displayed in the image preview.

- ◆ **Mode.** Displays the active layer In Front, Behind, or Blended with the other layers.

- ◆ **Opacity.** Determines the blending opacity between the individual layers.

5 Click **OK**.

Creating a Liquify Mesh

You may have noticed the Load Mesh and Save Mesh buttons, located at the top of the Liquify dialog box. A **mesh** is a predefined Liquify operation. When you activate the mesh option, a mesh or grid is placed over the image, and then as you use the Liquify tools, the mesh distorts and bends. After applying a lot of work to a particular image, it's quite possible you might want to use that exact Liquify on another image. That's where the Load and Save Mesh options come into play. With a click of a button you can create a mesh and use it over and over again.

Create a Liquify Mesh

1. Open a document.

2. Select the **Layers** palette, and then select the layer you want to liquify.

3. Click the **Filters** menu, and then click **Liquify**.

4. Select the **Show Mesh** check box.

5. Use the Liquify tools to adjust the image.

6. Click **Save Mesh**.

7. Enter a descriptive name, such as Fire, or Crashing Waves, for the mesh.

8. Click **Save**.

9. Click **OK**.

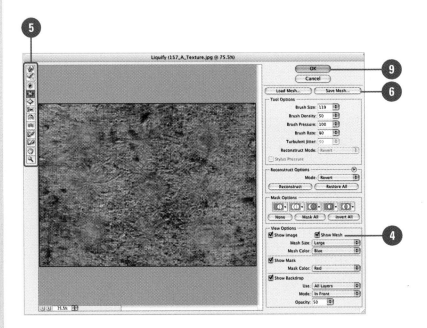

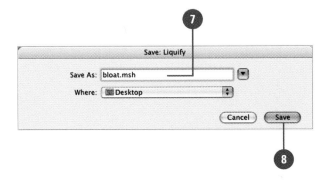

Did You Know?

You can display the distortion created by the Liquify tools. Check this option to display a mesh (grid) over the image preview. When you select the Show Mesh check box, a mesh is applied to an image, which distorts as you apply the Liquify tools. When you clear the Show Image check box (turning off the Image), you get a visual grid that represents the distortion values applied to the image.

Applying a Liquify Mesh

Applying a mesh to an image is a lot easier than redoing a particular Liquify operation and to be honest, it would be virtually impossible to reproduce a Liquify adjustment from scratch. That's why Adobe gives you the option of creating, saving, and loading your very own personalized meshes.

Apply a Liquify Mesh

① Open a document.

② Select the **Layers** palette, and then select the layer you want to liquify.

③ Click the **Filters** menu, and then click **Liquify**.

④ Select the **Show Mesh** check box.

⑤ Click **Load Mesh**.

⑥ Select a mesh.

⑦ Click **Open**.

The distortions generated by the mesh are applied to the image.

⑧ Click **OK**.

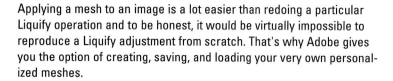
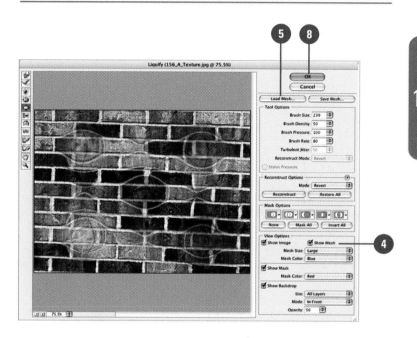

Did You Know?

You can modify a loaded mesh. Open a mesh, and then use the Liquify options to further distort the mesh pattern. That way you can create a generic mesh pattern and modify the pattern to fit any design need.

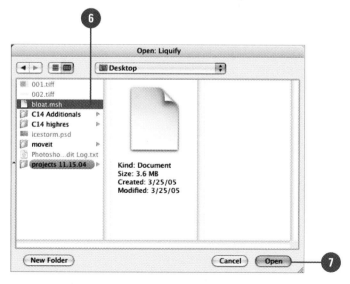

Using the Lens Blur Filter

The Lens Blur filter creates a varying depth of field so that certain objects stay in focus and others areas become blurred. What stays in focus and what blurs is determined by a user-defined selection or alpha channel. When the filter is activated, a depth map is created to determine the 3-dimensional position of the pixels in an image. If you use an alpha channel, the black areas in the alpha channel are at the front of the photo, and the white areas are in the distance. Experiment with selections and alpha channel masks to see how precisely you can control the visual effect of blurring in an image.

Use the Lens Blur Filter

1. Open a document.

2. Select the **Layers** palette, and then select the layer in which you want to apply the Lens Blur.

3. Create a selection or alpha mask to control the blur.

4. Click the **Filter** menu, point to **Blur**, and then click **Lens Blur**.

   The Lens Blur dialog box opens.

See Also

See "Using the Gaussian Blur and Despeckle Filters" on page 154 for information on using filters.

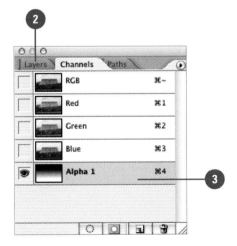

5 Select from the following options:

◆ **Preview.** Select Faster to generate quicker preview, or More Accurate to view the image with the filter applied.

◆ **Depth Map.** Select a source from the Source list arrow.

◆ **Blur Focal Distance.** Drag the slider to set the depth to which pixels are in focus. The higher the value the greater the effect.

◆ **Invert.** Inverts the selection or alpha channel.

◆ **Shape.** Select an iris option from the Shape list arrow.

◆ **Radius.** Drag the slider to add more blur.

◆ **Blade Curvature.** Drag the slider to smooth out the edges of the iris.

◆ **Rotation.** Drag the slider to rotate the iris.

◆ **Brightness.** Drag the slider to increase the brightness of the highlights.

◆ **Threshold.** Drag the slider to select a brightness cutoff so that all the pixels that are brighter than that value are treated as highlights.

◆ **Amount.** Drag the slider to add or remove noise.

◆ **Uniform or Gaussian.** Select one or the other to add noise to an image.

◆ **Monochromatic.** Adds noise without affecting the color in your image.

6 Click **OK**.

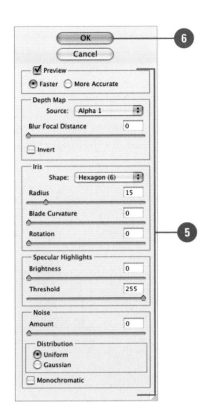

Image with Lens Blur filter applied

Working with Photo Filters

The Photo Filter command acts as if you placed a colored filter in front of the camera lens. Photographers place colored filters in front of a camera lens to adjust the color balance of the image and control the color temperature of the light transmitted through the lens. In addition to simulating a color filter, the Photo Filter command also lets you select a color preset and apply a specific hue adjustment to an image, and if you want to apply a custom color adjustment, the Photo Filter command lets you specify a user-defined color using the Adobe Color Picker.

Work with Photo Filters

1. Open a document.

2. Select the **Layers** palette, and then select the layer in which you want to apply the Photo Filter.

3. Click the **Image** menu, point to **Adjustments**, and then click **Photo Filter**.

4. Select the **Preview** check box to view the results of the color filter directly in the active document window.

5. Select from the following options:

   ◆ **Filter.** Click the list arrow, and then select from the available filter presets.

   ◆ **Color.** Click the color box, and then select a color using the Color Picker dialog box.

   ◆ **Density.** Drag the slider to increase or decrease the impact the color has on the image.

   ◆ **Preserve Luminosity.** Select the check box to prevent the image being darkened by adding a color filter (recommended).

6. Click **OK**.

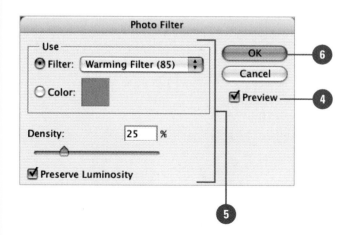

Blending Modes and Filter Effects

When Adobe introduced the Filter Gallery in Photoshop CS, it finally gave designers the ability to view the effects of multiple filters applied to a single image. While this changed forever how we apply filters to an image, there is one more creative way to work: Blending Modes. For example, make a copy of an image, then apply a separate filter effect to each layer, and then use the Blending Modes option to create a totally different image. While this is not a new technique, the results of combining two or more layers together, each with a different filter effect can produce quite stunning results.

Work with Blending Modes and Filters Effects

1. Open an image.

2. Select the layer containing the image you want to modify.

3. Press Ctrl (Win) or ⌘ (Mac) + J to create a copy of the selected layer.

4. Select the layers one at a time and apply a different filter to each layer.

5. Select the top layer.

6. Click the **Blending Modes** list arrow and experiment with the various blending options.

In this example, the Cutout and Find Edges filters were used on the separate layers, and then combined with the Linear Light Blending Mode.

> ### Did You Know?
>
> *You can use the Opacity option to further control the final image.* If the blending effect appears a bit too intense, simply lower the opacity of the top, or bottom layer to change the intensity of the filter effects.

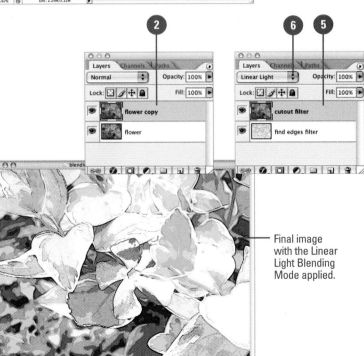

Final image with the Linear Light Blending Mode applied.

Building Custom Patterns

PS 2.6

Build Custom Patterns

1. Open a document.

2. Select the **Layers** palette, and then select the layer you want to use for a Pattern.

3. Click the **Filters** menu, and then click **Pattern Maker**.

4. Select the **Rectangular Marquee** tool on the toolbox, and then select a portion of the image.

5. Select the portion of the image you want to generate an image.

6. Click **Generate** to create a random pattern based on the selected sample.

7. Click **Generate Again** to generate another random pattern.

> **IMPORTANT** *All the generated patterns are stored in the History box, located on the bottom-right of the Pattern Maker dialog box.*

8. Select from the available Tile Generation options:

   ◆ **Use Clipboard As Sample.** Uses the pixel information contained in the Clipboard as the tile-generating pattern.

   ◆ **Use Image Size.** Creates a tile pattern the size of the original image.

The Pattern Maker filter lets you create you own distinctive patterns, based on image information in the active document, or clipboard memory. Since the pattern is based on a sample data, it shares the visual characteristics of the sample. For example, if you sample an image of a cloudy sky, the Pattern Maker generates a tile-like pattern that is different from the sample but is still retains the elements of a cloudy sky. You can even generate multiple patterns from the same sample.

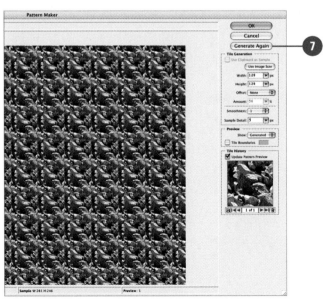

◆ **Width.** Enter a value (1 to 800), or click the black triangle and drag the slider left or right to define a width.

◆ **Height.** Enter a value (1 to 800), or click the black triangle and drag the slider left or right to define a height.

◆ **Offset.** Click the list arrow, and then click None, Horizontal, or Vertical.

◆ **Amount.** Enter a percentage value (1 to 100), or click the black triangle and drag the slider left or right.

◆ **Smoothness.** Click the list arrow, and then select a value of 1, 2, or 3.

◆ **Sample Detail.** Enter a value from 3 to 21, or click the black triangle and drag the slider left or right.

◆ **Show.** Click the list arrow, and then select between the generated sample, and the original image.

◆ **Tile Boundaries.** Select the check box to view the tile edges in the preview window. Click on the color box, and then select an alternate color.

9 Scroll through your tile patterns using the left/right arrow keys underneath the Tile History preview. Stop when you see the pattern you want.

10 Click **OK**.

IMPORTANT *When you click OK, the Pattern Maker filter over-writes the original image, so it's a good idea to make a copy of the image in a separate layer before using the Pattern Maker filter.*

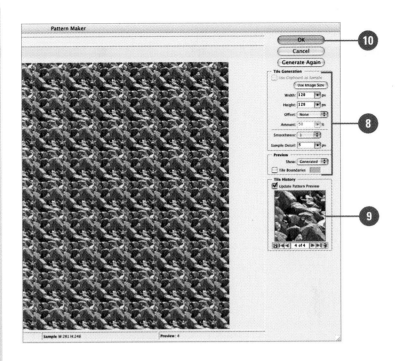

For Your Information

Using Pattern Maker

Custom patterns can be generated from any RGB, Grayscale, CMYK, or Lab mode graphic image. In addition, when you create a pattern the original image is overwritten with the new pattern, so you can use the generated pattern, reopen the Pattern Maker filter, and then create new patterns from the pattern you just created.

Using the Fade Command

Photoshop's Fade command is a one-shot chance to change you mind. For example, you've just applied a Find Edges filter to an image. You like the look but the effect is too dramatic. What you really want to do is slowly fade the effect. Unfortunately filter effects don't fade; they are simply applied to the image. You could create a copy of the original layer, apply the effect to the copy, and then use Layer transparency and blending mode options to merge the effect to the image, but there's an easier way, and that's using the Fade command.

Use the Fade Command

1. Open a document.

2. Select the **Layers** palette, and then select the layer you want to apply a filter.

3. Click the **Filters** menu, and then click **Filter Gallery**.

4. Apply any of Photoshop's filters to the active image.

5. Click **OK**.

6. Click the **Edit** menu, and then click **Fade**. The Fade command includes the name of the applied filter.

   IMPORTANT *The Fade command must be executed before performing any other command. Once you execute another command, the ability to modify the last filter is lost.*

7. Change the Opacity and Mode settings until you see the effect you're after.

8. Click **OK**.

Did You Know?

You can use the Fade command with almost any filter or drawing tool. Every time you draw, use a command or filter, the Fade command gives you a one-shot chance to fade and blend.

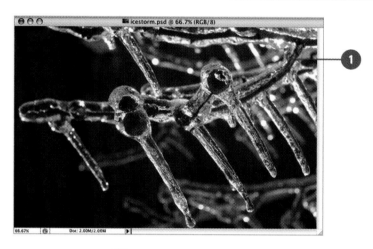

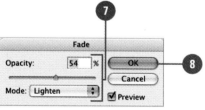

Filter effect and
Fade applied

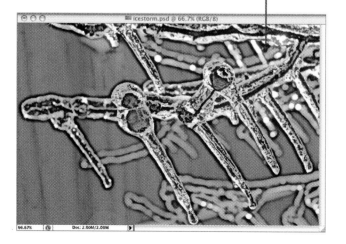

Controlling Filters Using Selection

When you apply a filter to an image, Photoshop applies the filter equally to the entire image. Unfortunately, that might not be what you had in mind. For example, you might want to apply the Gaussian Blur filter to a portion of the image. In that case, Photoshop's selection tools come to the rescue. The primary purpose of selection is to define a work area, and when you select an area before applying a filter, the only area impacted by the filter will be the selected area.

Control Filters Using Selection

1. Open a document.

2. Select the **Layers** palette, and then select the layer you want to apply a filter.

3. Click one of the selection tools on the toolbox, and then create a selection in the document window.

4. Click the **Filters** menu, and then click **Filter Gallery**.

5. Click any of Photoshop filters.

6. Adjust the filter options until you see the image you want.

7. Click **OK**.

   The filter is only applied to the selected areas of the image.

See Also

See Chapter 4, "Mastering the Art of Selection," on page 77 for more information on creating selections.

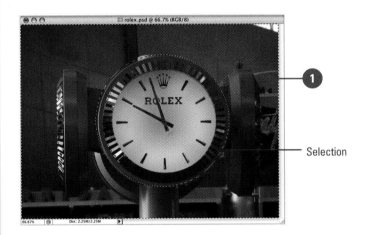

Selection

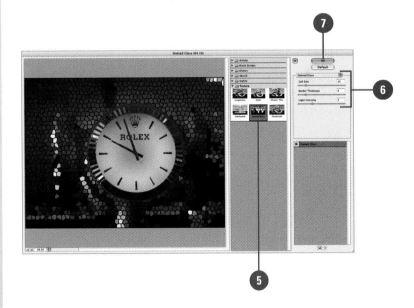

14

Using a Channel Mask to Control Filter Effects

Photoshop's filters can be applied to any raster image. In addition, filters can be controlled with the use of selections. You can use any of Photoshop's selection tools to define a working area. However, sometimes selections are somewhat limited in what they can do. Although selections can be feathered, they basically represent a cookie-cutter work area. What if you want to apply a filter in a completely different way? For example, you want to apply a filter that is more aggressive on the right side of the image, and slowly tapers off from left to right? In that case a simple selection won't help, but a Channel mask will do exactly what you need.

Use a Channel Mask to Control Filter Effects

1. Open a document.

2. Click the **Channels** palette, and then click the **Add New Channel** button.

3. Select the **Gradient** tool on the toolbox, click a linear gradient, default the foreground and background colors to black and white, and then drag left to right across the new channel mask.

   Photoshop creates a horizontal black to white, channel mask.

4. Select the **Layers** palette, and then select the layer containing the image you want to modify.

See Also

See Chapter 10,"Creating Layer and Channel Masks," on page 231 for information on using Channel Masks.

5 Click the **Select** menu, and then click **Load Selection**.

6 Click the **Channel** list arrow, select the new channel, and leave the other options at their default values.

7 Click **OK**.

8 Click the **Filters** menu, and then click **Filter Gallery**.

9 Click any of the available filters, and then adjust the options until you see what you want.

10 Click **OK**.

The gradient mask (black to white) creates a ramped percentage selection. The white area of the mask is fully selected and the black area is fully masked. As the mask moves to black, the image became less and less selected. When the filter was applied, it lost strength from left to right (matching the shades of gray in the mask).

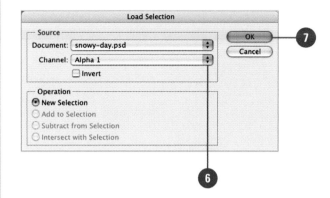

Protecting Images with Watermarks

Digital watermarks are designed to protect your intellectual property. When you embed a digital watermark, it actually inserts the watermark information as visible noise into the image. This means that someone can copy your image, scan it, and the watermark is still part of the image. To embed a digital watermark, you must first register with Digimarc Corporation; which maintains a database of artists, designers, and photographers and their contact information. You can then embed the Digimarc ID in your images, along with information such as the copyright year or a restricted-use identifier.

Protect Images with Watermarks

1. Open the image you want to watermark.

   IMPORTANT *The Embed Watermark filter won't work on an image that has been previously watermarked.*

2. If you're working with a layered image, you should flatten the image before watermarking it; otherwise, the watermark will affect the active layer only.

3. Click the **Filter** menu, point to **Digimarc**, and then click **Embed Watermark**.

4. If you're using the watermark for the first time, click **Personalize**. Get a Digimarc ID by clicking Info to launch your Web browser and visit the Digimarc Web site at *www.digimarc.com*.

   Enter a Digimarc ID and any other necessary information, and then click OK.

   The Personalize button becomes a Change button, allowing you to enter a new Digimarc ID.

5. Click the **Image Information** list arrow, select an option, and then enter a copyright year, Transaction ID, or Image ID for the image.

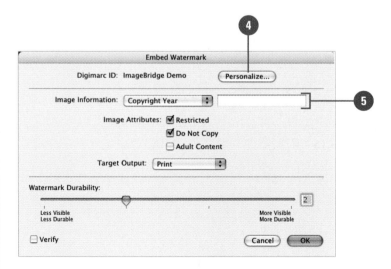

6 Select any of the following Image Attributes check boxes:

◆ **Restricted.** Select the check box to limit the use of the image.

◆ **Do Not Copy.** Select the check box to specify the image should not be copied.

◆ **Adult Content.** Select the check box to label the image contents as suitable for adults only.

7 Click the **Target Output** list arrow, and then specify whether the image is intended for Monitor, Web, or Print.

8 Drag the slider, or enter a value (1 to 4). The higher the number, the more aggressive the watermark.

9 To automatically assess the watermark's durability after it's embedded, select the **Verify** check box.

10 Click **OK**.

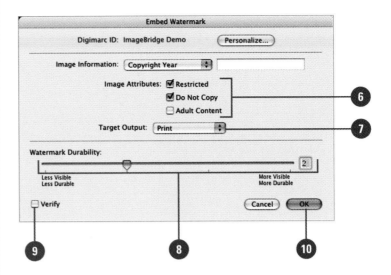

14

Viewing Various Filter Effects

Photoshop provides a bountiful selection of filters, 105 to be exact. Take a moment to view some of the various filter effects that Photoshop offers. The original image is shown to the right, and we've displayed some common filters on the following pages. A good thing to think about when using filters is your original image. Look at the background colors, and see if they will look good with some of the filters. The best thing to do is open an image that has a lot of various details, and then apply some filters to see what you like.

Various Filter Effects

Cutout

Dry Brush

Fresco

Palette Knife

Accented Edges

Glass

Diffuse Glow

Note Paper

Stamp

Glowing Edges

14

Grain

Spatter

Mosaic Tiles

Stained Glass

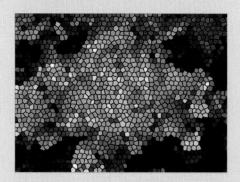

Graphic Pen

Plastic Wrap

Automating Your Work with Actions

Introduction

Actions are only one of the Adobe Photoshop Automate commands; however, they're so important to consistency and efficiency, they deserve their own chapter. Actions are Photoshop's way of relieving you of the mind-numbing task of repeating an operation over and over again. For example, you're recovering 55 images from your digital camera, and each image needs to be converted into a specific size and resolution. Instead of repeating the conversion process 55 times, you perform the conversion process once, and save it as a repeatable action.

Actions are similar to recording information on a tape; they record Photoshop commands and, like a tape recorder, can be played back at any time. Actions can be applied to any number of images. You can modify existing actions, and save them into a user-defined set. It's even possible to save them and send them to any other Photoshop user. Actions have been a part of Photoshop since version 5, and each evolution of the Actions palette has seen new features and abilities. In Photoshop, it's now possible to create an action out of almost any command, filter, or adjustment; including blending mode operations to layers. This chapter is dedicated to the masses of Photoshop users who are tired of doing something over and over again. If you have ever considered using actions as a part of your design workflow, then you're in for a wonderful journey of discovery.

You can also enhance your actions by creating a droplet. A **droplet** is an action that appears as a file on your hard drive. For example, you could create a droplet that performs a generic color correction operation. To perform the operation on a Photoshop document, you would not have to open Photoshop; you would simply drag the image file over the droplet, and release—the droplet does the rest.

Examining the
Actions Palette

 PS 8.1

The Actions palette is where you create, save, modify, and store all of your actions. The analogy of a tape recorder is used often in discussions of the Actions palette, but besides the overuse of the term, it's actually a good way to view actions. The action itself is a tape, and the Actions palette is the tape recorder. When you begin an action, the palette records each step in the process, saves them, and then lets you play them back on another image. In order to record and play actions, you need to understand how to use the Actions palette.

Examine the Actions Palette

1 Select the **Actions** palette.

2 Check the toggle box to toggle an action on or off.

3 Click the dialog box to toggle the dialog function on or off.

4 Click the **expand triangle** to expand or contract an action or set.

5 Click the **Actions Options** button to access all of the Actions palette options.

> **Did You Know?**
>
> **You can use the Window menu to display the Actions palette.** Click the Window menu, and then click Actions.

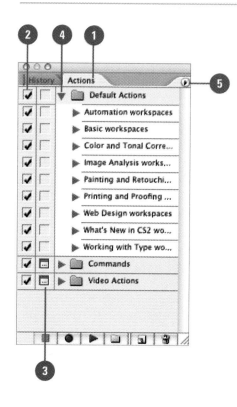

6 The following buttons are accessible at the bottom of the Actions palette, from left to right:

◆ **Stop.** Click to stop recording and save an action.

◆ **Record.** Click to begin recording an action.

◆ **Play.** Click to begin execution of the selected action.

◆ **Create New Set.** Creates a new action set.

Sets are like file folders; they store individual actions.

◆ **Create New Action.** Starts the process of creating a new action.

◆ **Delete.** Click to delete the selected action or set.

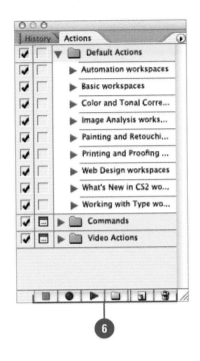

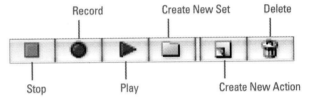

Record   Create New Set   Delete

Stop   Play   Create New Action

15

Building a New Action

 PS 8.1

Building an action is almost as simple as clicking the record button on a tape recorder. Actions are simply a series of program instructions. When you build an action, you're instructing Photoshop what to name the file, where to store it, and what functions keys, if any, will be used to activate the action. Since an action is simply a record of the work performed on an image, it's a good idea to plan out what you intend to do, and then build the action. Remember actions are tasks you plan to do repeatedly. It wouldn't make sense to create an action for a one-time use.

Build a New Action

1. Open a document.

2. Select the **Actions** palette.

3. Click the **Create New Action** button.

4. Enter a name for the action in the Name box.

5. Click the **Set** list arrow, and then select what set to save the Action.

6. Click the **Function Key** list arrow, and then click F1 - F12 to assign your new action to a function key.

7. Select the **Shift** or **Command** check boxes to require the pressing of the Shift key, or the Ctrl (Win) or ⌘ (Mac) key in conjunction with the function key.

   For example, F1, or Shift+F1, or Ctrl+F1, or Shift+Ctrl+F1.

8. Click the **Color** list arrow, and then select from the available colors.

9. Click **Record** to begin creating the action.

   IMPORTANT *If you choose a color for the action, they will only be available if the actions are viewed in Button Mode.*

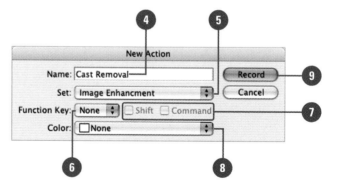

Recording an Action

PS 8.1

Once you've set up, or built the action, it's a simple matter of clicking the Record button and performing a pre-determined set of commands to the image. Photoshop watches you like a hawk; faithfully recording each step in the process. Once complete, Photoshop stores the file in the Actions palette, where it's ready when needed. When you end the action, Photoshop stores the program instructions in a file, and displays all the files, by name, in the Actions palette. Then it's a simple matter of clicking the Play button to apply the instructions to another document.

Record an Action

1. Open a document.

2. Select the **Actions** palette.

3. Specify the action settings.

4. Click **Record**.

5. Edit the image. Each time you perform an edit, such as filters, adjustments, or commands, the operation is listed as a step in the Actions palette.

   IMPORTANT *The Actions palette doesn't record the speed you perform a command, only you performed it. So take your time, and work carefully through the process. Creating an action right the first time, save editing hassles later.*

6. Click the **Stop** button on the Actions palette.

   The action is saved and listed in the current Action Set.

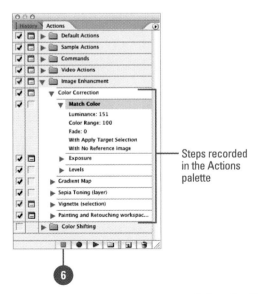

Steps recorded in the Actions palette

15

Adding a Stop to an Action

PS 8.1

There are times when you want to make changes, based on a specific image. For example, you create an action to balance the contrast in an image, and one of the commands you use is the Levels adjustment. Although all of the other commands do not need modification, the Levels adjustment is specific to each individual image. What you want is the action to perform (automatically) all of the action steps, except Levels. For the Levels adjustment, you want the action to stop, and let you make changes, and then after you click the OK button, to move on and complete the rest of the steps.

Add a Stop to an Action

① Open a document, and then select the **Actions** palette.

② Click the **expand triangle** of the action you want to modify.

③ Click the command directly above where you want to place the action.

④ Click the **Actions Options** button, and then click **Insert Stop**.

⑤ Enter a text message associated with the purpose of the stop action.

⑥ Select the **Allow Continue** check box to add a Continue button to the stop alert box.

⑦ Click **OK**.

⑧ Click the **Play** button on the Actions palette to run the action.

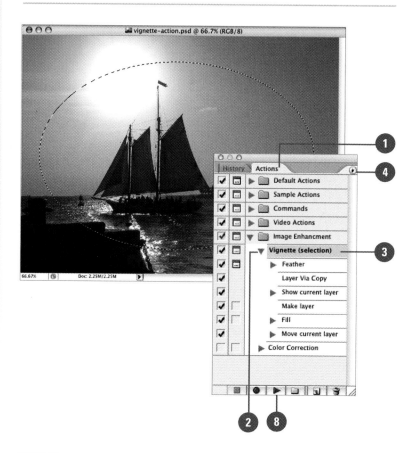

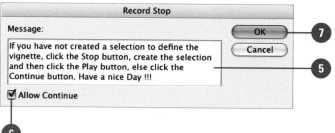

Controlling the Playback of a Command

Control the Playback of a Command

1. Open a document, and then select the **Actions** palette.

2. Click the **expand triangle** of the action you want to modify.

3. Uncheck the command or commands you do not want to execute.

4. Click the **Play** button on the Actions palette to run the action without executing the unchecked command.

5. Recheck the command to return it to executable status.

See Also

See "Working with Batch File Processing" on page 398 for information on applying an action to multiple files at once.

Not all actions are created perfect. Sooner or later, you'll work through the process of action building only to find out (after the action is saved), you forgot a step, or need to remove or modify an existing step. You might even need to change the order of the commands in the action. Fortunately, Photoshop doesn't make you recreate the action; all you have to do is modify it. When you create an action, all of the commands execute in the order they appear in the command list. However, it's possible you might occasionally want to skip one of the commands in the list, without permanently deleting it.

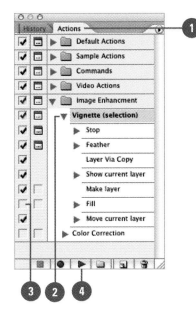

Adding a Command to an Action

PS 8.1

Actions are very versatile; in fact almost anything that can be done to an image can be placed into an action. You might find that as you perform an action, you need to add an additional command. You can do this with ease, that's why actions are so great to work with. For example, you might create an action to convert an image from the RGB to the CMYK mode, and after you save the action; you decide it would be great to include a Curves adjustment. You don't have to throw away the old action and start all over, all you have to do is select where the command will be inserted, restart the action and perform the new step. The Actions palette is a powerful time-saving tool, and if you forget a step, it's also a breeze to modify.

Add a Command to an Action

1. Open a document, and then select the **Actions** palette.

2. Click the **expand triangle** of the action you want to add the command.

3. Click the command directly above where you want to insert the new command.

4. Click the **Actions Options** button, and then click **Start Recording**.

5. Add the additional command by selecting the filter, adjustment, or any other Photoshop option.

6. When you're finished adding commands, click the **Stop** button on the Actions palette.

   The next time the action is run, the additional command will be performed.

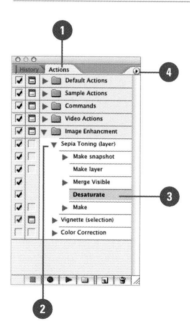

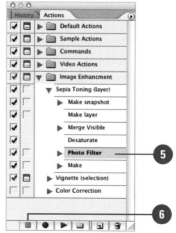

Deleting a Command from an Action

 **PS 8.1**

Occasionally, you may want to permanently delete a command from an existing action. If that's the case, Photoshop makes the process quick and easy. An action consists of a group of steps. As the action executes, each step is completed in the order that they appear within the action list. No one step is dependent upon another, so if the case arises you want to remove a step, it's a simple process of deletion. Once the command is removed the action will perform as if the deleted command never existed.

Delete a Command from an Action

① Open a document, and then select the **Actions** palette.

② Click the **expand triangle** of the action you want to delete the command.

> **IMPORTANT** *You cannot delete a command from a running action.*

③ Click the command you want to delete.

④ Select from three deletion methods:

- ◆ Drag the command over the **Delete** button.

- ◆ Click the command, click the **Delete** button, and then click **OK** in the Delete This Selection alert box.

- ◆ Click the command, and then hold down the Alt (Win) or Option (Mac) key, and then click the **Delete** button to delete the command without the alert box message.

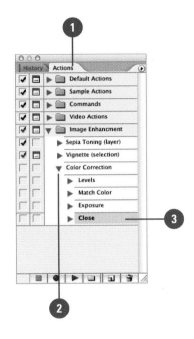

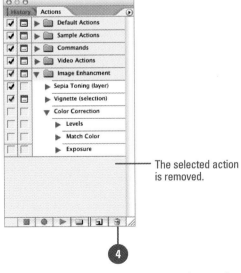

The selected action is removed.

15

Working with Modal Controls in an Action

PS 8.1

Modal controls are pauses in an action; which allow you to modify a command before proceeding with the action. Modal controls are available for every Photoshop command that utilizes a dialog box, or any command that requires the pressing of the Enter/Return key to process the effect. For example, you create an action that utilizes a Levels and Curves adjustment, and you want the option to control the Levels adjustment each time the action is run.

Work with Modal Controls

1. Open a document, and then select the **Actions** palette.

2. Click the **expand triangle** of the action you want to modify.

3. Click the second column from the left to activate the Modal Control button.

4. Click an existing modal control button to deactivate the control.

5. Click the **Play** button on the Actions palette to run the action.

   The action stops and lets you control the command.

6. Adjust the image using the Exposure dialog box.

7. Click **OK** to continue the action.

Changing the Order of Commands in an Action

 PS 8.1

When an action runs, it performs each command in the order that they appear in the action list. Since the order a filter or adjustment is applied to an image determine the final document, it's important to be able to adjust the order that the commands are executed. For example, if you create an action that contains a Curves adjustment followed by a Gaussian Blur filter, and you move the Gaussian Blur filter above the Curves adjustment, it will totally change the look of the final image. Since the order of execution is important to the outcome of the image, the Actions palette gives you the ability to change the order in which commands are executed.

Change the Order of Commands

1 Open a document, and then select the **Actions** palette.

2 Click the **expand triangle** of the action you want to change.

3 Drag the command you want to change up or down in the action stack.

4 Release the mouse when you see a dark line underneath the command you want the dragged one to be placed.

Did You Know?

You can choose the speed at which an action executes when you're playing it. Click the Actions Options button, and then click Playback Options. Click Accelerated, Step By Step, or Pause for a predetermined number of seconds. You can even have it pause for any audio annotations. Clicking a slower speed lets you view each step, and is useful when performing editing on an action.

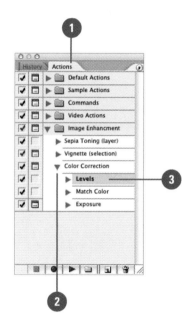

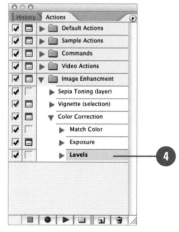

Copying an Action

PS 8.1

What if you need to create an action with several commands, and you need another similar action; possibly one action that performs several commands and ends with the Curves adjustment. And then another action that performs the same commands and ends with the Levels adjustment. If that's the case, there is no need to reinvent the wheel, just create the first action, make a copy, and then modify the copy.

Copy an Action

1. Open a document, and then select the **Actions** Palette.

2. Click the **expand triangle** of the action you want to change.

3. Select how you want to duplicate the action:

   ◆ Drag the action over the **Create New Action** button on the Actions palette.

   ◆ Select the action, click the **Actions Options** button, and then click **Duplicate**.

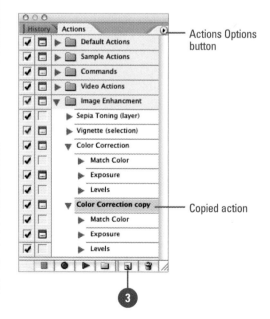

Actions Options button

Copied action

Running an Action Inside an Action

 PS 8.1

Run an Action Inside an Action

1. Open a document, and then select the **Actions** palette.

2. Click the **expand triangle** of the action you want to modify.

3. Click the command directly above where you want to insert the run step for the other action.

4. Click the **Record** button.

5. Click the action to be added.

6. Click the **Play** button to record the second action into the first action.

7. Click the **Stop** button.

The second action is recorded inside the first action.

IMPORTANT *When you click the Play button, the action executes on the active document, so you might want to perform this on a duplicate image.*

You can make an action run within another action, thus reducing action complexity. For example, you could create an action that performs a dozen or more commands (it's not unusual), or you could create two simpler actions, and have one action load and run the other action. That way, when it comes time to modify the action, you have a smaller list of commands to deal with. You can also call actions from more than one source, giving you the ability to create small action codes that can be used over and over again.

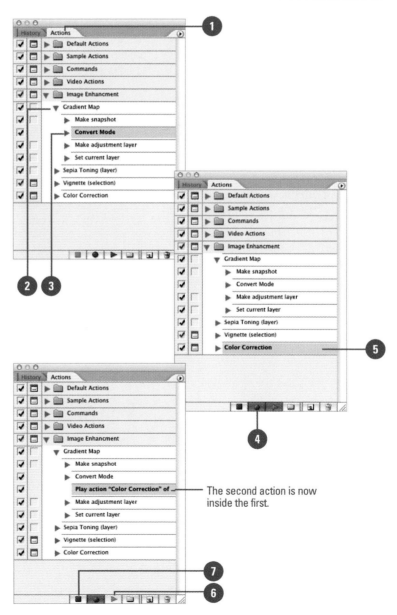

The second action is now inside the first.

Saving Actions into Sets

Once you discover the advantage to using actions, you'll be creating actions for all those dull, boring repetitive tasks, and life inside Photoshop will never be the same again. As the days go on, you'll see your list of actions growing longer and longer. Sooner or later (probably sooner), you'll develop so many actions that scrolling down the Actions palette to find you favorite actions becomes a job in itself. The Actions palette has the ability to hold as many actions as you need, and it also gives you the ability to organize those actions into sets. Action sets are like file folders; they hold groups of actions. For example, you might have a group of actions that perform image restoration, and another group for color correction. Using the Actions palette, you can create two sets, one for each kind. Once a set is created, it can be removed from the Actions palette, and reloaded when needed. Action sets can also be distributed to other users.

Save Actions into Sets

1. Open a document, and then select the **Actions** palette.

2. Click the **Create New Set** button.

3. Enter a name for the new set.

4. Click **OK**.

    The new set is added to the Actions palette.

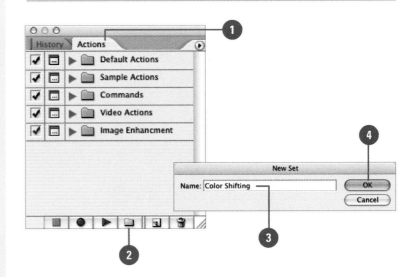

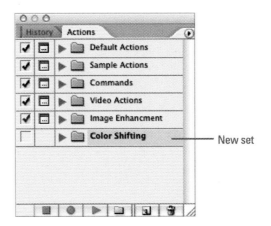

New set

Saving Actions as Files

PS 8.1

When you create a new set of actions, Photoshop displays the actions in the Actions palette, but the actions are not permanently saved to the hard drive. That means if you delete an unsaved action or action set, they will be gone forever. To stop that from happening, you need to save the sets. Not only does this give you the ability to save your precious actions, it lets you share you actions with other Photoshop users. For example, you have a friend that's having trouble performing color correction to an image. The problem is she lives 800 miles away. So you create an action that performs color correction, save the action as a file, and e-mail her the file. Now, all she has to do is click the Actions Options button, and then click Load Actions. She now has the action to color correct her images.

Save Actions as Files

1. Select the **Actions** palette.

2. Click the set you want to save.

3. Click the **Actions Options** button, and then click the **Save Actions**.

4. Enter a name for the action set.

   The default name will be the original name of the set.

5. Click the **Where** (Mac) or **Save In** (Win) list arrow, and then click where to save the set.

6. Click **Save**.

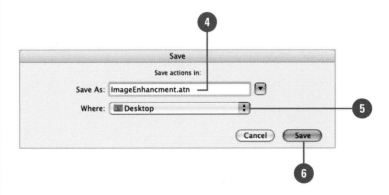

15

> **Did You Know?**
>
> **You can access your new Action Set directly from the Actions dialog box.** If you save the new action set in the Photoshop Actions folder, the actions appears at the bottom of the Actions Options dialog box.

Moving and Copying Actions Between Sets

PS 8.1

Once you've created an action set, it's a simple matter to organize all of your timesaving actions. Think of an action set as a file drawer. When you need a specific action, you expand the set, and then locate the proper action. You might want to create sets with names such as Color Correction or Special Effects, for easier retrieval. Then you can create new or move existing actions into your organized sets. Once the perfect action set is created it can be saved, and even e-mailed to other Photoshop users.

Move and Copy Actions Between Sets

1. Select the **Actions** palette.

2. Click a pre-existing set, and then click the **expand triangle** to open the set.

3. Use the following move or copy method:

   ◆ To move an action, drag the action from one set

   ◆ To copy an action, hold down the Alt (Win) or Option (Mac) key, and then drag the action from one set.

4. Release when your mouse hovers over another set.

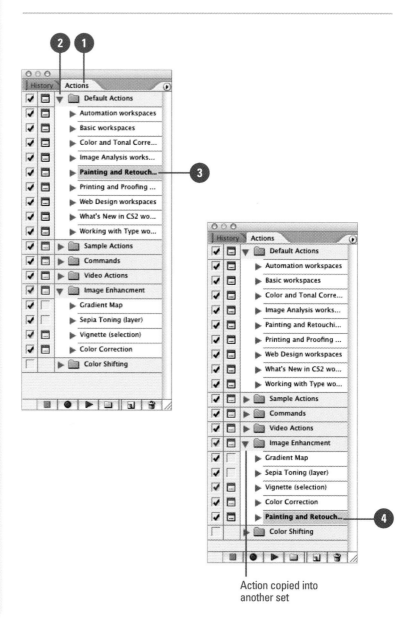

Action copied into another set

Inserting a Non-Recordable Command into an Action

When you create an action, you cannot record mouse movements, such as a brush stroke, or any of the view, and window commands. However, you can insert many non-recordable commands into an action using an Insert Menu Item command. The Insert Menu Item command can be used when recording an action or after it has been recorded. Inserted commands do not execute until the action is played, so the file remains unchanged when the command is inserted. This gives you the ability to experiment with different non-recordable commands without the possibility of damaging a valuable image.

Insert a Non-Recordable Command into an Action

1 Select the **Actions** palette.

2 Click an action, and click the **expand triangle**.

3 Click the name of the action to insert the item at the end of the action, or click an action step to insert the item after the selected step.

4 Click the **Actions Options** button, and then click **Insert Menu Item**.

5 Select a command from the available options (the command is selected by clicking and selecting an item from Photoshop's drop-down menu system).

6 Click **OK**.

The non-recordable command is added to the action steps.

IMPORTANT *When you use the Insert Menu Item command for a command that opens a dialog box, you cannot disable the modal control in the Actions palette.*

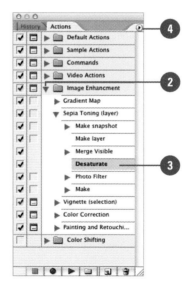

Using Enhanced Scripting

PS 8.4

Use Enhanced Scripting

1. Open a text editor, and then create the script using any approved scripting language.

2. Save the document with the correct extension. For example, ActiveLayer.js for JavaScript.

3. To access the script in Photoshop, click the **File** menu, point to **Scripts**, and then click **Browse**.

A **script** is a series of commands that instructs Photoshop to perform a set of specified actions or commands. These actions can be as simple as affecting only a single object or more complex, affecting many objects. The actions can call Photoshop alone or invoke other applications such as Adobe Illustrator. Scripts are useful for repetitive tasks and can be used as a creative tool to streamline tasks that are time consuming and boring. For example, you could write a script to access your digital camera. It could then process the images, create and save the documents in a folder that automatically includes the current date in the folder name, like Nikon 5700-12.12.2005. A scripting language lets you ask a question (an event), and use the answer to that question to perform any commands (an action) that are available in Photoshop. To create your own scripts you need a working knowledge of scripting languages such as JavaScript, and either a script-editing application or simply a text editor, such as NotePad (Win), TextEdit (Mac) BBEdit or even MS Word. The languages you can use to perform scripting are varied and include Visual Basic, AppleScript, and JavaScript, to name a few. As a matter of fact, the Scripts Events Manage (**New!**) lets you set JavaScript, and Photoshop Actions to run automatically when a specified Photoshop event occurs.

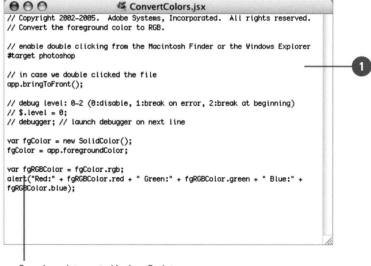

Sample script created in JavaScript

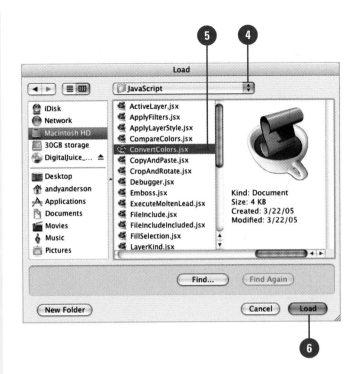

4 Click the **From** (Mac) or **Look In** (Win) list arrow, and then select your script editor file.

5 Click the script in which you want to run.

6 Click **Load** to run the script.

Your script appears in a browse window.

See Also

For more information on Enhanced Scripting, open the Photoshop applications folder, and then navigate to the Scripting Guide folder for access to several PDF tutorial files, and sample scripts.

For Your Information

Using Built-in Scripts

You can save time by automating repeated tasks, such as outputting your layers to files or saving Layer Comps as separate pages of an Adobe PDF file using user-defined or Photoshop's enhanced built-in scripts. Click the File menu, point to Scripts, and then select from the available option presets. For more information on how to write your own scripts, see the documentation available in your Adobe Photoshop CS2/Scripting Guide folder.

15

Enhancing the Process with Droplets

PS 8.2

When you apply an action to an image, you open Photoshop, open the document, open the Actions palette, select the action, and then click the Play button. While that process is easier than having to redo all the steps in a complicated action, there is simpler way, create a droplet. Droplets are Photoshop Actions that appear as a file on your hard drive, or organized within a folder. For example, you could create a droplet that performs a generic color correction operation. To perform the operation on a Photoshop document, you would not have to open Photoshop; simply drag the image file over the droplet, and release—the droplet does the rest.

Create a Droplet

1. Click the **File** menu, point to **Automate**, and then click **Create Droplet**.

   IMPORTANT *Droplets are created from existing actions.*

2. Click **Choose**, and then select a location to store the droplet.

3. Click the **Set** list arrow, and then select from the available sets.

4. Click the **Action** list arrow, and then select the action you want to convert into a droplet.

5. Select from the available Play options (see table).

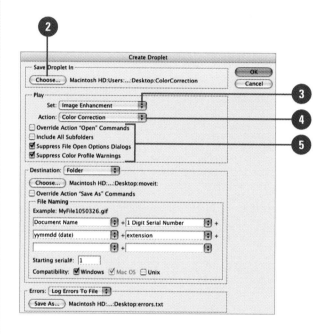

Available Play Options	
Option	**Purpose**
Override Action "Open" Commands	Overrides the batch Open command and uses an embedded Open command in the Action. The Action MUST have an Open command as one of the steps.
Include All Subfolders	Opens any subfolders within the selected folder and performs the action to any files found within.
Suppress File Open Options Dialogs	Do not show any File Open dialog boxes.
Suppress Color Profile Warnings	When a color profile mismatch occurs, do not display a warning dialog box, just continue.

6. Click the **Destination** list arrow, and then select from the following options:

   ◆ **None.** The file remains open after the droplet ends.

   ◆ **Save And Close.** The file is resaved (loss of original).

   ◆ **Folder.** The file is saved in a new folder (user selected), with the option of renaming the file and extension.

7. Select from the following File Naming options:

   ◆ **Document Name.** Use the original name of the document, or click to choose from the naming schemes; including incrementing the files by number (001, 002, etc).

   ◆ **Extension.** Use the original extension of the document, or click to choose from the extension options, such as using the date or sequenced serial number.

   ◆ **Starting Serial Number.** If you select to use a serial number, you can select a starting value for the sequence.

   ◆ **Compatibility.** Select the check boxes you want between Windows, Mac OS, or Unix.

8. To create an error log file, click the **Errors** list arrow, and then click **Log Errors To File**.

   The error log records any problems associated with applying the droplet to the image file.

9. To specify an error log file name and location, click **Save As**.

10. Click **OK**.

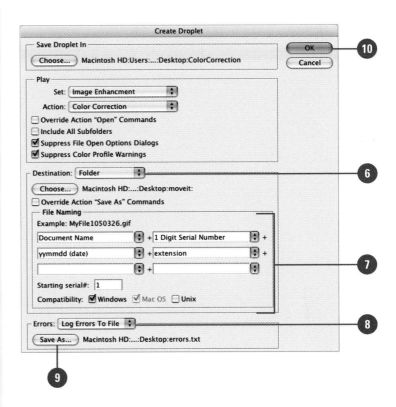

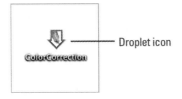

Droplet icon

Using a Droplet

PS 8.2

Use a Droplet

1 Open the folder that contains your droplets.

2 Open the folder that contains the image file, or files you need to convert.

3 Drag an image file directly over the droplet, and then release.

Photoshop automatically opens and performs the selected droplet.

Did You Know?

You can use droplets with more than one file. To use a droplet on more than one image file, hold down the Shift key, select all the image files you want to apply the single droplet, and then drag over the droplet. Photoshop performs the droplet on all selected files.

Once you've created a droplet, it's a simple matter of streamlining your workload. For example, you've created a droplet that converts an image into the grayscale color mode, and lowers the image to a monitor resolution of 72ppi. To convert an image file, just drag and drop. Droplets are files that hold the action instructions. Once a droplet is created, you can store them anywhere you can store a file. It's not a bad idea to create file folders that hold specific types of droplets, such as color correction droplets, or image enhancement droplets. To use a droplet, it's as easy as clicking an image file, dragging, and then dropping it over the droplet.

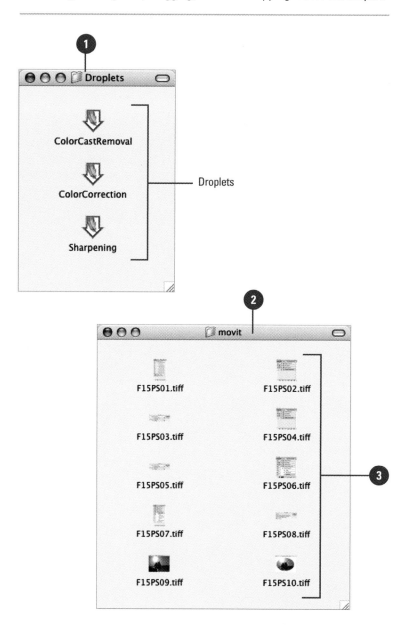

Controlling Image Output

Introduction

Once you create your Adobe Photoshop masterpiece, you will have to decide the output for the image file, and how the image will be printed. These are not easy considerations. For example, an image created with a resolution of 72ppi, might be fine if output to the Web, but would not be of sufficient quality for output to a high-quality laser printer. In addition, images saved in the RGB color space, would not work, if the image were to be printed on a 4-color (CMYK) press.

Raster images (Photoshop files) do not handle change very well, so it's important to design with a goal in mind. Designers call this process a workflow. When you start a Photoshop project you should have a good idea of where the project is headed to a press or inkjet printer, a copy machine, or a monitor. Knowing this information helps you design with the end in mind. That's not to say you can't make changes to a Photoshop document; however, when it comes to color space and resolution, the less change the better the output quality.

When preparing images for the Web, it's important to understand that file size and format are important considerations. People aren't very patient when it comes time to downloading Web pages. Creating good-looking, yet fast-loading images keeps visitors on your Web site, waiting for more. Photoshop gives you the ability to perform image compression using formats such as the JPEG (Joint Photographers Expert Group), and GIF (Graphics Interchange File) formats. That will make your images as small as possible, while still retaining great image quality. In image preparation it's all about control, and Photoshop gives you the tools to make the job easy.

What You'll Do

Work with Page Setup

Use Print With Preview

Print a Document

Print Part of a Document

Print One Copy

Understand File Formats

Save a Document with a Different File Format

Insert File Information into a Document

Understand File Compression

Prepare Clipart for the Web

Prepare a Photograph for the Web

Prepare an Image for the Press

Prepare an Image for the Inkjet or Laser Printer

Understand Monitor, Image, and Device Resolution

Working with Page Setup in Macintosh

Photoshop images can be printed out to virtually any device. For example, an image could find its way to a laser or inkjet printer, a 4-color press, even run-of-the-mill copy machines have input for image printing from application software. What you need is Photoshop, an open image, and a good idea of where you want the image displayed. This may seem easy, however, a few careful adjustments will make all the difference in the world.

Work with Page Setup in Macintosh

1 Open a document.

2 Click the **File** menu, and then click **Page Setup**.

3 Click the **Settings** list arrow, and then click **Page Attributes**.

4 Select from the various Page Attributes options:

◆ **Format For.** Click the list arrow, and then select a printer from the available options. If your printer is not accessible from the list, click the Edit Printer List, and then add your printer (you may need the printer CD, or access to the Internet, to load the latest drivers).

◆ **Paper Size.** Click the list arrow, and select from the available options. The default printer will determine the available paper sizes.

◆ **Orientation.** Click the Portrait, Landscape Left, or Landscape Right button.

◆ **Scale.** Enter a percentage value to increase (over 100) or decrease (under 100) the size of the printed document.

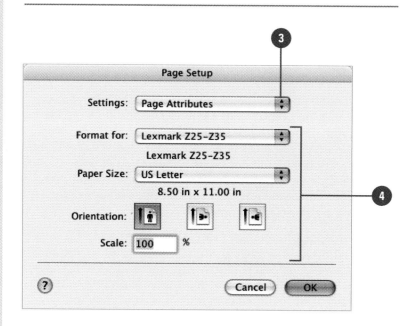

5 Click the **Settings** list arrow, and then click **Custom Paper Size**.

6 Select from the various Custom Paper Size options:

◆ **New.** Click to create a new custom paper size.

◆ **Duplicate.** Click to duplicate the selected custom item.

◆ **Delete.** Click to delete the selected custom item.

◆ **Save.** Click to save the selected custom item.

◆ **Paper Size.** Enter Width and Height values for the custom item.

◆ **Printer Margins.** Enter Top, Bottom, Left, and Right paper margins for the custom item.

7 Click the **Settings** list arrow, and then click **Summary** to view a text summary of your page setup options.

8 Click **OK**.

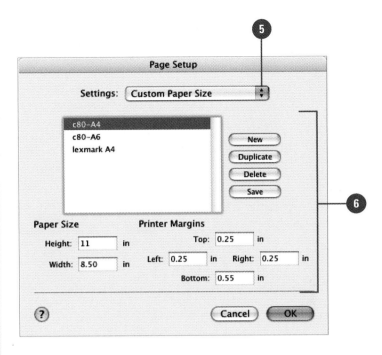

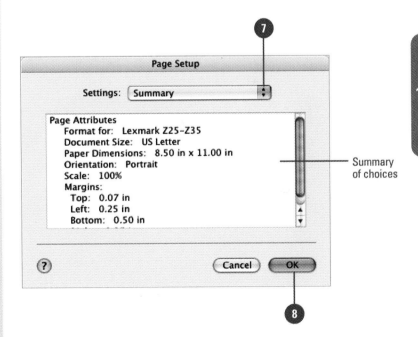

Summary of choices

Working with Page Setup in Windows

You can use the Page Setup dialog box in Windows to select the size and location in the printer of the paper you want to use. You can also select the page orientation (portrait or landscape) that best fits the entire document or any selection. **Portrait** orients the page vertically (taller than it is wide) and **landscape** orients the page horizontally (wider than it is tall). When you shift between the two, the margin settings automatically change. **Margins** are the blank space between the edge of a page and the image. The printer only prints within these margins. Different printer models support different options and features; the available options depend on your printer and print drivers.

Work with Page Setup in Windows

1 Open a document.

2 Click the **File** menu, and then click **Page Setup**.

3 Select from the various Page Setup options:

◆ **Size.** Click the list arrow, and then select from the available options. The default printer will determine the available paper sizes.

◆ **Source.** Click the list arrow, and then select from the available options.

◆ **Orientation.** Click the Portrait or Landscape option.

◆ **Margins.** Enter Top, Bottom, Left, and Right paper margins for the custom item.

4 Click **OK**.

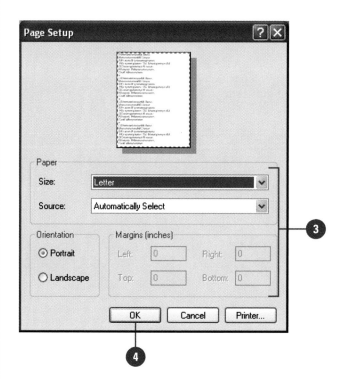

Set Printer Properties in Page Setup

1. Open a document.

2. Click the **File** menu, and then click **Page Setup**.

3. Click **Printer**.

4. Click the **Name** list arrow, and then select the printer you want to use.

5. Click **Properties**.

6. Select the printer options you want; each printer displays different options.

7. Click **OK** to close the Properties dialog box.

8. Click **OK** to close the Page Setup dialog box.

9. Click **OK** to close the Page Setup dialog box.

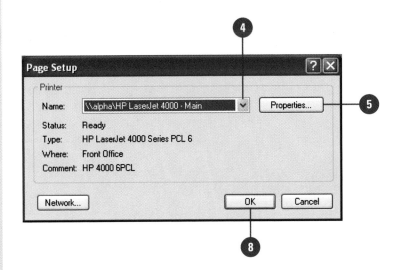

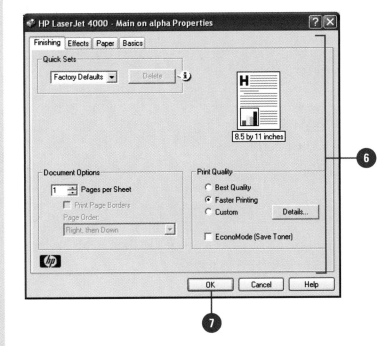

16

Using Print With Preview

PS 12.1, 12.2

The option to print with a preview gives you the opportunity to view the image (on screen), and decide whether to print or return to the drawing board. This is just one more way that Photoshop gives you to control your workflow. Although the image displays on a monitor, you still get to see an accurate representation of how the graphic, and all its associated layers, and effects will appear. Remember, a monitor uses additive color (RGB), and most output devices, such as printing presses, use subtractive color (CMYK). However, if you have a good, color-calibrated monitor, you should have a good idea of how the image will look when you click the Print button.

Use Print With Preview

1 Open a document.

2 Click the **File** menu, and then click **Print With Preview**.

3 Select from the various Position options:

◆ **Top.** Instructs the output device to print the image from the top of the page.

◆ **Left.** Instructs the output device to print the image from the left of the page.

◆ **Center Image.** Select the check box to instruct the output device to center the image on the paper.

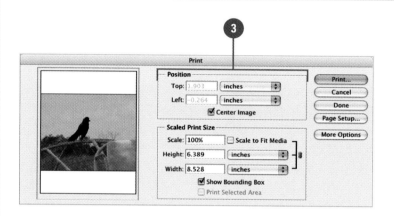

Did You Know?

You can manually scale and position an image. Select the Show Bounding Box check box, and then clear the Scale To Fit Media, and Center Image check boxes. Then simply drag the image in the View window to reposition, and then click and drag a corner to resize.

④ Select from the various Scaled Print Size options:

◆ **Scale.** Enter a percentage value.

◆ **Scale to Fit Media.** Select the check box to instruct Photoshop to scale the document to the selected paper size.

◆ **Height.** Enter a specific height for the image.

◆ **Width.** Enter a specific width for the image.

◆ **Show Bounding Box.** Select the check box to create a viewable bounding box around the image.

◆ **Print Selected Area.** Select the check box to only print the previously selected area of the image.

⑤ Click **More Options** to display additional options on color management.

⑥ Click **Page Setup** to set any set up options.

⑦ Click **Print** to open the Print dialog box.

⑧ Click **Done** to return to your document without printing.

See Also

See "Working with Page Setup" on page 370 (Mac) or 372 (Win) for more information on setting various page setup attributes.

Preview of active image

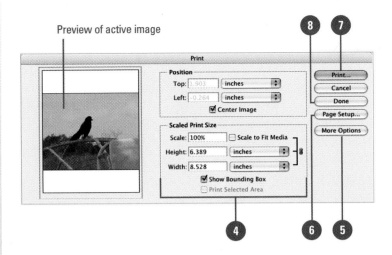

For Your Information

Taking Printing With Preview to the Next Level

When you click the More Options button in Print With Preview, Photoshop not only gives you access to its powerful color management tools, it also lets you create color bars, calibration marks, and even place a custom border around the image. Click the Color Management list arrow, and then click Output. Photoshop displays a listing of all the options available, including the ability to change document's encoding. It's just one more way that Photoshop gives you control over document output.

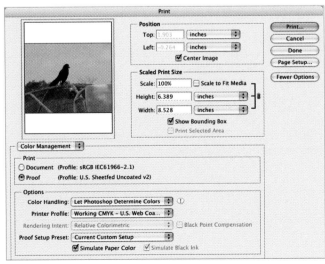

16

Printing a Document in Macintosh

The Print command is probably the most used of all Photoshop's print options. In addition to normal printing functions, such as Copies and Pages, the Print command gives you other menus that let you control specific printing functions, such as output ink and color management. Understand that the options available for the Print command will be partially determined by the default printer. For example, if your default printer uses more than one paper tray, you will see options for selecting a specific tray for the current print job. In spite of the differences, there are some universal options to all print jobs, and these are covered here.

Print a Document in Macintosh

1. Open a document.

2. Click the **File** menu, and then click **Print**.

3. Click the **Printer** list arrow, and then select from the available printer descriptions.

    IMPORTANT *Changes made here, override any changes made in the Page Setup dialog box.*

4. Click the **Presets** list arrow, and then select from the available preset options.

5. Click the **Print Options** list arrow, click **Copies & Pages**, and then select the various options: Number of copies, Collated, Print All or Range of pages.

6. Click the **Print Options** list arrow, click **Layout**, and then select the various options: Pages Per Sheet, Layout Direction, and if you want a Border.

7. Click the **Print Options** list arrow, click **Output Options**, and then select the various options: Save As File, and what Format you want the file.

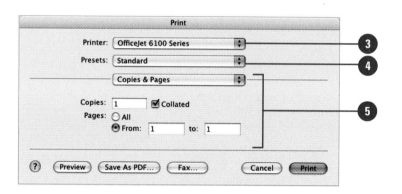

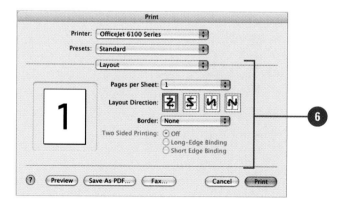

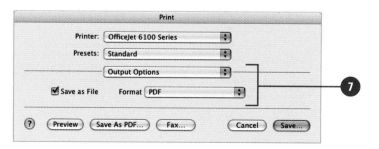

8 Click the **Print Options** list arrow, click **Paper Type/Quality**, and then select the various options located on the Paper, Color Options, Digital Photo, and Ink tabs.

◆ **Paper.** Click to control the document's paper type, quality, and whether to print the document in color or grayscale.

◆ **Color Options.** Click to print in color, to control the amount of saturation, brightness, and color tone applied to the image. If you choose to print in grayscale, select your options.

◆ **Digital Photo.** Click to artificially fill in dark areas of an image, like using a flash on a camera.

◆ **Ink.** Click to select Ink Density and drag the slider to adjust, or select Drying Time and drag the slider to adjust the wait time between pages when using 2-sided printing

9 Click the **Print Options** list arrow, click **Summary**, and then view the summary of settings.

10 Click the following options to finalize your print:

◆ Preview

◆ Save As PDF

◆ Fax

◆ Cancel

◆ Print

11 If you need additional help along the way, click the **Help** button.

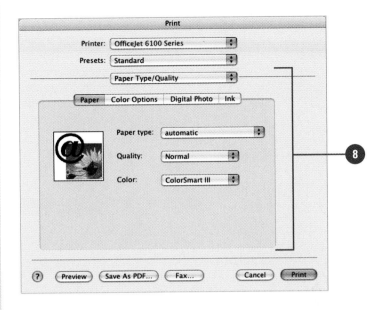

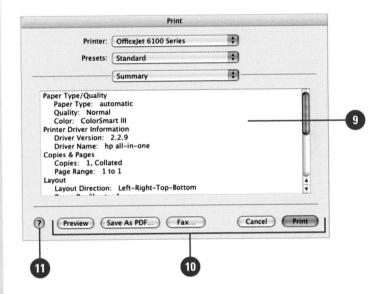

16

Printing a Document in Windows

 PS 12.2

Printing a paper copy is the most common way to preview and share your documents. You can use the Print dialog box to set how many copies to print, specify a range of pages to print, and print your document. Understand that the options available for the Print command will be determined by the default printer, and operating system. Different printers will display different options, there are some options that are fairly universal, and these options are covered here.

Print a Document in Windows

1 Open a document.

2 Click the **File** menu, and then click **Print**.

3 If necessary, click the **Name** list arrow, and then click the printer you want.

4 Type the number of copies you want to print.

5 Specify the pages to print:

- ◆ **All.** Prints the entire document.

- ◆ **Pages.** Prints the specified pages.

- ◆ **Selection.** Prints the selected item.

6 Click **OK**.

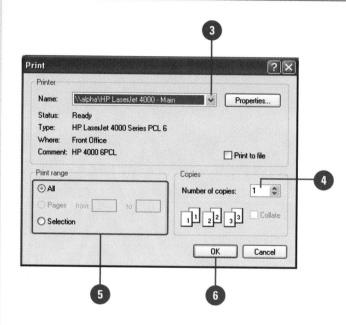

Printing Part of a Document

If you only want to print part of an image in a Photoshop document, you can use the Print Selected Area option in the Print With Preview dialog box to quickly perform the task. All you need to do is select the part of an image you want to print, select the Print With Preview command on the File menu, select the Print Selected Area check box, and then send it to the printer.

Print Part of a Document

1 Open a document.

2 Select the **Rectangle Marquee** tool on the toolbox.

3 Select the part of an image you want to print.

4 Click the **File** menu, and then click **Print With Preview**.

5 Select the **Print Selected Area** check box.

6 Click **Print**.

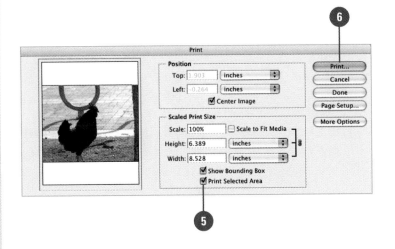

Printing One Copy

 Adobe Certified Expert PS 12.2

If you want it quick without any questions, then the Print One Copy command is for you. No hassle, just a printed copy of the image, using Photoshop's default print settings. The Print One Copy command does not open a dialog box, so when the option is selected, the printing process starts and attempts to print the document. If you try to print an image that is larger than the paper's printable area, an alert dialog box appears. If this happens, you have the option of continuing the printing process, or canceling. Otherwise, the Print One Copy command is a one click solution to a fast printed copy of your active document.

Print One Copy of a Document

1 Open a document.

2 Click the **File** menu, and then click **Print One Copy**.

Photoshop prints a single copy of the image without a dialog box.

IMPORTANT *If you have made any changes to Page Setup, or modified the printer settings in any way, Photoshop will ignore its defaults and print using your modified settings.*

Understanding File Formats

 PS 11.3

File Formats

Format	Usage
Photoshop	Uses a PSD (Photoshop) format (the default), which saves layers, channels, notes, and color profiles.
BMP	Uses a BMP (Bitmap) format.
CompuServe GIF	Uses a GIF (Graphic Interchange Format) format, which is used for clipart and text for the Web. A format for images on the Web that only use 256 colors. GIF's compress images by selectively disregarding color and repeating simple patterns. It supports transparency and animation.
Photoshop EPS	Uses a EPS (Encapsulated PostScript Format) format, which saves vector information - i.e. paths.
Large Document Format	Uses a PSB (Photoshop) format (for CS and CS2 only), which is used for saving documents up to 300,000 pixels in any dimension; this useful for saving High Dynamic Range images.
JPEG	Uses a JPG or JPEG (Joint Photographers Expert Group) format. A compression method used to reduce the size of image files primarily for the Web.
PCX	Uses a PCX (PC Paintbrush bitmap) format, which is used primarily in PC formats.
Photoshop PDF	Uses a PDF (Portable Document File) format, which creates a file that can be read by anyone who has a PDF reader program (such as Adobe).
Photoshop 2.0	Uses a PSD (Photoshop Document File) format, which is used to strip a file of all layers, an creates a flattened composite image.
Photoshop RAW	Uses a RAW format that is used for saving and transferring files between programs and computer platforms.
PICT File	Uses a PICT format that is used for the Macintosh operating system.
PICT Resource	Uses the PICT Resource format that lets you save the file that can be used as a Mac image resource.
Pixar	Uses the Pixar format for images that are high-end animation, and 3-D rendering programs.
PNG	Uses the PNG (Portable Network Graphic) format. This is used for saving images onto the Web that supports up to 16 million colors and 256 levels of transparency.
PBM	Uses the PBM (Portable Bit Map) format, which supports monochrome bitmaps (1 bit per channel), and is part of a family of bitmap formats supported by most applications.
Scitex CT	Uses the SCT (Continuous Tone) format in high-end Scitex image-rendering computers.
Targa	Uses a Targa format for high-end image editing on the Windows platform.
TIFF	Uses a TIFF or TIF Tagged Image File) format. This can be opened by almost any image-editing or layout program. a common format for printing and saving flat images without losing quality.
Photoshop DCS 1.0 & 2.0	Uses a DCS (Digital Color Separation) format. This is used by press operators to create the plates used in 4-color printing.

16

Saving a Document with a Different File Format

After all your hard work, you now need to save your document. The saving process involves selecting a specific file format, naming the file, and choosing a destination. Choose a file name, which will help identify the document (looking in a folder of 100 images and seeing files names, such as image_a, image_b, really doesn't help). Select a destination, such as a hard drive, removable media, or even rewritable CD or DVD. Determine the format of the document file. While name and location are important, the file format is crucial to the future of the image. The file format determines how the document is stored, and what information is saved with the file. Choosing the wrong format, may even prevent you from correctly outputting the file.

Save a Document with a Different File Format

1. Open a document.

2. Click the **File** menu, and then click Save As.

3. Enter a name in the **Save As** (Mac) or **File Name** (Win) box.

4. Click the **Format** list arrow, and then select a format.

   See the table on the previous page for assistance.

5. Click the **Where** (Mac) or **Save In** (Win) list arrow, and then select a location to save the document file.

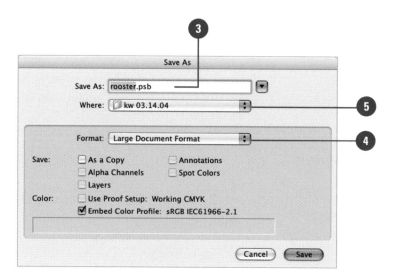

See Also

See "Understanding File Formats" on page 381 for information on the different file formats.

6 Select from the following Save options:

- ◆ **As A Copy.** Select the check box to save a copy of the file, while leaving the original open.

- ◆ **Alpha Channels.** Select the check box to save any alpha channel information.

- ◆ **Layers.** Select the check box to preserve all layers within the document.

- ◆ **Annotations.** Select the check box to save any audio, or note annotations with the document.

- ◆ **Spot Colors.** Select the check box to save any spot channel information.

7 Select from the following Color options:

- ◆ **Use Proof Setup (Win).** Select the check box to create a color-managed Windows document.

- ◆ **Embed Color Profile (Mac).** Select the check box to create a color-managed Macintosh document.

- ◆ **ICC Profile (Win).** Select the check box to create a color-managed Windows document.

8 Click **Save**.

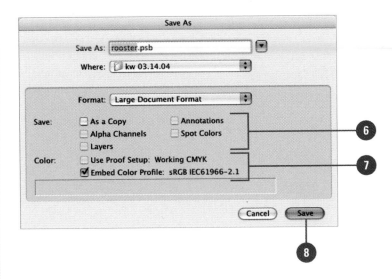

For Your Information

Organizing Documents

Organization is a big part of any Photoshop project. For example, you might be working on several images, along with a dozen supporting images and text. When you work on a project, create a project folder and save all the parts in that folder. That way everything is in one place, so it's easy to access, easy to move, and easy to store.

16

Inserting File Information into a Document

 PS 6.2

When you save a document, you have the ability to save more than just color information. You can save copyright, camera, and even image category information. This data is saved with the file as metadata in the XMP format (Extensible Metadata Platform), and can be accessed by any application that reads XMP data. In addition, if the image is a photograph, you can save data on the type of image, where it was shot, the camera used, even information on shutter speed and F-Stop. That information will not only protect your intellectual property, but will supply you with vital statistics on exactly how you created that one-of-a-kind image.

Insert File Information into a Document

1. Open a document.

2. Click the **File** menu, and then click **Info** (Mac) or **File Info** (Win).

3. Click **Description**, and then enter information concerning the author and any copyright information.

4. Click **Camera Data 1 and 2**, and then enter information about the camera that took the image.

   If the picture was taken with a digital camera that records Metadata, much of this information will already be filled out.

5. Click **History** to view historical information on the active document, such as last opened and saved, and a list of adjustments performed on the image.

6. Click **IPTC Contact**, **Content**, **Image**, and **Status** to enter information concerning the image's creator, description and keywords, image physical information such as: city and date created, copyright and usage terms.

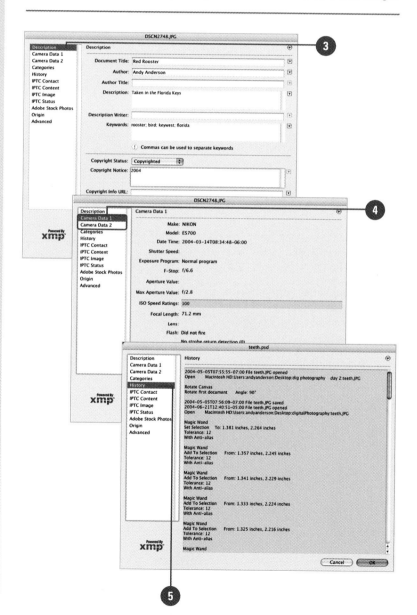

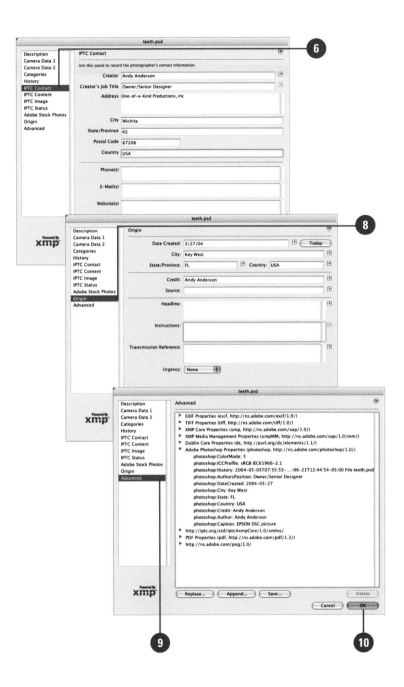

7 Click **Adobe Stock Photo** to display information about Stock Photo images.

8 Click **Origin**, and then enter data pertaining to the origin of the image.

9 Click **Advanced** to view high-end information on the active document, such as EXIF, and PDF document properties.

10 Click **OK**.

Did You Know?

You can add metadata to files saved in the psd, pdf, eps, png, gif, jpg, and tif formats. The information is embedded in the file using XMP (eXtensible Metadata Platform). This allows metadata to be exchanged between Adobe applications and across operating systems.

You can use the XMP Software Development Kit to customize the creation, processing, and interchange of metadata. You can also use the XMP kit to add fields to the File Info dialog box. For information on XMP and the XMP SDK, check the Adobe Solutions Network.

16

Understanding File Compression

Compression is Photoshop's way of reducing the size of a document file. Kind of like the ultimate weight-loss program... just click a button, and the file is half its original size. Photoshop employs two types of compress schemes: lossy and lossless. **Lossy** compression reduces the size of the file by removing color information... information that can never be restored to the saved document. Lossy compression schemes can achieve file reductions of 80 percent or greater.

The lossless method reduces file size by using compression algorithms that reduce the size of a file without removing image information. Lossy methods are used primarily for images displayed in browsers, or Web images. The relatively slow speed of the Internet forces Web designers, to employ lossy compression

methods to reduce images down to their smallest values. Lossless methods are used when the reduction of a file is important, but not so much that you would consider removing information. For example, reducing the size of a group of high-quality TIFF images, so they fit on a rewritable CD. Lossless compression methods can reduce files sizes up to 50 percent, or even a bit more.

Both methods compress documents based on the actual image information. For example, images that contain a lot of solid color information would compress quite well using the GIF (Graphics Interchange) or PNG8 formats; where an image with a lot of soft blending colors, such as a photograph, would be best compressed using the JPEG (Joint Photographic Experts Group) format.

Lossy

Lossless

Format Type, Compression Type, and Output Uses

Format	Compression	Output Use
JPEG	Lossy	**Web/Slide Presentations.** PDFs, photographs, and images that contain lots of colors that softly blend together.
GIF	Lossless	**Web.** Clipart, text, and any images that contain solid colors and images with hard edges.
PNG-8	Lossless	**Web.** Clipart, text, and any images that contain solid colors and images with hard edges.
PNG-24	Lossless	**Web/Slide Presentations/PDF/Print.** Photographs and images that contain lots of colors that softly blend together. Because the PNG-24 format is lossless, it cannot compress images as small as the JPEG format. Therefore, the JPEG format is still the format of choice for compressing images for the Web.
ZIP	Lossless	**Used on all image types for Image Storage and Transfer.** The Zip compression application lets you compress images without affecting image quality. To open a Zip image, you must have the Unzip application.
LZW	Lossless	**Used primarily on TIF images for Image Storage and Transfer.** The LZW compression scheme lets you compress images without affecting image quality. To open an LZW image, the opening application must have the proper LZW decompress utility.

16

Preparing Clipart for the Web

Clipart is defined as non-photographic image information, with a lot of solid-color areas. For this process the GIF or PNG8 formats would serve best. The GIF (Graphics Interchange File) and PNG (Portable Network Graphics) formats use an RLE (Run Length Encoding) scheme. When the file is saved areas of solid color are compressed into small units and then restored to the file when it is opened. The GIF format supports a maximum of 256 colors. While that may not seem like much, most GIF images, such as clipart and text, contain far less color information. By reducing the number of colors available for the GIF color table, you can significantly reduce the image's file size. For example, a GIF image of black text might only require a maximum of 2 colors (black and white). Experiment with the GIF Colors option to produce small, fast-loading image files. Since the GIF format has been around for a long time, using it almost guarantees the image will open on a visitor's browser. The PNG format is newer, and has some new encoding schemes that make even smaller files, but it is not supported by all Web browsers.

Prepare Clipart for the Web

1 Open a clipart document.

2 Click the **File** menu, and then click **Save As**.

3 Enter a name for the file in the Save As box.

4 Click the **Where** (Mac) or **Save In** (Win) list arrow, and then select a location to save the file.

5 Click the **Format** list arrow, and then click **CompuServe GIF**.

6 Click **Save**.

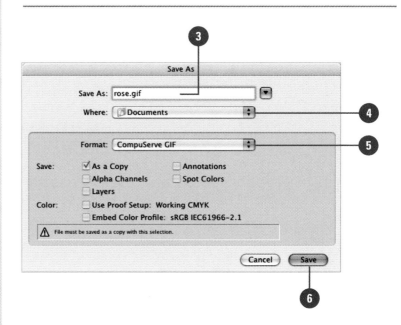

7 Select from the following Indexed Color options:

◆ **Palette.** Click the list arrow, and then select from the available color palette options, including Web (Safe), Mac, and Win System palettes.

◆ **Colors.** If you selected a local color, or custom palette, click to select the number of colors saved with the image. The maximum number of colors is 256.

◆ **Forced.** Click the list arrow, and then select what colors will be forced to remain in the image.

◆ **Transparency.** Select the check box to preserve any transparent areas.

◆ **Matte.** If the image contains transparent areas, clicking this list arrow lets you select a color to fill the areas. For example, you could fill all transparent areas of the image with black to match the black of a Web document.

◆ **Dither.** Click the list arrow, and then select how you want the remaining images color to mix.

◆ **Amount.** Enter an Amount percentage to instruct the GIF format how aggressively to Dither the image colors.

◆ **Preserve Exact Colors.** Select the check box to force the preservation of the original image colors (based on how many colors were chosen using the Palette option).

8 Click **OK**.

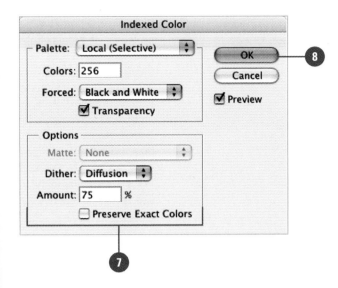

16

Preparing a Photograph for the Web

 PS 14.1

Reducing the size of a photograph presents its own particular set of problems, and Photoshop comes to the rescue with the solution. For Photographic images, the best format to use is the JPEG (Joint Photographic Experts Group) format. This format reduces file size by removing image information (lossy compression). For example, a 1MB uncompressed TIFF file, can be reduced to 20 or 30K using JPEG compression. That reduces the download time of the image on a 33K modem from15 minutes, to 10 seconds. While that is quite a reduction, it also means most of the image colors have been removed and the remaining color are used in a dithering scheme to fool the eyes into seeing colors that are no longer in the image. Highly compressed JPEG images look good on a monitor, but fair poorly when sent to a printer.

Prepare a Photograph for the Web

1 Open a photographic document.

2 Click the **File** menu, and then click **Save As**.

3 Enter a name for the file in the Save As box.

4 Click the **Where** (Mac) or **Save In** (Win) list arrow, and then select a location to save the file.

5 Click the **Format** list arrow, and then click **JPEG**.

6 Click **Save**.

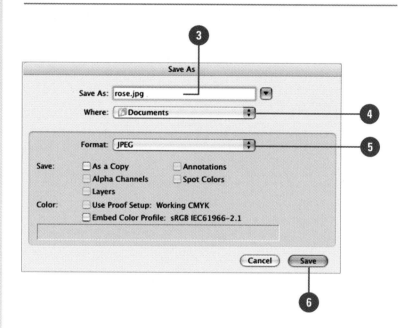

7 Select from the following JPEG Options:

- ◆ **Matte.** The JPEG format does not support transparency. Click the Matte list arrow, and then select what color to fill transparent areas within the active document.

- ◆ **Quality.** The Quality option determines the amount of image information loss. Enter a value from 1 to 12; the higher the value the more information is retained, thus creating a larger file.

- ◆ **Baseline (Standard).** The format is recognized by most browsers.

- ◆ **Baseline Optimized.** Produces optimized color, and a slightly smaller file size, but is not supported by older browsers.

- ◆ **Progressive.** Displays a series of increasingly detailed scans as the image downloads. The visual impression is of a blurred image, slowly coming into focus (not supported by older browsers).

- ◆ **Scans.** If Progressive is selected, select the number of scan passes for the image.

- ◆ **Size.** Allows you to view the download time of the image, based on standard Internet bandwidths.

8 Click **OK**.

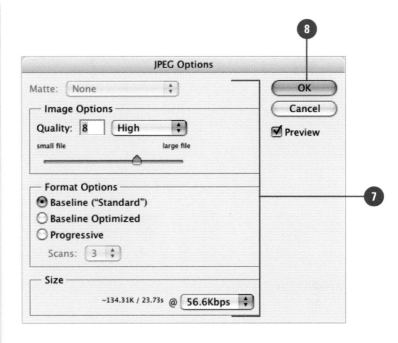

16

Preparing an Image for the Press

Images saved for press are in another world. For example, images displayed on a monitor use the RGB (additive) color space, while images sent to press use the CMYK (subtractive) color space. The format of choice is the DCS (Digital Color Separation) format. The DCS format is a version of the standard EPS format that lets you save color separations of CMYK images. DCS comes in two flavors, DCS 1.0 and DCS 2.0. Both create five separate files: one each for the four color plates, Cyan, Magenta, Yellow, and Black, and one for a combined, or composite image. However, the DCS 2.0 format allows you to save alpha and spot-color channels, as well as giving you the option of saving the five separate files under one combined file name. You can also use DCS 2.0 format to export images containing spot channels. It's important to understand that the only device that can print a DCS file is a PostScript printer. As with anything related to press operations, always contact your friendly press operator and ask what format to use.

Prepare an Image for the Press

1. Open a document.

2. Click the **File** menu, and then click **Save As**.

   IMPORTANT *Images saved in the DCS format must be in the CMYK color mode.*

3. Enter a name for the file in the Save As box.

4. Click the **Where** (Mac) or **Save In** (Win) list arrow, and then select a location to save the file.

5. Click the **Format** list arrow, and then click **Photoshop DCS 2.0**.

6. Click **Save**.

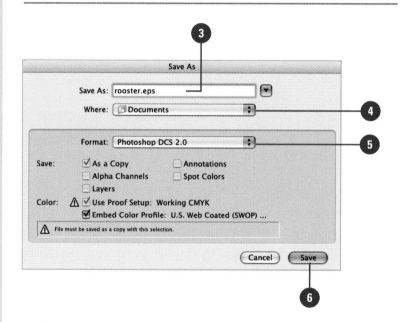

7 Select from the following DCS 2.0 Format options:

◆ **Preview.** Click the list arrow, and then select what type of low-resolution image to use in the layout application.

◆ **DCS.** Click the list arrow, and then select how you want the color plate information saved.

◆ **Encoding.** Click the list arrow, and then select how the image data is encoded for delivery to the output device (contact your service bureau).

◆ **Include Halftone Screen.** Select the check box to include any halftone screens.

◆ **Include Transfer Function.** Used with high-end commercial production jobs.

◆ **Include Vector Data.** Select the check box to include any vector data contained within the active image.

◆ **Image Interpolation.** Select the check box to create an anti-aliased version of the Preview image (does not impact printing).

8 Click **OK**.

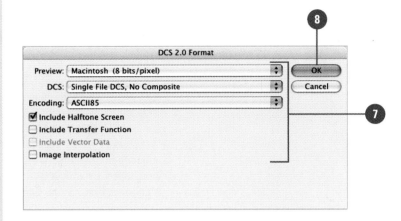

16

Preparing an Image for the Inkjet or Laser Printer

While not everyone has access to a 4-color press; even casual computer users have or have access to, an inkjet or laser printer. Inkjet and laser printers apply ink to the paper using dots of color. In fact, one of the measurements of quality for this type of output is its printing resolution. For example, a photo-quality inkjet or laser printer can run with a resolution of 1,400dpi and higher, or one thousand four hundred dots of color information per linear inch. There are several file format options for output to print, however none is so versatile as the TIFF format. The Tagged Image File Format, uses lossy or lossless compression, and lets you save multiple Photoshop layers, as well as alpha channel information. In addition, there is hardly a layout application in the marketplace, Macintosh or Windows, that will not open a TIFF saved image.

Prepare an Image for the Inkjet or Laser Printer

1. Open a document.

2. Click the **File** menu, and then click **Save As**.

3. Enter a name for the file in the Save As box.

4. Click the **Where** (Mac) or **Save In** (Win) list arrow, and then select a location to save the file.

5. Click the **Format** list arrow, and then click **TIFF**.

6. Click **Save**.

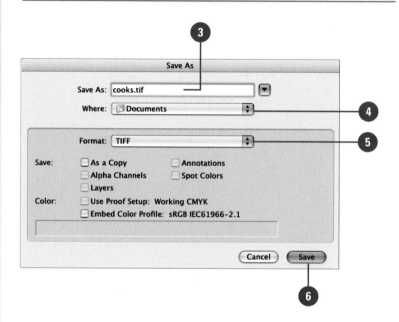

7 Select from the following TIFF Options:

- ◆ **None.** No compression is performed to the image.

- ◆ **LZW.** Performs lossless compression to the image. When used, the receiving application must have the corresponding LZW option or they will not be able to uncompress the file.

- ◆ **Zip.** Performs a standard Zip (lossless) compression to the image. Receiving application must have an unzip utility.

- ◆ **JPEG.** Performs lossy (image loss) compression to the image.

- ◆ **IBM PC.** Select PC if the image is to be used on an IBM system.

- ◆ **Macintosh.** Select Macintosh if the image is to be used on a Macintosh system.

- ◆ **Save Image Pyramid.** Check to save the image using several image resolutions, and lets you decide, when reopening the image, what resolution to use.

- ◆ **Save Transparency.** Check to preserves any transparent areas in the active image.

- ◆ **RLE.** Run Length Encoding (RLE) helps to compress solid areas of color across multiple layers.

- ◆ **ZIP.** Uses the Zip format to compress multiple layers.

- ◆ **Discard Layers And Save A Copy.** Creates a copy of the file without the layers, essentially saves a composite image file.

8 Click **OK**.

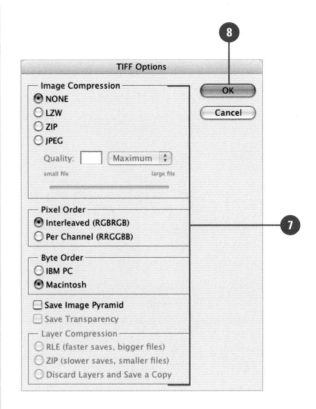

16

Understanding Monitor, Image, and Device Resolution

 PS 12.3

Remember that raster images are all about resolution. Images have a specific scanned resolution (spi, samples per inch), your monitor has a resolution (ppi, pixels per inch), and output devices such as inkjet printers (dpi, dots per inch), and high-end presses (lpi, lines per inch). While all these terms may seem a bit complicated, they're not; they simply explain how much resolution, or information is contained within the image.

Most computer monitors are set to a fixed resolution of 72 or 96 ppi. Say you scan an image a 4 by 4 inch image at 288spi (that's 4 times the resolution of a 72ppi monitor). If you attempted to display the image at 100 percent view, the monitor would take the image pixels and adjust the width and height to match its resolution, so the image would be 16 by 16 inches (288 divided by 72 = 4). With monitors 16 inches is not an exact number, but it's close enough for this example. If you attempt to reduce the zoom size of the image to make it fit the monitor size, Photoshop will have to remove pixels from the image to make it fit. This typically causes the image to generate jagged lines; especially around angles lines. The moral of this story is when adjusting an image for viewing on a monitor, for example a slide presentation, never change the zoom of the image to fit the monitor, always adjust the resolution by selecting Image menu, and clicking Image Size.

When it comes to output, such as to an inkjet print, the rules are a bit more forgiving. Many output devices have print resolutions of 1,440 or higher. However, we're not talking about fixed monitor pixels (ppi), we're talking about dot of ink hitting a piece of paper (dpi). Most inkjet printer, because of the dot gain of the inks (that's the amount of space a dot of ink spreads when it hits the paper), does not need image resolution greater than 300spi. Unlike a monitor, if you use higher resolutions than needed, the image typically will not suffer, quality wise, you'll just be printing an image with a larger file size. However, that can be a time-wasting problem. For example, a 300spi 8 by 10 image will have a file size of about 20MB, the same image scanned at 1200spi will produce a 329MB file size. When you print the two images, you will probably not notice any quality difference; however, it will take, on average, 6 minutes longer to print the 1200spi document on most mid-range printers.

The bottom line is that resolution represents the amount of information contained within a linear inch; however, various devices handle that same resolution number differently. The good news is that understanding those differences helps you to create a useable workflow. Knowledge is power.

Working with Automate Commands

Introduction

It's great when you hear about new tips and tricks that will save time. But it's never a good policy to shave time to sacrifice quality. Adobe Photoshop has come to the rescue with some great time-savers that will help you. The Automate commands give the ability to streamline your workflow, and make short work of repetitive tasks. The Automate commands let you process—Batch File Processing—hundreds of image files with the click of a button, create interactive Web documents of your images; and even lets you create a picture package from a precious image.

You can create a PDF file (presentation or document), or a photographic contact sheet. You can also use the Crop and Straighten Photo and Photomerge commands. Photoshop gives you the ability to convert a multi-page PDF file into a self-running slide show. Or how about those proof sheets with various size images on them? Now you can take an image and make your own photo sheet using the Picture Package command.

Think of an action as a batch of single commands all rolled up into one powerful authority. For example, to create a picture package without the Picture Package command would take dozens of steps to complete, and the results would be different every time you performed the steps. In the busy world of graphic design, with all the image processing you need to do on a daily basis, Photoshop's Automate commands give you the ability to deliver consistent results, over and over again with the click of a button.

You can also use many of the commands on the Automate menu in Adobe Bridge. The Tools menu in Bridge contains commands available with different Adobe Creative Suite program names, such as Photoshop or InDesign. For example, the Photoshop automation commands appear under the Photoshop submenu in Bridge.

Working with Batch File Processing

PS 8.2, 8.3

There is nothing more exciting than working on a new creative process, and watch as your designs come to life. Conversely, there is nothing more tiresome than having to apply that new creative concept to 50 other images. For example, you just spent three hours coming up with a procedure to color correct an heirloom photograph, and the process took two filters, and three adjustments. The photo looks great; however, you now have 50 other images with the exact problem. You could create an action, but you would still have to open and apply the action 50 times. The solution is to batch process the images, after you have created the action. Batch file processing lets you apply an action to an entire folder of images, and all you have to do is click a button. Now, what could be simpler than that?

Work with Batch File Processing

1 Create a new folder, and then move all the images into the folder.

> **IMPORTANT** *These files must be typical image files. There should not be any other files, such as text files, inside this folder.*

2 Create a second folder to hold the modified images (optional).

3 Open Photoshop (you do not need to open a document).

4 Click the **File** menu, point to **Automate**, and then click **Batch**.

5 Select from the following Play options:

◆ Click the **Set** list arrow, and then select the Set containing the Action you want to apply to the images.

◆ Click the **Action** list arrow, and then select the correct Action.

6 Click the **Source** list arrow, and then select an image-source option of Folder, Import, Opened Files, or File Browser.

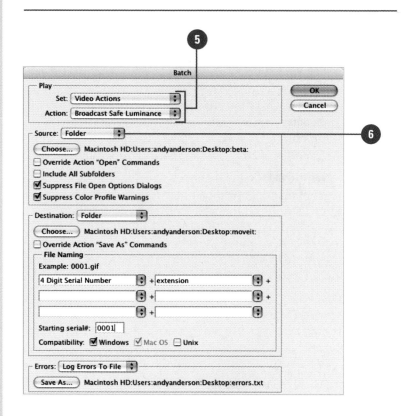

7 Click **Choose** (available if Folder is selected as the source), and then select the location of the image folder.

8 Check the various boxes you want:

◆ **Override Action "Open" Commands.** Select to use an open command embedded into the Action.

◆ **Include All Subfolders.** Select to batch process any images located in folders embedded into the main image folder.

◆ **Suppress File Open Options Dialogs.** Select to disable the File Open dialog box.

◆ **Suppress Color Profile Warnings.** Select to disable the Color Profile Mismatch dialog box.

9 Click the **Destination** list arrow, and then click **None**, **Save And Close**, or **Folder**.

10 Click **Choose** (available if Folder is selected as the source), and then select the destination of the modified images.

11 Select the **Override Action "Save As" Commands** check box to use a save command embedded into the Action.

12 If Folder is selected as destination, the File Naming options allows you to rename the modified files, and then select the required Compatibility options you want: Windows, Mac OS or Unix.

13 Click the **Errors** list arrow, select an errors option, and then click **Save As** to save your error information, if necessary.

14 Click **OK**.

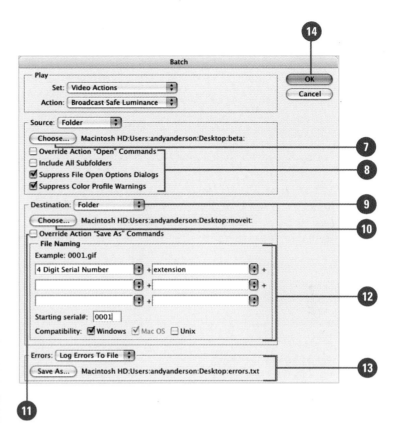

For Your Information

Things to Remember About Batch File Processing

There are many settings and requirements in order to make your batch file processing a success. Remember that before you begin, you need to have a created action. For more information on actions, you can refer to Chapter 15. After your action is created, and all the kinks are worked out, you can then set up your batch file processing. Knowing information such as where the source images are, where you'll be storing them (destination), having a naming convention, and other details will help to make your setup of the batch file processing a few easy steps.

17

Creating a PDF File

PS 8.2

There are times when you want to create a slide show of your latest summer vacation and distribute it via e-mail or CD. You have the entire image collection in a folder; they're ready to go, but you need a format to place all of the images, so that your Macintosh and Windows relatives can open. The answer is **PDF** (Portable Document File). The PDF format from Adobe lets you create a slide show presentation or individual documents that can be opened by literally any computer or operating system using Adobe Acrobat Reader (free at *www.adobe.com*). Photoshop and ImageReady recognize two types of PDF files: Generic PDF (multiple pages and images) and Photoshop PDF (single image only). Adobe provides standard presets (**New!**) to make PDFs quick and easy, and you can even create your own customized presets.

Create a PDF Presentation

1. Open Photoshop (it is not necessary to open a document).

2. Click the **File** menu, point to **Automate**, and then click **PDF Presentation**.

3. Select the **Add Open Files** check box to add any active files, or click **Browse** to select the files.

4. To remove any images from the current Source Files List, click a file, and then click **Remove**.

5. To change its presentation stacking order, drag a file in the list.

6. Click the **Presentation** option.

7. Select the **Advance Every XX Seconds** check box to select how long each image is displayed.

8. Select the **Loop After Last Page** check box to loop the show.

9. Click the **Transition** list arrow, and then select a slide transition.

10. Click **Save**.

11. Specify a name and location for the show, and then click **Save**.

   The Save Adobe PDF dialog box opens.

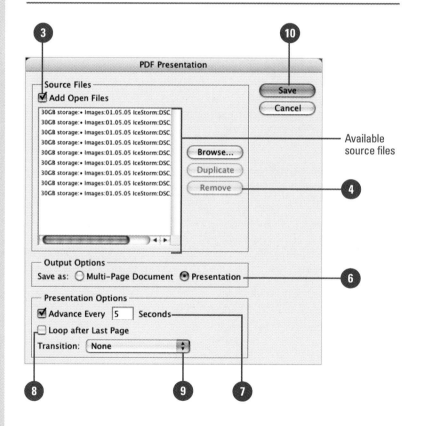

Available source files

12 Select from the general options (**New!**):

- ◆ **Adobe PDF Preset.** Click to select a pre-defined compression (Smallest File Size) recommended.

- ◆ **Standard.** Click to select the PDF standard to be compliant with (None, recommended).

- ◆ **Compatibility.** Click to select a version of the PDF reader application to be compatible with (5.0, recommended).

- ◆ **Description.** Enter a new description, if desired.

13 Select from the other PDF options (**New!**):

- ◆ **Preserve Photoshop Editing Capabilities.** Disabled for PDF presentations.

- ◆ **Embed Page Thumbnails.** Check to add thumbnails to the presentation (larger file size, and not necessary).

- ◆ **Optimize For Fast Web Preview.** Check to optimize for viewing on the Web (recommended).

- ◆ **View PDF After Saving.** Check to view the presentation, after it's created.

14 Click **Compression** to modify compression values (typically not required), **Output** to set color management and PDF/X (for pre-press/postscript) options, **Security** to set passwords and print options, and **Summary** to review your settings.

15 To create your own presets, click **Save Preset**, enter a name, and then click **Save**.

16 Click **Save PDF** to start your PDF presentation.

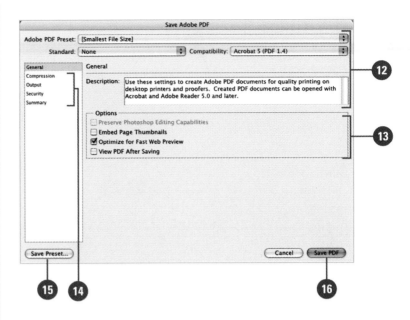

For Your Information

Saving a File in PDF Format

In addition to creating a PDF presentation with multiple images, you can save an individual file in Photoshop PDF format (**New!**). Instead of using the PDF Presentation command, you use the Save As command; the process is very similar. Open the document you want to use, click the File menu, click Save As, click the Format list arrow, click Photoshop PDF, select a Color option (if you want to embed a color profile or use the profile with the Proof Setup command), and then click Save. If necessary, click OK to the override alert message. In the Save Adobe PDF dialog box, select the options you want (see steps 12-14 on this page for details), and the click Save PDF.

Creating and Working with Custom PDF Presets

If you need to create specialized PDFs, you can create your own PDF presets (**New!**) to make the job easier. Click the Edit menu, click Adobe PDF Presets, click New to create a preset, or select a preset and click Edit (you can't edit the default presets). In the Save Adobe PDF dialog box, select the options you want (see steps 12-14 for details), name and save (if necessary), and then exit the dialogs. Adobe PDF presets are saved as files with a .joboptions extension, which can be used by all CS2 programs using the Load button.

17

Creating a Contact Sheet

 PS 8.2

Photoshop's Contact Sheet II provides you with a way to view multiple images in a contact sheet format. Traditional photographers used to create contact sheets in the darkroom by placing a group of negatives on a piece of light-sensitive photographic paper, laying a piece of glass over the top, and exposing the glass and negative paper sandwich to light. After processing, you had a contact sheet with thumbnails of your images. Now with Photoshop, you can create your contact sheet without the darkroom requirements.

Create a Contact Sheet

1 Create a folder, and then move in the images you want to create a contact sheet for into the folder.

2 Open Photoshop (it is not necessary to open a document).

3 Click the **File** menu, point to **Automate**, and then click **Contact Sheet II**.

4 Click the **Use** list arrow, and then select from the available Source Images options:

   ◆ Current Open Documents

   ◆ Folder

   ◆ File Browser

5 Click **Choose**, and then select the folder containing the images (available only if Folder is selected) for your source images.

6 Select the **Include All Subfolders** check box to add images from folders embedded into the original source folder.

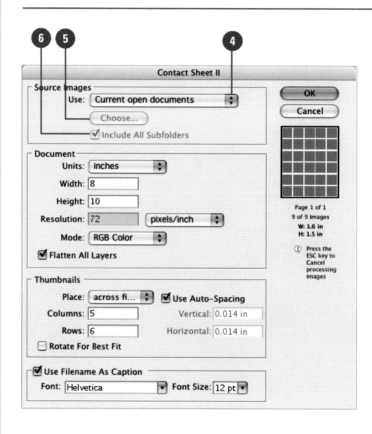

Did You Know?

You can start the Contact Sheet II command from Bridge. Select the images you want, click the Tools menu, point to Photoshop, and then click Contact Sheet II.

7 Select from the Document options (these options determine the characteristics of the output document):

- ◆ **Units.** Click the list arrow, and then select a measurement system for the output paper document.

- ◆ **Width/Height.** Enter a width and height for the contact sheet.

- ◆ **Resolution.** Enter a resolution for the output document.

- ◆ **Mode.** Click the list arrow, and then select a color mode for the output document.

- ◆ **Flatten All Layers.** Select to create a contact sheet as a composite (flattened) image. Leave unchecked to place the images in a separate layer.

8 Select from the Thumbnail options:

- ◆ **Place.** Click the list arrow, and then select an option to determine whether the contact images run top-to-bottom or left-to-right.

- ◆ **Use Auto-Spacing.** Check to let Photoshop control the placing of the images on the page.

- ◆ **Columns/Rows.** Enter a value for rows and columns.

- ◆ **Rotate For Best Fit.** Check to let Photoshop rotate images for best placement on the page.

9 Select the **Use Filename As Caption** check box to use as the caption for the thumbnail, and then set the font type and size for the caption (recommended).

10 Click **OK**.

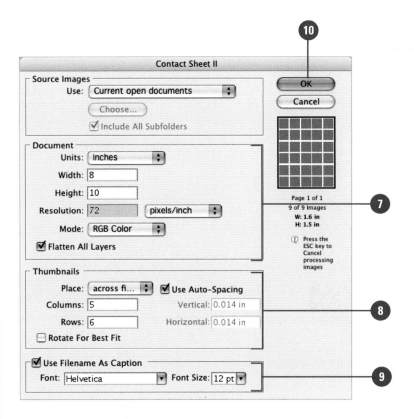

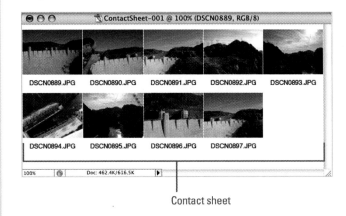

Contact sheet

Working with Conditional Mode Change

 PS 8.2

Work with Conditional Mode Change

1 Open a document.

2 Start the recording of an Action.

> **IMPORTANT** *To make a conditional mode change, you must have a document open and an available Action to change.*

3 Click the **File** menu, point to **Automate**, and then click **Conditional Mode Change**.

4 Select the check boxes with the possible modes for the source image; you can click **All**.

5 Click the **Mode** list arrow, and then select the Target mode you want the image converted to.

6 Click **OK**.

7 Add any additional commands to the action.

8 Click the **Stop Recording** button, and then save the action.

See Also

See "Building a New Action" and "Recording an Action" on pages 350-351 for information on starting the recording of an action.

The Conditional Mode Change command lets you specify the conditions for changing the mode of an image in an action. When you create an action that changes modes, it can cause a problem when you run the action. For example, you create an action and one of the commands is to convert the image from RGB to Grayscale. Running the action against a file that is not RGB will cause an error. But, what if you want to use the same action to convert a CMYK image to grayscale? You can if you make the mode change within the action using Conditional Mode Change. Using this option guarantees that you will never have a problem using an action to change the mode of an image.

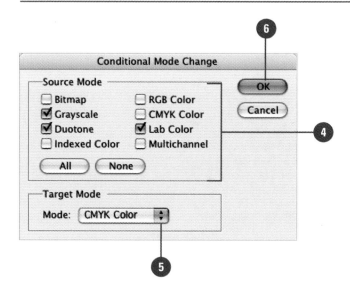

Using the Crop and Straighten Photos Command

PS 8.2

Use the Crop and Straighten Photos Command

1 Open a document.

2 Click the **File** menu, point to **Automate**, and then click **Crop And Straighten Photos**.

Photoshop automatically creates separate images from the available image information in the active document, and then places the images into individual files.

Did You Know?

You can control the Crop And Straighten Photos command through selection. Use the Rectangular Marquee tool to select a portion of the image before using the Crop And Straighten Photos command, and then Photoshop will only work within the selection.

The Crop and Straighten Photos command is a nifty way to quickly straighten and make separate image files out of one image. For example, you have a photograph of two people standing side-by-side, and you want a separate image of each person. Or you have a scanned image that wasn't quite straight on the platten. The Crop and Straighten Photos command works best when the images in the document are separated by some space. When you apply the command to an image, it looks for areas to divide based on shifts in color; no selection is required.

1

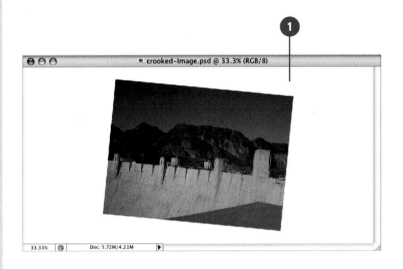

Image cropped and straightened

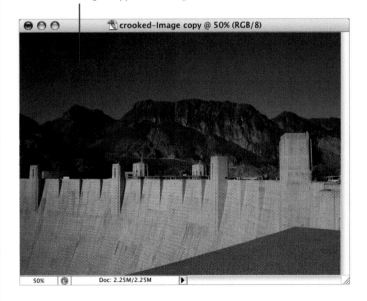

17

Converting a Multi-Page PDF to PSD

 PS 8.2

Photoshop's list of automation features is impressive, and it gets longer and better with each new version of the program. One of the features that will come in handy is the ability to convert a multi-page PDF directly into multiple Photoshop image files. You have this great Adobe PDF document that contains images you want to use in a Photoshop design. The PDF format is a versatile file format that saves both vector and bitmap data, as well as contains electronic document search and navigation features. Some PDF files contain a single image, while other PDF files contain multiple pages and images. When you open a PDF file, you can choose which pages to open, as well as specify a specific rasterization process (how to convert the image from vector to raster). Although Adobe moved this process from the Automation palette to the Open dialog box (**New!**), it still rates a spot in automation.

Work with Multi-Page PDF to PSD

1. Open Photoshop (it is not necessary to open a document).

2. Click the **File** menu, and then click **Open**.

3. Select a document in the Photoshop PDF format, and then click **Open**.

4. Click the **Select** list arrow, and then choose to open whole pages, or images.

5. Select from the following Page Options:

   ◆ **Name:** Enter a name for the new document

   ◆ **Crop To:** Click the list arrow, and then select from the various cropping options.

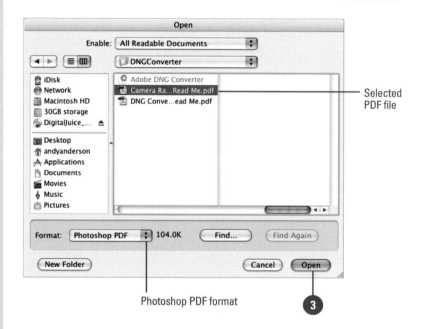

Selected PDF file

Photoshop PDF format

See Also

See "Creating a PDF File" on page 400 for information on the different types of PDF formats.

- ◆ **Resolution:** Choose a resolution for Photoshop to use when it rasterizes the PDF document.

- ◆ **Mode:** Click the list arrow, and then select a color mode for the output document.

- ◆ **Bit Depth:** Click the list arrow and then select 8 or 16 bit color depth.

- ◆ **Anti-aliased:** Select the check box to use anti-aliasing smoothing techniques during the conversion.

- ◆ **Suppress Warnings:** Select the check box to prevent the operation from stopping on alert dialog boxes.

6 Shift+click to select contiguous pages, or Ctrl+click (Win) or ⌘+click (Mac) to select separate pages.

7 Click **OK**.

Photoshop creates separate PSD files from each specified page within the PDF document, and places the text and/or images on a transparent layer.

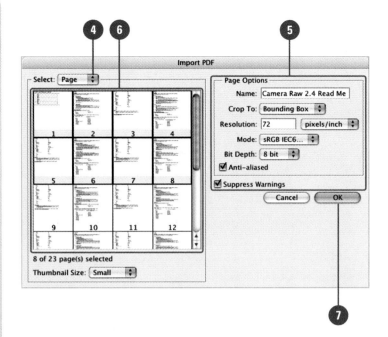

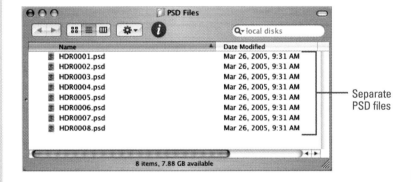

Separate PSD files

Did You Know?

You can convert Photoshop image into PDF documents. Photoshop gives you the option to save the document in the Photoshop PDF file format (**New!**). Photoshop documents saved as PDF files preserve shape information as vector data, and you have the option of preserving type layers.

Designing a Personalized Picture Package

PS 8.2

The Picture Package command gives you the ability to generate a group of pictures from one or more images. Whatever you want, and in whatever sizes you need, Photoshop's Picture Package can deliver them right from your computer and a good photo-quality printer. You can modify existing layouts or create new layouts using the Picture Package Edit Layout feature. Your custom layouts are saved as text files. The Picture Package Edit Layout feature uses a graphic interface that eliminates the need to write text files to create or modify layouts. Just select a standard layout from the available options, and then make the necessary changes.

Design a Personalized Picture Package

1. Open Photoshop (it is not necessary to open a document).

2. Click the **File** menu, point to **Automate**, and then click **Picture Package**.

3. Click the **Use** list arrow, and then select the source for the document or documents to be used in the picture package.

4. Click **Choose**, and then select the folder containing the images (available only if File is selected for Source Images).

5. Select the **Include All Subfolders** check box to include images from subfolders (available only if File is selected for Source Images).

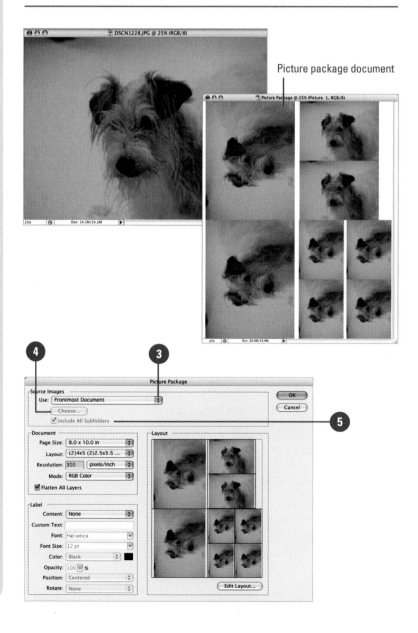

Picture package document

Did You Know?

You can change an individual image in the Picture Package set. Click on any thumbnail in the Picture Package image preview, and Photoshop lets you select an alternate image for that spot in the package.

You can start the Picture Package command from Bridge. Select the images you want, click the Tools menu, point to Photoshop, and then click Picture Package.

6 Click to select from the Document options:

 ◆ **Page Size.** Click to select a page size for the picture package document.

 ◆ **Layout.** Click to select from the available image layouts.

 ◆ **Resolution.** Select a resolution for the picture package.

 IMPORTANT *If you're planning on printing the package, the resolution should be higher than the default resolution of 72pp.*

 ◆ **Mode.** Click to select a color mode for the document.

 ◆ **Flatten All Layers.** Select the check box to create a composite (flattened) picture package document.

7 Click to select from the Label options to determine what will be printed with the images:

 ◆ **Content.** Click to select from the available label content options.

 ◆ **Custom Text.** Generate custom text for the images.

 ◆ **Font And Size.** Click to select a font and size for the label text.

 ◆ **Color.** Click to select a color for the label text.

 ◆ **Opacity.** Enter a percentage value for the label text.

 ◆ **Position.** Click to select a position for the label text.

 ◆ **Rotate.** Click to rotate the text.

8 Click **OK**.

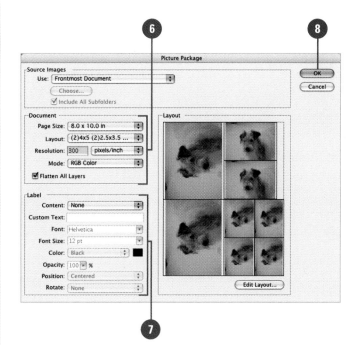

17

Using the Web Photo Gallery Command

 PS 8.2

Photoshop's Web Photo Gallery takes the drudgery out of creating those thumbnail Web pages. The pages display small thumbnails of a group of images—when you click on an image, a larger version is displayed within another window, or section of the page. If your goal is to show the world your photographs, but you don't want to write all the HTML code involved in making that happen, then the Web Photo Gallery is just what you need.

Use the Web Photo Gallery Command

1. Create a folder with the images you want to use to generate the photo gallery.

2. Open Photoshop (it is not necessary to open a document).

3. Click the **File** menu, point to **Automate**, and then click **Web Photo Gallery**.

4. Click the **Styles** list arrow, and then select from the available styles (watch the preview to see how each style appears).

5. Enter an e-mail address in the Email box. This gives the visitor the ability to click and send you an e-mail message (optional).

6. Click the **Use** list arrow, and then select the location of the Source Images.

7. Click **Choose**, and then locate the folder containing the images (available only if Folder is selected).

8. Select the **Include All Subfolders** check box to include images from subfolders (available only if File is selected for Source Images).

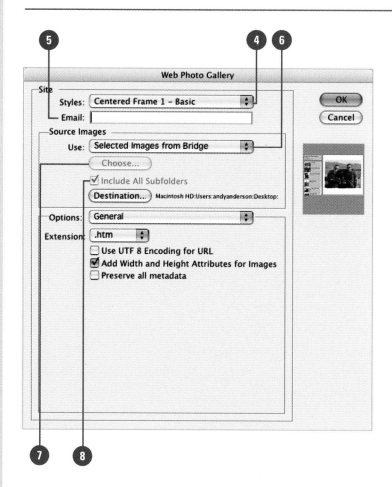

9️⃣ Click **Destination**, and then select a destination for the HTML document and images.

🔟 Click the **Options** list arrow, and then design the final HTML document based on the following options:

- ◆ General
- ◆ Banner
- ◆ Large Images
- ◆ Thumbnails
- ◆ Custom Colors
- ◆ Security

1️⃣1️⃣ Click **OK**.

Did You Know?

You can create a new Web Photo Gallery style. Use an HTML editor, create the necessary HTML template files, and then store them inside the style folder (located in the Photoshop applications folder). The new style appears as an option in the Styles dialog box and in the Web Photo Gallery dialog box. Creating your own styles does require knowledge of HTML and Web design techniques.

You can start the Web Photo Gallery command from Bridge. Select the images you want, click the Tools menu, point to Photoshop, and then click Web Photo Gallery.

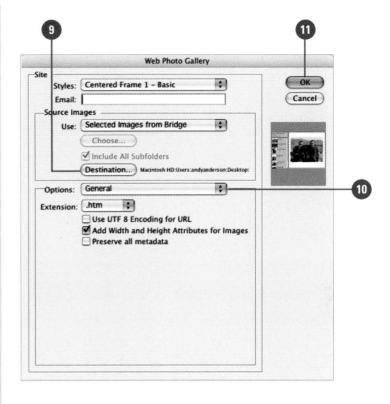

Web Photo Gallery

17

Using Photomerge

PS 8.2

Use Photomerge

1 Open Photoshop (it is not necessary to open a document).

2 Click the **File** menu, point to **Automate**, and then click **Photomerge**.

3 Click the **Use** list arrow, and then select from the following options:

- ◆ **Files.** Select the files to include in the merge document. Click the Browse button, and then select the images.

- ◆ **Folder.** Select a folder that contains all the images. Click the Browse button, and then select the folder containing all the images.

- ◆ **Open Files.** Selects the currently open Photoshop images.

4 To remove any images from the list, click the file name, and then click **Remove**.

Did You Know?

You can start the Photomerge command from Bridge. Select the images you want, click the Tools menu, point to Photoshop, and then click Photomerge.

Ever wanted to create a panoramic photograph? Panoramas are those great looking images that encompass a wide area into one photograph. For example, you want to create a single photograph of the Grand Canyon, but the lens on your camera doesn't go that wide. So you start at the left of the canyon wall, and take a photo. Then you move slightly to the right and take another photo, and another, until you have reached the far right canyon wall. So, now you have four or five separate images on the Grand Canyon, and you want to stitch them together into a single panoramic view. If you have Photoshop, you have what you need to make it happen.

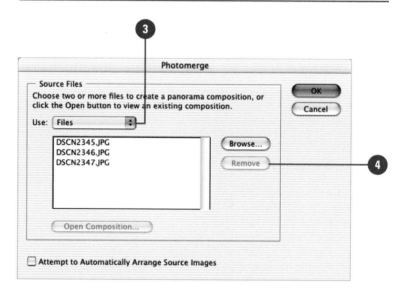

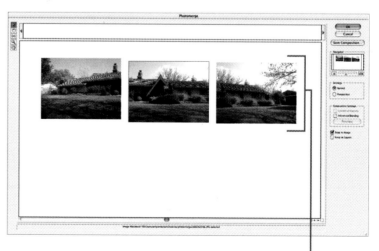

3 separate images

5 Select the **Attempt To Automatically Arrange Source Images** check box to let Photoshop try to stitch the images together.

If left unchecked, Photoshop opens the Composition editor, and then lets you manually arrange the images (recommended).

6 Click **OK**.

7 If you did not check the option in step 5, arrange the images, and then click **OK**.

Photoshop merges the images into a single panoramic document file.

Did You Know?

You can add and remove files from the Photomerge Source Files list. Click the Browse button, select the correct source files, and then click Open. To remove a file from the Source Files list, select the file and then click the Remove button.

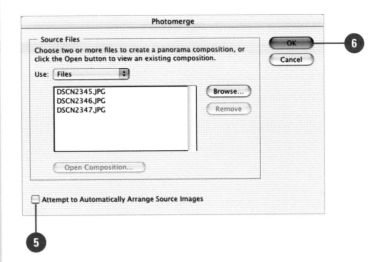

When manually arranging, click OK.

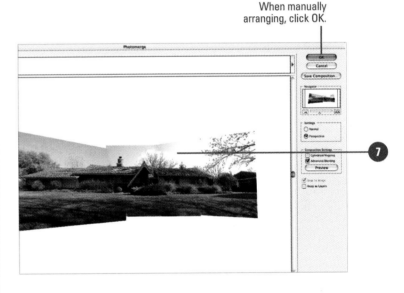

Single panoramic document

17

Merging Images to HDR

PS 6.2, 6.3, 8.2

The Merge To HDR command (**New!**) allows you to combine multiple images (of different exposures) of the same image or scene, or a bracketed exposure. HDR (High Dynamic Range) creates 32-bit high-end digital quality images. The Merge To HDR command takes the best elements of each photograph and combines them to create a single HDR image with more dynamic range than possible with a single digital image. Since several photos will be combined to create a single image, it's important to place the camera on a tripod (so it won't move), and then take enough photographs (3 minimum) at different exposures to capture all the dynamic range of the scene.

Use the Merge To HDR Command

1 Click the **File** menu, point to **Automate**, and then click **Merge To HDR**.

2 Click the **Use** list arrow, and then select from the following options:

◆ **Files.** Select the files to include in the merge document. Click the Browse button, and then select the images.

◆ **Folder.** Select a folder that contains all the images. Click the Browse button, and then select the folder containing all the images.

◆ **Open Files.** Selects the currently open Photoshop images.

3 To remove any images from the list, click the file name, and then click **Remove**.

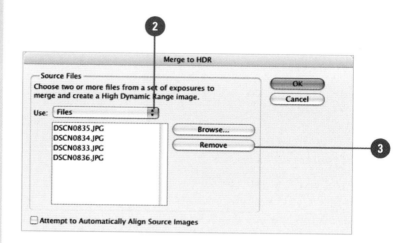

Did You Know?

You can start the Merge To HDR command from Bridge. Select the images you want, click the Tools menu, point to Photoshop, and then click Merge To HDR.

4 Select the **Attempt to Automatically Align Source Images** check box to let Photoshop try to align the images together (always try this option first).

5 Click **OK**.

6 If you did not check the option in step 4, specify any of the following options, and then click **OK**.

◆ **Select Files.** Select or clear the check box under each thumbnail to specify which images to use.

◆ **Bit Depth.** Click the Bit Depth menu, and then select a bit depth for the merged image.

◆ **Histogram.** Drag the slider to set the white point for previewing the merged image.

Photoshop attempts to combine the elements of all the images.

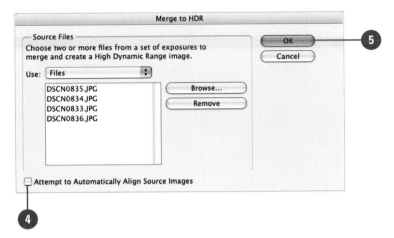

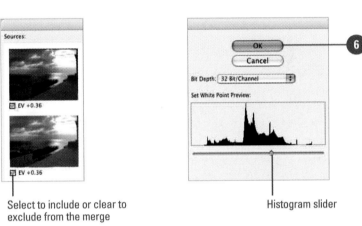

Select to include or clear to exclude from the merge

Histogram slider

Merge to HDR image

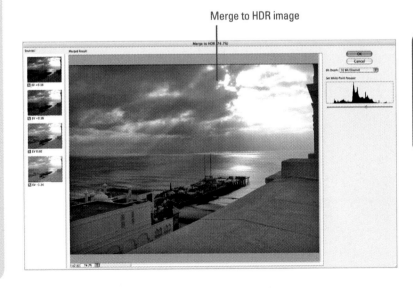

17

Processing Multiple Image Files

The Image Processor command (**New!**) in Photoshop allows you to convert and process multiple files without first creating an action, which is something you need to do with the Batch command. The Image Processor commands makes it easy to convert a set of files to either JPEG, PSD, or TIFF, or all three formats at the same time. When you take a lot of digital pictures, you can process the camera raw files all at once using the same options. If you are working on a collage with specific size and color requirements, you can use Image Processor to resize images to specific dimensions and embed a color profile or change the color mode to sRGB (the default working space for most Adobe color settings; recommended for Web and digital camera images). In addition, you can include copyright metadata into any of the converted images.

Use the Image Processor Command

1 Click the **File** menu, point to **Scripts**, and then click **Image Processor**.

2 Click the **Use Open Images** option or click **Select Folder** to select the images or folder to process.

3 Select the **Open First Image To Apply Settings** check box to apply the same settings to all the images.

This allows you to adjust the settings in the first image, and then apply the same settings to the rest of the images.

4 Click the **Save In Same Location** option or click **Select Folder** to select the location to save processed images.

If you process the same file multiple times to the same location, each file is saved with a unique file name, so it's not overwritten.

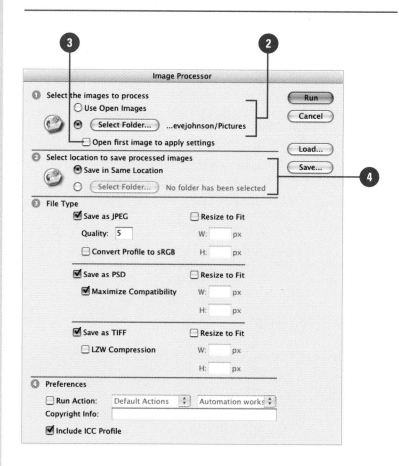

5 Select from the following options:

◆ **Save As JPEG.** Saves image in JPEG format.

◆ **Quality.** Enter a quality value between 0 and 12 (3 or 4 recommended for Web graphics)

◆ **Resize To Fit.** Resizes the images to fit the width and height in pixels.

◆ **Convert Profile To sRGB.** Converts the color profile to sRGB; select the Include ICC Profile check box to save it.

◆ **Save As PSD.** Saves images in the PSD Photoshop format.

◆ **Maximize Compatibility.** Saves a composite of a layer image for programs that can't read layered images.

◆ **Save As TIFF.** Saves images in the TIFF format.

◆ **LZW Compression.** Saves TIFF files using the LZW compression scheme.

6 Select from the following preferences options:

◆ **Run Action.** Runs a selected Photoshop action.

◆ **Copyright Info.** Includes file information entered in the IPTC copyright metadata

◆ **Include ICC Profile.** Embeds the color profile with the saved image files.

7 To save your settings, click **Save**, enter a name, and then click **Save**.

8 To load saved settings, click **Load**, select the settings file, and then click **Open**.

9 Click **Run**.

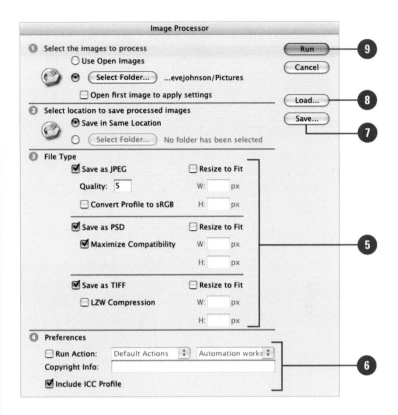

For Your Information

Batch Renaming Files with Bridge

You can rename files and folders in a batch, or group, to save time. With Bridge, you can select the same settings for all the files you want to process. Launch Bridge from the desktop or Photoshop, select the files you want to rename or select a folder in the Folders panel that contains the files you want to rename, set options in any of the following areas, and then click Rename: Destination Folder (rename, move, or copy), New Filenames (choose elements from menus or enter text to create file names; click plus (+) to add and minus (-) to remove), Preserve file name in XMP Metadata, or Operating System Compatibility.

17

Using the Fit Image Command

 PS 8.2

The Fit Image command is a quick way to adjust an image to a specific width and height without changing its current aspect ratio. While the same process can be accomplished using Photoshop's Image Size dialog box, this way is quicker and works more reliably when used to change the size of an image within an action. Like another one of the Automate commands called Conditional Mode Change, the Fit Image command is designed to work best when incorporated into an action. When the action is executed, the Fit Image command will adjust the image's size without opening any dialog boxes, or requiring you to answer any formatting questions.

Use the Fit Image Command

1. Open a document.

2. Click the **File** menu, point to **Automate**, and then click **Fit Image**.

3. Enter a Width and Height for the transformation.

   Photoshop maintains the image's aspect ratio.

4. Click **OK**.

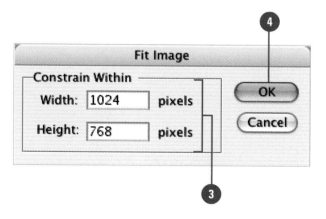

Managing Color from Monitor to Print

Introduction

Color management has changed a lot in the last few years, standards have been set up, and Adobe is at the forefront of this new technology. No longer do you have to fear color management, because Adobe Photoshop has taken all (or at least most) of the guesswork out of the equation. Adobe's color management system (CMS) translates, known as rendering intents, color discrepancies between the input device and the output device using color profiles to avoid color-matching problems.

When you work on a computer monitor, you're viewing color information in the RGB (red, green, and blue), additive color space. When you move into the world of the 4-color press, you're viewing color information in the CMYK, subtractive color space. While a standard color press uses 4 colors, in reality, CMY (cyan, magenta, and yellow) are the opposites of RGB. A press to generate a true black uses the K plate (K stands for black, or key plate). Monitors display RGB colors very differently; when you factor in monitor resolutions, and the different types of monitors in the marketplace, what you see on a computer monitor is seldom what anyone else sees on their monitors. And that's not all, everyone that owns a computer, has the ability to adjust or calibrate the colors on their monitors, further confusing the issue.

While nothing is perfect, the world of print is more controlled. For example, when you're working on a color document moving to press, you use a predetermined set of colors, such as, the Pantone Color Matching System. The Pantone colors come printed on special card stock. When you're looking for a specific color, you make the determination from the card stock, and then that information is transferred to the press operator. This type of control, even including the type of paper, keeps you in charge of the process of moving from monitor to print.

Producing Consistent Color

 PS 13.1, 13.4

Producing Consistent Color

You can create consistent color in Photoshop by following some basic steps:

1. If you are working with a production company, consult with them to make sure they provide you with any software and hardware configuration and color management settings.

2. Calibrate and profile your monitor. See "Calibrating a Monitor" on this page.

3. Add color profiles to your computer for your input and output devices, such as a printer or scanner. Color profiles are typically added to your computer when you install the device. Photoshop use the profile to help determine how the device produces color in a document.

4. Set up color management in Adobe programs. See "Working with Color Management" on page 428.

5. Preview colors using a soft-proof (optional). See "Setting Up Soft-Proof Colors" on page 422.

6. Use color management when printing and saving files. See "Saving a Document on page 28 and "Using Print With Preview" on page 374.

Calibrating a Monitor (Manually)

Photoshop contains its own color management system; however, before you can successfully use color management, you must first calibrate your monitor to a predefined standard. There are several methods available to you for monitor calibration. One is to purchase a 3rd party calibration system, another is to use Photoshop's built in color calibrator in

Windows. While this section deals with manual calibration of your monitor, it is highly recommended that you purchase calibration equipment, or hire someone to calibrate your system. The reason is that the human eye is not the best device to color manage a system.

Before beginning the calibration process, let your monitor warm up for thirty minutes to an hour, and calibrate under the same lighting system that you'll be using when you work. To manually calibrate your computer monitor, on Windows, select the Adobe Gamma utility, located in the Control Panel. For Macintosh users, select the Calibrate Utility by opening System Preferences, clicking the Display tab, and then clicking the Color tab. After you launch the calibration application, you will be instructed to manually balance the monitor for shades of red, green, and blue, or to pick from a set of pre-determined calibration settings. Since the human eye is not the best device for adjusting color, this method produces less-than-desirable results.

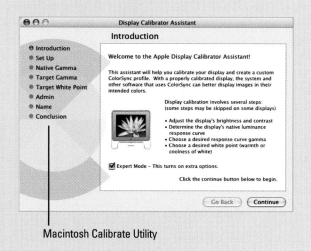

Macintosh Calibrate Utility

Calibrating Using Hardware and Software

 PS 13.1, 13.4

The digital tools available today are so sophisticated that just 10 years ago, no one would have thought them possible. Color calibration falls into three categories: Input (digital cameras, scanners), Processing (monitors), and Output (printers, presses), and each category requires calibration, to create a workflow between devices. Remember a few things before you calibrate your system: Let monitors warm up for about an hour before doing the calibration, and calibrate the system using the same lighting levels that you will be designing. Once the calibration of all your devices is complete, you can expect the best color consistency that technology can provide. Several companies market color calibration hardware and software; one of them is ColorCal at *www.colorcal.com*.

Calibrate a Monitor (Processing)

To calibrate a monitor, you will need to purchase a digital spyder: (also called a colorimeter, or spectrophotometer). When you launch the calibration software, it typically displays a color target in the middle of the monitor. You would then attach the spyder to the monitor, directly over the color patch, and follow the step-by-step instructions. When complete, the software creates a digital color profile for the monitor, and PostScript output devices use that profile to accurately print color images.

Calibrate a Scanner and Digital Camera (Input)

Calibration of a scanner and digital camera requires the scanning or shooting a reference color target, of known color values. For example, the Kodak Q-60, IT8.7 color target has 240

color patches, and a 24-step grayscale, and an image of flesh tones. The calibration software reads the scanned colors and compares them to known color values to create a table of how the camera or scanner performs. Scanning a color target is easy: You lay the target on the scanner, close the lid and push the button. Digital cameras are a bit more difficult because you have to deal with the lighting conditions at the time the target was shot. With studio cameras this isn't a problem; however, taking photographs in the real world involves different times of day, sunny versus cloudy, and incandescent versus fluorescent lighting. Yet, even factoring in the potential problems, calibrating your camera goes a long way in stabilizing color information on a digital camera.

Calibrate a Printer

To calibrate a printer, you will need a digital target file. The file is sent directly to the printer. Once printed, the results are checked with a spectrophotometer, and then the software measures the colors against the target values and creates a profile. There are many variables involved in the printing process, such as purchasing new inks, and the type of paper used for printing. Therefore, calibration is performed based on the fact that you will be using the same paper, and the calibration process should be performed each time you purchase new ink cartridges.

18

Setting Up Soft-Proof Colors

 PS 13.4

In the traditional publishing workflow, you print a hard proof of your document, and visually preview how the colors look. Then you sign off on the proof, and the press operator begins the run. In Photoshop, you can use color profiles to soft-proof the document. Color profiles are a way to display the colors of a specific device directly on your monitor. While not exact as a hard proof, it can go a long way to getting the colors of a CMYK document into the range of the output device. It's important to understand that the reliability of the soft-proof is directly dependent on the quality of your monitor. When you soft-proof a document, you're temporarily assigning a color profile to the document.

Understand How to Soft-Proof Colors

1. Open a document (to use soft proofing, the document does not have to be in the CMYK color mode).

2. Click the **View** menu, point to **Proof Setup**, and then click **Custom**.

3. Click the **Custom Proof Condition** list arrow, and then select from the available customized setups (check with your press operator).

4. Click the **Device To Simulate** list arrow, and then select from the available color output devices.

5. Select the **Preserve Numbers** check box to simulate how the colors will appear without conversion.

6. Click the **Rendering Intent** list arrow, (available if Preserve Numbers is unchecked), and then select from the available options to view how the colors will convert using the proof profile colors, and not the document profile.

7. Select the **Black Point Compensation** check box to map the full dynamic range of the source space (recommended).

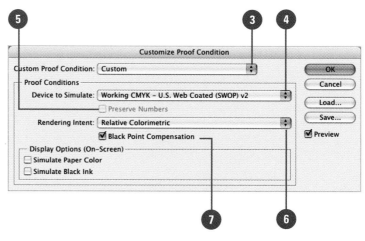

8 Select the **Simulate Paper Color** check box to simulate the visual conditions of white paper as defined by the current profile.

9 Select the **Simulate Black Ink** check box to map the full dynamic range of black as defined by the current profile.

10 To save a customized profile setup, click **Save**.

11 To load a previously saved profile setup, click **Load**.

Check with your press operator; in many cases they have profiles set up to match the dynamic range of their presses.

12 Click **OK**.

13 Click the **View** menu, and then click **Proof Colors** to view the color profile on the active document.

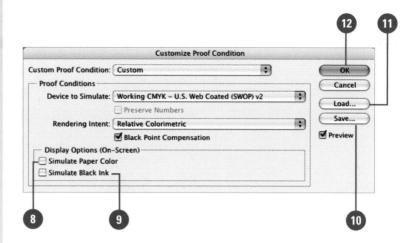

18

Changing from Additive (RGB) to Subtractive (CMYK) Color

RGB (red, green, blue) is defined as an additive color space. RGB is the color space of computer monitors, televisions, and most PDA's and cell phones with built-in color screens. A monitor uses pixels (small square or rectangular bricks), and each pixel mixes a combination of red, green, and blue to project (additive) a specific color to your eyes. Pixels use (on average) 24 switches to hold color information, and can produce 1 of 16,777,216 separate colors. CMYK (cyan, magenta, yellow, black) is defined as a subtractive color space. CMYK is the color space of high-end inkjet, laser, and professional presses. A press uses plates that define each of the 4 colors; as a piece of paper passes through the press, the colors are applied from each plate. The term subtractive comes from the fact that a piece of paper requires a light source to bounce off the paper, and reflect back up to your eyes. Since a press cannot generate the intense saturation of an electronic pixel, the number of possible colors is reduced into the thousands. However, when used correctly, you can produce some stunning results. It's a simple matter to convert a Photoshop document into the CMYK mode; however, good planning will ensure the colors you want will be the color you get.

Change from RGB to CMYK Color

1. Open a document.

   IMPORTANT *You cannot convert a Bitmap or Multi-channel document directly into CMYK mode. Convert a Bitmap image to Grayscale, and then to CMYK; convert a Multi-channel to RGB, and then to CMYK.*

2. Click the **Image** menu, point to **Mode**, and then click **CMYK**.

   Photoshop converts the RGB image into CMYK.

   If the RGB colors are not supported by the CMYK color space, they will be converted into the closest subtractive color values.

Image converts to CMYK

Working with Rendering Intent

PS 13.5

Rendering intent deals with how the color profile selected is converted from one color space into another. When you define rendering intent you are specifying how the colors should be displayed, even at the expense of the original gamut (colors) within the active document. The rendering intent you choose depends on whether colors are critical in an image and on your preference of what the overall color appearance of an image should be. Many times the intent of the images color gamut is different than how the original image was shot.

Work with Rendering Intent

1 Open a document.

2 Click the **View** menu, point to **Proof Setup**, and then click **Custom**.

3 Click the **Rendering Intent** list arrow, and then select from the following options:

◆ **Perceptual.** Preserves the natural colors of an image, as viewed by the human eye, sometimes at the expense of the true color values. Good for photographic images.

◆ **Saturation.** Produces vivid colors in an image, without paying attention to the original color values of the image. Good for business graphics, and charts where you want the colors to pop.

◆ **Relative Colorimetric.** Shifts the color space of the document to that of the maximum highlight values of the destination. Useful for photographic images, and preserves more of the original color than Perceptual.

◆ **Absolute Colorimetric.** Clips any colors in the destination image that do not fall into the color gamut of the destination. Use to proof images sent to devices, such as 4-color presses.

4 Click **OK**.

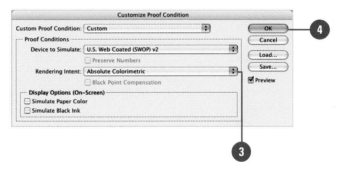

Image with a Web coating profile.

18

Printing a Hard Proof

 PS 13.4

In the language of the print world, a soft-proof is viewed on a monitor, and a hard proof (sometimes referred to as a match print) is viewed on a piece of paper, typically printed on the device that is less expensive than the final output, such as an inkjet, or laser printer. In the last few years, many inkjet printers now have the resolution necessary to produce inexpensive prints that can be used as hard proofs, which previously had to be printed on high-end printing presses, or expensive high-resolution laser printers. A hard proof gives you something you can hold in your hands, and is not only useful for viewing colors, but even evaluating the layout. Since a monitor typically displays a document at a different size, you now have an exact size match to the final document.

Print a Hard Proof

1. Open a document.

2. Click the **View** menu, point to **Proof Setup**, and then click **Custom**.

3. Click the **Device To Simulate** list arrow, and then select a specific proof set.

4. Click **OK**.

5. Click the **File** menu, and then click **Print With Preview**.

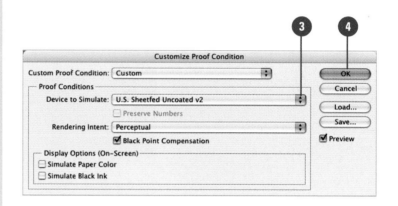

See Also

See "Setting Up Soft-Proof Colors" on page 422 for information on using color profiles.

6 Click the **More Options** button.

Button name changes to Fewer Options, which you can click to display a smaller dialog box with less options.

7 Click the **Proof** option (it should display your chosen proof setup).

8 Click the **Color Handling** list arrow, and click **Let Photoshop Determine Colors**.

9 Click the **Printer Profile** list arrow, and then select your output device from the available options.

10 Click the **Rendering Intent** list arrow, and then select from the available options (disabled when you select the Proof option, step 6).

11 Click the **Proof Setup Preset** list arrow, and then click **Current Custom Setup**.

12 Click **Print**.

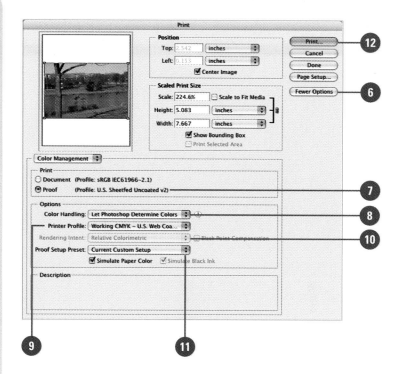

See Also

See "Working with Rendering Intent" on page 425 for more information on using the intent option.

Working with Color Management

PS 13.1, 13.3

Colors in an image many times will appear different when you view them using different monitors. They may also look very different when printed on your desktop printer or when printed on a professional printing press. If your work in Photoshop requires you to produce consistent color across different devices, managing color should be an essential part of your workflow. Photoshop gives you a group of pre-defined color management systems, which are designed to help you produce consistent color. These management systems are recognized by other Adobe products, and by most professional printing services. In most cases, the pre-defined sets are all you will need to manage color workflow or, as you become more advanced at managing color, they can be used as a basis for creating your own customized sets. The power of color management lies in its ability to produce consistent colors with a system that reconciles differences between the color spaces of each device.

Work with Color Management

1. Open Photoshop (it is not necessary to open a document).

2. Click the **Edit** and then click **Color Settings**.

3. Click the **Settings** list arrow, and then select from the available options:

   ◆ **Custom.** Create you own customized set (requires a good knowledge of color management, and color theory).

   ◆ **Monitor Color.** For creating content for video and on-screen presentations.

   ◆ **North America General Purpose 2. (default).** For creating consistent workflow with Adobe applications used in North America.

   ◆ **North America Prepress 2.** The defaults for common pre-press operations in the U.S.

   ◆ **North America Web/Internet.** Manages color-space content for documents published on the Web.

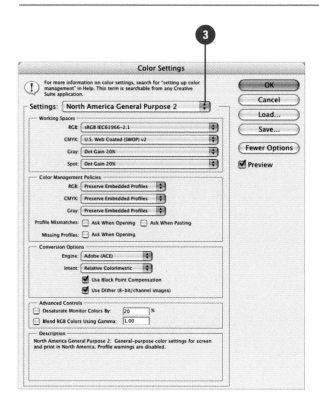

- ◆ **More Settings.** Click the More Options button, and then click Settings list arrow to see more options for Japan and Europe.

④ Create your own customized color sets using the following options:

- ◆ **Working Spaces:** Defines the working color profiles for each color model. Working Spaces can be used for images that were not previously color-managed, or for newly created color-managed documents.

- ◆ **Color Management Policies:** Defines how the colors in a specific color model are managed. You can choose to embed or convert the selected profile, or to ignore it.

- ◆ **Conversion Options:** Defines exactly how you want the conversion process handled. Using a color-defined Engine, and color conversion Intent. You can adjust for black point when converting color spaces, and dither color channel information when converting between color spaces.

- ◆ **Advanced Controls:** Desaturate Monitor Colors gives you the ability to control the viewing of a color space on different monitors; however, if activated, images will print differently than viewed. You can decide what Gamma level is used when blending RGB values.

⑤ To save color settings as a preset, click **Save**, and then save the file in the default location.

⑥ To load a color settings preset not saved in the standard location, click **Load**.

⑦ Click **OK**.

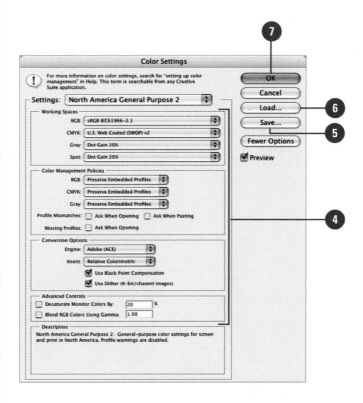

For Your Information

Synchronizing Color Settings Across CS2

When you set up color management using Adobe Bridge, color settings are automatically synchronized across all Adobe Creative Suite programs (**New!**), which makes sure colors look consistent. It's a good idea to synchronize color settings before you work on new or existing documents, so the color settings match from the start. Launch Bridge, click the Edit menu, click Creative Suite Color Settings, select a color setting from the list, and then click Apply. If the default settings don't suite your needs, select the Show Expanded List Of Color Settings Files option to view additional settings. To install custom color settings, click Show Save Color Settings Files.

18

Embedding ICC Color Profiles

When you work on a color document, you're viewing the image using your computer, with a specific version of Photoshop, and a unique monitor calibration. What you need is a way to preserve the visual settings of the document. In other words, you want someone else, to see what you see. The ICC Color Profile system is a universal way of saving a color profile (called tagging or embedding), and has a reasonable certainty that the document will display correctly on other devices. Although there are several modes that accept ICC profiles, the two most common modes are RGB and CMYK.

Embed ICC Color Profiles

1. Open a document.

2. Click the **View** menu, point to **Proof Setup**, and then click **Custom**.

3. Click the **Device To Simulate** list arrow, and then select a color profile for the image.

4. Click **OK**.

5. Click the **File** menu, and then click **Save As**.

6. Enter a file name.

7. Click the **Format** list arrow, and then select one of the following formats: Photoshop, Photoshop EPS, JPEG, Photoshop PDF, or TIFF.

   IMPORTANT *To save the file with the newly created custom profile, the file must be saved as an EPS, DCS, or PDF.*

8. Click the **Where** (Mac) or **Save As** (Win) list arrow, and then select a location to save the file.

9. Select the **Embed Color Profile** (Mac) or **ICC Profile** (Win) check box.

10. Click **Save** to save the file as a copy, and embed the new profile.

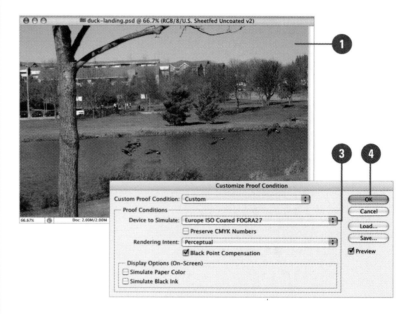

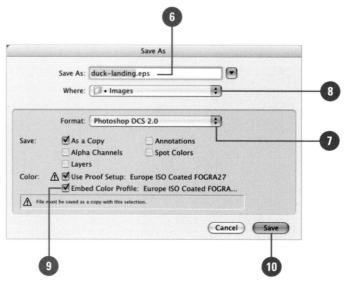

Assigning a Different Profile to a Document

Assign or Remove a Profile

① Open a document.

② Click the **Edit** menu, and then click **Assign Profile**.

③ Select from the following options:

◆ **Don't Color Manage This Document.** Select the option to remove any assigned profile (the document becomes untagged).

◆ **Working RGB.** Select the option to tag the document with the current working space profile.

◆ **Profile.** Select the option, click the list arrow, and then select a new color profile, which removes the old one.

④ Click **OK**.

See Also

See "Changing from Additive (RGB) to Subtractive (CMYK) Color" on page 424 for more information on using and working with CMYK.

Photoshop's color management system must know the color space of the image so it can decipher the meaning of the color values in the image. When assigning a profile to an image, the image will be in the color space described by the particular profile. For example, a document's profile can be assigned by a source device, like a digital camera or a scanner, or assigned directly in Photoshop. When using the Assign Profile command, color values are mapped directly into the new profile space.

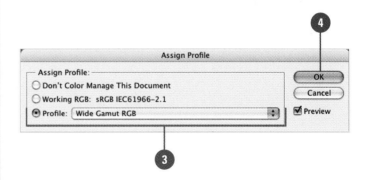

Converting the Color Space to Another Profile

PS 13.1, 13.2

There are times when you will open a document that contains an embedded profile, and you need to convert it. Photoshop gives you the option of tagging the document with another profile without converting the colors, or removing the old profile and converting the color space. Photoshop's Convert To Profile command gives you the ability to remove, reassign, or change the profile in a document. In addition, you may want to prepare a document for a different output destination, such as an ink jet printer or 4-color press.

Convert the Color Space to Another Profile

1. Open a document.

2. Click the **Edit** menu, and then click **Convert To Profile**.

3. Click the **Profile** list arrow, and then select a new color profile.

   The document will be converted and tagged with the new color profile.

4. Click the **Engine** list arrow, and then select:

   ◆ **Adobe (ACE).** Adobe color management (default).

   ◆ **Microsoft ICM.** Windows color management.

   ◆ **Apple ColorSync.** Mac OS color management.

   ◆ **Apple CMM.** Mac OS color management.

5. Click the **Intent** list arrow, and then select an option.

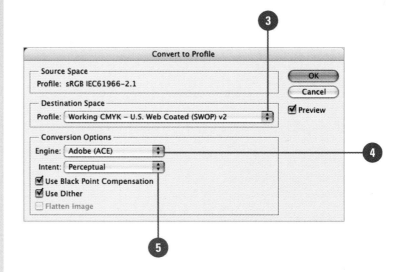

See Also

See "Working with Rendering Intent" on page 425 for more information on using the intent option.

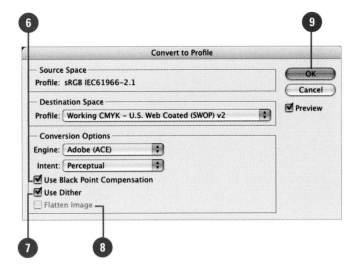

6 Select the **Use Black Point Compensation** check box to map the full color range of the source to the full color range of the destination profile.

7 Select the **Use Dither** check box to use with 8-bit color channel images; if you select the option, Photoshop dithers color pixels when converting between source and destination color profiles.

8 Select the **Flatten Image** check box to flatten a multi-layered document.

9 Click **OK**.

18

Working with the Out-Of-Gamut Command

One of the biggest problems with images displayed on a computer monitor is that they don't accurately represent the color space of a 4-color press. There are ways that we can reduce the possibility of colors not printing correctly, but in the end the RGB and CMYK color spaces are different—in fact, they're exactly the opposite of each other. Photoshop understands this, and gives you a way to view out-of-gamut colors. The term **Gamut** is used to define a color that will reproduce on a press. The out-of-gamut test is performed on an image before the conversion into the CMYK mode. Once you convert an image to CMYK it's too late to test, because Photoshop has already made the conversion.

Work with the Out-Of-Gamut Command

① Open an RGB image.

② Click the **Edit** (Win) or **Photoshop** (Mac) menu, point to **Preferences**, and then click **Transparency & Gamut**.

③ Select a Gamut Warning color, and then enter an Opacity percentage value (1 to 100).

Gamut Warning is the color Photoshop uses to mask the out-of-gamut areas of the image.

④ Click **OK**.

⑤ Click the **View** menu, and then click **Gamut Warning**.

Photoshop displays any color outside the CMYK gamut with a predefined color mask.

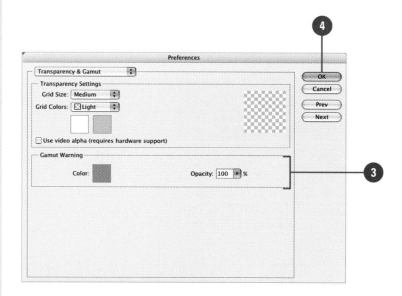

Color displayed outside CMYK gamut.

Printing a Target Image

When you work in the world of computer monitors and output devices, what you see on your monitor, is seldom what you get when you print. The color spaces are different—monitors are additive color, and paper is subtractive color. In addition, monitors use pixels to generate colors, and printers use inks. However, you can create a target print, and then use that to generate a custom profile. A target document with specific color swatches and information is used to create the target document and is supplied as part of a third-party color management software package. When printing a target, you want to turn off all color management in both Photoshop and the print driver. Once the target is printed, it is scanned by a third-party measuring instrument to create the custom profile. Photoshop supplies a target document *Ole' No More Moiré* you can use to print the target document, and companies such as Color Cal (*www.colorcal.com*) provide electronic measurement systems to analyze the image and create the profile. If you have more than one output device, you will have to print a target for each document.

Print a Target Image

1. Open a color target document (such as Photoshop's Ole' No More Moiré).

2. Click the **File** menu, and then click **Print With Preview**.

3. Click the **More Options** button.

4. Click the list arrow, and then select **Color Management**.

5. Click the **Document** option.

    This reproduces colors as interpreted by the profile currently assigned to the document.

6. Click the **Color Handling** list arrow, and then click **No Color Management**.

7. Click **Print**.

8. Click the **Printer** list arrow, and then select the correct output device.

9. Select any other print related options as needed.

10. Click **Print**.

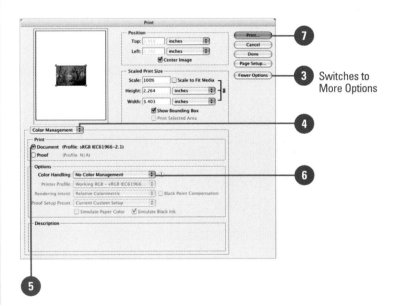

Switches to More Options

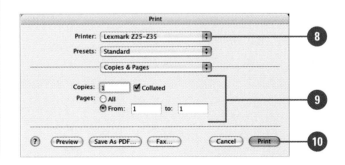

Using the Hue/Saturation for Out-Of-Gamut Colors

Once you've established your document contains colors outside the CMYK color space, it's up to you to decide exactly how to correct the problem. There are as many ways to correct color problems as there are tools, and each Photoshop user has their favorites. Two methods that are simple and powerful, are using the Hue/Saturation Adjustment, and Photoshop's Sponge tool. Understand that the primary reason a color won't move into the CMYK color space is due to the saturation values of the ink. A monitor can produce more saturation to a pixel, than a 4-color press can produce by mixing inks.

Use the Hue/Saturation Method

1. Open an RGB image.

2. Click the **View** menu, and then click **Gamut Warning**.

   Photoshop displays any color outside the CMYK gamut with a predefined color mask.

3. Click the **Image** menu, point to **Adjustments**, and then click **Hue/Saturation**.

4. Drag the **Saturation** slider to the left until all the gamut masks disappear.

5. Record the Saturation Value used.

6. Click **Cancel**.

7. Click the **Select** menu, and then click **Color Range**.

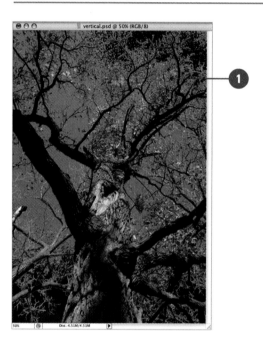

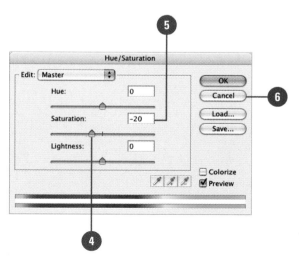

8 Click the **Select** list arrow, and then click **Out-Of-Gamut**.

9 Click **OK**.

The out-of-gamut areas of the image are now selected, and isolated from the rest of the image.

10 Click the **Select** menu, and then click **Feather**.

11 Enter a Feather value of .5.

This softens the desaturation of the out-of-gamut areas of the image.

12 Click **OK**.

13 Click the **Image** menu, point to **Adjustments**, and then click **Hue/Saturation**.

14 Enter the Saturation value you recorded from step 5.

15 Click **OK**.

16 Press Ctrl+D (Win) or ⌘+D (Mac) to deselect the image areas.

The image is now ready for conversion to CMYK.

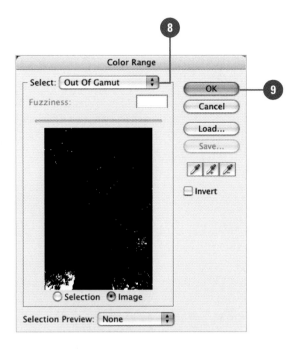

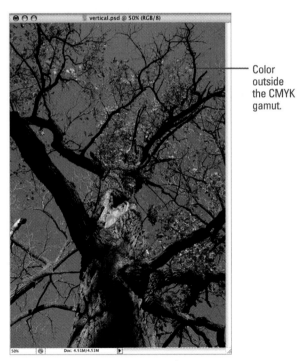

Color outside the CMYK gamut.

18

Using the Sponge Tool for Out-Of-Gamut Colors

The Sponge tool method is a bit more work intensive; however, it gives you precise control over each out-of-gamut area of the image. Since the Sponge tool removes saturation values from the image based on the speed the tool is dragged across the image, the key to successfully using the Sponge tool to restore out-of-gamut colors is to choose a soft-edged brush, and smooth, even strokes. Practice is the key to good image restoration, and using a drawing tablet as opposed to the mouse will help in the control of the tool.

Use the Sponge Tool Method

1. Open an RGB image.

2. Click the **View** menu, and then click **Gamut Warning**.

   Photoshop displays any color outside the CMYK gamut with a predefined color mask.

3. Select the **Sponge** tool.

4. Click the **Brush** list arrow, and then select a soft, round brush tip with a small diameter from the brush tip options.

5. Click the **Mode** list arrow, and then click **Desaturate**.

6. Enter a Flow value of 60 percent.

7. Click the **Select** menu, and then click **Color Range**.

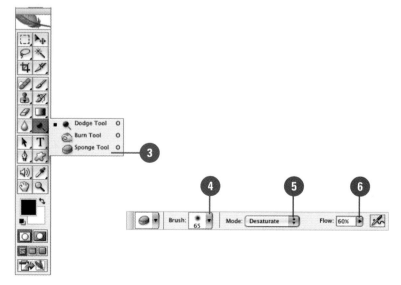

Original RGB image

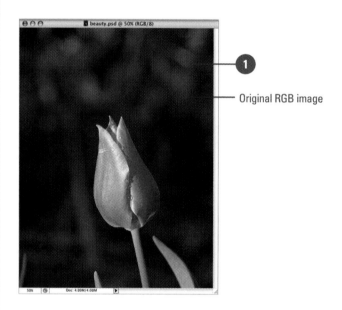

8 Click the **Select** list arrow, and then click **Out-Of-Gamut**.

9 Click **OK**.

The out-of-gamut areas of the image are now selected, and isolated from the rest of the image.

10 Click the **Select** menu, and then click **Feather**.

11 Enter a Feather value of .5.

This softens the desaturation of the out-of-gamut areas of the image.

12 Click **OK**.

13 Slowly drag the **Sponge** tool over an out-of-gamut area until the color mask disappears.

Continue through the document until all the areas have been corrected.

14 Press Ctrl+D (Win) or ⌘+D (Mac) to deselect the image areas.

The image is now ready for conversion to CMYK.

Did You Know?

You can hide selection marquees.
If the selection marquee is getting in the way of seeing small out-of-gamut areas, press Ctrl+H (Win) or ⌘+H (Mac) to temporarily hide the selection marquee, and then repeat the command to restore the marquee.

Out-Of-Gamut colors masked

Out-Of-Gamut removed with the Sponge tool

18

Using Online Services to Print or E-Mail Photos

Photoshop's Online Services (**New!**) lets you to print or e-mail photos directly from Adobe Bridge to a remote online service provider. The Online Photo Printing and Online Sharing services give you a great advantage over having the hassle of saving, storing, and shipping images to local outlets. The Online Services make it easy to manage addresses and accounts to stream-line the process; it's only a few clicks. Since the images used in high-end printing involve a lot of physical information (big file sizes), it's important to have access to a high-speed Internet connection. Services such as DSL or broadband (cable) help to make the process of sending information faster and more reliable.

Use Online Services to Print or E-Mail Photos

1 Click the **Go To Bridge** button on the Options bar to open the Bridge.

2 Select the files that you want to print.

3 Click the **Tools** menu, point to **Photoshop Services**, and then click **Photo Prints** or **Photo Sharing**.

   The Online Services Web site appears; a Web connection is required.

4 Follow the on-screen instructions to complete the process.

   You only need to enter account information once.

5 Click **Next** to continue to each screen, and then click **Done** when you're finished.

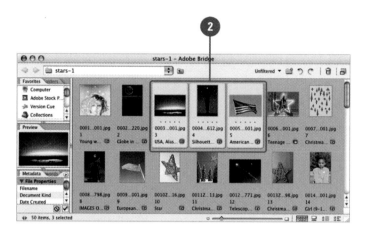

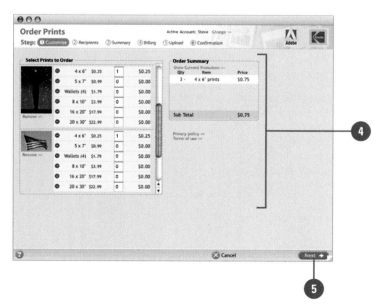

Designing for the Web

19

Introduction

If you need to manipulate a photographic image, there's not a better program on the market than Adobe Photoshop that will do the job for you. But Adobe didn't stop with Photoshop; they realized that there are many users wanting to design images for the Internet, so they came up with ImageReady. ImageReady is Adobe's answer to creating great images for the Internet. And not just images, with ImageReady you can create animated GIF's, JavaScript rollovers, and much more. ImageReady is truly a program for anyone interested in creating Web friendly documents.

Photoshop uses various document formats such as JPEG, GIF, PNG, and WBMP, to save images for the Web. For example, the JPEG format is used primarily for compressing photographic images, while the GIF format is used for compressing clipart and text. Each format is designed to serve a purpose, and knowing when to use a specific format will help you design fast-loading, dynamic Web documents.

However, saving files in a specific file format is not the only way Photoshop helps you create Web-friendly images, you can also slice images. When you slice an image, you're cutting the image into several pieces. Since the Internet handles smaller packets of information more efficiently than one large piece, slicing an image makes the whole graphic load faster, and ImageReady helps you slice images with ease.

Saving for the Web

PS 14.2

Photoshop's Save For Web command is a dream come true for prepping images for the Internet, or even for saving images in a quick-loading format for PowerPoint slide presentations, and you don't even have to leave Photoshop. The Save For Web command lets you open any Photoshop document, and convert it into a Web friendly format using the GIF, JPEG, PNG, or WBMP formats. You can even try different optimization settings or compare different optimizations using the 2-Up or 4-Up pane. In addition, the dialog area below each image provides optimization information on the size and download time of the file.

Save for the Web

1. Open a document.

2. Click the **File** menu, and then click **Save For Web**.

3. Click the **Original**, **Optimized**, **2-Up**, or **4-Up** palettes to view the document using different layouts.

4. Click one of the sample images to change its default format.

   IMPORTANT *If you're viewing the document using 2-Up or 4-Up the first image is the original. You can't change the original, only one of the sample images.*

5. Click the **Preset** list arrow, and then select a new format from the available options.

6. Click the **Format** list arrow, and then select from the following options:

   ◆ **GIF.** The Graphic Interchange File Format is useful for clipart, text, or images that contain a large amount of solid color. GIF uses lossless compression.

   ◆ **JPEG.** The Joint Photographers Expert Group format is useful for images that contain a lot of soft colors, like photographs. JPEG uses lossy compression.

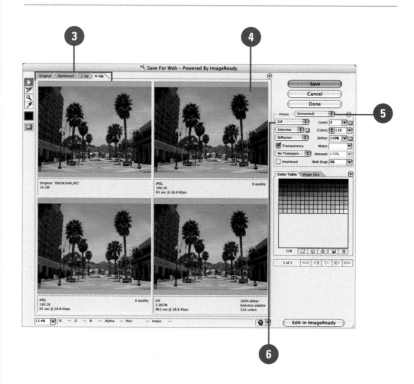

- ◆ **PNG-8.** The Portable Network Graphic 8-bit, functions in a manner similar to the GIF format. PNG uses lossless compression.

- ◆ **PNG-24.** The Portable Network Graphic 24-bit functions in a manner similar to the JPEG format. PNG-24 uses lossless compression.

- ◆ **WBMP.** The Web Bitmap format, converts an image into black and white dots, for use on some output devices, like cell phones, and PDA's.

7 Select from the various options that change based on your File Format selection.

8 Click the **Color Table** palette (available for the GIF, and PNG-8 formats), and add, subtract, or edit colors in the selected document.

9 To change the selected image's width and height, select the **Image Size** palette, and then make adjustments.

10 To move the selected image directly into the ImageReady application, click the **Edit In ImageReady** button.

11 Click **Save**.

12 Enter a name, and then select a location to save the image file.

13 Click **OK**.

Photoshop saves the modified file, and returns you to the original image.

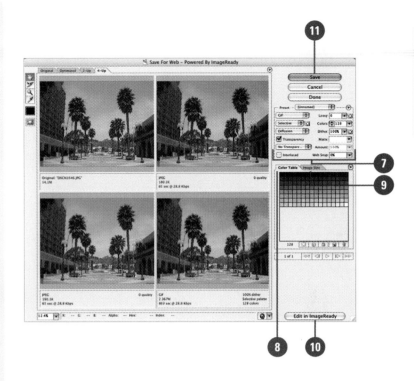

For Your Information

Working with Matte and Transparency

The Matte option, when available, specifies the background color used to fill anti-aliased edges that lie adjacent to transparent areas of the image. When the Transparency option is selected, the matte is applied to edge areas to help blend the edges with a Web background of the same color. When the Transparency option is not selected, the matte is applied to transparent areas. Choosing the None option for the matte creates hard-edged transparency if Transparency is selected; otherwise, all transparent areas are filled with 100% white. The image must have transparency for the Matte options to be available.

Working with Save For Web Options

When you work with Save For Web, the intention is to prepare the image, in one of four Web formats: GIF, JPEG, PNG, and WBMP. Save For Web comes with options, which will help you through the process. For example, if you choose the JPEG format, you can select the amount of compression applied to the image or if you select the GIF format, you can choose how many colors are preserved with the image. The PNG format lets you save images in an 8-bit (256 colors) or a 24-bit (millions of color) format. The options available with Save For Web give you the control you need to produce small image files with the quality.

Work with Save For Web Options

1. Open a document.

2. Click the **File** menu, and then click **Save For Web**.

3. Select from the various Save For Web tools:

   ◆ **Hand Tool.** Drag the image, to change the view of a document.

   ◆ **Slice Selection Tool.** Select a predefined image slice.

   ◆ **Zoom Tool.** Click on the image to expand the view size.

   ◆ **Eyedropper Tool.** Drag the image to perform a live sampling of the image.

4. Click the **Thumbnail Options** button, and then select color profile and bandwidth options for the selected document.

5. Click the **Zoom** list arrow, and then select a view size for the sample images.

6. Click the **Toggle Slice Visibility** button to show or hide the image slices.

7. Click the **Preview In Default Browser** list arrow, and then select the image.

8. Click **Save**.

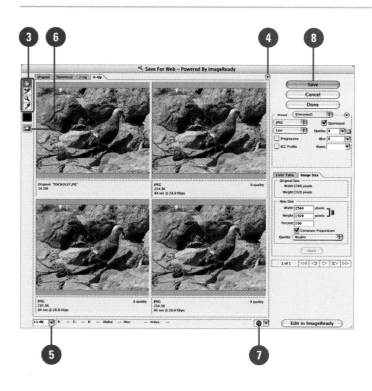

Optimizing an Image to File Size

The Save For Web dialog box has many options to help you create the exact image you need—including helping you compress an image down to a specific file size. For example, you've just created an image you want to display on the Web, but the maximum file size you can use is 35k. You could open the image, and experiment with Save For Web's compression options, or you could use the Optimize To File Size option.

Optimize an Image to File Size

1. Open a document.

2. Click the **File** menu, and then click **Save For Web**.

3. Click the **2-Up** palette, and then select the sample image.

4. Click the **Format Options** button, and then click **Optimize To File Size**.

5. Enter a file size in the Desired File Size data box.

6. Click the **Current Settings** option or the **Auto Select GIF/JPEG** option to let Photoshop choose between the JPEG or GIF format.

7. Click the following Use options:

   ◆ Current Slice

   ◆ Each Slice

   ◆ Total Of All Slices

8. Click **OK**.

   Photoshop compresses the selected sample.

9. Click **Save** to save the compressed image.

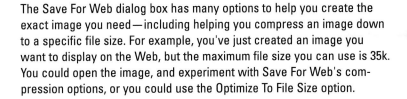

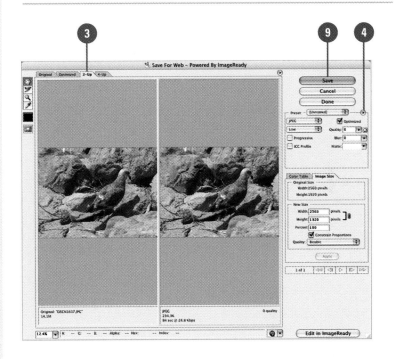

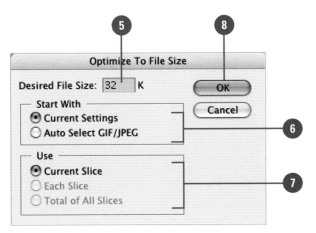

Working with Web File Formats

PS 14.1

If you design Web documents, you know that the size of your images is very important. ImageReady gives you the option of compressing images in one of four Internet formats: GIF, JPG, PNG, and WBMP. The GIF format compresses images that contain solid colors with sharp, definable edges, such as clipart, and text. The JPG format reduces the size of image files that contain a lot of soft transitional colors, such as photographs. The PNG format is a hybrid format designed to take the place of the GIF and JPG format. Finally, the WBMP format was created to display images on low-resolution devices like cell phones, and PDA's by converting the image into dots of black and white. Whatever format you need to create stunning Web images, ImageReady is the program that will help you get there.

Work with Web File Formats

1. Open a document in ImageReady by first opening the image in Photoshop and then click the **Jump To ImageReady** button.

2. Click the **Original**, **Optimized**, **2-Up**, or **4-Up** palettes to view the document using different layouts.

3. Select one of the samples.

4. Select the **Optimize** palette.

5. Click the **Format** list arrow, and then select a format from the available options.

6. Click the **Quality**, **Transparency**, and **Options triangles** to change the image's compression, and color options.

7. Click the **File** menu, and then click **Save Optimized As**.

Did You Know?

You can use the Window menu to open the Optimize palette. Click the Window menu, and then click Optimize.

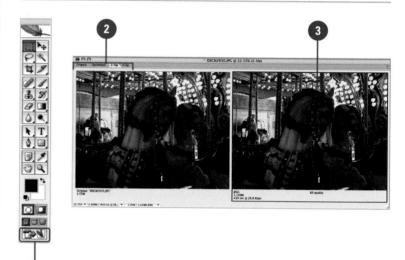

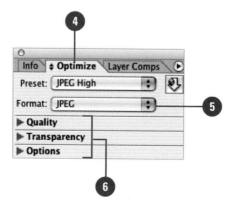

8 Enter a file name in the Save As box.

9 Click the **Format** list arrow, and then select to save the image in HTML And Images, Images Only, or HTML Only.

10 Click the **Where** (Mac) or **Save In** (Win) list arrow, and then select the location to save the file.

11 Click the **Settings** and **Slices** list arrows to further define the output files (if you save a single image without slices, you can leave these settings at their default values).

12 Click **Save**.

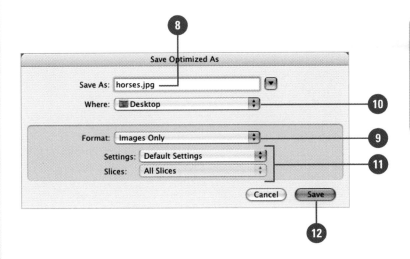

For Your Information

Creating an HTML File for an Image

When you save an optimized file using the Save Optimized As command, you can choose to generate an HTML file for the image. This file contains all the necessary information to display your image in a Web browser.

Optimizing a JPEG Document

PS 6.2, 14.1

ImageReady comes complete with everything you will need to properly compress any JPEG Document. The Internet is typically a slow device, and your visitors typically do not have much patience. When you compress a JPEG image, you're essentially removing information from the image to reduce its file size. The unfortunate results of that reduction is loss of image quality. Internet graphics are not always the best for quality; however, reducing file size is a necessary evil, to keep visitors from clicking off your site, and moving to another. To keep the visitors happy, your JPEG images must load fast, and ImageReady is just the application to help you accomplish that goal.

Optimize a JPEG Document

1 Open a document in ImageReady by first opening the image in Photoshop and then click the **Jump To ImageReady** button.

2 Click the **Original**, **Optimized**, **2-Up**, or **4-Up** palettes to view the document using different layouts.

3 Click one of the sample images to change its default format.

4 Select the **Optimize** palette.

5 Click the **Format** list arrow, and then click **JPEG**.

6 Click the **Quality** arrow (if necessary), and then select from the following options:

- ◆ **Quality.** Click the list arrow, and then select a preset JPEG quality from Low (poor quality) to Maximum (best quality).

- ◆ **Amount.** Enter a JPEG quality compression value (0 to 100). The lower the value, the more information (color) is sacrificed for image size.

- ◆ **Blur.** JPEG images compress better when the image has soft edges. Apply the Blur option to increase the softness of the image (at a sacrifice to image quality).

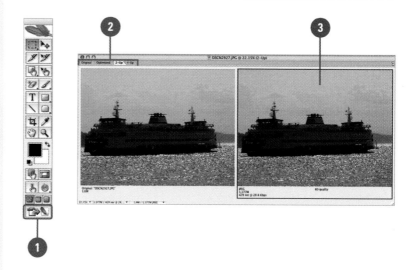

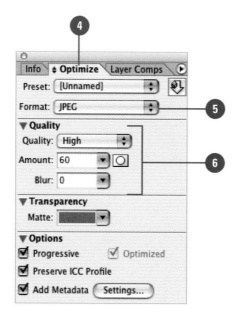

7 Click the **Transparency** arrow (if necessary), click the **Matte** list arrow, and then select from the available options.

JPEG images do not support transparency. If you image contains transparent areas, use the Matte option to fill them in using a specific color.

8 Click the **Options** arrow (if necessary), and then select from the following options:

- **Progressive.** Select the check box to load a JPEG in three progressive scans. Not supported by all browsers.

- **Optimized.** Select the check box to further compress the image. Not supported by all browsers.

- **Preserve ICC Profile.** Select the check box to embed an ICC color profile into the JPEG image. This increases file size but helps maintain color consistency between monitors, and operating systems.

- **Add Metadata.** Select the check box to embed recoverable data about the files colors, creation, and even author information. Click Settings to specify the data you want.

9 Click the **File** menu, and then click **Save Optimized** to save the current image.

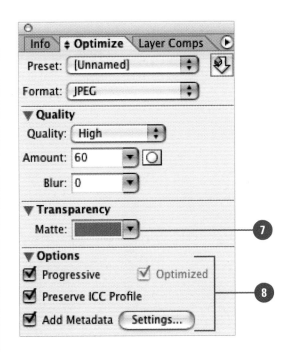

Optimizing a GIF Document

The GIF file format is used primarily for images that contain solid colors with sharp edges, such as clipart, text, line art, and logos. Since the Internet is a slow device, using the GIF format on images significantly reduces their file size, and will create fast-loading graphics. The GIF format utilizes an 8-bit pixel, and creates a document with a maximum of 256 colors (the less colors the smaller the file size). The GIF format has been around long enough for it to be considered an Internet "native" format. A **native format** is one that does not require a specific plug-in for the browser to display the file.

Optimize a GIF Document

1. Open a document in ImageReady by first opening the image in Photoshop and then click the **Jump To ImageReady** button.

2. Click the **Original**, **Optimized**, **2-Up**, or **4-Up** palettes to view the document using different layouts.

3. Click one of the sample images to change its default format.

4. Select the **Optimize** palette.

5. Click the **Format** list arrow, and then click **GIF**.

6. Click the **Color Table** arrow, and then select from the following options:

   - **Reduction.** Click to select a visual reduction method for the image colors.

   - **Colors.** Enter or select a value from 2 to 256 maximum colors.

   - **Web Snap.** Enter or select a value from 0 to 100 to instruct the GIF compression utility how many of the image colors should be Web safe.

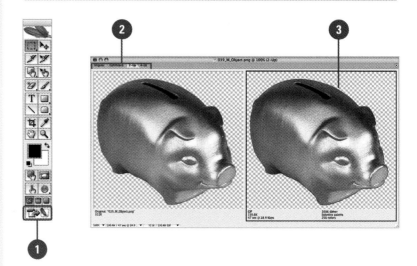

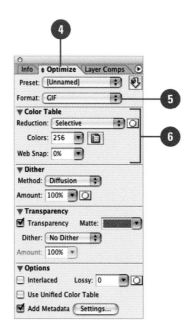

7 Click the **Dither** arrow, and then select from the following options:

◆ **Method.** Click the list arrow, and then select from the available dithering schemes. Dithering is how the GIF format mixes the available image colors.

◆ **Amount.** Enter or select a value from 0 to 100 to instruct the GIF compression utility how many of the image colors should dither.

8 Click the **Transparency** arrow, and then select from the following options:

◆ **Transparency.** Check to make the transparent areas of a GIF image transparent.

◆ **Matte.** Click to fill the transparent areas of a GIF image.

◆ **Dither.** Click to select a dithering scheme, and enter an amount for the mixing of the matte color.

9 Click the **Options** arrow, and then select from the following options:

◆ **Interlaced.** Check to have the GIF image load in three scans.

◆ **Lossy.** Enter or select a value from 0 to 100 to instruct the GIF compression utility how much image loss is allowed.

◆ **Use Unified Color Table.** Check to have the GIF format apply a universal color table to all images used in a rollover image.

◆ **Add Metadata.** Check to embed recoverable data about the files colors, creation, and even author information.

10 Click the **File** menu, and then click **Save Optimized**.

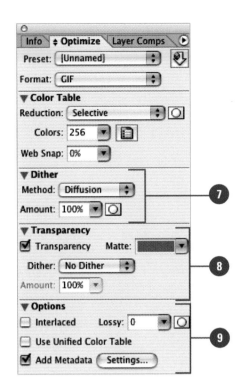

Optimizing a PNG-8 Document

 PS 6.2, 14.1

The PNG-8 file format is used primarily for images that contain solid colors with sharp edges—clipart, text, line art, and logos—and was designed as an alternative to the GIF file format. Since the PNG-8 format generates an image with a maximum of 256 colors, it significantly reduces an images file size. While similar to the GIF file format, the PNG-8 format is not completely supported by older browsers. However, it is considered a native format to the creation of Flash animation movies.

Optimize a PNG-8 Document

1. Open a document in ImageReady by first opening the image in Photoshop and then click the **Jump To ImageReady** button.

2. Click the **Original, Optimized, 2-Up,** or **4-Up** palettes to view the document using different layouts.

3. Click one of the sample images to change its default format.

4. Select the **Optimize** palette.

5. Click the **Format** list arrow, and then click **PNG-8**.

6. Click the **Color Table** arrow, and then select from the following options:

   ◆ **Reduction.** Click to select a visual reduction method for the image colors.

   ◆ **Colors.** Enter or select a value from 2 to 256 maximum colors.

   ◆ **Web Snap.** Enter or select a value from 0 to 100 to instruct the PNG-8 compression utility how many of the image colors should be Web safe.

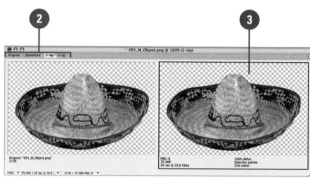

7 Click the **Dither** arrow, and then select from the following options:

- ◆ **Method.** Click the list arrow, and then select from the available dithering schemes. Dithering is how the PNG-8 format mixes the available image colors.

- ◆ **Amount.** Enter or select a value from 0 to 100 to instruct the PNG-8 compression utility how many of the image colors should be dithered.

8 Click the **Transparency** arrow, and then select from the following options:

- ◆ **Transparency.** Check to make the transparent areas of a PNG-8 image transparent.

- ◆ **Matte.** Click to fill the transparent areas of a PNG-8 image.

- ◆ **Dither.** Click to select a dithering scheme, and enter an amount for the mixing of the matte color.

9 Click the **Options** arrow, and then select from the following options:

- ◆ **Interlaced.** Check to have the PNG image load in three scans.

- ◆ **Use Unified Color Table.** Check to have the PNG-8 format apply a universal color table to all images used in a rollover image.

- ◆ **Add Metadata.** Check to embed recoverable data about the files colors, creation, and even author information.

10 Click the **File** menu, and then click **Save Optimized**.

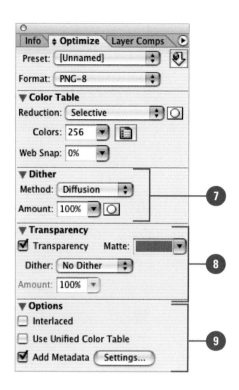

Optimizing a PNG-24 Document

PS 6.2, 14.1

The PNG-24 file format is used primarily for images that contain lots of colors with soft transitional edges, such as photographs, and was designed as an alternative to the JPEG file format. The PNG-24 format generates an image with millions of colors, and still manages to reduce the size of a file. While similar to the JPEG file format, the PNG-24 uses lossless compression, and does not compress files as small as the JPEG format. So for the time being, most designers are still using the JPEG format for creating fast-loading Web graphics.

Optimize a PNG-24 Document

1 Open a document in ImageReady by first opening the image in Photoshop and then click the **Jump To ImageReady** button.

2 Click the **Original**, **Optimized**, **2-Up**, or **4-Up** palettes to view the document using different layouts.

3 Click one of the sample images to change its default format.

4 Select the **Optimize** palette.

5 Click the **Format** list arrow, and then click **PNG-24**.

6 Click the **Transparency** arrow, and then select from the following options:

 ◆ **Transparency.** Check to make the transparent areas of a PNG-24 image transparent.

 ◆ **Matte.** Click to fill the transparent areas of a PNG-24 image.

7 Click the **Options** arrow, and then select from the following options:

 ◆ **Interlaced.** Check to have the PNG-24 image load in three scans.

 ◆ **Add Metadata.** Check to embed recoverable data about the files colors, creation, and even author information.

8 Click the **File** menu, and then click **Save Optimized**.

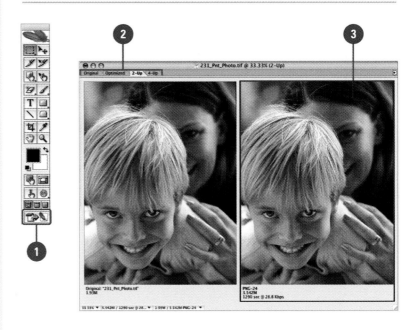

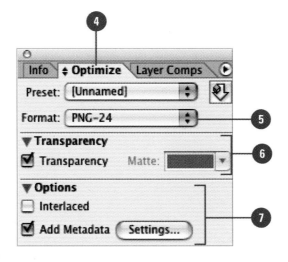

Optimizing a WBMP Document

The WBMP file format creates images from 2-color pixels, and is used for images that are displayed on small hand-held devices such as PDA's and cell phones. The WBMP format generates an image with 2 colors (black and white) and significantly reduces the images file size. The WBMP format is new to the world of wireless devices, and while it creates small images, the black and white pixels create very low-quality images.

Optimize a WBMP Document

1. Open a document in ImageReady by first opening the image in Photoshop and then click the **Jump To ImageReady** button.

2. Click the **Original**, **Optimized**, **2-Up**, or **4-Up** palettes to view the document using different layouts.

3. Click one of the sample images to change its default format.

4. Select the **Optimize** palette.

5. Click the **Format** list arrow, and then click **WBMP**.

6. Click the **Dither** arrow, and then select from the following options:

   ◆ **Method.** Click the list arrow, and then select from the available dithering schemes. Dithering is how the WBMP format mixes the available image colors.

   ◆ **Amount.** Enter or select a value from 0 to 100 to instruct the WBMP compression utility how many of the image colors should be dithered.

7. Click the **File** menu, and then click **Save Optimized**.

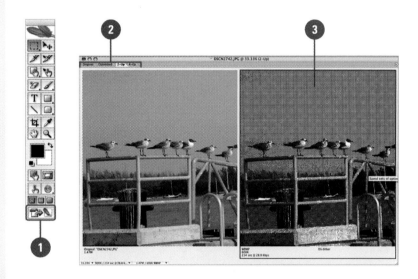

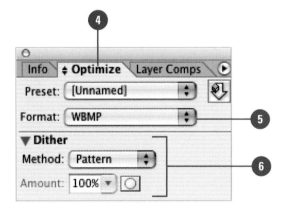

Creating an Animated GIF in Photoshop

Adobe is moving a lot of the features available in ImageReady over to Photoshop, and one of those is the ability to create an animated GIF file (**New!**). An **animation** is a sequence of images, or frames, that vary slightly to create the illusion of movement over time. The process is very similar to creating the animated GIF in ImageReady; however, since Photoshop is not primarily an animation program there is a bit of difference in how you compress and save the final file. Nevertheless, since Photoshop has more drawing tools than ImageReady, it's not a bad idea to do your animated GIF creations directly in Photoshop.

Create an Animated GIF from Scratch in Photoshop

1. Open Photoshop.

2. Click the **File** menu, and then click **New**.

3. Enter a name in the Name box.

4. Click the **Preset** list arrow, and then select from the available presets, or enter in a customized Width and Height, and Resolution.

5. Click the **Color Mode** list arrow, and then select a color mode for the image.

6. Click the **Bit Size** list arrow, and then choose a bit depth for the image (8-bit recommended).

7. Click **Background Contents**, and then click **White**, **Background Color**, or **Transparent** (animated GIF files look best using Transparency).

8. Click **OK**.

9. Create the first image for the animated GIF.

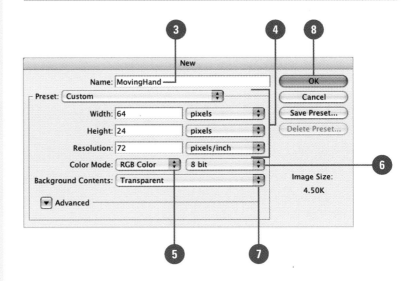

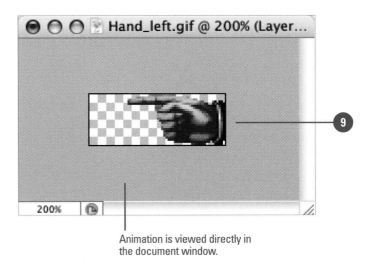

Animation is viewed directly in the document window.

10 Press Ctrl+J (Win) or Alt+J (Mac) to create a copy of your first animation in a separate layer.

11 Modify the second image (animations are essentially the same image, modified slightly between each animation frame or, in this case each layer).

12 Repeat steps 10 and 11 until you have enough cells for the animation.

13 Click the **Window** menu, and then click **Animation**.

14 Click the **Animation Options** button on the Animation palette, and then click **Make Frames From Layers**.

15 Click the **Play** button to view your animation in the document window.

16 Click the **Save** button, and then click **Save For Web**.

17 Fine-tune the image using the available options.

18 Click **Save**.

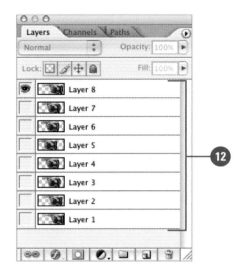

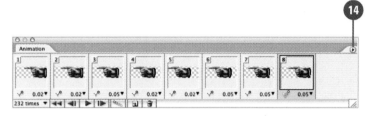

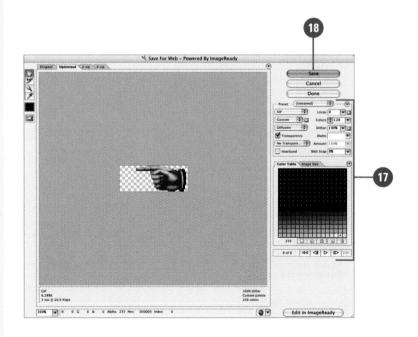

See Also

See "Creating an Animated GIF in ImageReady," on page 458 for more information on creating an animated GIF in another way.

See Chapter 19, "Designing for the Web," on page 441 for more information on using the various options.

Creating an Animated GIF in ImageReady

PS 14.5

There are many ways to make things move on a Web page; however, one of the most Internet compatible ways is the animated GIF. The original designation, GIF89a, gives you an idea of how long this format has been around. You can create an animated GIF directly in Photoshop, but if you prefer using ImageReady, you can use it too. The steps are similar, but not the same. If you use ImageReady to create an animation, you may still need Photoshop, which has more drawing tools to create each image, or frame, of the animation.

Create a GIF from Scratch in ImageReady

1. Open ImageReady.

2. Click the **File** menu, and then click **New**.

3. Enter a name in the Name box.

    Even if you name the file in the New dialog box, you will still have to save the file.

4. Click the **Size** list arrow, and then select from the available presets, or enter in a customized width and height.

5. Click **White**, **Background Color**, or **Transparent** options to determine the contents of the first layer (animated GIF files work best using the Transparent option).

6. Click **OK**.

7. Select the **Optimize** palette, click the **Format** list arrow, and then click **GIF**.

8. Create the first image for the animated GIF, or click the **Edit In Photoshop** button on the toolbox to move the new document into Photoshop.

    Since Photoshop has more drawing tools, moving into Photoshop to create the animation image is a good idea.

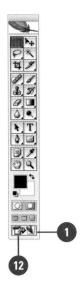

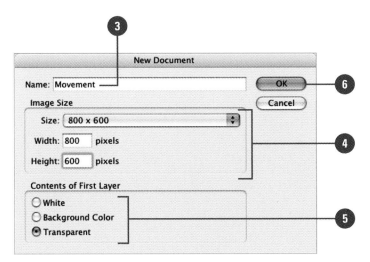

9 Press Ctrl+J (Win) or ⌘+J (Mac) to create a copy of your first animation in a separate layer.

10 Modify the second image (animations are essentially the same image, modified slightly between each animation frame or, in this case each layer).

11 Repeat steps 9 and 10 until you have enough cells for the animation.

12 If you created the animation layers in Photoshop, click the **Edit in ImageReady Jump** button.

13 Click the **Window** menu, and then click **Animation**.

14 Click the **Animation Options** button, and then click **Make Frames From The Layers**.

15 Click the **Play** button to view your first animation.

8 First image

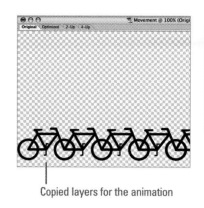

Copied layers for the animation

Did You Know?

You can perform frame-to-frame optimization on an animated GIF.
Click the Animation Options button, and then click Redundant Pixel Removal to make transparent all pixels in a frame that are unchanged from the preceding frame. This greatly reduces the file size of the animated GIF.

See Also

See Chapter 9, "Using the Paint, Shape Drawing, and Eraser Tools," on page 205 for more information on using the various drawing tools.

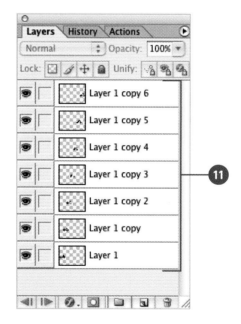

11

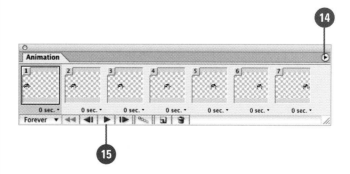

14

15

19

Opening an Existing Animated GIF

 PS 14.5

The great thing about ImageReady is that is doesn't make you reinvent the wheel. You can have this really great looking animated GIF and you want another one just like it, but with some slight modifications. Or you copy an animated GIF off the Internet, and you want to see how the designer created it. Either way, ImageReady is ready to help you get the task completed.

Open an Existing Animated GIF

1. Open ImageReady.

2. Click the **File** Menu, and then click **Open**.

3. Select an animated GIF, and then click **Open**.

4. Click the **Original**, **Optimized**, **2-Up**, or **4-Up** palettes to view the document using different layouts.

5. Select the **Animation** palette to view the individual frames in the animation.

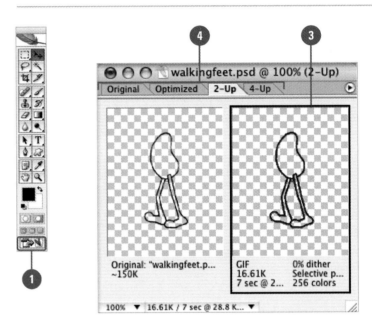

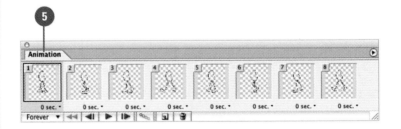

Did You Know?

You can reverse the order of an animated GIF. Open the animation in ImageReady, click the Animation Options button, and then click Reverse Frames to instruct ImageReady to reverse all the frames in the animation.

Modifying an Animated GIF File

PS 14.5

Modifying an animated GIF file is as easy as remembering that each one of the frames in the animation is stored as a separate layer in the Layers palette. Once you figure that out, it's a simple matter of selecting the layer you want to modify, and make the changes. You can even add or delete layers, it's simple when you work through the Layers palette. Since Photoshop has more editing tools to work with, you can jump back and forth between ImageReady and Photoshop.

Modify an Animated GIF File

1. Open an animated GIF file in ImageReady.

2. Open the **Animation** and **Layers** palettes.

3. Click the **2-Up** palette, and then select the original image (you can not modify an optimized image).

4. Use the **Layers** palette to select the layer (animation frame) you want to modify.

5. Use any of the options available to add to the layers—layer masks, layer styles, opacity, and blending modes.

6. Click the **Edit In Photoshop Jump** button on the toolbox to modify the image using Photoshop's vast array of editing tools.

7. When you're done in Photoshop, click the **Edit In Image Ready Jump** button.

8. Click the **File** menu, and then click **Save Optimized**.

   Your animation changes have been saved.

See Also

See Chapter 5, "Working with Layers," on page 97 for information on using and modifying layers.

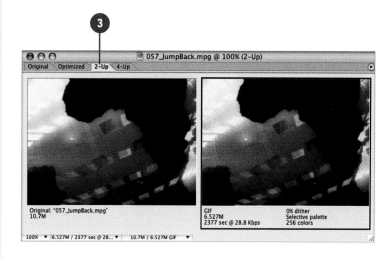

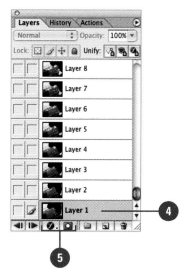

Slicing Images the Easy Way

PS 14.4

ImageReady allows you to slice a document into smaller image pieces. There are several reasons you might want to slice an image. One reason would be to create interactive links from the pieces. Another would be to reduce the size of the image file by individually compressing the separate pieces. Some designers even slice their artistic files to protect them from being easily copied off the Internet. However, one of the best reasons is speed. You can create layer-based slices when working with rollovers to help minimize file size, user-based slices allow you to cut the image into several pieces. Several Web studies show that the Internet can handle smaller packets of information more efficiently than one large packet, so slicing images is a good thing to do.

Slice Images the Easy Way

1. Open a document in ImageReady.

2. Select the **Slice** tool on the toolbox.

   IMPORTANT *To make slicing a little easier, drag a few guides from the Ruler bar to help guide your slicing tool.*

3. Drag and release the slice tool in the document to create a rectangular or square slice.

4. Continue to drag and release until you have the image correctly sliced.

Did You Know?

You can slice images in Photoshop. ImageReady is not the only program with a slicing tool. If you slice the image in Photoshop and you click the Jump To ImageReady button, the slices are preserved during the transfer to ImageReady.

5 Select the **Slice Select** tool on the toolbox, and then drag the corner or side nodes of the selected slice to select and modify a slice.

6 Click the **File** menu, and then click **Save Optimized As**.

7 Click the **Format** list arrow, and then select whether to save the images in HTML And Images, Images Only, or HTML Only.

8 Click the **Slices** list arrow, and click **All Slices**.

9 Click **Save**.

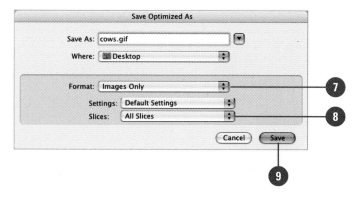

Modifying and Compressing Individual Slices

Not only does ImageReady make slicing an image easy, it also gives you the ability to modify the slices. Remember that each slice is an individual image file—it can be compressed, or modified in the same way as any other image file. When you compress an image, the image can only be compressed down based on the most complex area of the image. You can create a smaller image by slicing and compressing each slice down to its maximum values. When you work with ImageReady's slicing options, you can actually create several smaller images, which will load faster than the original.

Modify and Compress Individual Slices

1 Open a document in ImageReady.

2 Select the **Slice Selection** tool on the toolbox.

3 Click on the slice you want to modify.

4 Select the **Slice** palette, and then select from the following options:

◆ **Name.** Enter a name for the slice or use the default.

◆ **URL.** Enter a URL (Uniform Resource Locator) for the selected slice.

◆ **Target.** Select a target for the URL, such as _blank (load the URL into a separate browser window).

◆ **Alt.** Enter the alternate text for the selected image slice.

5 Click the **Dimensions** arrow, and then select the following options:

◆ **X and Y.** Enter precise values for the X and Y coordinates of the slice.

◆ **Width and Height.** Enter precise values for the width and height of the slice.

◆ **Constrain Proportions.** Check to maintain the aspect ratio of the selected slice.

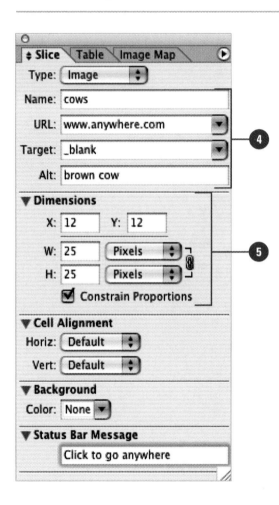

6 Click the **Cell Alignment** arrow, and then select from the following options:

◆ **Horizontal.** Click to instruct the HTML table document where to place the slice horizontally.

◆ **Vertical.** Click to instruct the HTML table document where to place the slice vertically.

7 Click the **Background** arrow, click the **Color** list arrow, and then select a color for the transparent areas of the selected slice.

8 Click the **Status Bar Message** arrow, and then enter a text message that appears in the status bar of the visitor's browser window.

Did You Know?

You can select more than one slice, using ImageReady's Slice Selection tool. Hold down the Shift key, and then click on two or more slices. You can save time by applying similar compression settings to the temporary group.

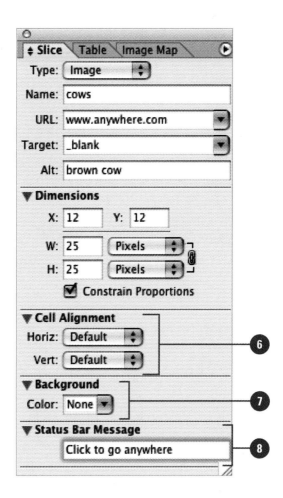

Creating a JavaScript Rollover

JavaScript rollovers are a dynamic way to display a button on the Internet. Essentially, the Rollover button has two or three states. State one represents the button before the visitors moves their mouse over the button, state two would be how the button looks as the visitor hovers over, and state three would be the look of the button when the visitor click their mouse. Rollovers are great, they really make a Web site come alive, and ImageReady makes it easy to create a Rollover. To create a rollover button, you will need the three states of the button. These typically are GIF images of a button in an up, over, and down state, and you can create the buttons in Photoshop or ImageReady.

Create a JavaScript Rollover

1. Open ImageReady.

2. Click the **File** menu, and then click **New**.

3. Enter a name in the Name box.

4. Click the **Size** list arrow, and then select from the available presets, or enter in a customized width and height.

5. Click the **White**, **Background Color**, or **Transparent** option to determine the contents of the first layer.

6. Click **OK**.

7. Click the **2-Up** palette, and then select the original image.

8. Create the normal state of the button.

9. Use the **Create New Layer** button to create the over state and the down state of the button.

> **IMPORTANT** *If the button states are similar with only a small modification like the changing of a shadow, then press Ctrl+J (Win) or ⌘+J (Mac) to create a copy of the original layer, and then modify the copy.*

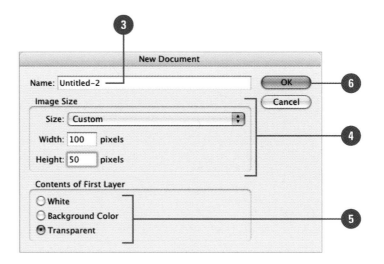

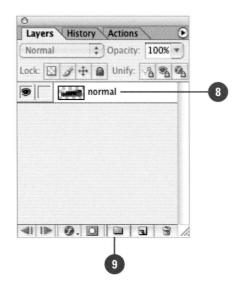

10 Open the **Web Content** palette.

11 Select the normal state of the button in the Layers palette.

12 Click the **Options** button in the Web Content Palette, and then click **Create Layer Based Rollover**.

13 In the Layers palette, select the over state of the button, and repeat step 12.

14 In the Layers palette, select the down state of the button, and repeat step 12.

15 Double-click on the state icons in the Web Content palette to open the Rollover State Options dialog box, and change the states to Up, Over, or Down.

The Rollover State Options dialog box appears each time. Click OK to set the state for each icon.

16 Click the **File** menu, and then click **Save Optimized As**.

17 Enter a file name in the Save As box.

18 Click the **Format** list arrow, and then click **HTML and Images**.

19 Click the **Where** (Mac) or **Save In** (Win) list arrow, and then select the location to save the file.

20 Click the **Settings** and **Slices** list arrows and make your selections.

21 Click **Save**.

ImageReady saves the three states of the button, including the JavaScript code in an HTML document.

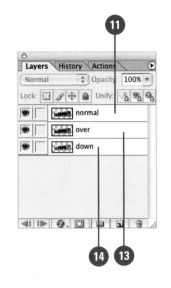

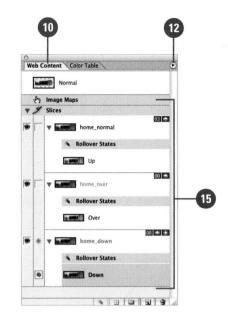

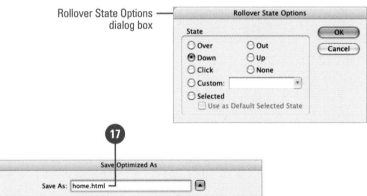

Rollover State Options dialog box

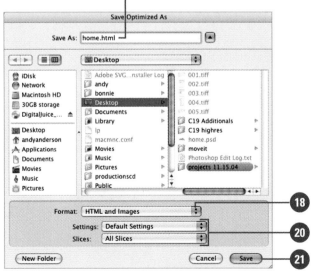

19

Defining and Editing Web Data Variables

When you work with images in ImageReady, or now Photoshop (**New!**), you can define variables to drive the graphics in your Web document. Data-driven graphics make it possible to create multiple versions of an image fast and precise. For example, you need to produce several Web banners using the same template. Instead of creating each banner, one at time, you can use data-driven graphics, to generate Web banners using variables and data sets. Any image can be converted into a template for data-driven graphics by defining variables for layers in the image. A **data set** is a collection of variables and associated data. You can switch between data sets to upload different data into your template. When you combine a Defined layer with a data set, you can use the information to swap images based on input variables.

Define a Data Driven Graphic

1. Open a document in Photoshop or ImageReady.

2. Select the layer in which you want to define variables.

3. Click the **Image** menu, point to **Variables**, and then click **Define**.

4. Select from the available options:

   ◆ **Visibility.** Select to show or hide the content of the layer.

   ◆ **Pixel Replacement.** Select to replace the pixels in the layer with pixels from another image file.

   ◆ **Text Replacement.** Select to replace a string of text in a type layer. (Available when a text layer is selected.)

   ◆ **Name.** Enter names for the variables. Variable names must begin with a letter, underscore, or colon.

5. To define variables for an additional layer, choose a layer from the Layer list arrow.

6. Click **OK**.

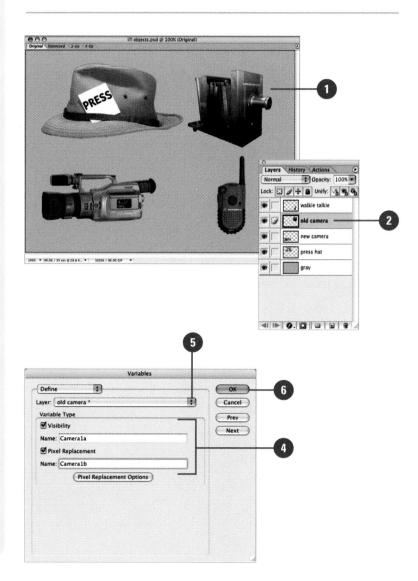

Create a Data Set

1. Open a document in Photoshop or ImageReady.

2. Select the layer in which you want to define variables.

3. Click the **Image** menu, point to **Variables**, and then click **Data Sets**.

4. Select a pre-defined data set from the list arrow.

5. Select a variable from the available listed objects.

6. Edit the following variable data (each available when selected as the definition for the file):

   ◆ **Visibility.** Select Visible or Invisible to show or hide the layer's content.

   ◆ **Pixel Replacement.** Click Browse, and then select a replacement image file.

   ◆ **Text Replacement.** Enter a text string in the Value box.

7. Repeat Steps 5 and 6 for each variable in the template.

   The Image's visibility, a type layer's text, or swapping images, can now be controlled through changing variables.

8. Click **OK**.

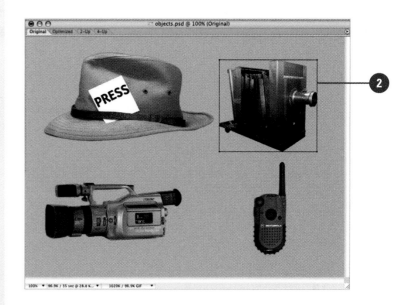

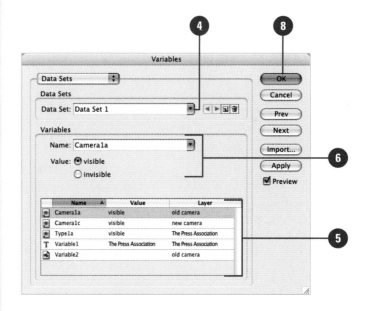

Exporting Directly to Flash

ImageReady lets you export a document as into the Flash SWF file format, that can then go directly to the Web or be imported into Macromedia Flash. If the document is a multilayered Photoshop file, each layer can be exported as a single SWF object file, or each layer can be exported as separate SWF files (using Layers As Files). If a multi-layered document file is exported into one SWF file, any animation frames are exported automatically as SWF animation frames. However, slices, image maps, and rollovers are not converted and are ignored.

Export Directly to Flash

1 Open a document in ImageReady.

   If the document is an animation, the frames will be visible in the Animation palette.

2 Click the **File** menu, point to **Export**, and then click **Macromedia Flash SWF**.

3 Select from the following Export options:

   ◆ **Preserve Appearance.** Retains the appearance of the Photoshop file and may rasterize a text or shape layer if they cannot be exported natively to the SWF format.

   ◆ **SWF bgcolor.** Click to select a color used for the background of the generated SWF file.

   ◆ **Generate HTML.** Select the check box to create an HTML document, that will house the SWF file.

   ◆ **Enable Dynamic Text.** Select the check box to map text variables to SWF dynamic text.

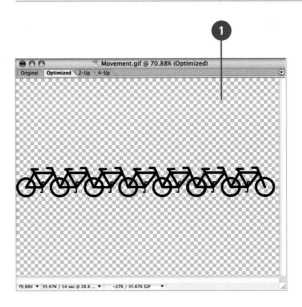

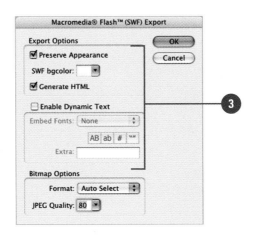

- **Embed Fonts.** Click to select not to embed, embed a full character set, or a partial set. If partial is selected choose whether to add all upper-case, all lower-case, all numbers, or all punctuation.

- **Extra.** Enter special characters to include in the generated set.

- **Format.** Click to select a formatting option for any of the images.

- **JPEG Quality.** Enter a JPEG quality compression value (0 to 100). The higher the value the larger the file, but less information is lost to the compression scheme.

4 Click **OK**.

5 Enter a name, and then select a location to save the SWF file.

6 Click **Save**.

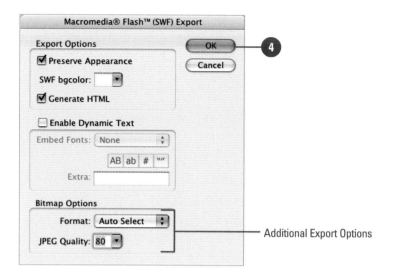

Additional Export Options

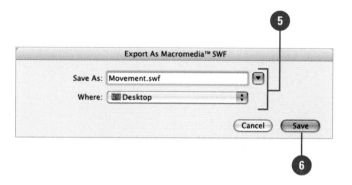

Andy's Workshop

Introduction

Andy's Workshop is all about being creative and thinking outside of the box. These workshops will help your right-brain soar, while making your left-brain happy; by explaining why things work the way they do. Exploring Photoshop's possibilities is great fun; however, always stay grounded with knowledge of how things work. Knowledge is power.

Getting and Using the Project Files

Each project in Andy's Workshop includes a start file to help you get started with the project, and a final file to provide you with the results of the project so you can see how well you accomplished the task.

Before you can use the project files, you need to download them from the web. You can access the files at *www.perspection.com* in the software downloads area. After you download the files from the web, uncompress the files into a folder on your hard drive to which you have easy access from Photoshop.

Project 1: Creating a Sketch from Scratch

Skills and Tools: Multiple Layers, Gaussian Blur, and Blending Modes

Photoshop has a ton of filters. In fact, there are 105 filters located under the Filters menu. Filters perform a wealth of special-effects operations; everything from artistic, distort, and even sketch effects, and while filters are very creative, and fun to use, there is a limit to what they can do. For example, Photoshop has no less than 14 Sketch filters, and while they do creative things to an image they can't do everything. What if you want to create what looks like a sketch effect and none of the sketch filters do what you want? If you don't know how to do things from scratch, you're stuck with the limitations of the filters. The technique you are about to learn will not only let you create an awesome sketch effect, but will give you a better understanding of how blending modes work with multiple layers. There are a lot of steps to this process; however, the end result is more than worth the effort. In addition, if this process seems familiar, they are; many of the steps used in the sharpening workshop are similar to this effect, until you get to the end.

The Project

In this project you'll take a photograph and through the judicious use of multiple layers, and blending modes convert in into a beautiful colorized sketch. There are a lot of steps in this workshop, but the final results are more than worth the journey.

The Process

1 Open the file **sketch_start.psd** in Photoshop, and then save it as **my_sketch.psd**.

2 Create a duplicate of the image by dragging the layer over the Create New Icon.

3 Click the **Image** menu, point to **Adjustments**, and then click **Desaturate**. The copied layer is converted into shades of gray.

4 Create a copy of the desaturated layer, and select it.

5 Click the **Image** menu, point to **Adjustments**, and then click **Invert**. The image layer becomes a grayscale negative (leave the negative image selected).

6 Click the **Blending Mode** list arrow on the Layers palette, and then click **Color Dodge**. The image appears to change to white.

Note: If you see areas of the image that do not change to white, but are pure black, don't worry, those areas of the image were originally pure black, and they will never convert to white.

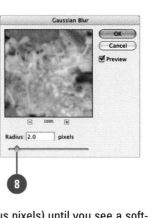

7 Click the **Filter** menu, point to **Blur**, and then click **Gaussian Blur**.

8 Very slightly blur the image (just a few radius pixels) until you see a soft-ghosted outline of the image.

9 Click **OK**.

10 Select the top layer in the Layers palette, click the **Layers Options** button, and then click **Merge Down**, or press Ctrl+E (Win) or ⌘+E (Mac).

You should now be left with the original image (the bottom layer), and the softly ghosted image (the top layer), which I've named, Sketch Effect.

11 Create a copy of the layer named Sketch Effect, and select it.

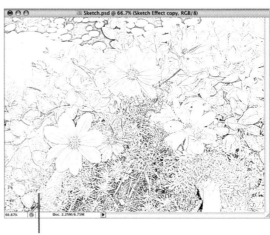

Softly-ghosted image

12. Click the **Blending Mode** list arrow on the Layers palette, and then click **Multiply**. The two copies combine to create a darker image.

13. Continue to make copies of the Sketch Effect layer until the image darkens to your taste (this might be 3 layers, or it might be 10).

14. Merge all the Sketch Effect layers together, but do not merge the original image layer into the Sketch Effect layers.

   Note: You can quickly merge layers by using the Merge Down shortcut. Select the top layer, and then press Ctrl+E (Win) or Ctrl+E (Mac). This merges the top layer into the layer directly underneath. Continue using the Merge Down shortcut until all the Sketch layers are merged.

15. Create another copy of the merged Sketch Effect layer, and select it.

16. Click the **Blending Mode** list arrow on the Layers palette, and then click **Multiply**.

17. Click the **Filter** menu, point to **Blur**, and then click **Gaussian Blur**.

18. Add a small amount of Gaussian Blur to taste (1 or 2 Radius). This will soften the edges of the sketch image and create visually softer sketch lines.

19. Click **OK**.

20. Merge the two Sketch Effects layers together.

21. To colorize the image, select the top layer (Sketch Effect), click the **Blending Mode** list arrow, and then click **Luminosity**.

The Results

Finish: Compare your completed project file with the image in **sketch_fnl.psd**.

Tweaking the Image

The subjective items that will influence the final sketch image are how much you Gaussian Blur the image, and how many additional copy layers you create. Creating more blur enhances the sketch lines, and adding more copy layer, increases the overall density of the final sketch image.

Good to Know: You can increase or decrease the intensity of the Sketch Effect by selecting the Sketch Effect layer and lowering its opacity.

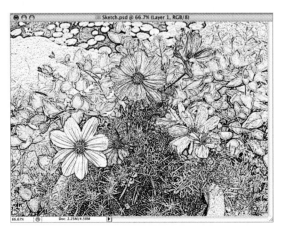

Project 2: Creating a Sharper Image

Skills and Tools: Multiple Layers, Blending Modes, Layer Opacity, and Paint Brush

In the world of photography, not everything has to be in focus. In fact, smart photographers know that placing image elements out of focus will help to draw the eye to the focused areas. However, there are times when you will take a photograph and the image was accidentally, not intentionally, out of focus (I hate it when that happens). Photoshop has several filters that help you create a sharper image. As a matter of fact, Photoshop has five sharpen filters: Sharpen, Sharpen Edges, Sharpen More, Smart Sharpen, and Unsharp Mask. Of these filters, Smart Sharpen (**New!**), and Unsharp Mask are considered the two most powerful sharpening filters. Unfortunately, all the sharpen filters have one major flaw; they do not separate the sharpening effects from the image, as in an adjustment layer. So, when you click the OK button, you're stuck with the results. That's not necessarily a bad thing; however, there is another way. The technique you're about to learn for sharpening an image does not require any of the sharpening filters, its effect on the image creates a more believable sharpening effect, and the changes to the image are contained within a separate layer. That gives you the control you need to be creative, and get the best visibly pleasing sharpening results possible.

The Project

In this project you'll take an out-of-focus image and sharpen it by creating an editable sharpening layer. Separating the sharpening adjustments from the image, gives you creative control over the entire process.

The Process

1. Open the file **lighthouse_start.psd** in Photoshop, and then save it as **my_lighthouse.psd**.

2. Create a duplicate of the image by dragging the layer over the **Create New Layer** button, or by selecting the layer and pressing Ctrl+J (Win), or ⌘+J (Mac).

3. Click the **Image** menu, point to **Adjustments**, and then click **Desaturate**. The copied layer is converted into shades of gray.

   Note: If the image is originally a grayscale image, you can skip step 3.

4. Create a copy of the desaturated layer and select it.

5. Click the **Image** menu, point to **Adjustments**, and then click **Invert**. The image layer becomes a grayscale negative (leave the negative image selected).

6. Click the **Blending Mode** list arrow on the Layers palette, and then click **Color Dodge**. The image appears to change to white.

Note: If you see areas of the image that do not change to white, but are pure black, don't worry, those areas of the image were originally pure black, and they will never convert to white.

7 Click the **Filter** menu, point to **Blur**, and then click **Gaussian Blur**.

8 Very slightly blur the image (just a few radius pixels) until you see a soft-ghosted outline of the image.

9 Click **OK**.

10 Select the top layer in the Layers palette, click the **Layers Options** button, and then click **Merge Down**, or press Ctrl+E (Win) or ⌘+E (Mac).

You should now be left with the original image (the bottom layer), and the softly ghosted image (the top layer), which I've named, unsharp mask.

11 Click the **Blending Mode** list arrow on the Layers palette, and then click **Multiply**. The white areas of the ghosted image change to transparent, and the darker lines are blended in with the original image, creating the illusion of sharpness.

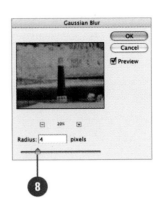

Softly-ghosted image

The Results

Finish: Compare your completed project file with the image in **lighthouse_fnl.psd**. ☞

Tweaking the Image

It's possible that the sharpening effect is too intense. If that's the case, simply reduce the opacity of the top layer to reduce its effect on the image. If, however, the effect is less than you

hoped for, simply create a copy of the top layer to double the effect. Additionally, if you want to remove some of the sharpening effects from portions of the image, just select your Paintbrush tool, and paint the top layer using white, in the areas you want removed.

Good to Know: It is actually impossible to sharpen a photograph. Photographs are two-dimensional representations of a three-dimensional world. Since there are no optics in a two-dimensional world there can be no sharpening. What happens in this technique is that the unsharp mask layer actually creates visible lines of force around the out-of-focus areas of the image, and the mind interprets those lines as being a sharper image.

Project 3: Restoring Life to Heirloom Images

Skills and Tools: Levels Adjustment Layer

There is nothing more important to a family than its history. History is found in many ways, places, and formats. For example, you may have historical documents that relate to who you are, or you might have physical artifacts from your ancestors. However, nothing strikes an emotional cord more than a photograph. A picture is indeed worth a thousand words. Yet even while an image freezes a moment in time, the actual photograph is traveling through time and unfortunately, Father Time can do major damage to a photographic image. Fortunately for us we have Photoshop. Adobe Photoshop is your time machine for restoring old images. While there are many methods for restoring an old grayscale image, one of the most consistently successful methods is through the use of a Levels Adjustment layer.

The Project

In this project you'll take an old image, and through the use of Photoshop's amazing Adjustment layers, restore the image. It's not that difficult, and the final results are awesome.

The Process

1. Open the file **three_girls_start.psd** in Photoshop, and then save it as **my_three_girls.psd**.

   Important: Always scan old grayscale images as RGB, not Grayscale. Most old images begin taking on a color as they age, such as: brown, sepia, or yellow. Although you will want to remove that color, it is information that Photoshop can use to correct the image.

2. Click the **Create New Fill Or Adjustment Layer** button (half-moon icon), and then click **Levels**.

   The Levels dialog box represents the brightness values of the pixels within the image. The data is called a Histogram, and is similar to a bar chart.

3. Click the **RGB Channel** selector, and then click the **Red** channel.

4. Drag the **black input** slider to just below the visible rise of the histogram (that's where black has moved to after all those years).

5. Drag the **white input** slider to just below the visible rise of the histogram (that's where white has moved to after all those years).

6 Once you have established the position of black and white, increase the input value of the white slider by 4, and decrease the value of the black slider by 4.

The value of 4 is an average, and based on the image; however, backing down both sliders, you help keep the light and dark areas of the image from blowing out (going pure white or black).

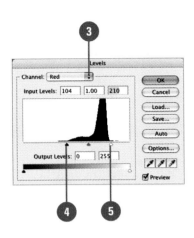

7 Click the **RGB Channel** selector, click the **Green** channel, and then repeat steps 4 thru 6.

8 Click the **RGB Channel** selector, click the **Blue** channel, and then repeat steps 4 thru 6.

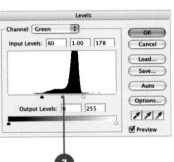

9 If the image still appears a bit to dark or light, return the **RGB Channel** selection to the RGB option, then drag the middle gray slider to correspondingly lighten or darken the image in the mid-tones.

10 Click **OK**.

11 Click the **Create New Fill Or Adjustment Layer** button (half-moon icon), located at the bottom of the Layers palette, and then click **Hue & Saturation**.

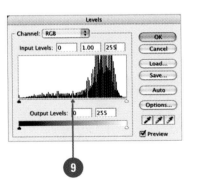

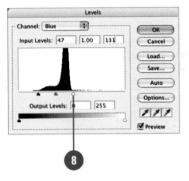

12 Drag the **Saturation** slider to the far left.

13 Click **OK**.

This has the effect of removing any unwanted colorcasts from the image.

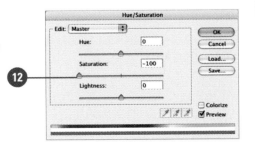

The Results

Finish: Compare your completed project file with the image in **three_girls_fnl.psd**.

Tweaking the Image

Like all adjustments in Photoshop, nothing is perfect, and no two images are ever adjusted in exactly the same way. Your results will depend on the physical information left within the scanned image. However, with a bit of practice, and knowing exactly how to move the Levels Input sliders, you will achieve fairly consistent results.

Good to Know: The brightness levels of a pixel range from 0 (black) to 255 (white), when you move the input sliders, you're redefining where black and white are within the active image. As an image ages the original values of black and white shift. The purpose of Levels is to reestablish those positions. Once that's completed, Levels can approximate the positions of all the other remaining pixels, and balance the image.

Project 4: Enhancing Image Contrast

Skills and Tools: Curves Adjustment Layer, Layer Masks, and Paintbrush

Contrast enhancement differs from sharpening. When you sharpen an image, you're attempting to fool the eye into seeing a sharper edge. In other words the image looks more in focus. When you enhance contrast, you're attempting to give the image more separation between the shadows and highlights. In other words, you want your whites whiter, and your darks darker. While Photoshop has an Auto Contrast adjustment (click the Image menu, point to Adjustment, and click Auto Contrast), you will gain much more control over the process if you perform the operation using Curves. The technique you are about to learn will give you a greater understanding of how Curves performs, and let you, not Auto Contrast, decide exactly what areas of the image are to be enhanced. You should understand that enhancing contrast essentially, compresses tonal values within the image. This technique is called a standard "S" contrast curve, and will work to increase the contrast on almost any image. Before you get started, remember, if you are too aggressive, the image will being to look a bit posterized, and you will see banding occur within transitional shadows. Therefore, a soft hand on the controls is recommended.

The Project

In this project you'll bump the contrast of a dull image. The process is simple to accomplish, and will help to kick up the contrast values of any image.

The Process

1 Open the file **colorado_start.psd** in Photoshop, and then save it as **my_colorado.psd**.

2 Click the **Create New Fill Or Adjustment Layer** button (half-moon icon), located at the bottom of the Layers palette, and then click **Curves**.

3 Create a mid-tone point by clicking on the middle of the diagonal curves adjustment line.

This allows you to lock the mid-tone values of the image.

4 Create a quartertone highlight point by clicking halfway between the mid-tone point, and the top point on the line.

5 Create a quartertone shadow point by clicking halfway between the mid-tone point, and the bottom point on the line.

6 Drag the quartertone highlight point straight up the curves grid (about 1 grid).

Note: If you want to remove a point, click the point and drag it off the grid, or hold the Ctrl (Win) or ⌘ (Mac) key, and then click the point.

Smart Tip: When you select a point on the Curves grid, you do not have to drag the point using your mouse, instead you can control the active point using your keyboard up, down, left, right arrow keys.

7 Drag the quartertone shadow point straight down the curves grid (about 1 grid).

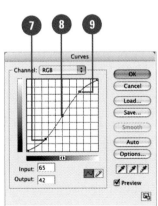

8 Since you locked the mid-tones, you will create what looks like an "S" curved line. This will lighten up the mid-tones of the image, and correspondingly darken the mid-tones.

9 Continue raising or lowering the quartertone and highlight points until you see the desired results.

10 Click **OK**.

Good to Know: If some of the areas of the images do not need the contrast sharpening supplied by the Curves Adjustment layer, simply use you paintbrush on the built in mask to isolate areas of the adjustment. Remember, painting with black masks out the Curves adjustment to the image, and painting with white restores the adjustment.

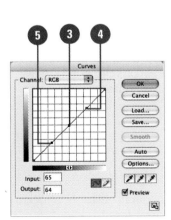

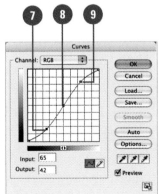

The Results

Finish: Compare your completed project file with the image in **colorado_fnl.psd**. 👉

Tweaking the Image

It's possible that you may need to work with the mid-tone point as well. The mid-tone point will not increase or decrease contrast, but will lighten or darken the mid-tones. Therefore, if after enhancing the contrast of the image, you feel overall it's a bit too dark or light, then click and drag the mid-tone point up or down.

Factoid: The human eye looks for the effect of contrast based on the speed in which tonal values shift. By opening the Curves Adjustment layer, and performing a standard "S" contrast enhancement curve, you are essentially increasing the rate in which the tonal values shift, and fooling the eye into believing there is more contrast.

Project 5: Colorizing a Grayscale Image

Skills and Tools: Multiple Layers, Blending Modes, Layer Opacity, and Paintbrush

Have you ever wanted to colorize an old grayscale image? Well, if you've ever wanted to add color to an old image, or ever change the colors within a new color image, then you've come to the right place. There are a lot of ways to colorize an image, and Photoshop knows them all. The technique you are about to learn will help you control the colorization process through the use of layers, blending modes and opacity. As a matter of fact, you will be able to control each color within the image and, later change those colors with the click of a button. This method is so powerful that with a little bit of patience and care, the image won't just look colorized; it will look like an original color image. Just remember this simple item: every time you add a new color to the image, you will add a new layer. This means that a single image may contain twenty or more layers; however the final results are worth it.

The Project

In this project you'll take a old, or new grayscale image, and through the use of multiple layers and blending modes create a colorized image that looks like it was taken with color film.

The Process

1. Open the file **colorization_start.psd** in Photoshop, and then save it as **my_colorization.psd**.

2. Click the **Create New Layer** button, located at the bottom of the Layers palette, and name the layer to correspond to the area of the image you're coloring.

3. Click the **Blending Mode** list arrow, and then click **Color**.

4. Select the **Paintbrush** tool.

5. Select the color you want to use to paint a specific area of the image within the new layer.

6. Use the **Paintbrush** tool to paint an area of the image.

   Note: Since you changed the blending mode of the layer to Color, the image retains its details, and only the color (Hue) of the information changes.

7. Depending on the color you chose, slightly lower the opacity of the layer to make it appear natural.

   Note: Different colors require different opacity settings to appear natural. This occurs because of the saturation of the color, and the detail within the areas you are painting. Experiment with opacity settings until the image looks correct.

8. Repeat steps 2 thru 7 for each individual color within the image.

The Results

Finish: Compare your completed project file with the image in **colorization_fnl.psd**. ☞

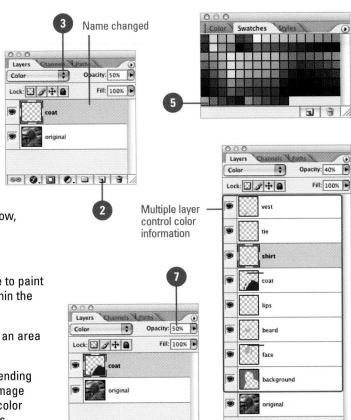

Name changed

Multiple layer control color information

Tweaking the Image

Since you are using individual layers to control the colorization process, if you over paint an area, it's a simple matter to use your eraser tool and remove the offending color information.

Smart Tip: When you change the opacity of a layer, it's not necessary to click the triangle button, located to the right of the Opacity input box, to access the triangular slider. All you have to do is click the word, Opacity, and drag left or right. It's that simple.

Project 6: Removing Complex Image Information with Extract

Skills and Tools: Multiple Layers and Extract

Extract has been a part of the Photoshop application since version 5.5, and it's improved in every version. The primary purpose of the Extract filter is to remove areas of image information from the selected image layer. For example, removing the sky from an image bordered by mountains is not too difficult; owing to the sharp nature of the sky against the mountains. However, what about removing the sky from between the branches of a large tree, or removing the background around a model with wind-tossed hair. It's problems like that the separate the serious Photoshop user from the tourist. In this workshop you will gain understanding of exactly how the Extract tool performs its magic on removing selective areas of image information. Just remember, it's not about color; it's about contrast.

The Project

In this project you'll learn the secret to removing simple and complex backgrounds from images using Photoshop's awesome Extract tool.

The Process

1. Open the file **old_tree_start.psd** in Photoshop, and then save it as **my_old_tree.psd**.

2. Click the **Filter** menu, and then click **Extract**.

3. Select the **Highlighter** tool and proceed to highlight the areas that contain the edge. As you can see in this example, the highlight tool is used to fill in the entire branch structure of the tree.

   Important: This is absolutely the most important step in the Extract process. You are highlighting where the edges of the image interact with the background that you want to remove; in this case the sky. Get this part wrong, it nothing else will work.

4. Select the **Paintbucket** tool.

5. Click to fill in all the areas that are to be saved.

6 Drag the **Smoothness** slider to **80** percent.

The Smoothness slider helps to create a softer transitional edge between the areas to save, and the areas to extract.

7 Click the **Preview** button to view a preview of the Extract.

The black areas are removed (extracted), and the Paintbucket areas are saved. The only place Photoshop will look for the extraction edge is in the original highlight.

8 Click **OK**.

9 Open the file **clouds.psd** in Photoshop, and then save it as **my_clouds.psd**.

10 Drag the sky layer into the extract document.

11 Drag the sky layer below the extract layer to view the results.

The Extract tool removed the sky from around the individual branches of the image, and allowed you to replace it with another sky image.

The Results

Finish: Compare your completed project file with the image in **old_tree_fnl.psd**. 👉

Tweaking the Image

If you are not entirely happy with how the Extract tool performed, you might look at how you highlighted the edge,

and try again, or if there is too much missing information, you might still click the OK button, and then use the History brush to fill in small amounts of missing information.

Project 7: Managing Images with Masks

Skills and Tools: Multiple Images, Layer Masks, Paintbrush, and Selection

Layer masks are one of those powerful features in Photoshop that have been around for a long time. The technique you are about to learn will give you a greater understanding of Layer masks, and how they can be used to combine image elements from multiple images. Layer masks let you control the visible elements of a layer by simply painting on the mask. Think of the mask as a piece of black construction paper. You take a pair of scissors and cut a shape out of the construction paper, and lay it directly over the image. The area cut out of the construction paper becomes the visible elements of the image, and the black areas of the construction paper mask everything else. When you work with a Layer mask, you paint with black, white, and shades of gray. Areas of the mask painted black appear transparent, areas painted white are visible (the cutout in the construction paper), and shades of gray produce values of transparency. For example, painting with fifty percent gray, produces fifty percent transparency. Each layer in an image can have its own layer mask, and the mask will control only the elements in the layer they're attached. As you can see Layer masks are a very powerful, and creative tool.

The Project

In this project you'll learn the creative potential of using layer masks to control the visible portions of any layer in Photoshop.

The Process

1 Open the file **lake_start.psd** in Photoshop, and then save it as **my_lake.psd**.

2 Click the **Add Layer Mask** button, located at the bottom of the Layers palette.

   Photoshop creates a mask, and places it to the right of the image thumbnail.

3 Select the **Paintbrush** tool.

4 Select Black as your Foreground color by clicking the **Default Colors** button.

   Important: A layer with an attached mask has two elements: The image thumbnail, and the mask thumbnail. If you want to edit the image, click the image thumbnail, if you want to edit the mask, click the mask thumbnail.

5 Click the mask thumbnail to select it.

6 Move into the document window, and begin painting. As you paint the black color converts the image information to transparent.

   Note: White painted areas of the mask become 100 percent visible, and painting with shades of gray produces various percentages of transparency, depending on the shade of gray.

7 Continue painting using black, white, and shades of gray, until you have completely isolated the sky portions of the image.

Smart Tip: You can create a mask by first using selection. Open the image, and before creating the mask, use your selection tools to select the visible areas of the image. Now, when you click the Add Layer Mask button, the mask will be created for you.

8 Open the **sky.psd** image in Photoshop, save it as **my_sky.psd**, and then click in its document window.

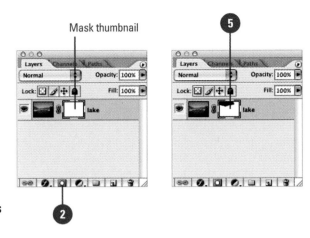

Mask thumbnail

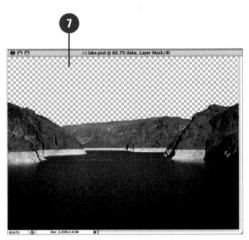

9 Move to the Layers palette, and drag the sky layer into the document window of the image containing the mask. You have just made a copy of the sky layer in the masked image.

10 Close the sky image.

11 Click the sky layer in the Layers palette and drag it underneath the masked layer.

The image, which is now defined as a composite, appears with its new sky.

The Results

Finish: Compare your completed project file with the image in **lake_fnl.psd_fnl.psd**.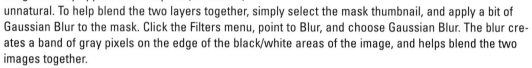

Tweaking the Image

It's possible that the visible edge of the masked image and sky appear too sharp and, therefore, unnatural. To help blend the two layers together, simply select the mask thumbnail, and apply a bit of Gaussian Blur to the mask. Click the Filters menu, point to Blur, and choose Gaussian Blur. The blur creates a band of gray pixels on the edge of the black/white areas of the image, and helps blend the two images together.

Good to Know: By default, a mask and image move and transform as a unit. If you want to adjust the mask independently of the image (or vise versa), click once on the chain icon, located between the image and mask thumbnail. The icon will disappear, and the mask and thumbnail can be adjusted or transformed independently.

Icing on the Cake: If you really want to get fancy, you might want to create a reflection of the clouds on the water. To accomplish this, create a copy of the sky layer, select the Edit menu, point to Transform, and then click Flip Vertical. Now, create a mask that only reveals the areas of the water, use the Overlay Blending mode, and slightly lower the opacity. The **lake_fnl.psd** image contains a sample reflection in a separate layer.

What More Projects

You can access and download more workshop projects and related files at *www.perspection.com* in the software downloads area. After you download the files from the web, uncompress the files into a folder on your hard drive to which you have easy access from Photoshop.

Get Everything on CD

Instead of downloading everything from the web, which take a while depending on your Internet connection speed, you can get all the files used in this book and much more on a Photoshop CS2 On Demand CD. The CD contains task and workshop files, tips and tricks, keyboard shortcuts, and other goodies from the author.

To get the Photoshop CS2 On Demand CD, go to *www.perspection.com*.

New! Features

Adobe Photoshop CS2

Adobe Photoshop CS2 with ImageReady CS2 means superior results faster, with new features and enhancements that help you create and manage your images more easily and efficiently. The indispensable new and improved features help graphic web designers, photographers, and video professionals create the highest quality images, with the control, flexibility, and capabilities that you expect from the professional standards in desktop digital imaging.

Photoshop CS2 for All Users

♦ **Adobe Update Manager (p. 4, 24-25)** Set Adobe update preferences for Photoshop and its related programs to automatically search for updates on a monthly basis.

♦ **Status Bar (p. 10)** Displays status information for 32-bit exposure and Version Cue.

♦ **Adobe Dialog (p. 11)** Open and save files using the Adobe dialog box. You can quickly switch between the operating system and Adobe versions.

♦ **Adobe Bridge (p. 12-13, 55)** Use Bridge—a stand-alone program that comes with Photoshop—to organize, browse, and locate the different types of images you need to create content for print, the web, and even mobile devices. Use Bridge to view, open, process, and batch images from any Adobe Creative Suite 2 program.

♦ **Video Preview (p. 16)** Display documents on a display device, such as a standard or DVD screen, using a Firewire link.

♦ **Pixel Aspect Ratio (p. 17)** Adobe adds 3 Pixel Aspect Ratio options: D4/D16 Standard (0.95), HDV Anamorphic (1.333), and D4/D16 Anamorphic (1.0).

♦ **Multi-image Camera Raw (p. 18-19)** Process an entire photo shoot in a fraction of the time. With support for a comprehensive range of digital cameras, you can automatically adjust settings, convert to universal Digital Negative (DNG) format, and apply nondestructive edits to batches of images.

♦ **Smart Objects (p. 21)** Perform transforms of embedded vector (e.g. Adobe Illustrator files) and of pixel data without losing original image data in Photoshop. Create multiple instances of embedded data and easily update all instances at once.

- ◆ **Adobe Help Center (p. 26)**   Display help topics in an integrated Adobe CS2 stand-alone viewer that floats like a palette. In addition to the encyclopedic help information, Adobe includes more task-based content that addresses how to accomplish common tasks quickly. The database and search engine provides better searching (e.g. a search for "hazy" would reveal "blurry").

- ◆ **Adobe Version Cue 2.0 (p. 32)**   Manage files and versions as a single user or in a small workgroup. Integrate with Adobe Bridge to manage files for your Photoshop and Adobe Creative Suite projects.

- ◆ **Info Palette (p. 43-44)**   Displays information such as: Document Size, Efficiency, Scratch Sizes, and whether the image uses 8-, 16-, or 32-bit color channels.

- ◆ **Font Size User Interface Customization (p. 54, 70)**   Customize the size of text in the Options bar, palettes, and the Layer Style dialog box.

- ◆ **File Handling (p. 56-57)**   Set a preference to enable the use of the Large Document format (PSB), which is designed for Photoshop CS and CS2.

- ◆ **Customizable User Interface (p. 54, 74-75)**   Customize menus and save customized sets in workspaces. Show and hide menu items, color-code menu items, and save workspaces that contain menu, keyboard, and/or palette layouts. Use and switch between presets (e.g. Basic, Automation, and What's New in CS2) to customize Photoshop to suit your needs.

- ◆ **Japanese Type Features (p. 70)**   Format text with new character alignment (Mojisoroe) and more Kinsoku Shori types.

- ◆ **Layer Visibility Undoable (p. 121)**   Set a preference to make layer visibility changes undoable.

- ◆ **WYSIWYG Font menu (p. 298)**   Preview font families and font styles directly in the Font menu. Font names are listed in the regular system font, and a sample word ("Sample") is listed next to each font name in the font itself.

Photoshop CS2 for Photographers

- ◆ **Adobe Stock Photos (p. 32)**   An integrated service available within Adobe Bridge that lets you search, view, try, and buy over 230,000 professional royalty-free stock photographic images.

- ◆ **Integrated Adobe Online Services (p. 32, 440)**   Search, view, and download professional images from Adobe Stock Photos within Adobe Bridge, and share and print online with Adobe Photoshop Services.

- ◆ **Noise Reduction (p. 147)**   Reduce digital image noise, JPEG artifacts, and scanned film grain. Use controls to reduce noise found in individual channels while preserving edge detail.

- ◆ **Lens Distortion Correction (p. 150-151)**   Correct typical problems caused by lenses, such as barrel and pincushion distortion, chromatic aberration, and lens vignetting. Easily correct image perspective using the filter's grid.

- ◆ **Blur Filters (p. 152-153)**   Apply blur effects using new blur filters: Box Blur, Shape Blur, and Surface Blur.

- **Smart Sharpen Filter (p. 156-157)**   Fix common types of blurring in images. Smart Sharpen improves edge detection and reduce sharpening halos and provides controls to sharpen images in the highlights and shadows.

- **Spot Healing Tool (p. 162)**   Quickly heal spots and blemishes with selecting source content.

- **Red-Eye Correction (p. 163)**   Automatically fix red eyes problems with a single click (much more easily than was possible painting with the Color Replacement tool) using the Red Eye tool. Set options to adjust pupil size and darkening amount.

- **High Dynamic Range (HDR) (p. 168-169, 201, 414-415)**   Work with images in 32-bits-per-channel, extended dynamic range. Photographers can capture the full dynamic range of a scene with multiple exposures and merge the files into a single image.

Photoshop CS2 for Designers

- **Brush Options (p. 58-59)**   Set preference to use a full size brush tip and show a crosshair in the center of the brush tip.

- **Smart Guides (p. 64, 94)**   Align the content of layers as you move them using guidelines that appear only when you need them.

- **Image Wrap (p. 88-89)**   Wrap an image around any shape or stretching, curling, and bending an image. The wrap options (such as Custom, Twist, Bulge, Flag, Fisheye, Inflate, etc.) can be manipulated by dragging control points or by editing settings in the Options bar. Warps applied to Smart Objects remain fully re-editable.

- **Vanishing Point (p. 148-149)**   Paste, clone, and paint image elements that automatically match the perspective planes in an image.

- **Multiple Layer Control (p. 102)**   Work with layers as objects. Select multiple layers and move, group, align, and transform them. Use Shift-click or drag-select to select multiple layers, and then perform various image operations, such as move, scale, rotate, and group into a layer set.

Photoshop CS2 for the Web and Workgroups

- **Photoshop PDF Format (p. 400-401)**   Save an image as a PDF Photoshop document, which is compatible with PDF 1.6/Acrobat 7.0. Use customizable presets to make the process quick and easy.

- **Image Processor (p. 416-417)**   Process a batch of files to multiple file formats.

- **Color Management (p. 429)**   Maintain common color settings throughout the Adobe Creative Suite components. Print with the simplified printing interface for color management.

- **Animation (p. 456-457)**   Create animated GIF files in Photoshop as you do in ImageReady.

- ◆ **Script and action event manager (p. 364-365)** Set JavaScripts and Photoshop actions to run automatically when a specified Photoshop event occurs.

- ◆ **Improved Creative Suite integration (p. 20, 32, 429)** Place Illustrator (raster) images into Photoshop as Smart Objects; share color swatches between Photoshop, Illustrator, and InDesign; create PDFs in Photoshop; and synchronize color management settings for all CS2 programs in Bridge.

- ◆ **Variables (p. 468-469)** Create data-driven graphics in Photoshop as you now do in ImageReady. Import data from spreadsheets, databases, etc., automatically replace text and pixel data, and generate files.

What's Changed

In addition to the new features, Photoshop CS2 also changed the way some features worked from the previous version, Photoshop CS.

- ◆ **File Browser (p. 12-13)** Adobe Bridge handles all the tasks that you previously did in the File Browser. Flagging is now handled by star ratings. Files previously flagged are marked with one star. In Bridge, Ctrl+D (Win) or ⌘+D (Mac) duplicates an image rather than deselecting it in the thumbnail view.

- ◆ **Placing a File (p. 20)** Files that you place into Photoshop with the Place command now become Smart Objects.

- ◆ **Clipping Mask Visibility (p. 100)** To hide all layers except the clipping mask layer and the layer it is clipped to, Alt+click (Win) or Option+click (Mac) the layer's visibility icon. Previously, Alt+clicking or Option+clicking hid all layers.

- ◆ **Multiple Layer Selection (p. 102)** To add or subtract layers from a selection in the Layers palette, Shift+click (or drag) in the document with the Move tool and the Auto Select Layer check box selected. Previously, Shift+clicking linked and unlinked layers.

- ◆ **Layer Grouping (p. 103)** You can group layers using the keyboard shortcut Ctrl+G (Win) or ⌘+G (Mac). The shortcut for creating a clipping mask is now Ctrl+Alt+G (Win) or ⌘+Option+G (Mac).

- ◆ **Loading a Selection (p. 104)** To load a layer as a selection, Ctrl+click (Win) or ⌘+click (Mac) the layer's thumbnail in the Layers palette. Previously, you could click anywhere in the layer.

- ◆ **Merging Layers (p. 110)** To merge all visible layers into a new layer, press Alt (Win) or Option (Mac), click the Layer menu, and then click Merge Visible. Previously, you created a new layer and selected it before merging. To merge any two layers, select them in the Layers palette, click the Layer menu, and then click Merge Layers. You can still merge two adjacent layers in the Layers palette by selecting the top layer and then choosing Layer Merge Down.

- ◆ **Layer Linking (p. 111)** The layer linking column was removed. To link layers, select multiple layers and click the Link Layers button at the bottom of the Layers palette. Some menu commands that work on linked layers have been changed to work on multiple layers.

Adobe Certified Expert

About the Adobe Certified Expert (ACE) Program

The Adobe Certified Expert (ACE) program is for graphic designers, Web designers, systems integrators, value-added resellers, developers, and business professionals seeking official recognition of their expertise on Adobe products.

What Is an ACE?

An Adobe Certified Expert is an individual who has passed an Adobe Product Proficiency Exam for a specific Adobe software product. Adobe Certified Experts are eligible to promote themselves to clients or employers as highly skilled, expert-level users of Adobe software. ACE certification is a recognized worldwide standard for excellence in Adobe software knowledge. There are three levels of ACE certification: Single product certification, Specialist certification, and Master certification. To become an ACE, you must pass one or more product-specific proficiency exam and sign the ACE program agreement. When you become an ACE, you enjoy these special benefits:

- Professional recognition
- An ACE program certificate
- Use of the Adobe Certified Expert program logo

What Does This Logo Mean?

It means this book will prepare you fully for the Adobe Certified Expert exam for Adobe Photoshop CS2. The certification exam has a set of objectives, which are organized into broader skill sets. Throughout this book, content that pertains to an ACE objective is identified with the following Adobe Certified Expert logo and objective number below the title of the topic:

 PS 3.1, 3.3

Photoshop CS2 ACE Exam Objectives

Objective	Skill	Page
1.0	**Working with the Photoshop user interface**	
1.1	Describe the advantages of saving workspaces	72
1.2	Given a view in Adobe Bridge, explain when you would use that view	12-13
1.3	Describe the basic functionality provided by the Preset Manager, and explain how to use the Preset Manager to manage libraries	71
1.4	Customize menus and keyboard shortcuts by selecting options in the Keyboard Shortcuts and Menus dialog box	73-75
2.0	**Painting and retouching**	
2.1	Given a tool, paint an object by using that tool. Tools include: Brush Tool, Pencil Tool, and Eraser	214-215, 224-226
2.2	Given a tool, retouch an image by using that tool. Tools include: Healing Brush, Patch Tool, Color Replacement Tool, and Red Eye Tool	160-161, 163, 230
2.3	Adjust the tonal range of an image by selecting the proper options and using a levels adjustment layer	164-165, 190-191
2.4	Adjust the tonal range of an image by selecting the proper options and using a curves adjustment layer	191-193
2.5	Explain how blending modes are used to control how pixels are effected when using a paint or editing tool	98-99, 112, 142-143
2.6	Create and use patterns	336-337
2.7	Create and use gradients	198, 227-229
2.8	Given a setting in the Exposure dialog box, explain how that setting affects an image	201
2.9	Create and edit a custom brush	211-212
3.0	**Creating and using layers**	
3.1	Create and arrange layers and groups	100-103
3.2	Explain the purpose of layer comps and when you would use one	116, 139
3.3	Explain how or why you would use a clipping group	266
3.4	Explain how or why you would use a layer mask	232-233
3.5	Create and save a layer style	274-293
3.6	Select and work with multiple layers in an image	108-110, 113-114
3.7	Given a scenario, edit layer properties	115, 118
3.8	Create and use Smart Objects	21
4.0	**Working with selections**	
4.1	Create and modify selections by using the appropriate selection tool	78-87
4.2	Save and load selections	243, 246-247

Choosing a Certification Level

There are three levels of certification to become an Adobe Certified Expert.

- **Single product certification.** Recognizes your proficiency in a single Adobe product. To qualify as an ACE, you must pass one product-specific exam.

- **Specialist certification.** Recognizes your proficiency in multiple Adobe products with a specific medium: print, Web, or video. To become certified as a Specialist, you must pass the exams on the required products. To review the requirements, go online to *http://www.adobe.com/support/certification/ace_certify.html*.

- **Master certification.** Recognizes your skills in terms of how they align with the Adobe product suites. To become certified as a Master, you must pass the exam for each of the products in the suite.

Preparing for an Adobe Certified Expert Exam

Every Adobe Certified Expert Exam is developed from a list of objectives, which are based on studies of how an Adobe program is actually used in the workplace. The list of objectives determine the scope of each exam, so they provide you with the information you need to prepare for ACE certification. Follow these steps to complete the ACE Exam requirement:

1. Review and perform each task identified with a Adobe Certified Expert objective to confirm that you can meet the requirements for the exam.

2. Identify the topic areas and objectives you need to study, and then prepare for the exam.

3. Review the Adobe Certified Expert Program Agreement. To review it, go online to *http://www.adobe.com/support/certification/ace_certify.html*.

   You will be required to accept the ACE agreement when you take the Adobe Certified Exam at an authorized testing center.

4. Register for the Adobe Certified Expert Exam.

   ACE testing is offered at more than a thousand authorized Pearson VUE and Thomson Prometric testing centers in many countries. To find the testing center nearest you, go online to *www.pearsonvue.com/adobe* (for Parson VUE) or *www.2test.com* (for Prometric). The ACE exam fee is US$150 worldwide. When contacting an authorized training center, provide them with the Adobe Product Proficiency exam name and number you want to take, which is available online in the Exam Bulletin at *http://www.adobe.com/support/certification/ace_certify.html*.

5. Take the ACE exam.

Getting Recertified

For those with an ACE certification for a specific Adobe product, recertification is required of each ACE within 90 days of a designated ACE Exam release date. There are no restrictions on the number of times you may take the exam within a given period.

To get recertified, call Pearson VUE and Thomson Prometric. You will need to verify your previous certification for that product. If you are getting recertified, check with the authorized testing center for discounts.

Taking an Adobe Certified Expert Exam

The Adobe Certified Expert exams are computer-delivered, closed-book tests consisting of 60 to 90 multiple-choice questions. Each exam is approximately one to two hours long. A 15-minute tutorial will precede the test to familiarize you with the function of the Windows-based driver. The exams are currently available worldwide in English only. They are administered by Pearson VUE and Thomson Prometric, independent third-party testing companies.

Exam Results

At the end of the exam, a score report appears indicating whether you passed or failed the exam. Diagnostic information is included in your exam report. When you pass the exam, your score is electronically reported to Adobe. You will then be sent an ACE Welcome Kit and access to the ACE program logo in four to six weeks. You are also placed on the Adobe certification mailing list to receive special Adobe announcements and information about promotions and events that take place throughout the year.

When you pass the exam, you can get program information, check and update your profile, or download ACE program logos for your promotional materials online at:

http://www.adobe.com/support/certification/community.html

Getting More Information

To learn more about the Adobe Certified Expert program, read a list of frequently asked questions, and locate the nearest testing center, go online to:

http://www.adobe.com/support/certification/ace.html

To learn more about other Adobe certification programs, go online to:

http://www.adobe.com/support/certification

Index

A